1985

# Advances in Bilingual Education Research

# Advances in Bilingual Education Research

*Eugene E. Garcia*
*Raymond V. Padilla*
*Editors*

The University of Arizona Press
Tucson

## About the Editors

EUGENE E. GARCIA has been director of the Center for Bilingual/ Bicultural Education at Arizona State University since 1980. Before joining the faculty at ASU, he taught both at the University of Utah and the University of California. He is author of several books including *Early Childhood Bilingualism* published in 1983, and he has edited and written for numerous linguistics, psychology, and education journals.

RAYMOND V. PADILLA has been an associate professor in the Department of Higher and Adult Education at Arizona State University for several years. His primary research has been in bilingual education policy analysis, higher education, and microcomputer applications to research and teaching. He worked in the Chicano Persistence Project that piloted Freireian techniques of field research and in the development of an interactive video project for limited English-proficient students.

THE UNIVERSITY OF ARIZONA PRESS

Copyright © 1985
The Arizona Board of Regents
All Rights Reserved

This book was set in 10/12 Linotron 202 Times Roman.
Manufactured in the U.S.A.

Library of Congress Cataloging-in-Publication Data

Main entry under title:

Advances in bilingual education research.

  Bibliography: p.
  Includes index.
  1. Education, Bilingual—United States—Addresses, essays, lectures. 2. Hispanic Americans—Education—United States—Addresses, essays, lectures. 3. Code switching (Linguistics—United States)—Addresses, essays, lectures. 4. Bilingualism in children—United States—Addresses, essays, lectures. I. García, Eugene E., 1946–    . II. Padilla, Raymond V.
LC3731.A58  1985      371.97'00973      85-13956
ISBN 0-8165-0922-0 (alk. paper)

# Contents

# Introduction

THIS COLLECTION OF PAPERS was selected by reviewers, who are themselves researchers in bilingual education, from manuscripts prepared in response to a national call for papers on bilingual education research. The competitive, peer review process that was used to make the selections was intended to net "the best" of the available research that has been done in the field of bilingual education to date. High-quality research is highlighted in both traditional and emerging areas.

In spite of the national interest in bilingual education, especially among communities where non-English languages are spoken, little systematic research of high quality has been carried out in the United States. (Canadians, for example, have a much better record in this area.) As a result, a host of issues of great importance to language minority communities (particularly in the areas of theory, technology, and public policy related to bilingual education) have been relegated to the backwash of mainstream research. One of the purposes of this volume, therefore, is to focus on research related to bilingual populations, particularly in the United States.

Consistent with our epistemological perspective on bilingual phenomena, we signaled to potential contributors our particular interest in receiving papers relating to theory, technology, and public policy in bilingualism and bilingual education. Further, we advised that papers focusing on empirical research, critical reviews of literature, and well-documented conceptual frameworks would be especially relevant to our interests. Not surprisingly, we received submissions in all three substantive areas and from the perspectives indicated. Each submission was forwarded to two external reviewers, who themselves are established scholars in bilingual education, in an effort to identify the most valuable papers for publication. The resulting selections, incorporated in this volume, are consistent with our aim of helping to establish a cumulative knowledge base about bilingual phenomena. However, one potential disadvantage in this approach to building a volume is that the articles collectively may not cast a fine-grained thematic pattern. We hope that the results show that in the present case the disadvantage has been minimized.

The book supports also the notion that paradigmatic research in bilingual education is highly desirable. Paradigms are fundamentally the distilled perspectives of organized adherents who generate knowledge within a systematized framework. In most well-established fields of inquiry, competing paradigms sooner or later arise. The resulting competitive process tends to accelerate the rate of knowledge production and accumulation. Our intent is to help the field of bilingual education move toward paradigmatic research by contributing to the accumulation and dissemination of knowledge that is necessary as a precondition to the definition and creation of paradigms.

The volume reflects a strong bias towards the United States and is not particularly inclusive of important developments internationally. Our intent is not to deny the importance of international research on bilingualism but rather to focus on issues of immediate concern to language minority communities in the United States. Since the greatest incidence of bilingualism in this country is English/Spanish, it is not surprising that there is also a Hispanic flavor to the volume, although multiethnic issues are by no means ignored. Given the great diversity of non-English languages prevalent in the United States, we recognize the need to maintain a research effort across various languages. Still, research does not always proceed evenly across all linguistic groups, and this volume clearly reflects that unevenness in research production.

The study is organized into three distinct sections: Language and Culture; Educational Perspectives; and Policy Issues. These sections represent organizationally the pattern of cumulative work that has addressed bilingual education in the United States. That is, theory and research which have incorporated issues related to language and culture for bilingual students have been related directly to educational practices. These, in turn, have generated educational policy at national, state, and local levels. Not always is there a direct relationship between research/theory and educational practice/policy. But for bilingual education in the United States, an attempt to integrate these elements characterizes the field. The organization of this volume, therefore, reflects this separation for purposes of communication while clearly understanding that all three sections represent the integrated nature of bilingual education.

The first section presents five chapters that discuss first and second language development, code-switching, language use, and personality development in multilingual/multicultural populations. Maez presents a study of the linguistic development of Hispanic children with emphasis on the phonological variations exhibited by the children under investigation. The acquisition of Spanish as a mother tongue by Mexican children in an English-language environment presents some unique insights into early childhood bilingualism. It is one of a few studies highlighting native language acquisition which focuses on Spanish as a first language. Berdan and Garcia employ quantitative analytical techniques to examine linguistic patterns of bilingual children of school age over a period of several years. This work considers the natural language context important as it relates to the probability of specific utterance length. Previous work in this area attempting to document the development of morphological and syntactic milestones with bilinguals may be directly confounded with context variables these authors identify as relevant. Madrid and Garcia integrate and present in a cohesive way research results related to the acquisition of a second language with particular emphasis on interlanguage transfer. Particularly, they demonstrate that the relative proficiency status of each language is related to the nature of interlanguage transfer in bilingual Spanish/English preschoolers. This work adds to the emerging conceptualizations that the linguistic character of the bilingual is much more complex than previously indicated. Wald extends previous work with young children focusing on the functions and intended meaning of code-switching and code-mixing. This work focuses on code-switching exhibited by preadolescents from a bilingual Hispanic community. This investigation of code-switching phenomena takes into consideration both social context and topic by providing a selective analysis of natural speech in nonschool, community situations. By doing so, the work provides a systematic investigation of code-switching not previously available. To conclude this section Gutierrez presents a series of models of immigrant personality, a potentially significant topic related to ethnolinguistic group populations in the United States. This psychological conceptualization of "culture" recognizes as significant the personality dimensions relevant to the status of "immigrant," a characteristic which embodies many bilingual populations in the United States. Therefore, the author argues, what we might have once considered as a combination of Mexican and American cultural attributes in bilingual students might be better understood as attributes of immigrant status.

The second section, Educational Perspectives, provides five chapters characterized by specific reference to teaching and learning. This section represents a special effort to provide research that is relevant to practitioners. Moll and Diaz offer a psychosocial approach to the understanding of cognitive development of minority children based on Vygotsky's "zone of proximal development." Jacobson raises extraordinarily urgent issues of language use in bilingual classrooms along with a discussion of the optimization of conditions to develop genuine bilingualism. In particular, Jacobson suggests that optimal conditions regarding the educational support of bilingual students is directly related to the form in which the two languages are utilized during instruction. He provides evidence which implicates first language retrieval and development strategies with instructional methods as significant in overall linguistic and academic gains of bilingual students. Villamil-Tinajero and Gonzalez-Baker address the practical and important concerns of bilingual clinical-teacher supervision such as the "match" between supervisors and teachers in areas of curriculum philosophy and implementation. Aguirre's chapter presents the results of his work assessing the perspectives of parents and educators on bilingual education. This piece provides a "public" perspective of programmatic developments which have characterized the practice of bilingual education. In the last chapter Garcia discusses issues of language and cultural maintenance, a newly perceived public goal (and highly accepted private goal) of bilingual education.

The last of the three sections is entitled Policy Issues. Pol gives projections of ethnolinguistic group populations. These estimates, along with the variables associated with them, present inescapable future concerns for education. Along with the accelerated growth of the bilingual population in the United States, these data suggest that the geographical concentration, "youthfulness," and economic characteristics of this population must be taken into consideration by educational planners. Craig's paper on the twin subjects of the California public school system as an employer of Hispanics and the difficulty in determining educational policy via-à-vis widespread equity, ethnicity, and unemployment concerns provides a broader look at the institutionalization of bilingual education. Navarro's paper presents an analysis of the political context of bilingual education. He suggests that simplistic solutions sometimes are proposed to resolve complex problems. However, he concludes that the role of the educator as a policy-change agent in the arena of bilingual education can no longer be questioned.

Finally, it is important to note that this volume should be placed in a broad context. Numerous educational, demographic, and economic reports highlight the continued population growth of ethnolinguistic group students throughout the United States. The 1980 census indicates that nationally some fourteen million families report the use of a language other than English as their home language. This is an increase of four million families over the 1970 census. In some ten or twelve states, within the next five to ten years, an estimated fifteen to twenty-five percent of school-age children will be entering public schools with a home language other than English. Fortunately, this population of bilingual students has not been completely ignored by national and state legislation, local school district policies, and federal court adjudications concerning bilingual education. Yet, as is the case with many educational initiatives, the influence of bilingual education on the children it has served remains difficult to assess. Still, bilingual education has been, and continues to be, one of the major educational initiatives of the last two decades in the United States. In this sense, bilingualism clearly has made its mark on an important institution of society. It is our hope that this volume, through its research emphasis, will have a beneficial influence on the field of bilingual education and the children that it serves.

EUGENE E. GARCIA
RAYMOND V. PADILLA

# PART ONE
# Language and Culture

# 1.
# The Acquisition of
# the Spanish Sound System by
# Native Spanish-Speaking Children

*Lento Maez*

CHILDREN'S PRELINGUISTIC DEVELOPMENT is traditionally considered to begin at birth. Kagan and Lewis (1965) observed that infants as young as two
weeks of age appear to be able to differentiate between their mother's speech
and other auditory signals. Wolff (1966) suggests that the human voice is
more effective than inanimate sounds in eliciting smiling and vocalizing in
infants. Kaplan and Kaplan (1971) have proposed four stages that appear to
describe the child's early productive language abilities. The first stage begins
with the birth cry. This cry is characterized by a rising and falling frequency
contour. Parents appear to be able to infer a meaning from the variants of the
child's cry. Empirical evidence to substantiate such claims, however, is lacking. The second stage consists of cooing and vocalizations other than crying.
This stage begins at the end of the first or second month after birth. The third
stage begins at approximately six months of age and consists of babbling.
This stage is characterized by the development of units of utterances that
spectrographic analysis shows to be of the same duration as those of an adult
(Nakazima 1962). However adultlike these utterances may be, there are still
no identifiable morphemes produced. The fourth stage begins at approximately 12 to 18 months of age and is characterized by an initial phase of silence followed by a decrease in the variety of sounds produced. It is during
this stage that a few adultlike lexical entries, using single words to express
whole thoughts, emerge. The fourth stage has been called "patterned speech"
by Kaplan and Kaplan.

A child learning a language must learn the sound system of that language.
In all languages the minimal unit of sound is the phone (Jakobson and Halle
1956). How sounds are produced is called articulatory phonetics. And how a
child perceives, organizes, and produces the sounds in that language spoken
around him is only partially understood. To date, two approaches have been

utilized to understand the child's phonological development. One approach has been to isolate and describe the set of sounds the child uses and to focus on the gradual development of the set. The second method is to determine the relationship between the child's speech and the adult model he is attempting to reproduce (Menyuk 1969).

Determining the child's phonemic inventory at the early stages is not an easy task. This situation is complicated by the age of the child. It is usually impossible to appeal to the child's intuitive knowledge of the sounds he is acquiring. In addition, the sounds the child makes must be caught on the fly, so to speak. As a consequence, the relatively few studies of phonemic development have been done by linguists on their own children (Moskowitz 1970).

These studies have cautiously proposed that as early as a few months after birth the child's acquired sound system is a structured one. Jakobson (1968) is credited with being the first to suggest a universal order for the successive differentiation of distinctive features. He proposed that the first three contrasts to appear and be acquired are oral-nasal (/b/ versus /m/), labial-dental (/p/ versus /t/), and fricative-stop (/f/ versus /p/), in that order. Jakobson also proposed the "law of irreversible solidarity." For example, "the acquisition of the velar and palatal consonants presupposes the acquisition of labials and dentals, and . . . the presence of palatovelars implies the simultaneous existence of labials and dentals." "The presence of labials and dentals does not imply the presence of palatovelars" (Jakobson 1962:77). A third principle proposed by Jakobson is that phoneme acquisition is determined in part by the frequency of occurrence in the languages of the world and not how frequently the phoneme occurs in the particular language.

Velten (1943) is credited with being the first to put Jakobson's theory on phonemic acquisition to the test. What Velten found was that the first three phonemic contrasts to be acquired were as Jakobson had predicted. However, Velten proposed that the order of acquisition was labial-dental, fricative-stop, and oral-nasal.

In essence, the child's acquisition of phonemic distinctions is considered to occur sequentially by classes, for example, stops precede fricatives. This "rigid regularity in the sequence of these acquisitions" appears to be universal "no matter if the children are French or English, Scandinavian or Slavic, German or Japanese, Estonian or New Mexican Indian" (Jakobson 1968:77). Velten (1943) agreed with Jakobson that "this process is identical for children of all linguistic communities." Moreover, Velten suggested that "some children have acquired the standard phonological system of their parents' speech at the age of eighteen months" (p. 83). However, little documented evidence exists for such sequential acquisition for Spanish. The present analysis constitutes a step in filling the void.

Jakobson's principles governing the order of acquisition of sounds (as synthesized by Ervin-Tripp (1966:68–69) are as follows:

1. Vowel-consonant (/a/ *vs* /p/) contrasts are possibly the first to be acquired.
2. Stop-continuants (a continuant can be a nasal /m/ or a fricative /f/) appear to be among the earliest acquired by children.
3. Stops precede fricatives in initial position (/p/ *vs* /f/).
4. If two consonants are alike in manner of articulation, one will be labial and the other dental or aveolar (/p/ *vs* /t/).
5. Contrasts in place of articulation usually precede voicing contrasts.
6. Affricates (/č/ as in *church* or /ǰ/ as in *judge*) and liquids (/l/ as in *lane* or /r/ as in *race*) may appear later than the stops and nasals.
7. In Russian and French /l/ precedes a vibrant (trilled) /r̄/.
8. A contrast between low and high vowels (/a/ *vs* /i/) precedes a front versus back contrast (/i/ *vs* /u/).
9. Oral vowels precede nasal vowels and are a late acquisition.
10. Consonant clusters (/tr/ as in *truck*) are also acquired late.
11. Consonant contrasts usually appear to be made earlier in initial positions rather than in medial or final positions.

From the broad principles proposed by Jakobson in the early 1940s to studies in the 1980s unresolved questions remain concerning how a child's phonological development occurs. A second strategy utilized in attempting to explain the child's phonological development is focusing on the relationship between the child's phonemic production and the adult forms. This approach basically focuses on the substitutions, additions, and deletions of sounds found in the child's utterances in attempts to approximate the adult speech heard around him. The data appear to suggest that these substitutions are highly regular and can be considered rule governed (Oller 1974).

Dale (1976:216) has summarized some of the most common types of processes involved in the production of child utterances:

1. Processes of substitution
   - (a) Final devoicing  
     bag [bæk]  
     Final voiced consonants, if not completely omitted (see 3 below), are generally unvoiced.
   - (b) Initial stopping  
     sandwich [tæwiš]  
     Initial fricatives are changed to corresponding stops.
   - (c) Gliding  
     rabbit [wæbIt]  
     Substitutions of glides /w/ and /y/ for liquids /l/ and /r/.

|  |  |
|---|---|
| (d) Fronting<br>key [ti]<br>thick [fɪk] | Substitution of front conso-<br>nants for back ones. |

2. Process of cluster reduction

|  |  |
|---|---|
| (a) Deletion<br>stop [tɒp]<br>play [pey] | Typically when a stop is<br>combined with a fricative or<br>a liquid, only the stop is<br>produced. |
| (b) Epenthesis<br>blue [bəlú] | Less frequent than deletion;<br>both consonants may be<br>produced but with a vowel<br>added between them. |

3. Process of final-consonant<br>avoidance

|  |  |
|---|---|
| (a) Deletion<br>cat [kʰæ] | Self-explanatory. |
| (b) Epenthesis<br>pit [pʰigæ] | Less frequent than deletion;<br>the consonant may be re-<br>tained but a vowel added<br>after it. |

4. Process of assimilation

|  |  |
|---|---|
| (a) Assimilation<br>lamb [næm] | Some sounds are modified to<br>make them more similar to<br>other sounds. In the ex-<br>ample, /l/ becomes nasal,<br>like /m/, but is still produced<br>at the same point in the<br>mouth as /l/; hence /n/. It<br>is more common for early<br>sounds to be assimilated to<br>later ones, but the reverse<br>frequently occurs. |
| (b) Reduplication<br>bottle [baba] | An entire syllable being<br>reduplicated. |

Research on the acquisition and development of the phonological system of the child's language system is in its infancy (Menyuk 1971). The summaries by Ervin-Tripp and Dale suggest some tentative conclusions on children's phonological development. However, the sequence of acquisition of distinctive features both as the child perceives and produces them, as well as the process of acquisition of phonological rules, both intra-morphemic and intra-sententially, is yet to be understood.

The study of the acquisition of Spanish by native Spanish speakers is a relatively new field of inquiry. Research in this area has been undertaken from two major perspectives: that of sociolinguistics and that of psycholinguistics. An example of the application of sociolinguistic principles is the analysis of

Spanish/English codeswitching among bilinguals (García, Maez, González, and Ibañez 1980). The psycholinguist has attempted to examine acquisition of the grammatical, syntactic, cognitive, semantic, and pragmatic constraints that operate on the Spanish language (González 1970, 1975, 1978, 1980; Pfaff 1975; García 1979, 1980). Both disciplines have made contributions toward understanding the complex nature of Spanish as acquired and used by native Spanish speakers in an English-speaking country. The area of early childhood acquisition (18 to 24 months of age) of Spanish by native Spanish speakers, however, has been sadly neglected.

During the past decade there have been a few studies on Spanish language acquisition. An early study by González (1968) profiles the sounds found in the speech of thirteen six-year-old Spanish-speaking Mexican American children from Corpus Christi, Texas. The following is a composite of the consonants and vowels found in the speech of the children; however, as González clearly states, "not all the sounds appeared in any one child's inventory."

From these data González was able to isolate the labiodental voiced fricative [v] and found that it was in free variation with [ɓ] as opposed to the variant [b] which occurred consistently after a nasal. The labiodental [v], which has been ignored as a speech sound in traditional descriptions of Spanish, appears to be a part of the phonology of the speech of the children in his study. González also found the often omitted sound [š] in free variation with [č] and is quick to point out that it was present in only two informants' speech and occurred in noncontrastive distribution with [č] (González 1968:3).

These studies on the native Spanish-speaking child's use of Spanish as a first language have addressed issues of late acquisition (age two and older). The majority has described elicited rather than natural speech and none of the studies systematically characterizes patterns of acquisition for beginning learners (18 months and older). Additionally none of the studies has established the acquisition of the Spanish sound system as a criterion.

The intent of the present study was to analyze spontaneous language data gathered from three children whose first language experience was Spanish. In doing so, it provides one of the first detailed analyses of the acquisition of the Spanish sound system by children whose first language experience is Spanish in an English speaking country.

## GENERAL SUBJECTS AND PROCEDURE DESCRIPTION

The subjects of the study were female; each was eighteen months of age when spontaneous utterances in their home environments were first recorded. Their primary language experience was Spanish. The children were also exposed to English during this investigation, from television, in particular.

**TABLE 1.1**
**Spanish Consonants**

| | Labial | Labio-Dental | Dental | Alveo-Palatal | Velar | Glottal |
|---|---|---|---|---|---|---|
| Stops | [p]<br>[b] | | [t]<br>[d] | | [k]<br>[g] | |
| Affricates | | | | [č] | | |
| Fricatives | | [f]<br>[v]<br>[ƀ] | [đ]<br>[s]<br>[z] | [š] | [x]<br>[ǧ] | [h] |
| Nasals | [m] | [ɱ] | [n] | [ñ] | [ŋ] | |
| Laterals | | | [l] | | | |
| Semi-Consonants | [w] | | [y] | | | |
| Vibrants | | Tap<br>Trilled | [r]<br>[r̄] | | | |

**Spanish Vowels**

| | Front | Central | Back |
|---|---|---|---|
| High | [i] | | [u] |
| Mid | [e] | | [o] |
| Low | | [a] | |

However, all three sets of parents said that they made a concerted effort to speak only Spanish to their children. This was confirmed by the recordings.

Prior to obtaining the parents' permission, the purpose of the investigation was explained as follows: to record the children's spontaneous utterances for the purpose of determining their acquisition of Spanish as a first language. This was to occur while the mother and/or father and the child interacted; interactions were to be as natural as possible. The only instructions to the parents were to play with the children and attempt to get them to talk. Each recording session took place in the child's home.

Usually a few items such as blocks, balls, books, and dolls were made available to facilitate the interaction. A cassette recorder, placed near the child, was used to record all verbal interactions. As the interactions unfolded, notes on the context of the child's utterances were taken to aid in the extrapolation of questionable sounds.

The recording sessions were twenty minutes in length, every two weeks for a period of six months. The first recording session for Karina and Celena was January 23, 1980. This was the day they both turned 18 months of age. For Ana C. that day and the first recording session was March 11, 1980.

This procedure worked well throughout the investigation; at times the investigator was not present to note the context of a child's utterance. On those occasions the investigator listened to the tape with the caretaker present, usually no more than a day later. This allowed the caretaker to fill in the context as best she could while her comments were recorded. After the recording session and/or consultation with the caretaker, the tape was transcribed. If a question arose during the transcription of the tape, the caretaker was called and asked for clarification.

A total of thirteen recordings per child, each twenty minutes in length, was collected for analysis. Each recording was reviewed prior to the next session to assure sufficient clarity for analysis. If a recording happened to be unclear, garbled or otherwise of poor quality, the investigator returned the following day and secured a second tape. A phonetic transcription was not attempted at this time. The transcriptions were done in normal Spanish orthography. These transcribed recordings yielded approximately 3400 utterances for each child. The following analysis is based on this data.

## RESULTS OF THE STUDY

All 39 transcriptions (13 per child) were analyzed; however, to make the data manageable, the children's utterances were grouped into three age levels: 18 months of age (the beginning of the investigation); 21 months of age (the mid-point); and 24 months of age. In addition, the two transcriptions per child for each age level were transcribed phonetically to facilitate the study of the acquisition of sounds and the sound substitutions made by each child.

The data were analyzed from two perspectives. The first involved the use of the sound in question in obligatory contexts. The second examined the sound substitutions made by the children in the hope of capturing intermediate stages in the acquisition of problematic sounds or sound sequences. Thus, in addition to determining at what age certain sounds are acquired, substitution analysis revealed what transition stages are involved in establishing the sounds.

Since the children's sound system will be compared to an adult model or form, a table of Spanish sounds (Table 1.2), an adaptation from Bowen and Stockwell (1969:133), is included. The reference Spanish sounds on the left column represent the phones normally occurring in the Southwest dialect of Spanish. The next four columns contain examples of words, with the phones, respectively, in utterance initial position, utterance medial position, intervocalic, and in an utterance final position. For the purpose of this study an utterance is defined as a string of meaningful speech sounds bounded by

**TABLE 1.2**
**Spanish Consonants and Their Privilege of Occurrence**

| Sound | *Utterance Initial | *Utterance Medial | Intervocalic | *Utterance Final |
|---|---|---|---|---|
| [p] | pato | carpa | copa | †— |
| [t] | tu | canto | pito | — |
| [k] | kilo, casa, que | escoba | taco | — |
| [b] | beso, vamos | ambas | — | — |
| [d] | donde | mundo | — | — |
| [g] | gota | mango | — | — |
| [č] | chino | marcha | coche | — |
| [f] | fijo | cofre | cofa | — |
| [b̵] | — | abre | iba, uva | — |
| [h] | jabon | — | cojo | — |
| [đ] | — | podré | dedo | ciudad |
| [s] | ser | farsa | rosa | mas |
| [g̵] | — | sagrado | lago | — |
| [z] | — | desde | — | — |
| [m] | mala | arma | cama | — |
| [n] | no | antes | vena | con |
| [ñ] | ñudo | ñisñil | niño | — |
| [ŋ] | — | chango | — | — |
| [l] | lata | nublado | sala | sol |
| [w] | huevo | laurel | — | — |
| [y] | ya, llave | pleito | allá | rey |
| [r] | — | — | cara | — |
| [r̄] | rana | partir | perro | por |

*For the purpose of this study an utterance is defined as a string of meaningful speech sounds bounded by silence.
†The dash (—) denotes the absence of that consonant in that particular position in Spanish.

silence. The focus on the four utterance positions is dictated by the occurrence of the significant Spanish allophones in these positions. Standard Spanish does not allow certain speech sounds in certain positions, for example, stops [p, t, k, b, d, g] and all affricates and fricatives [except s, l, n, d] cannot occur in an utterance final position. Also, certain phones do not occur in this dialect in utterance final position, for example, [b̵, đ, g̵, ŋ] (Phillips 1976). Those speech sounds not occurring at the utterance position indicated by the column are distinguished by a dash (—).

It should be pointed out that in standard Spanish /b/ has two variants [b] and [b̵] (Bowen and Stockwell 1969:54). For the Southwest dialect, the situation is compounded by the addition of a voiced labiodental fricative [v], which occurs in free variation with [b̵] (González 1968). The Southwest dialect thus makes use of either [b̵] or [v] in the intervocalic position or utterance medial position.

**TABLE 1.3**
**Speech Sounds Found at 18 Months of Age for**
**Karina (K), Celena (C), and Ana (A)**

| | | | Consonants | | | |
|---|---|---|---|---|---|---|
| | Labial | Labio-Dental | Dental | Alveo-Palatal | Velar | Glottal |
| Stops | [p] K,C,A<br>[b] K,C,A | | [t] K,C,A<br>[d] K,C,A | | [k] K,C,A<br>[g] K,C,A | [ʔ] C |
| Affricates | | | | [č] K,C,A | | |
| Fricatives | | [f] K,C<br>[v] K,C,A<br>[ƀ] K,C,A | [đ] K,C<br>[s] K,C,A<br>[z] K | | [g] K | [h] K,C,A |
| Nasals | [m] K,C,A | | [n] K,C,A | [ñ] A | [ŋ] C | |
| Laterals | | | [l] K,C,A | | | |
| Semi-Consonants | [w] K,C,A | | | [y] K,C,A | | |
| Vibrants | | | Tap<br>Trilled | [r] K,C,A<br>[r̄]   — | | |
| | | | Vowels | | | |
| | Front | | Central | | Back | |
| High | [i] K,C,A | | | | [u] K,C,A | |
| Mid | [e] K,C,A | | | | [o] K,C,A | |
| Low | | | [a] K,C,A | | | |

Tables 1.3, 1.4, and 1.5 provide a sketch of the speech sounds found in the three children at 18, 21, and 24 months of age respectively. The sounds in the table are arranged according to mode and place of articulation. Alongside each sound is the initial letter of the child's first name, identifying those sounds each child produced at the different age levels.

Table 1.3 shows that at 18 months the three children were producing the five basic Spanish vowels [i, e, a, o, u] while certain consonants had yet to appear individually for the three children. This lends support to Jakobson's first principle that vowel-consonant contrasts are possibly the first to be acquired. Since the children appeared to have mastered all five Spanish vowels at this age, we were unable to document Jakobson's sequence of acquisition between low and high vowels (/a/ *vs* /i/) preceding the front versus back contrast (/i/ *vs* /u/). However, we can see from Table 1.3 that all three children were producing stop/continuants (nasals) prior to the fricatives. The continuants [m, n] appeared in all three children's inventories of sounds while Ana alone did not produce an [ñ]. This occurred in her rendition of [neño] for "Lento" (proper name). Celena was the only child to produce the velar [ŋ].

This occurred in the utterance [waŋi] and in [ŋui]. In spite of parental assistance, it was impossible to determine what she was trying to say with those two utterances. Celena's production of the velar [ŋ] was unusual in that the velar [ŋ] is expected to occur only before other velars as in *chango* (monkey). Celena was also the only child to produce a glottal stop [ʔ] at this time. From the model sounds in Table 1.1 we can see that a glottal stop is not ordinarily part of the Spanish sound system. Its use appeared to be idiosyncratic in that Celena's glottal stops were produced indiscriminately throughout the first three recordings; that is to say, there was no evidence of a consistent linguistic environment for their occurrence. They occurred spontaneously in her speech. The affricate [č] and the lateral [l] were co-occurring with the stops, hence the affricate/liquid/stop contrasts appeared to have been established at this time. The only other group of consonants produced by all three children were the semi-consonants [w, y] and the tap [r]. The appearance of the tap [r] was unusual in that it should appear later than the stops; in fact González (1968) found it to occur erratically in the speech of children six years of age. According to Jakobson's principles, in Russian and French the lateral [l] precedes the vibrant [r̄]; this also appeared to be the case in these children's acquiring of Spanish as a first language.

Table 1.4 shows that within three months' time all three children were in the process of developing the full inventory of Spanish consonants. At 21 months of age the stop/fricative contrasts were still developing. Celena and Ana had completed their inventory of stops, while certain fricatives were still missing. Jakobson suggested that if two consonants are alike in manner of articulation, one will be labial and the other dental or aveolar. This principle, observed at 18 months, continued to be present at 21 months. It is of interest that at this age the affricate [č], which had co-occurred with the stops at 18 months of age, still appeared prior to the full inventory of nasals and not afterwards, as predicted by Jakobson. For all three children the lateral [l] did precede the vibrant [r̄] as suggested by Jakobson and as documented in the Russian and French languages. Individually, the children's sound systems changed significantly, as indicated in Table 1.4. For Karina, the only new addition at 21 months of age was the alveo-palatal nasal [ñ], which appeared in the utterance [níña] (feminine for 'child'). At this point the consonants missing in Karina's inventory of Spanish sounds were the trilled [r̄] and the velar nasal [ŋ]. The missing trilled [r̄] showed that vibrants are a late acquisition, as predicted by Jakobson. For Celena, the only new additions were the velar [g] and the dental [z]. Still missing in her inventory of sounds at 21 months of age were the alveo-palatal [ñ], the velar [ŋ], and the trilled [r̄], which is expected to be a late acquisition. Of interest is that Celena did produce the velar [ŋ] at 18 months of age, yet it did not occur again at 21 months of age. She produced

**TABLE 1.4**
**Speech Sounds Found at 21 Months of Age for**
**Karina (K), Celena (C), and Ana (A)**

| | | | | | | |
|---|---|---|---|---|---|---|
| Consonants | | | | | | |
| | Labial | Labio-Dental | Dental | Alveo-Palatal | Velar | Glottal |
| Stops | [p] K,C,A<br>[b] K,C,A | | [t] K,C,A<br>[d] K,C,A | | [k] K,C,A<br>[g] K,C,A | [ʔ] C |
| Affricates | | | | [č] K,C,A | | |
| Fricatives | | [f] K,C,A<br>[v] K,A<br>[b] K,A | [đ] K<br>[s] K,C,A<br>[z] K,C | | [g] K,C,A | [h] K,C,A |
| Nasals | [m] K,C,A | | [n] K,C,A | [ñ] K | [ŋ] A | |
| Laterals | | | [l] K,C,A | | | |
| Semi-Consonants | [w] K,C,A | | | [y] K,C,A | | |
| Vibrants | | | Tap<br>Trilled | [r] K,C,A<br>[r̄] — | | |
| Vowels | | | | | | |
| | Front | | Central | | Back | |
| High | [i] K,C,A | | | | [u] K,C,A | |
| Mid | [e] K,C,A | | | | [o] K,C,A | |
| Low | | | [a] K,C,A | | | |

only one incidence of a glottal stop [ʔ] at this age. As with earlier occurrences, the parents' help was sought to ascertain what she meant, without success. For Ana, the new sounds added to her repertoire were the alveo-palatal affricate [č] and the velar [ŋ], both of which she uttered in [čáŋgo] (monkey); the labio-dental fricative [f] uttered in [fío] for *frío* (cold); the lateral [l] which appeared in [klábo] (nail); and [pélo] (hair). The sounds still missing from Ana's inventory of Spanish sounds were the dental fricatives [d, z], along with the alveo-palatal [ñ].

Table 1.5 shows that the only Spanish consonant missing in the sample for all three children was the trilled [r̄]. For Karina, the velar [ŋ] appeared between 21 and 24 months of age in the word [čáŋgo] (monkey). For Celena, the alveo-palatal [ñ] and velar [ŋ] appeared in [níña], and [čáŋgo], respectively. No new incidences of glottalizing by Celena were evident at this time. For Ana, the dental fricatives [d,s,z] appeared in [dédo] (finger), and [es] (is), respectively, which she pronounced with a [z] as well as with an [s] when she requested a label for something. For example, she would point to a picture or object and utter [ez, es] meaning ¿*Qué es?* (what is it?). The alveo-palatal [ñ] reappeared for Ana at 24 months in the word [níña].

**TABLE 1.5**
**Speech Sounds Found at 24 Months of Age for**
**Karina (K), Celena (C), and Ana (A)**

| | Labial | Labio-Dental | Dental | Alveo-Palatal | Velar | Glottal |
|---|---|---|---|---|---|---|
| | | | Consonants | | | |
| Stops | [p] K,C,A<br>[b] K,C,A | | [t] K,C,A<br>[d] K,C,A | | [k] K,C,A<br>[g] K,C,A | |
| Affricates | | | | [č] K,C,A | | |
| Fricatives | | [f] K,A<br>[v] K,C,A<br>[b] K,C,A | [đ] K,C,A<br>[s] K,C,A<br>[z] K,C,A | | [g] K,C,A | [h] K,C,A |
| Nasals | [m] K,C,A | | [n] K,C,A | [ñ] K,C,A | [ŋ] K,C,A | |
| Laterals | | | [l] K,C,A | | | |
| Semi-Consonants | [w] K,C,A | | | [y] K,C,A | | |
| Vibrants | | | Tap<br>Trilled | [r] K,C,A<br>[r̄]  — | | |

| | Front | Central | Back |
|---|---|---|---|
| | | Vowels | |
| High | [i] K,C,A | | [u] K,C,A |
| Mid | [e] K,C,A | | [o] K,C,A |
| Low | | [a] K,C,A | |

The first three tables indicate that the five basic vowels in Spanish [i,e,a,o,u] were produced early by the children. This documents that the vowel-consonant contrast is the first to be acquired. Tables 1.3, 1.4, and 1.5 show that the stop consonants were the first to be fully established for all three subjects, as evidenced by their appearance at 18, 21, and 24 months of age. As a class, the fricatives appeared to be the most troublesome in terms of acquisition, judging by their fluctuation in appearance at 18, 21, and 24 months of age; as will be shown later, the children's sound substitutions were not representative of a particular category. The trilled [r̄] was not established in the three subjects by 24 months of age, which falls within the prediction made by Jakobson that vibrants are a late acquisition. All three children's production of nasals suggests that if two consonants are alike in manner of articulation, one will be labial and the other dental or alveolar. A degree of creativity was noted in the children's use of sounds not normally found in standard Spanish, for example [ʔ,š,ǰ], and in the use of Spanish sounds in positions not normally expected, such as the velar nasal [ŋ] before a vowel, rather than before another velar [k,g]. Non-Spanish sounds were gradually phased out as the children more closely approximated the adult Spanish model.

Up to now, the term *acquisition* has been used somewhat loosely. For the remainder of this paper, a sound will be considered *acquired* when it is produced correctly 90 percent of the time in obligatory contexts. For example, if a Spanish utterance requires a certain phone in the utterance initial, utterance medial/intervocalic, or utterance final position, and if the child produces that phone correctly in 90 percent of the utterances requiring that particular sound at any age level, then it can be said that the child had *acquired* that particular sound. It should be pointed out that, due to the children's age, lexical inventories are relatively limited and some sounds such as [č,f,đ,ɓ,ǧ,z,ñ,n,ř] occur infrequently. A child's production of a certain sound may reach criterion at one age, yet utterances at subsequent age levels may not call for the production of that same sound. For example, Celena reached criterion for the phone [f] at 21 months, yet produced no utterances containing that same phone at 24 months (see Tables 1.9 and 1.10).

The sound substitutions a child makes when attempting to produce certain sounds can possibly reveal stages in the child's phonological development. By combining the information on such sound substitutions with that of sound/ phones occurring in spontaneous speech over time and meeting the criterion mentioned in the preceding paragraph, it is possible to derive some notions about the children's phonological development.

Tables 1.6, 1.7, and 1.8 trace each child's sound substitutions at 18, 21, and 24 months of age. The model phone found in normal adult speech is listed on the left column for comparison purposes. The next three columns contain the substituted sound found in utterance initial position, utterance medial/intervocalic, and in utterance final position. Tables 1.9, 1.10, and 1.11 show the total number of Spanish utterances for each child at 18, 21, and 24 months of age. In addition, they show the number of occurrences of each sound, the number of substitutions for each sound, and the percent of correct productions for each child. The tables also indicate when the sounds ceased to be substituted and, hence, presumably acquired. Table 1.12 shows the percent of correct production of consonants for Karina, Celena, and Ana at 18, 21, and 24 months. The term *substitution* includes both a phone substitution for another phone, [p] for [b], for example, and consonant cluster reduction. The consonant cluster reductions are of the type $C_1C_2 \Rightarrow C_1$ (*frío=fío*), $C_1C_2 \Rightarrow C_2$ (*frío=río*), $C_1C_2 \Rightarrow C_3$ (*frío-bío*), and in some instances $C_1C_2 \Rightarrow \emptyset$ (*frío-ío*).

At 18 months the children's lexical inventories were relatively limited and some sounds occurred infrequently. The phones that did appear at this age and were substituted, appeared with greater frequency in the utterance initial position. However, Jakobson suggested that consonant contrasts usually appear earlier in the utterance initial position rather than in medial or final position.

**TABLE 1.6**
**Substitutions Found at 18 Months of Age for**
**Karina (K), Celena (C), and Ana (A)**

| Sound | Utterance Initial | Utterance Medial | Intervocalic | Utterance Final |
|---|---|---|---|---|
| | | Substitutions | | |
| [p] | [b,m] C | — | — | N/A |
| [t] | [m] C | [Ø] A | — | N/A |
| [k] | [ʔ,g] C [t] K | — | — | N/A |
| [b] | [v] K,C | — | N/A | N/A |
| [d] | [t] K [đ] C | [Ø] K | N/A | N/A |
| [g] | — | — | N/A | N/A |
| [č] | — | — | — | N/A |
| [f] | [b] C | — | — | N/A |
| [ƀ] | N/A | — | — | N/A |
| [v] | N/A | — | — | N/A |
| [h] | [n] C | N/A | — | N/A |
| [đ] | [d] K,C | [Ø] K | [d] C | — |
| [s]  [t] A | $\begin{bmatrix} š,b,č \\ t,ž \end{bmatrix}$ K $\begin{bmatrix} t,b,n \\ Ø,g \end{bmatrix}$ C | [Ø] C | [đ,č,g] K | [l] C [h] K |
| [ǥ] | [g] K,C | — | — | N/A |
| [z] | [h] [Ø] K | — | N/A | N/A |
| [m] | [Ø] K | — | — | N/A |
| [n] | — | [ñ] A | — | — |
| [ñ] | — | — | [l] C [n] K,C,A | N/A |
| [ŋ] | N/A | — | N/A | N/A |
| [l] | [n] A | — | [n] C | — |
| [w] | — | — | [b] K,C,A | N/A |
| [y] | — | — | — | — |
| [r] | — | [Ø] K,C,A | — | N/A |
| [r̄] | [d,l] K [r] C | [Ø] K | [l] K,C | — |

Table 1.6 suggests that by 18 months the subjects had still to develop consonant contrasts in initial position, as evidenced by the relatively high substitution rate by all three children. But, as Tables 1.7 and 1.8 show, these contrasts, measured by substitution rate, appear to be established by 21 months of age.

The second major set of substitutions occurred in the inter–vocalic position, when *niña* was rendered as *nina*, wherein the [ñ] was substituted by [n] between the vowels [i] and [a]. The fricative [s] was the only phone substituted in the word final position. Karina produced the word *más* (more) as [mah], substituting the [h] for [s]. There appeared to be three major types that were substituted by the children; the first were the stops. Of these, ten out of a total of sixteen substituted stops in the utterance initial position were produced by Celena. She substituted [b] for [p] in [bata] for *pata* (foot) and produced four instances of [m] for [p] in [mapá] for *papá* (father). However,

**TABLE 1.7**
**Substitutions Found at 21 Months of Age for**
**Karina (K), Celena (C), and Ana (A)**

| Sound | Substitutions | | | |
|---|---|---|---|---|
| | Utterance Initial | Utterance Medial | Intervocalic | Utterance Final |
| [p] | — | — | — | N/A |
| [t] | — | — | — | N/A |
| [k] | [Ø] A | — | — | N/A |
| [b] | — | — | N/A | N/A |
| [d] | [n,Ø] C | — | N/A | N/A |
| [g] | — | — | N/A | N/A |
| [č] | — | — | — | N/A |
| [f] | — | — | — | N/A |
| [ƀ] | N/A | — | — | N/A |
| [v] | N/A | — | — | N/A |
| [h] | — | N/A | — | N/A |
| [đ] | — | — | [n] C | — |
| [s] | — | [Ø] K,C,A | [š] A | [Ø] A |
| [ǥ] | [Ø] A | — | — | N/A |
| [z] | — | — | N/A | N/A |
| [m] | [Ø] A [n] C | — | — | N/A |
| [n] | — | — | — | — |
| [ñ] | — | — | [d] C | N/A |
| [ŋ] | N/A | — | N/A | N/A |
| [l] | [Ø] A | — | [Ø] A | — |
| [w] | — | — | — | N/A |
| [y] | [Ø] C | — | — | — |
| [r] | — | [Ø] C,A | [Ø] C | N/A |
| [r̄] | [Ø] A [d] K | — | [y,r] K | — |

out of the 288 utterances (See Table 1.8), Celena correctly used the phone [p] in the utterance initial position in *pato* (duck) four times, and *pata* (foot) five times. For the remainder of the stops [t,k,b,d,g] she substituted [m] for [t] once in *toalla* (towel) which she rendered as [mobáyah], [?] and [g] for [k] in *qué* [what] which she produced as [ge] and [?e] once each, and [d] for [d] once in *Diana* [đyána].

Karina's 175 utterances at the age of 18 months included substitutions of [t] for [k] once in *cayó* (fell) produced as [tayó] and [t] for [d] once in *dile* (tell him) produced as [tíle]. No substitutions for stops at utterance initial position were found in Ana's 133 utterances.

The next major grouping to be substituted at 18 months of age was the fricative class [f,v,đ,s,z,ǥ,h], in particular the dental fricative [s]. For Karina, the substitutions of [b,č,t] for the [s] in the utterance initial position were found in [bí], [čí], and [tí] for *sí* (yes). In the intervocalic position the dental fricative [s] was rendered as [š] in [dóša] for *Rosa* (her mother's name) and [č] in [ačina] for *asina*, dialect form of *así* (this way). Karina substituted [h] for

**TABLE 1.8**
**Substitutions Found at 24 Months of Age for**
**Karina (K), Celena (C), and Ana (A)**

| | Substitutions | | | |
|---|---|---|---|---|
| Sound | Utterance Initial | Utterance Medial | Intervocalic | Utterance Final |
| [p] | [Ø] A | — | — | N/A |
| [t] | — | — | — | N/A |
| [k] | [Ø] A | — | — | N/A |
| [b] | [Ø] A | [Ø] A | N/A | N/A |
| [d] | [Ø] K,C | [Ø,l] C | N/A | N/A |
| [g] | [d] A | — | N/A | N/A |
| [č] | — | — | — | N/A |
| [f] | — | — | — | N/A |
| [ɓ] | N/A | — | — | N/A |
| [v] | N/A | — | — | N/A |
| [h] | — | N/A | — | N/A |
| [đ] | — | — | — | — |
| [s] | [t] A  [c,š] C | [Ø] K,C,A | — | [Ø] A |
| [ǥ] | — | — | — | N/A |
| [z] | — | — | N/A | N/A |
| [m] | — | — | — | N/A |
| [n] | — | [Ø] C,A | — | — |
| [ñ] | — | — | — | N/A |
| [ŋ] | N/A | — | N/A | N/A |
| [l] | [Ø,n] A | — | [Ø] C,A | — |
| [w] | — | — | — | N/A |
| [y] | — | — | — | — |
| [r] | — | [Ø] A | [Ø] K,C | N/A |
| [r̄] | [l] K,C,A  [n] A | — | — | — |

[s] in the utterance final position once in the word *más* which she produced as [máh]. Celena substituted [t,n,g,Ø] for [s] in the utterance initial position, producing the following for *sí*: [tí], [ní], and [gí]. Ana substituted [t] for [s] in the utterance initial position only, in [tí] for *sí* (yes).

Table 1.9 shows the number of occurrences of each sound, the number of substitutions for each sound, and the percent correct production of each sound for Karina (K), Celena (C), and Ana (A) at 18 months of age. For Karina, the only stop that did not reach criterion was the dental stop [d], with 60 percent correct production. Karina only reached criterion on three fricatives, [h], [ɓ] and [z], with the lowest percent of correct production being the dental fricative [s] (16 percent). No instances of production occurred for the nasals [ñ] and [ŋ], while the [m] and [n] reached criterion at this age. Karina reached criterion on the lateral [l] and the semi-consonant [y], but did not reach criterion on the semi-consonant [w] and the vibrants [r] and [r̄]. Celena reached criterion on the stops [k,b,g] and on the fricatives [h,ɓ]. No occurrence ap-

**TABLE 1.9**
**Comparison of Substitutions to Incidences of Sounds Produced**
**for Karina, Celena, and Ana at 18 Months of Age**

| Sound | Karina (n = 175) | | | Celena (n = 228) | | | Ana (n = 133) | | |
|---|---|---|---|---|---|---|---|---|---|
| | Number of Occurrences | Number of Substitutions | % Correct | Number of Occurrences | Number of Substitutions | % Correct | Number of Occurrences | Number of Substitutions | % Correct |
| [p] | 25 | 0 | 100.0 | 18 | 5 | 72.3 | 5 | 1 | 80.0 |
| [t] | 40 | 0 | 100.0 | 23 | 4 | 82.6 | 5 | 4 | 20.0 |
| [k] | 32 | 3 | 90.6 | 37 | 2 | 95.6 | 1 | 0 | 100.0 |
| [b] | 13 | 1 | 92.3 | 39 | 1 | 97.4 | 38 | 0 | 100.0 |
| [d] | 5 | 2 | 60.0 | 10 | 2 | 80.0 | 1 | 0 | 100.0 |
| [g] | 4 | 0 | 100.0 | 8 | 0 | 100.0 | 0 | 0 | — |
| [č] | 2 | 0 | 100.0 | 1 | 0 | 100.0 | 1 | 0 | 100.0 |
| [f] | 4 | 3 | 25.0 | 2 | 1 | 50.0 | 0 | 0 | — |
| [đ] | 4 | 3 | 25.0 | 4 | 3 | 25.0 | 0 | 0 | — |
| [h] | 5 | 0 | 100.0 | 22 | 1 | 95.5 | 8 | 0 | 100.0 |
| *[b̵] | 2 | 0 | 100.0 | 4 | 0 | 100.0 | 1 | 0 | 100.0 |
| [s] | 25 | 21 | 16.0 | 19 | 15 | 21.1 | 2 | 1 | 50.0 |
| [ǧ] | 4 | 3 | 25.0 | 0 | 0 | — | 1 | 1 | 0.0 |
| [z] | 2 | 0 | 100.0 | 0 | 0 | — | 0 | 0 | — |
| [m] | 54 | 2 | 96.3 | 65 | 0 | 100.0 | 73 | 0 | 100.0 |
| [n] | 25 | 0 | 100.0 | 87 | 0 | 100.0 | 65 | 4 | 93.8 |
| [ñ] | 0 | 0 | — | 6 | 6 | 0.0 | 1 | 1 | 0.0 |
| [ŋ] | 0 | 0 | — | 4 | 4 | 0.0 | 0 | 0 | — |
| [l] | 21 | 0 | 100.0 | 20 | 1 | 95.0 | 5 | 4 | 20.0 |
| [w] | 1 | 1 | 0.0 | 39 | 2 | 94.9 | 5 | 1 | 80.0 |
| [y] | 13 | 0 | 100.0 | 21 | 0 | 100.0 | 10 | 0 | 100.0 |
| [r] | 26 | 4 | 84.7 | 7 | 6 | 14.3 | 2 | 1 | 50.0 |
| [r̄] | 7 | 7 | 0.0 | 2 | 2 | 0.0 | 0 | 0 | — |

*This represents a combination of [b̵,v] since they occurred in nonobligatory contexts (free variation) in the children's utterances.

peared in the data for the fricatives [ǧ] and [z]. Two nasals, [m,n], reached criterion in Celena's productions while the nasals [ñ] and [ŋ] did not. For the remainder of the Spanish consonants, Celena reached criterion on [l,w,y], but not on [r,r̄]. Ana reached criterion on three stops [k,b,d], while no instances occurred for [g]. Of the fricatives, only [h] and [b̵] reached criterion; no occurrence of [z] was noted. As with the other two children, the only nasals to reach criterion at this time for Ana were [m,n]. Ana reached criterion on the semi-consonant [y] but did not on the [w]. She failed to reach criterion on the vibrants [r,r̄], as did the other two subjects.

Table 1.7 shows the substitutions the children made at 21 months. At this time Karina made fewer substitutions; her utterances came closer to the adult model, although she was still having difficulty with the dental fricative in the utterance medial position. For example, she produced *Rosa* as [dóša], also substituting the [d] for the trilled [r̄]. The affricate [č] was rendered once in the utterance initial position as [š] in *chile* [šíle]. The trilled [r̄] was substituted by a tap [r] and the semi-consonant [y] once each in *arriba* (on top) resulting in [aríɓa] and [ayiba], respectively. Celena also made fewer substitutions at age 21 months than at the previous age level. The only stop for which she provided a substitution was the dental [d] in utterance initial position in [déɗo] (finger). Her attempt resulted in [néɗo]. The nasal [n] also was substituted for the interdental fricative [ɖ] in the intervocalic position for the same word in a different utterance, resulting in the reduplication of the initial consonant and rendering [neno]. The tap [r] was dropped in *quiero* (I want) when Celena uttered [kío]. One incidence of [y] being substituted by [Ø] occurred in the utterance initial position in the word *llama* (call) which she produced as [áma]. Ana's number of utterances increased at 21 months of age and this perhaps resulted in a greater incidence of substitutions. Of the substitutions she made, two were of the type [Ø] for a consonant in the utterance initial position such as [ápis] for *lápiz* (pencil), [ána] for *rana* (frog).

At this age the children also produced various instances of consonant cluster reduction. Karina produced *gusta* (like) as [gúta] and [patél] for *pastel* (cake), for the category $C_1C_2 \Rightarrow C_2$. Ana produced [bávo] for *bravo* (exclamation of approval), in which $C_1C_2 \Rightarrow C_1$. In words of three syllables or more she produced only the last two syllables. She produced *mariposa* (butterfly), *gatito* (kitten), and *manzana* (apple) as [pósa], [títo], and [sána], respectively.

From Table 1.7 it is evident that the children produced fewer substitutions overall while their utterances increased in number from the previous age. In addition, Table 1.10 shows that more Spanish consonants were acquired [met the 90 percent criterion] by the three children by 21 months of age. Karina had acquired [p,t,k,b,g,č,h,ɓ,z,m,n,l,y] at 18 months; at 21 months, she added [d,f,ɓ,ɖ,g,ñ,ŋ]. Celena had acquired [k,b,g,č,h,ɓ,m,n,l,w,y] at 18 months, and acquired [p,t,f,ñ,ŋ] by 21 months of age. Ana's acquisitions at 18 months were [k,b,d,č,h,ɓ,m,n,y]; by 21 months, she had added [p,t,f,z,ŋ,l,w].

Table 1.8 presents the sound substitutions made by Karina, Celena, and Ana at two years of age. Karina made a total of five substitutions at this age. Her utterances continued to draw closer to the adult model. In fact the substitutions she made were deviations only when compared to the standard Spanish model, following instead the adult dialect model: [ónde] for *donde* (where), [pa] for *para* (for), [toy] for *estoy* (I am), [tas] for *estás* (you are), and [táɓas] for *estabas* (you were) (Phillips 1976). Celena continued to substitute for the dental fricative [s] in the following utterances: [čí] and [ší] for *sí* (yes), [číŋko] for *cinco* (five), [čyéte] for *siete* (seven), [do] for *dos* (two), and

**TABLE 1.10**
**Comparison of Substitutions to Incidences of Sounds Produced**
**for Karina, Celena, and Ana at 21 Months of Age**

| Sound | Karina (n = 280) | | | Celena (n = 175) | | | Ana (n = 168) | | |
|---|---|---|---|---|---|---|---|---|---|
| | Number of Occurrences | Number of Substitutions | % Correct | Number of Occurrences | Number of Substitutions | % Correct | Number of Occurrences | Number of Substitutions | % Correct |
| [p] | 34 | 0 | 100.0 | 9 | 0 | 100.0 | 24 | 0 | 100.0 |
| [t] | 46 | 2 | 95.6 | 11 | 0 | 100.0 | 20 | 0 | 100.0 |
| [k] | 26 | 0 | 100.0 | 15 | 0 | 100.0 | 33 | 1 | 97.0 |
| [b] | 33 | 1 | 97.0 | 6 | 0 | 100.0 | 8 | 0 | 100.0 |
| [d] | 25 | 0 | 100.0 | 4 | 1 | 75.0 | 9 | 0 | 100.0 |
| [g] | 7 | 0 | 100.0 | 2 | 0 | 100.0 | 4 | 1 | 75.0 |
| [č] | 12 | 1 | 91.7 | 5 | 0 | 100.0 | 4 | 0 | 100.0 |
| [f] | 5 | 0 | 100.0 | 7 | 0 | 100.0 | 2 | 0 | 100.0 |
| [đ] | 5 | 0 | 100.0 | 0 | 0 | — | 0 | 0 | — |
| [h] | 13 | 0 | 100.0 | 10 | 0 | 100.0 | 17 | 0 | 100.0 |
| *[ƀ] | 7 | 4 | 42.9 | 0 | 0 | — | 0 | 0 | — |
| [s] | 23 | 4 | 82.6 | 20 | 6 | 70.0 | 17 | 2 | 88.2 |
| [ǥ] | 2 | 0 | 100.0 | 0 | 0 | — | 0 | 0 | — |
| [z] | 4 | 0 | 100.0 | 0 | 0 | — | 1 | 0 | 100.0 |
| [m] | 50 | 2 | 96.0 | 39 | 0 | 100.0 | 25 | 1 | 96.0 |
| [n] | 83 | 0 | 100.0 | 19 | 0 | 100.0 | 31 | 0 | 100.0 |
| [ñ] | 4 | 0 | 100.0 | 2 | 0 | 100.0 | 0 | 0 | — |
| [ŋ] | 1 | 0 | 100.0 | 1 | 0 | 100.0 | 2 | 0 | 100.0 |
| [l] | 21 | 0 | 100.0 | 2 | 0 | 100.0 | 9 | 0 | 100.0 |
| [w] | 1 | 0 | 100.0 | 17 | 0 | 100.0 | 8 | 0 | 100.0 |
| [y] | 17 | 0 | 100.0 | 4 | 0 | 100.0 | 2 | 0 | 100.0 |
| [r] | 38 | 11 | 71.1 | 8 | 5 | 37.5 | 9 | 4 | 55.6 |
| [ř] | 12 | 12 | 0.0 | 0 | 0 | — | 6 | 6 | 0.0 |

*This represents a combination of [ƀ,v] since they occurred in nonobligatory contexts (free variation) in the children's utterances.

[dyed] for *diez* (ten). Celena also produced *duele* (it hurts) as [wéle] substituting [Ø] for [r] utterance initially, [mía] for *mira* (look) substituting [Ø] for [r] intervocalically. Her consonant cluster reduction consisted of the type $C_1C_2 \Rightarrow C_2$ in the following: [éte] for *este* (this one). She uttered three words of more than two syllables, of which one, *elefante* (elephant), maintained the last two syllables, resulting in [fante]. The other two, *grabando* (recording) and *Rodríguez* (proper last name), approximated the adult model more closely. The word *grabando* was produced with the medial [d] absent, rendering [grabáno]. She rendered *Rodríguez* as [lolíges] substituting the trilled [ř] and the consonant cluster with the lateral [l] (reduplication).

Ana's utterances and substitutions continued to increase numerically. She maintained, with regularity, the last two syllables in words of three or more syllables, for example, [lóta] for *pelota* (ball), [sía] for *policía* (police),

TABLE 1.11
Comparison of Substitutions to Incidences of Sounds Produced
for Karina, Celena, and Ana at 24 Months of Age

| Sound | Karina (n = 389) | | | Celena (n = 285) | | | Ana (n = 317) | | |
|---|---|---|---|---|---|---|---|---|---|
| | Number of Occurrences | Number of Substitutions | % Correct | Number of Occurrences | Number of Substitutions | % Correct | Number of Occurrences | Number of Substitutions | % Correct |
| [p] | 39 | 0 | 100.0 | 41 | 0 | 100.0 | 18 | 1 | 94.4 |
| [t] | 72 | 0 | 100.0 | 22 | 0 | 100.0 | 68 | 0 | 100.0 |
| [k] | 86 | 0 | 100.0 | 38 | 0 | 100.0 | 27 | 2 | 92.6 |
| [b] | 18 | 0 | 100.0 | 7 | 0 | 100.0 | 22 | 2 | 91.0 |
| [d] | 19 | 1 | 94.7 | 24 | 3 | 87.5 | 26 | 0 | 100.0 |
| [g] | 2 | 0 | 100.0 | 5 | 0 | 100.0 | 7 | 2 | 71.4 |
| [č] | 2 | 0 | 100.0 | 4 | 0 | 100.0 | 4 | 0 | 100.0 |
| [f] | 1 | 0 | 100.0 | 0 | 0 | — | 3 | 0 | 100.0 |
| [đ] | 5 | 0 | 100.0 | 2 | 0 | 100.0 | 3 | 0 | 100.0 |
| [h] | 20 | 0 | 100.0 | 5 | 0 | 100.0 | 2 | 0 | 100.0 |
| *[b] | 5 | 0 | 100.0 | 4 | 0 | 100.0 | 5 | 0 | 100.0 |
| [s] | 72 | 3 | 95.8 | 42 | 10 | 76.2 | 43 | 3 | 93.0 |
| [ǧ] | 6 | 0 | 100.0 | 16 | 1 | 93.7 | 4 | 2 | 50.0 |
| [z] | 4 | 0 | 100.0 | 2 | 0 | 100.0 | 3 | 1 | 66.6 |
| [m] | 52 | 0 | 100.0 | 35 | 0 | 100.0 | 42 | 0 | 100.0 |
| [n] | 97 | 1 | 99.0 | 41 | 1 | 97.5 | 58 | 1 | 98.2 |
| [ñ] | 2 | 0 | 100.0 | 1 | 0 | 100.0 | 3 | 0 | 100.0 |
| [ŋ] | 1 | 0 | 100.0 | 2 | 0 | 100.0 | 3 | 0 | 100.0 |
| [l] | 61 | 0 | 100.0 | 9 | 1 | 88.8 | 38 | 3 | 92.1 |
| [w] | 4 | 0 | 100.0 | 3 | 0 | 100.0 | 7 | 0 | 100.0 |
| [y] | 33 | 0 | 100.0 | 14 | 0 | 100.0 | 10 | 1 | 90.0 |
| [r] | 30 | 1 | 96.6 | 10 | 2 | 80.0 | 26 | 3 | 88.4 |
| [r̄] | 7 | 5 | 28.6 | 6 | 6 | 0.0 | 9 | 9 | 0.0 |

*This represents a combination of [b,v] since they occurred in nonobligatory contexts
(free variation) in the children's utterances.

[bása] for *calabaza* (pumpkin), [báyos] for *caballos* (horses), [jamín] for
*Benjamin* (proper name), and [bóles] for *árboles* (trees). Ana also continued
to have difficulty with the dental fricative [s] in the utterance initial position
and in the utterance final position, for example, [tápo] for *sapo* (toad), and
[ápi] for *lápiz* (pencil). The trilled [r̄] had not appeared for the children at this
time; as a consequence Ana substituted [n] for [r̄] in *rana* (frog) rendering
[nána] (reduplication), and [l] for [r̄] in *rico* (rich) rendering [líco].

Table 1.11 shows that at 24 months of age the children had acquired a high
percentage of the Spanish consonants. At this age Karina had acquired all but
the trilled [r̄], yet she managed to produce it correctly twice out of seven attempts. Celena had acquired 18 of the 23 consonants. She still had to acquire
the stop [d], the fricative [s], the lateral [l], and the vibrants [r,r̄]. Ana also

TABLE 1.12
**Percent Correct Production of Consonants**
**for Karina, Celena, and Ana at 18, 21, and 24 Months of Age**

| Sound | % Correct at 18 Months | | | % Correct at 21 Months | | | % Correct at 24 Months | | |
|---|---|---|---|---|---|---|---|---|---|
| | Karina (n = 175) | Celena (n = 288) | Ana (n = 133) | Karina (n = 280) | Celena (n = 175) | Ana (n = 168) | Karina (n = 389) | Celena (n = 285) | Ana (n = 317) |
| [p] | 100.0 | 72.3 | 80.0 | 100.0 | 100.0 | 100.0 | 100.0 | 100.0 | 94.4 |
| [t] | 100.0 | 82.6 | 20.0 | 95.6 | 100.0 | 100.0 | 100.0 | 100.0 | 100.0 |
| [k] | 90.6 | 95.6 | 100.0 | 100.0 | 100.0 | 97.0 | 100.0 | 100.0 | 92.6 |
| [b] | 92.3 | 97.4 | 100.0 | 97.0 | 100.0 | 100.0 | 100.0 | 100.0 | 91.0 |
| [d] | 60.0 | 80.0 | 100.0 | 100.0 | 75.0 | 100.0 | 94.7 | 87.5 | 100.0 |
| [g] | 100.0 | 100.0 | — | 100.0 | 100.0 | 75.0 | 100.0 | 100.0 | 71.4 |
| [č] | 100.0 | 100.0 | 100.0 | 91.7 | 100.0 | 100.0 | 100.0 | — | 100.0 |
| [f] | 25.0 | 50.0 | — | 100.0 | 100.0 | 100.0 | 100.0 | 100.0 | 100.0 |
| [đ] | 25.0 | 25.0 | — | 100.0 | — | — | 100.0 | 100.0 | 100.0 |
| [h] | 100.0 | 95.5 | 100.0 | 100.0 | 100.0 | 100.0 | 100.0 | 100.0 | 100.0 |
| *[b] | 100.0 | 100.0 | 100.0 | 42.9 | — | — | 100.0 | 100.0 | 100.0 |
| [s] | 16.0 | 21.1 | 50.0 | 82.6 | 70.0 | 88.2 | 95.8 | 76.2 | 93.0 |
| [ǧ] | 25.0 | — | 0.0 | 100.0 | — | — | 100.0 | 93.7 | 50.0 |
| [z] | 100.0 | — | — | 100.0 | — | 100.0 | 100.0 | 100.0 | 66.6 |
| [m] | 96.3 | 100.0 | 100.0 | 96.0 | 100.0 | 96.0 | 100.0 | 100.0 | 100.0 |
| [n] | 100.0 | 100.0 | 93.8 | 100.0 | 100.0 | 100.0 | 99.0 | 97.5 | 98.2 |
| [ñ] | — | 0.0 | 0.0 | 100.0 | 100.0 | — | 100.0 | 100.0 | 100.0 |
| [ŋ] | — | — | 0.0 | 100.0 | 100.0 | 100.0 | 100.0 | 100.0 | 100.0 |
| [l] | 100.0 | 95.0 | 20.0 | 100.0 | 100.0 | 100.0 | 100.0 | 88.8 | 92.1 |
| [w] | 0.0 | 94.9 | 80.0 | 100.0 | 100.0 | 100.0 | 100.0 | 100.0 | 100.0 |
| [y] | 100.0 | 100.0 | 100.0 | 100.0 | 100.0 | 100.0 | 100.0 | 100.0 | 90.0 |
| [r] | 84.7 | 14.3 | 50.0 | 71.1 | 37.5 | 55.6 | 96.6 | 80.0 | 88.4 |
| [ř] | 0.0 | 0.0 | — | 0.0 | — | 0.0 | 28.6 | 0.0 | 0.0 |

*This represents a combination of [b,v] since they occurred in nonobligatory contexts (free variation) in the children's utterances.

had acquired 18 of the 23 consonants. She still had not acquired the velar stop [g], the velar fricative [ǧ], the fricative [z], and the vibrants [r,ř].

Table 1.12 is a composite of Tables 1.9, 1.10, and 1.11 showing the percent correct production of consonants for Karina, Celena, and Ana at 18, 21, and 24 months of age.

Table 1.6 reveals that there was no discernible pattern in the children's sound substitutions. That is to say, no one group of sounds, for example, stops, substituted wholesale for other groups of sounds, for example, fricatives. For example, the dental fricative [s] was substituted for by nasal (continuant) stops, other fricatives, or was dropped altogether in the utterances the children attempted. In addition, Table 1.9 shows that the number of occurrences of sounds versus the number of substitutions made for that sound were relatively small in number. The only exception was the dental fricative [s] which was substituted 21 out of 25 times by Karina, 15 out of 19 times by Celena, and only once of two times by Ana. Tables 1.7, 1.8, 1.10 and 1.11 show that the children reduced the number of substitutions across succeeding age levels. Since the substitutions were not representative of a particular category and since most of them occurred at 18 months of age, it was impossible to identify intermediate stages in the acquisition process.

In summary, the children's production of the five basic Spanish vowels suggests that the vowel consonant contrasts may well be the first to be acquired in Spanish. Table 1.3 revealed that the stop/continuant (nasal) contrast was also among the earliest acquired by the children. This study suggests that stops precede fricatives not only in the initial position, as suggested by Jakobson, but also in the utterance medial position, as well as intervocalically. In addition, Table 1.3 reveals that if two consonants are alike in manner of articulation, one will be labial and the other dental (recall that Spanish does not have alveolars). The affricate [č] reached criterion quite early while the lateral [l] was substituted by a nasal, lending partial support to Jakobson's principle that laterals appear later than nasals. In Spanish, as in Russian and French, the [l] preceded the vibrants [r,ř].

Due to the children's early acquisition of the Spanish vowels, it was impossible to determine if the contrast between low and high vowels (/a/ *vs* /i/) preceded front versus back contrasts (/i/ *vs* /u/). From the rate of substitutions the children made (Table 1.9) it was determined that consonant clusters are a late acquisition. In addition, consonant contrasts in general appeared to be made earlier in the medial and final position rather than the initial positions suggested by Jakobson (see Table 1.6). Finally, since consonantal substitutions were not limited to a particular category and since most of them occurred at 18 months of age it was impossible to identify clear–cut intermediate stages in the acquisition process.

This investigation documented the early phonological development of three children acquiring Spanish as a first language at an early age (18–24 months).

In analyzing the phonological data it was discovered that some of Jakobson's principles were applicable systematically for these three children, while they refuted some, and appeared to provide tentative evidence on others. Principles 1, 3, 4, 7, 10 received substantial support from these data; principles 6 and 11 were refuted. The data were inconclusive on 2, 5, and 8. Principle 9 does not apply, since Spanish does not utilize nasal vowels. Since there were no discernible patterns in the children's sound substitutions, this study was also unable to document intermediate stages in the Spanish phonological development of these children.

## REFERENCES

Bowen, J. D., and Stockwell, R. P. *Patterns of Spanish pronunciation.* Chicago, Ill.: University of Chicago Press, 1969.

Dale, P. S. *Language development: Structure and function.* University of Washington, Seattle: Holt, Rinehart and Winston, 1976.

Ervin-Tripp, S. Language development. In *Review of child development research,* L. W. Hoffman and M. L. Hoffman, eds., vol. 2. New York: Russell Sage Foundation, 1966, pp. 55–105.

Ferguson, C. A., and Slobin, D. I., eds. *Studies of child language development.* New York: Holt, Rinehart and Winston, 1973.

García, E. Research in review: Bilingualism in early childhood. *Young Children* 35 (1980):52–66.

García, E. E., Maez, L., González, G., and Ibañez, J. *A national study of early childhood bilingualism: An age by region analysis of Spanish/English MLU.* Paper presented at the National Association for Bilingual Education Conference. Seattle, Washington, May 1980.

González, G. *A linguistic profile of the Spanish–speaking first–graders in Corpus Christi.* Unpublished M.A. Thesis, University of Texas, Austin, 1968.

———. *The acquisition of Spanish grammar by native Spanish speakers.* Ph.D. Dissertation, University of Texas-Austin, University Microfilm No. 71-11540, 1970.

———. The acquisition of grammatical structures by Mexican-American children. In *El lenguaje de los chicanos.* E. Hernández-Chávez, A. D. Cohen, and A. F. Beltramo, eds. Arlington, VA: Center for Applied Linguistics, 1975, pp. 220–237.

———. *The acquisition of Spanish grammar by native Spanish speaking children.* Rosslyn, VA: National Clearinghouse for Bilingual Education, 1978.

———. The acquisition of verb tenses and temporal expressions in Spanish: Age 2;0–4;6. Los Angeles: National Dissemination and Assessment Center, California State University, 4, 1980.

Jakobson, R. Why "mama" and "papa?" In *Selected writings of Roman Jakobson.* The Hague: Mouton, 1962, pp. 538–45.

———. Translated by Keiler, A. *Child language, aphasia, and phonological universals.* The Hague: Mouton, 1968.

Jakobson, R., and Halle, M. *Fundamentals of language.* The Hague: Mouton, 1956.

Kagan, J., and Lewis, M. Studies of attention. *Merril Palmer Quarterly of Behavior and Development* 2 (1965):95–127.

Kaplan, E., and Kaplan, G. The prelinguistic child. In *Human development and cognitive processes.* J. Elliot, ed. New York: Holt, Rinehart and Winston, 1971, 359–81.

Menyuk, P. *Sentences children use.* Cambridge: M.I.T. Press, 1969.

———. *The acquisition and development of language.* New York: Prentice-Hall, 1971.

Moskowitz, A. I. The two-year-old stage in the acquisition of English phonology. *Language* 46(1970):426–41.

Nakazima, S. A comparative study of the speech developments of Japanese and American English in childhood. *Studia Phonologica* 2.

Oller, D. K. Simplification as the goal of phonological processes in child speech. *Language Learning* 24 (1974):299–303.

Pfaff, C. W. Syntactic constraints on code-switching: A quantitative study of Spanish/ English. Paper read at Linguistic Society of America meeting, San Francisco, December, 1975. Also *Papers in Sociolinguistics*, 35.

Phillips, R., Jr. The segmental phonology of Los Angeles Spanish. In *Studies in southwest Spanish*. J. D. Bower and J. Ornstein, eds. Rowley, Mass.: Newbury House, 1976.

Velten, H. V. The growth of phonemic and lexical patterns in infant language. In *Child language: A book of readings*. A. Bar-Adon and W. F. Leopold, eds. Englewood Cliffs, N.J.: Prentice-Hall, Inc., 1972, pp. 82–91.

Wolff, P. H. The natural history of crying and other vocalizations in early infancy. In *Determinants of infant behavior*. B. M. Foss, ed., vol. 4. London: Methuen, 1966.

# 2.
# Discourse-Sensitive Measurement of Language Development in Bilingual Children

*Robert Berdan and Maryellen Garcia*

THE MEASUREMENT OF ORAL LANGUAGE DEVELOPMENT in school-aged children poses a number of perplexing issues. When the children of interest are in the process of learning two languages, the issues become even more complicated, particularly as the children grow older and fluency increases. In part, this complexity derives from the fact that language, and in particular language more broadly construed as *communication*, is itself an extremely complex phenomenon.

This complexity, and the variety of purposes for which measurement must serve, has given rise to considerable controversy over what aspects of language provide the most appropriate indicators of overall language development (Erickson 1981). Using data from Spanish and English speaking children, this paper deals chiefly with length of utterance as an indicator of language development. The focus, however, is not on length per se, but on the dependencies between length of utterance and discourse context. It is expected that the relationship between length and discourse context reported here will be replicated to one degree or another with virtually all quantitative measures derived from language samples, including such measures as: structural complexity scores (McCarthy 1930; Davis 1933a), length complexity index (Shriner 1967), t-units (Hunt 1970), syntactic density measures (Kidder 1974), mean word morpheme index (Tyack and Gottsleben 1974), and complexity scores (Herbert 1979).

Syntactic length has been used as a measure of language development for well over half a century. McCarthy (1954), in a largely positive review of length studies, attributes their beginning to the work of Smith (1926). Summarizing the findings of her review, McCarthy concluded that:

The use of the measures has been criticized by some writers, and a few substitute measures have been suggested, but none seems to have super-seded the mean length of sentence for a reliable, easily determined, ob-jective, quantitative, and easily understood measure of linguistic matu-rity (1954:550).

A subsequent review by Shriner (1969) is considerably less sanguine, citing problems of both reliability and validity. By that time, of course, the study of language development had shifted largely to the study of language structure, and Shriner (1967) was advocating use of a combined length-complexity measure.

Throughout this time measures of length have been used in a great variety of language studies, including early language development (Brown 1973), school-age language development (Davis 1937), bilingual language develop-ment (Garcia, Maez, and Gonzalez 1981), atypical language development (Shriner 1969), and literary stylistics (Yule 1938).[1] The general tendency is to report the *mean* number of lexical units (words, morphemes) per syntactic unit (sentence, utterance). Some studies also report other characteristics of length distribution, including the number of one-word utterances, the length of the longest utterance, the mean of the five longest utterances (Davis 1937b), and the standard deviation of length (Minifie, Darley and Sherman 1963). Only the stylistics studies attempt to deal with the full distribution of sentence lengths (Williams 1969; Buch 1969). With the exception of the sty-listics literature, however, the focus is chiefly on the single measure of central length tendency, the mean.

There seems to be a highly consistent linear relationship between increase in age and utterance length, when looking at the means of populations, but a great deal of instability when looking at repeated measures of individuals. Thus, studies of oral language such as McCarthy (1930), Davis (1937) and Templin (1957), have all found consistent relationships between increases in age and increases in group mean length scores. The same has been true of studies of written language, for example, Stormzand and O'Shea (1924), Heider and Heider (1940), Hunt (1965), and O'Donnell, Griffin and Norris (1967).

Application of these studies in educational and clinical settings, however, requires reliable indicators of individual performance. Several clinical studies

---

1. These various areas overlap somewhat, but in general they have developed as quite sepa-rate literatures, using slightly different terminologies and procedures. For example, the early lan-guage development tends to be measured in terms of morphemes rather than words, across a do-main termed an *utterance*. The atypical or clinical language studies tend to count either words or morphemes, in a domain termed a *response*. The stylistics literature also counts words, but deals with sentences. The school–aged development studies are variable in terminology, but many stud-ies, following Hunt, count words in t–units (terminable units).

have looked at the variability of length scores within age cohorts. Minifie, Darley, and Sherman report not only group means, but also standard deviations and the range of scores found at each grade level. The range of scores for individuals at any age level was sufficient "to place a given child as much as two years ahead or two years behind his age level (1963, 146)."[2]

Studies using repeated samples from the same children, collected under similar circumstances, have shown rather conflicting results. Fisher (1954), using samples of fifty sentences from twenty-three subjects, drawn at each of two times a month apart, found a correlation of only 0.58 for mean length. Minifie, Darley, and Sherman (1963) found reliability coefficients of .82 and .77 respectively for their samples of five-year-olds and eight-year-olds.

These problems of variability occur even when there have been attempts to maintain consistency in the elicitation procedure. The introduction of systematic variation in either setting or topic also shows that measures of length are sensitive to characteristics of the situation under which they were elicited. Scott and Taylor (1978) collected samples of 125 utterances from each of twelve normal preschoolers in home and in clinical settings. They found significantly longer mean lengths in the home setting. Kramer, James and Saxman (1979) did a similar study for preschool children who had been referred to a clinic for speech and language evaluations. They found that mean utterance length averaged about two-thirds longer in the home setting than in the clinical setting.

These studies strongly suggest that syntactic length cannot be interpreted solely as characteristic of an individual, abstracted from the particular situation in which the language use is observed. The consistent reporting only of mean length scores, however, obscures another major indicator of variability in sentence length. Rarely, if ever, is the standard error of the mean, standard deviation, or any other indicator of internal variability given (but Winitz 1959). Darley and Moll (1960) show that the reliability of samples of five to ten sentences is extremely low ($r = .36 - .53$), but that as sample size approaches fifty sentences, the usual size reported in the clinical literature, reliability reaches .85, and increases relatively little with increased sample size. Even larger samples are needed, however, before structural complexity scores begin to stabilize.

In addition to the differences related to setting, shifts of topic or stimulus material within a single setting can have an effect on length. Most studies using language samples employ a variety of toys, pictures, and questions to

2. It should be noted, however, that the sample for this study was drawn to yield "a cross-sectional sampling of the socioeconomic levels present in Iowa City" (Minifie, Darley, and Sherman 1963:141). The relationship of social status to sentence length was documented as early as the studies by Davis and by Templin. Minifie, et al., do not provide any information which might link variability at any age with their sampling pattern.

elicit language from children, but the exact stimulus material is rarely controlled. Cowan, Weber, Hoddinott, and Klein (1967) used popular magazine covers as stimulus materials with 96 five- to eleven-year-olds. They found significant differences in sentence length depending on which picture the children were talking about. Mean lengths for the pictures ranged from 8.85 to 13.44, and the range was greater than that for the means of the age groups. They had anticipated that children would talk more about some pictures than about others, but were at a loss to explain why some pictures would elicit longer sentences than others.

In addition to this variability related to context or topic, it should be pointed out that lengths of successive utterances for any one speaker in any situation are extremely variable. Virtually all speakers occasionally use one-word utterances, and their longest utterances may be far greater than the mean across a large number of utterances (Templin 1957). Minifie, Darley, and Sherman (1963) show that the standard deviation of sentence lengths within samples for individuals tends to be greater than the difference between the means of samples for five-and-a-half and eight-year-olds.

Explanation of the variation in length, either variation related to various aspects of the discourse situation, or variation internal to any particular portion of a discourse, has been extremely limited. As Brown pointed out, increments in length relate in a rather general sense to different processes at different points in development:

> Increases in MLU could perfectly well be produced solely by increases in the number of functors or grammatical morphemes (like inflections, articles, prepositions, auxiliary verbs). Or they could be solely produced by embedding one simple sentence in another or by coordinating two or more simple sentences. And in fact, in later stages, the continued rise of MLU values is strongly affected by all these factors more or less in turn (1973, 185).

There can be no doubt that syntax, and in particular, ratios of subordinate clauses to main clauses, is highly related to length measured in lexical units (Shriner 1967). But these syntactic measures are perhaps best thought of as covariants, or alternate measures of length, rather than as explanations for variation in length itself.

Ultimately syntax fails as an explanation for variation in lexical measures of length, because the different measures are defined across the same linguistic domain, the sentence. Explanation must come from some higher level of the integration of discourse. Rather than look to setting or topic, as in the studies cited above, the functions which utterances serve in discourse are considered in this study.

The clinical literature does provide some hint that length may be related to function, but does not explicitly pursue that possibility. Scott and Taylor (1978) observed that the children in their sample asked more questions in home environments than in the clinic. It is also apparent from their tables that questions were of shorter length than were other utterances in their samples. The higher incidence of the shorter questions in the home environment would tend to confound their overall finding that utterances were longer in the home environment, masking some of that environmentally related difference.

In addition to asking questions, there are, of course, many other functions that utterances perform in a discourse (Dore 1979). How these different functions relate to length has not been studied previously. In connected dialog, each successive turn is generally contingent on the preceding turn in several ways. For example, turns that provide specific information are generally, but not always, in response to requests for specific information.

Both the function of a particular turn, and the function of the immediately prior turn in the discourse, may influence what information is exchanged, and also influence the length and complexity of the utterances. This is apparent in the following exchange:

> Interviewer: Do you like science?
> Child: Yes. I like it.
> Interviewer: What else do you learn in your science class?
> Child: About water.
> Interviewer: What about water?
> Child: Water becomes a liquid and the gas, no the air, becomes water.

The interviewer's first question is a request for a specific piece of information. It is a yes/no question; it can be answered appropriately with a single word, or, as in this case, with a pronominalized rephrasing of the question. The interviewer's second question is another request for information, referring to a prior topic in the conversation. It is readily answered with a simple noun phrase. The third question is a request for elaboration on the child's immediately preceding turn. The child's response could vary widely in the amount of elaboration provided, but almost all of the alternatives would require a full sentence as a response. The request for elaboration is also an invitation for the child to provide an extended response on a topic introduced by the child. Utterances in such a discourse context tend to be longer than responses to requests for specific information.

In addition to these functional contingencies across turns, there may be syntactic contingencies as well. The most important of these for any study of length is ellipsis.

The rules for ellipsis in English discourse are rather complex (Halliday and Hassan 1976). Ellipsis may be characterized generally, however, as the *non-repetition of identical information across adjacent turns in a conversation.* Consider the following exchange:

> Interviewer: What do you think they're going to do after they finish eating?
> Child: Play. (full ellipsis)

This response contains just one word. Yet it is fully as appropriate for the discourse as would any of the following have been:

> I think they're going to play after they finish eating. (no ellipsis)
> I think they're going to play. (partial ellipsis)
> After they finish, they're going to play. (partial ellipsis)

The more extended responses might have offered positive evidence of fairly well-developed English fluency; the use of the most elliptic form, however, offers no negative evidence. In some instances the failure to use ellipsis where it is possible makes the conversation sound unnatural.

In summary, elliptic utterances may be considerably shorter than their non-elliptic paraphrases, but offer no evidence for less well-developed language proficiency. Conversely, some very short elliptic utterances indicate ability to comprehend and use dialogue appropriately, thus showing greater language proficiency than some equally short, but nonelliptic utterances. Clearly, this phenomenon confounds the use of utterance length as a measure of language development. Reliable measure based on length must either control the relative frequency of ellipsis in the sample of language analyzed, or it must provide a means of weighting utterances of the same length differently in order to compensate for ellipsis effects.

## METHODOLOGY

Continued analysis of data generated by the National Center for Bilingual Research (NCBR) Longitudinal Studies of Language Development in Bilingual Contexts (Garcia, Veyna-Lopez, Siguenza and Torres 1982) provided the findings reported here. Data collected includes monthly tape recordings and participant-observation of naturalistic interaction by children in home and school settings. Over the course of the study, the children ranged in age from approximately four to ten years and were observed in their use of English, as well as in the language of the home, Spanish or Korean. The study was undertaken to document the nature of the language development process for children in bilingual contexts, with particular interest in relating that process to educational practice.

*Participants.* The sixteen children included in this analysis ranged in age from 3;8 to 9;8 at the time the language samples were collected in the summer of 1981. The children are eight sibling pairs from the greater Los Angeles area, whose home language ranged from almost exclusively Spanish to largely English. The children who were in school had access to a range of bilingual services and some, but not all, were in bilingual classrooms. Characteristics of the children, their homes, and their schools are detailed in Garcia et al. (1982). For the longitudinal study, these children are visited by a bilingual fieldworker monthly in their homes and in their schools. Each session is audio tape recorded.

*Elicitation procedures.* The data for this analysis were elicited using the picture description and story-telling task of the Basic Inventory of Natural Language (BINL) (Herbert 1979). Following the general procedures for the administration of the BINL, the children were asked to describe various pictures which they selected from a set of culturally diverse color pictures. The sessions were conducted in the children's homes; both focal siblings were present throughout and were encouraged to interact during the course of the session. In some cases another family member or neighborhood children participated. The sessions were tape recorded and subsequently transcribed and edited. Each child, in turn, described and discussed the pictures. Conversation between siblings was included as part of the sample. The fieldworker directed that for each child the task was to be done first in English and then in Spanish. The goal of the session was to elicit at least fifty utterances in English and in Spanish from each child. In some cases this was not possible, particularly in the weaker language of the younger children. Three of the children did not produce even ten utterances in English, and were excluded from the analysis of the English data.

*Coding.* After transcription and editing, utterances were extracted from the transcripts in each language in accordance with BINL procedures. The lists of extracted utterances were then sent to the BINL publisher for machine scoring. In that process the utterances were edited to exclude sentence partials that did not conform to the BINL definition of utterance.[3] Words borrowed from the non-test language were also excluded from the count. Utterances were then scored for length in words.

In addition to being coded for length and language (English or Spanish),

---

3. The BINL is scored in terms of mean number of words per *language sample*, for example, sentence, and the complexity of the language used. Eliminated from the word count are such things as repetitions, corrections, fillers, and words substituted from another language. Borrowed words, that is, vocabulary incorporated from another language, are counted, as are proper names. Contractions are counted as two words.

each utterance was coded for several discourse-related characteristics. These included the function of the child's discourse turn, the function of the previous turn, presence of ellipsis in the child's utterance, status of the speaker of the previous turn, number of clauses in the child's utterance, and number of clauses in the preceding turn. This set of characteristics is referred to here as the *discourse context of an utterance*.

*Function.* The term discourse function refers to the informational content and the effect of the utterance in the interaction. Other function classification systems were considered but were found to be oriented to classroom interaction (Sinclair and Coulthard 1975, 40–44; Dore 1979, 354–55; Peters, Ostman, Larsen, and O'Connor 1982). The discourse functions described below are not in all cases speech acts, but reflect the demands of the speech situation under analysis, in other words, a language elicitation interview. The two variables which take discourse function into account are the function of the child's own turn and the function of the previous relevant turn in the discourse. Both variables used the following set of values:

| | |
|---|---|
| Agreement or disagreement response. | An utterance which contradicted or agreed with what was said in the last relevant utterance. |
| Request for specific information. | A question which required a point of fact or conjecture from the next speaker. |
| Elaboration. | An utterance which advanced the narrative or added new information to a previous point in the discourse. |
| Information response. | An utterance which provided the specific factual or conjectural information requested by the previous speaker. |
| Solicitation. | An utterance which was procedural in nature, selecting the next speaker or otherwise indicating that the next turn be taken. |
| Request for clarification. | An utterance which required the speaker of the previous relevant turn to clarify or repeat what was said in that turn. |
| Bid or attention getter. | An utterance which was either a bid for the floor, joke, or other means of getting attention in the interaction. |

*Ellipsis.* Utterances differ with respect to ellipsis in a number of different ways. They may be fully elliptic, with all redundant forms excluded, partially elliptic, or they may show no ellipsis at all. Ellipsis is not always possible in discourse; generally only the first utterance of a turn may be elliptic, and then the potential for ellipsis depends, among other things, on the syntactic and lexical relationship to the preceding turn. Thus utterances were scored both for the presence of ellipsis and for the eligibility for ellipsis according to the following categories: *completely elliptical, partially elliptical, not elliptical* (but ellipsis possible), or *ellipsis not appropriate* (by the rules of discourse).

*Speaker of the Previous Turn.* Generally, but not always, a child's utterance in the sample is related to a previous turn in the discourse. The speaker of this previous turn may have been any one of the persons present during the elicitation session. The particular individuals present varied from family to family, but could all be classified into one of the following categories: *sibling* of the child, *peer* of the child, *usual fieldworker, companion fieldworker, adult relative,* or *no relevant previous turn.*

*Syntax.* In addition to the more straightforward discourse characteristics given above, two gross syntactic analytical devices were included. These measures the length of the child's utterance and the length of the previous turn in the discourse, counting the number of clauses. The following categories were used: less than one full clause, one full clause, two clauses, and three clauses or more.

*Distribution of data set.* The one-way tabulation on each of the variables shows that the distribution of utterances across functions is extremely uneven (Table 2.1). For example, for Function of Turn, there were 584 examples of Elaboration, but only six examples of Request for Elaboration across all sixteen children. Cross tabulation of all variables produced numerous empty cells. Because of this, the number of categories was reduced for each variable by conflation of logically similar categories. This recording formed the basis for the analyses.[4]

*Holistic ratings of language proficiency.* Excerpts of approximately ten pages were then selected from the transcript of each child's session in each language, which contained an average of forty-five turns per focal child. Five adult judges who are fluently bilingual in English and Spanish and who had not had direct contact with the children in the study were asked to rate each child's language on a scale of one to ten, with the following instruction:

> We would like to get an idea of how well the children in our study speak English and Spanish. On the basis of your impressions from looking at the transcript provided, please rank the two children (whose initials or

---

4. It may be noted in Table 1.1 that in recoding, the values elaboration and information responses were not conflated for function of turn but were for function of previous turn. Elaboration and information response are themselves quite different with respect to length, but do not seem to differentially affect the subsequent turn.

**TABLE 2.1**
**Distribution and Mean Length of Utterances by Discourse Variables**

| Variable | Value | N | Mean Length | Recoded Value | Mean Length English | Length Spanish |
|---|---|---|---|---|---|---|
| Ellipsis | Partial | 26 | 4.12 | Ellipsis | 3.10 | 3.85 |
| | Full | 473 | 3.48 | | | |
| | No ellipsis | 75 | 5.01 | No ellipsis | 4.36 | 5.28 |
| | Not appropriate | 721 | 5.91 | | | |
| Function of Turn | Request Specific Information | 130 | 4.85 | Request Information | 3.69 | 4.07 |
| | Request Elaboration | 6 | 4.67 | | | |
| | Request Clarification | 27 | 2.81 | | | |
| | Elaboration | 584 | 6.39 | Elaboration | 5.36 | 5.86 |
| | Information Response | 410 | 3.38 | Information Response | 3.26 | 3.66 |
| | Clarification | 54 | 3.42 | Attention to Interaction | 3.66 | 4.03 |
| | Agree—Disagree | 43 | 4.74 | | | |
| | Bid-Attention Getter | 24 | 3.54 | | | |
| | Evaluative remark | 17 | 5.18 | | | |
| Function of Previous Turn | Request Specific Information | 442 | 3.57 | Request Information | 3.34 | 3.74 |
| | Request Clarification | 52 | 3.73 | | | |
| | Request Elaboration | 326 | 5.89 | Prompt | 4.88 | 5.93 |
| | Solicitation | 145 | 7.48 | | | |
| | Elaboration | 90 | 5.17 | Elaboration/ Information | 4.08 | 4.31 |
| | Information Response | 94 | 4.26 | | | |
| | Clarification | 24 | 4.17 | Attention to Interaction | 4.13 | 4.86 |
| | Agree—Disagree | 52 | 5.21 | | | |
| | Bid-Attention Getter | 19 | 6.47 | | | |
| | Evaluative Remark | 51 | 5.20 | | | |
| Number of Clauses of Turn | Less than 1 | 474 | 2.31 | Less than 1 | 2.57 | 2.32 |
| | 1 full clause | 644 | 5.16 | 1 full clause | 5.31 | 4.57 |
| | 2 clauses | 143 | 10.34 | 2 or more clauses | 3.51 | 2.92 |
| | 3 or more clauses | 34 | 15.18 | | | |
| Number of Clauses of Previous Turn | Less than 1 | 434 | 5.30 | Less than 1 | 5.08 | 4.50 |
| | 1 full clause | 703 | 4.71 | 1 full clause | 4.69 | 4.12 |
| | 2 clauses | 125 | 4.93 | 2 or more clauses | 4.70 | 4.24 |
| | 3 or more clauses | 29 | 5.59 | | | |
| Speaker of Previous Turn | Usual fieldworker | 713 | 5.69 | Fieldworker | 4.09 | 5.07 |
| | Companion fieldworker | 212 | 2.84 | Other adult | 3.17 | 4.39 |
| | Adult relative | 17 | 4.24 | | | |
| | Sibling/Peer | 353 | 4.73 | Peer | 4.58 | 3.89 |

names appear above) on a scale of 1–10, with 10 being *excellent*, 5 being *average*, and 1 being *poor*. Use your own criteria as the basis for these evaluations/rankings.

To verify that judges were responding in reasonably comparable ways to the task, we converted the ratings to ranks, and calculated Kendall's Coefficient of Concordance (Siegel 1956) for both the English and the Spanish samples. There was significant concurrence across judges for each sample (English: Kendall's $W = 0.531$, $X^2(12) = 31.87$, p < .01; Spanish: Kendall's $W = 0.488$, $X^2(15) = 36.66$, p < .001).

*Analytic Procedures.* The questions underlying this study, and the nature of the data set, require several different analytic approaches. One problem was determining which of the discourse variables related to differences in utterance length. Another was separating effects on length due to discourse context from the more general utterance length characterization of each child in both Spanish and English.

Natural language data sets tend to be plagued by a number of distributional characteristics which call into question the appropriateness of some conventional statistical procedures, such as analysis of variance. The chief problems are the numerous empty cells and the grossly unequal number of observations per cell. The variables which seem to be most meaningful in differentiating the effects of discourse context cross classify in such a way that there is extremely low probability of occurrence of utterances in some cells, while in other cells utterances occur at high frequency.

The following strategy was used to circumvent these problems. Each of the six discourse variables was treated separately, one at a time, by analysis of variance. Lack of significant effect for any variable suggested that it be ignored in consideration of the overall relationship of discourse context to length. Because the variables were analyzed separately, however, there was the possibility that any one of them was a recording of some other variable. For instance, an effect related to request for information as a function of the previous turn might be indistinguishable from an effect related to information response as a function of the turn itself. Thus these analyses of variance allowed the discarding of irrelevant variables but did not identify redundant variables.

To do that, it was necessary to look at the remaining discourse variables simultaneously, for which a multinomial maximum likelihood procedure was indicated, with data aggregated across children. The maximum likelihood estimates provided expected frequency distributions of all utterance lengths for each discourse context.[5] This overall approach of successive analyses is simi-

---

5. A somewhat parallel multiple regression analysis of these data is presented in Berdan and Garcia (1982).

lar to that used for analysis of primary linguistic variables by Berdan (1975) and Garcia (1981).

Sociolinguists who have used quantified approaches to the study of natural language variability have long been frustrated by the distributional characteristics of most language variables, with many contexts of great interest occurring naturally at very low frequencies (Labov 1966). Maximum likelihood models can accommodate these distributional problems and provide a means for considering all of the discourse variables simultaneously. The use of maximum likelihood techniques for estimating effects of linguistic environments was introduced by Cedergren and Sankoff (1974).[6] For this approach the data of interest were the frequency with which utterances of each length occurred in each discourse context. The distribution of lengths was regarded as a multinomial function (Edwards 1972).[7]

The object of the maximum likelihood procedure is to derive a multinomial function for each factor in each factor group and to calculate the *likelihood* that these functions adequately characterize the data set.[8] Whether or not the use of additional factor groups significantly improves the characterization of the data set may be tested by comparing likelihoods across solutions. It is also possible to estimate the probability of occurrence of utterances of each length category in each discourse context from the functions defining each factor.

To reduce the number of parameters estimated in the multinomial and to balance the data set, length was recoded into the following ten categories:

### Length Category

| L1 | L2 | L3 | L4 | L5 | L6 | L7 | L8 | L9 | L10 |
|----|----|----|----|----|----|----|-----|-------|-------|
| 1  | 2  | 3  | 4  | 5  | 6  | 7  | 8–9 | 10–11 | 12–31 |

6. The several models which these researchers estimated by maximum likelihood have more recently been replaced by a model based on logistic transformation (Cox 1970; Lindsey 1975) of proportions (Rousseau and Sankoff 1976). This model has been extended to the description of polychotomous variables by Jones (1975). The introduction of this latter model to the treatment of language variation follows the development of the necessary computer programming by Pascale Rousseau at the University of Montreal, to whom the authors are grateful for providing a copy of the program and related documentation.

7. In a sense, treatment as a multinomial degrades the information in the data set, since length is treated as a nominal rather than interval scale. However, the treatment of length as an ordinal scale is itself troublesome, since longer utterances do not result simply from incrementing shorter utterances, but from a complex change in the semantic and syntactic integration of information. Whatever limitations there may be in the linguistic or cognitive interpretation of a multinomial model of length, other models of this secondary language measure seem at least equally opaque, and do not share many of the useful properties of this approach.

8. Terminology in the related sociolinguistic literature diverges from that of other statistical treatments. *Factor group* and *factor* are used analogously to the analysis of the terms *variable* and *level*, respectively. Within a factor group, factors give a mutually exclusive and exhaustive

This results in a compression of the upper end of the length scale, but affects a relatively small proportion of the data set.

## RESULTS

*Analyses of Variance.* For the analyses of variance, children were grouped according to school-grade level: preschoolers, first graders and third graders. Utterances for each child were grouped separately by language. Then, each of the remaining six discourse variables was treated in turn in a grade by language by discourse variable design. For each analysis, utterances were reclassified by the levels of the discourse variable in the analysis. Mean MLUs across grade levels are shown for each discourse level of each of the variables in Table 2.1. The significant effects (p < .05) for each of the six analyses are summarized in Table 2.2. Five of the six discourse variables show significant effect on the length of utterance: ellipsis, function of turn, number of clauses, function of the previous turn, and speaker of the previous turn. The sixth variable, number of clauses of the previous turn, showed no significant effect. As shown in Table 2.2, there is a significant main effect for grade level, but only in the analysis by function of turn. In none of the analyses is there a significant main effect for language. There are several interactions, but for none of them are all of the relevant main effects significant. Inspection of the cell means suggests that there is some tendency for shorter utterances by preschool children, particularly in English. In general, the preschool children did not use multiple clause utterances in English. However, given that the six analyses are simply reclassifications of the same data set, grade and language effects, which are not consistent across analyses, are highly suspect.

These analyses lend strong support to the general contention that discourse context is an important intervening variable in the interpretation of the relationship of MLU to language development. Analyzing the discourse variables separately, however, presents the possibility that one or more of the observed effects is nothing more than a re-labelling of some other logically prior effect. Considering the discourse variables simultaneously, however, introduces the distributional problems referred to earlier. For this reason a maximum likelihood procedure was used.

*Maximum likelihood estimates.* Maximum likelihood can be estimated using all the discourse variables (factor groups) or any subset of them. The choice of factor groups is, in effect, a hypothesis of the underlying dimensions of the data set: what factors best and most parsimoniously account for the ob-

---

characterization of all observations. Any given observation is defined by one factor from each factor group and, in this case, by a category corresponding to length.

**TABLE 2.2**
**Summary of Significant Effects (p < .05) for Six Analyses**
**of Variance (Grade × Language × Discourse Variable)**

| Variables (Levels) | Mean Square | df | f | p |
|---|---|---|---|---|
| Analysis 1: Ellipsis | | | | |
| Ellipsis (2) | 27.363 | 1,12 | 36.40 | .0001 |
| Analysis 2: Function of Turn | | | | |
| Grade (3) | 26.801 | 2,12 | 5.29 | .0225 |
| Function (4) | 23.283 | 3,36 | 20.25 | .0000 |
| Analysis 3: Number of Clauses | | | | |
| Clauses (3) | 42.384 | 2,24 | 16.20 | .0000 |
| Analysis 4: | | | | |
| Function of Previous Turn | | | | |
| Language (2) × Grade (3) | 41.493 | 2,12 | 4.05 | .0452 |
| Function (4) | 14.718 | 3,36 | 9.28 | .0001 |
| Analysis 5: | | | | |
| Speaker of Previous Turn | | | | |
| Speaker (3) | 3.010 | 2,24 | 4.30 | .0254 |
| Language (2) × Speaker (3) | 6.788 | 2,24 | 5.66 | .0097 |
| Analysis 6: | | | | |
| Number of Clauses, Previous Turn | | | | |
| Grade (3) × Language (2) | | | | |
| × Clauses (3) | 5.695 | 4,24 | 4.01 | .0125 |

served differences in utterance lengths. From among all of the logically possible combinations of factor groups, sampled here are two combinations of five factor groups and two combinations of four factor groups; and finally, the data set has been split by language. Separate estimates were run for each language set using three factor groups each. The combinations of factor groups used in each analysis are shown in Table 2.3.

In spite of the difficulty of interpreting the number of clauses as an independent variable, we retained it in Analysis 1, but not in the subsequent treatments. Analyses 3 and 4 alternate between function of the previous turn and speaker of the previous turn. In each of these estimates, language (Spanish and English) was also maintained as a factor group.[9] For Analyses 5a and 5b, the data set was split by language, and separate estimates were run for each set. Otherwise these are identical in factor groups to Analysis 3. For each of the analyses, utterances are aggregated across speakers.

*Comparing Alternative Analyses.* The absolute measure of goodness of fit of any particular set of factor groups is very difficult, if not impossible, on a

9. This was done in spite of the failure to show a language effect in the analyses of variance. For the ultimate purpose of modeling language development, the appropriateness of aggregating across languages is open to serious question, and it is preferable to demonstrate similarity (or difference) across languages, rather than assume it.

**TABLE 2.3**
**Factor Groups Used for Each Maximum Likelihood Estimate**

| Factor Groups | Log Likelihood |
|---|---|
| Analysis 1:<br>　　Language<br>　　Ellipsis<br>　　Function of Turn<br>　　Function of Previous Turn<br>　　Number of Clauses | −2263.15 |
| Analysis 2:<br>　　Language<br>　　Ellipsis<br>　　Function of Turn<br>　　Function of Previous Turn<br>　　Speaker of Previous Turn | −2643.56 |
| Analysis 3:<br>　　Language<br>　　Ellipsis<br>　　Function of Turn<br>　　Function of Previous Turn | −2682.03 |
| Analysis 4:<br>　　Language<br>　　Ellipsis<br>　　Function of Turn<br>　　Speaker of Previous Turn | −2667.16 |
| Analysis 5a: (English data only)<br>　　Ellipsis<br>　　Function of Turn<br>　　Function of Previous Turn | −1303.92 |
| Analysis 5b: (Spanish data only)<br>　　Ellipsis<br>　　Function of Turn<br>　　Function of Previous Turn | −1336.88 |

data set such as this, which has many empty cells and many cells with very low expected frequencies. An alternative to such absolute tests of goodness of fit are *relative* tests, comparing alternative solutions. Solutions are preferred which both maximize the log likelihood, and minimize the number of parameters estimated from the data set. This was tested by computing twice the difference in log likelihoods for any two solutions, and comparing that figure with the $X^2$ distribution, with degrees of freedom equal to the change in degrees of freedom between the two solutions. The log likelihoods for each of the solutions tested here are given in Table 2.3.

By the above criterion, first choice among the solutions is Analysis 1, incorporating number of clauses as a factor group. Its log likelihood is significantly greater than that of any other solutions. Analysis 2 is significantly better than Analysis 3 [$X^2$ (2,9) = 79.94], but not better than Analysis 4 [$X^2$

$(3,9) = 23.60$]. Splitting the data set by languages in Analyses 5*a* and 5*b* nearly doubles the number of parameters estimated, but does not significantly improve the log likelihood [$X^2$ $(6,9) = 41.23$] over Analysis 3. All of this suggests that for the alternative solutions compared here, it is not possible to reduce the number of factor groups by which the data are modeled without significantly reducing the adequacy of the model.[10]

## SEPARATING THE EFFECTS OF DISCOURSE CONTEXT

The findings presented here show the significant effect of discourse context on length of utterance. This strongly suggests that any attempt to relate length of utterances in a language sample to a child's language development must either control for discourse context, or develop a system for accommodating the influences of discourse contexts which are external to the child. These analyses provide a basis by which the influences of discourse context can be partialled out.

From the maximum likelihood estimates it is possible to calculate the probabilities that utterances of any particular length will be observed in each discourse context.[11] Actually, we are not interested in the probability of occurrence of an utterance of a particular length, but in the probability that an utterance of *at least* that particular length will occur in a given discourse context. To calculate the discourse effects estimated by the maximum likelihood procedure, we use the following weighting procedure; one minus the estimated probability that an utterance will be at least as long as that observed in any particular discourse context.

From each of the maximum likelihood estimates, weights based on the estimated cumulative probability were derived for each sentence. Mean weights were then calculated for each child in each language under each of the maximum likelihood analyses (Table 2.4). These mean weights provide a basis for at least an initial test of whether the general notion of weights based on frequency of occurrence and discourse context are of utility in estimating language development. One problem, of course, is the identification of an independent standard of language development, such that the proposed measure can be evaluated. No satisfactory standard is available for this data set, so two general indicators will be considered, both separately and jointly. These are chronological age, and judges' holistic ratings of language proficiency.[12]

---

10. The specific effects related to each factor in each analysis are displayed in Berdan and Garcia (1982).

11. These procedures are detailed in Berdan and Garcia (1982).

12. A third indicator, scores on the BINL proficiency measure, that is, their complexity

*Age as an independent measure of language development.* Age is an extremely precarious predictor of language development for a bilingual population. The children in this sample have highly diverse experiences in each of their languages. Some of the children are from homes where Spanish was the primary, perhaps the only, language until they entered school. Others are from homes where English is the primary language for at least some dyads. Some of the children are in full bilingual programs in school; others are in regular programs, with or without extra instruction in English. Nonetheless, we expect that there will be a generally positive relationship between age and language development in both languages. The age of each child at the time the language sample was collected is given in Table 2.4.

*Judges' ratings of language proficiency.* The judges' ratings for each child were converted to ranks, with all of the English data being considered separately from all of the Spanish data. Ranks were then summed across judges for each child in each language. These resulting scores are shown in Table 2.4.

*Patterns of relationships among the measures of language development.* Correlations for age, mean judge's proficiency rating, MLU, and mean weights calculated under each of the maximum likelihood procedures are given in Tables 2.5a and 2.5b for English and Spanish, respectively. The straight measure of length, MLU, is significantly correlated with age only in English. MLU does not correlate significantly with the judges' rankings in either language. Thus MLU by itself does not seem to show a particularly consistent relationship to development. For both languages, the judges' rankings correlate with age at about $r = .6$. The length measures which variously accommodate discourse context produce results which do not differ greatly from MLU; all but one correlate with MLU in the $r = .85 - .95$ range. The one exception is Analysis 1 in Spanish, $r = .687$.

The patterns for the maximum likelihood weights are somewhat mixed. All except Analysis 1 correlate significantly with age in English; exactly the opposite is true in Spanish. There, only Analysis 1 correlates significantly with age. Analysis 3 correlates with the judges' rankings in both languages. Analysis 5a also correlates significantly with both age and judges' rankings in English, but not in Spanish.

Recognizing that in this sample of children there are numerous situations which intervene in the expected relationship between age and language development, the various indicators derived from length with age and the judges' proficiency ratings, considered jointly, were compared. Separate multiple regressions were computed for MLU and for each of the weightings from the

---

scores, was not considered. The correlation of these complexity scores with MLU approaches unity (English, $r = .998$; Spanish, $r = .975$) and they cannot be treated as independent indicators.

**TABLE 2.4**
**Individual Scores on Language Measures**

| Child ID* | Age (Year, Month) | Judges' Profic. Rating | English Length Mean | Std. Error | Mean Weights, Max Likelihood Analyses 1 | 2 | 3 | 4 | 5a |
|---|---|---|---|---|---|---|---|---|---|
| PA | 9;8 | 23.5 | 8.1 | .72 | .50 | .58 | .58 | .59 | .57 |
| RR | 9;3 | 52.5 | 6.24 | .48 | .46 | .45 | .47 | .45 | .46 |
| NF | 8;11 | 52.5 | 5.94 | .46 | .41 | .49 | .51 | .48 | .52 |
| MS | 8;8 | 49.0 | 5.51 | .74 | .32 | .49 | .45 | .49 | .45 |
| JH | 8;7 | 31.0 | 5.96 | .65 | .40 | .44 | .46 | .45 | .46 |
| BF | 7;6 | 38.5 | 6.32 | .48 | .44 | .52 | .54 | .53 | .53 |
| SR# | 7;5 | | | | | | | | |
| VM | 7;5 | 39.5 | 5.86 | .41 | .46 | .48 | .51 | .49 | .49 |
| JT | 7;2 | 32.0 | 4.50 | .34 | .33 | .42 | .47 | .42 | .45 |
| VS | 7;2 | 23.0 | 3.12 | .34 | .30 | .35 | .29 | .35 | .29 |
| ER | 6;11 | 50.5 | 5.05 | .42 | .46 | .43 | .45 | .43 | .45 |
| LA | 6;9 | 20.0 | 2.78 | .34 | .29 | .17 | .17 | .17 | .18 |
| MR# | 5;6 | | | | | | | | |
| GH# | 5;0 | | | | | | | | |
| RT | 4;8 | 17.5 | 5.38 | .43 | .47 | .39 | .42 | .40 | .41 |
| TM | 3;8 | 15.5 | 2.48 | .25 | .18 | .27 | .20 | .26 | .20 |
| Mean | 7;5 | 34.2 | 5.17 | .47 | .39 | .42 | .42 | .42 | .42 |
| S.D. | 4;5 | 13.8 | 1.59 | .15 | .09 | .10 | .12 | .11 | .12 |

*From Garcia, et al. 1982.
# Could not respond to BINL in English; not included in English tabulations.

Maximum Likelihood Estimations in English and in Spanish, with Age and Judges' Ranks as independent variables. These are summarized in Table 2.6.

## DISCUSSION

The general conclusions of a large literature that relates increased length of utterance to increased age are only weakly supported by the findings. The analyses of variance showed a significant grade level effect only when utterances were categorized by the discourse function they served. Length did correlate with age for the samples of English utterances but did not for Spanish. The limitedness of this relationship, however, is made less significant by the small number of children involved in the study. Nonetheless, failure to show a strong relationship between age and length leaves open the question of whether in this sample of bilingual children, development of a particular language is not closely related to age, or whether length is an imperfect indicator of language development. There seem good reasons to believe both are true. The children in this sample have not all had the same opportunity to use English in their home and community environments. For some of the older children,

| Judges' Profic. Rating | Spanish | | | | | | | |
|---|---|---|---|---|---|---|---|---|
| | Length | | | Mean Weights, Max Likelihood Analyses | | | | |
| | Mean | Std. Error | 1 | 2 | 3 | 4 | 5b |
| 70.0 | 6.62 | .75 | .45 | .58 | .59 | .58 | .57 |
| 29.0 | 5.50 | .63 | .35 | .45 | .47 | .46 | .47 |
| 51.0 | 5.72 | .53 | .41 | .45 | .47 | .45 | .48 |
| 51.0 | 3.54 | .45 | .42 | .54 | .44 | .55 | .45 |
| 54.5 | 3.61 | .53 | .30 | .35 | .37 | .35 | .36 |
| 55.0 | 5.73 | .63 | .43 | .45 | .48 | .46 | .48 |
| 48.5 | 5.30 | .56 | .33 | .39 | .41 | .39 | .41 |
| 46.5 | 3.94 | .27 | .31 | .36 | .39 | .36 | .38 |
| 53.0 | 10.54 | .34 | .40 | .71 | .72 | .72 | .73 |
| 28.0 | 2.79 | .29 | .27 | .37 | .30 | .38 | .30 |
| 20.5 | 4.84 | .47 | .46 | .50 | .47 | .50 | .64 |
| 64.0 | 5.38 | .56 | .35 | .48 | .51 | .48 | .49 |
| 35.0 | 2.07 | .18 | .17 | .14 | .16 | .14 | .17 |
| 30.5 | 2.82 | .34 | .22 | .26 | .28 | .25 | .28 |
| 32.0 | 9.21 | .76 | .41 | .64 | .66 | .65 | .66 |
| 11.5 | 1.91 | .18 | .18 | .20 | .13 | .20 | .13 |
| 42.53 | 4.97 | .47 | .34 | .43 | .43 | .43 | .44 |
| 16.28 | 2.39 | .18 | .09 | .15 | .15 | .15 | .16 |

Spanish is no longer an instructional language, and its use in school environments is limited. These differences in language-use opportunities may well confound the relationship between age and language development.

The tendency to report the *means* of utterance lengths has obscured the fact that successive utterances in connected discourse tend to vary greatly in length, at least for speakers as old and as proficient as those included in this sample. For many of the children, the standard error of the mean is great enough to suggest that for samples of fifty utterances, the means will be subject to considerable sampling fluctuation, and smaller samples may be highly unstable. This may raise serious questions about the practice of basing language proficiency assessment on very small samples, that is, ten utterances in the case of the BINL proficiency test.

A significant portion of the variability of utterance length relates directly to discourse context. The effect of discourse on length can be identified variously in terms of function of turn or function of previous turn, or syntactically in terms of ellipsis or number of clauses. When number of clauses is considered, the effect of ellipsis is largely obviated, but the effects of discourse function are largely unchanged. Noting the speaker of the previous turn does not

**TABLE 2.5a**
**Correlation Coefficients for Age and Seven Indicators of Language Proficiency**

| | | | | English | | | | |
|---|---|---|---|---|---|---|---|---|
| | | | | | Max Likelihood Estimates | | | |
| | Age | Judges | MLU | 1 | 2 | 3 | 4 | 5a |
| Age | — | .602 | .693 | .495 | .649 | .638 | .643 | .661 |
| Judges | * | — | .442 | .402 | .537 | .556 | .510 | .579 |
| MLU | * | n.s. | — | .853 | .909 | .930 | .920 | .936 |
| Residual | * | n.s. | ** | .629 | .937 | .864 | .935 | .872 |
| M.L. 1 | n.s. | n.s. | ** | — | .707 | .808 | .728 | .807 |
| M.L. 2 | * | n.s. | ** | * | — | .962 | .998 | .964 |
| M.L. 3 | * | * | ** | ** | ** | — | .966 | .998 |
| M.L. 4 | * | n.s. | ** | ** | ** | ** | — | .966 |
| M.L. 5a | * | * | ** | ** | ** | ** | ** | — |

**TABLE 2.5b**

| | | | | Spanish | | | | |
|---|---|---|---|---|---|---|---|---|
| | | | | | Max Likelihood Estimates | | | |
| | Age | Judges | MLU | 1 | 2 | 3 | 4 | 5b |
| Age | — | .627 | .195 | .579 | .406 | .406 | .405 | .398 |
| Judges | ** | — | .384 | .474 | .464 | .504 | .448 | .483 |
| MLU | n.s. | n.s. | — | .684 | .886 | .934 | .882 | .940 |
| M.L. 1 | * | n.s. | ** | — | .852 | .859 | .854 | .859 |
| M.L. 2 | n.s. | n.s. | ** | ** | — | .965 | .999 | .967 |
| M.L. 3 | n.s. | * | ** | ** | ** | — | .961 | .998 |
| M.L. 4 | n.s. | n.s. | ** | ** | ** | ** | — | .965 |
| M.L. 5b | n.s. | n.s. | ** | ** | ** | ** | ** | — |

$*p < .05; **p < .01$

seem to be preferable to noting the function of the previous turns. Nothing is gained by considering both speaker and function jointly because of the interdependence of their relationship.

Any attempt to draw inferences related to language development from examination of measures of length must accommodate these effects, at least for children as old as those observed here. These findings are completely consistent with the conclusions of Cowan, et al., that "the implicit assumption that magnitude of MLR (mean length of response) is a property of the subject independent of his setting should be permanently discarded" (1967, 203). These findings go beyond that, however, to suggest that length–related measures may yet be viable indicators of language development if the effects of discourse context are accounted for. What remains to be determined, however, is whether the kinds of situational and topical sensitivity of MLU which

**TABLE 2.6**
**Summary of Multiple Regressions of Length Measures**
**on Age and Judges' Proficiency Rankings**

| Dependent Measure | Multiple R | $R^2$ | Standard Error |
|---|---|---|---|
| | English | | |
| MLU | .694 | .482 | 1.259 |
| M.L. 1 | .512 | .262 | 0.089 |
| M.L. 2 | .674 | .454 | 0.088 |
| M.L. 3 | .673 | .453 | 0.103 |
| M.L. 4 | .662 | .438 | 0.092 |
| M.L. 5a | .699 | .488 | 0.096 |
| | Spanish | | |
| MLU | .388 | .151 | 2.364 |
| M.L. 1 | .597 | .356 | 0.081 |
| M.L. 2 | .486 | .237 | 0.142 |
| M.L. 3 | .517 | .268 | 0.148 |
| M.L. 4 | .476 | .226 | 0.146 |
| M.L. 5b | .498 | .248 | 0.149 |

Cowan, et. al., and others have demonstrated are artifacts of different distributions of discourse contexts, as defined here, within the different elicitation environments that they identified.

The differences observed across languages seem fairly small overall. There was language effect in the analyses of variance. Under maximum likelihood, language factors were also fairly small. When the data set was partitioned by language, the factors for function differed. These differences, however, had essentially no effect on the derived weightings: Analysis 3 and Analyses 5a and 5b produced almost identical results. This in no way minimizes the effect of discourse context, but suggests that those effects are highly consistent across both languages of these bilingual children.

Considering that measures of length are now used much less frequently with children in this age range, it may seem rather pointless to demonstrate yet one more problem in the relationship of length to language development. Measures of length continue to be highly susceptible to the criticism that they measure nothing that is of direct linguistic interest. As Barlow and Miner point out,

The fact remains, however, that after MLR (Mean length of response) is computed, all the clinician has is a numerical score for linguistic performance. It tells nothing about the grammatical structures a child has, or his ability to generate grammatical rules (1969, 248).

What the authors seem not to have noticed is that precisely the same criticism must be leveled against all of the structure–based indices used with language samples. Once scores have been summed across any combination of structures, all direct linguistic information is lost. In addition, it seems highly probable that relationship of length measures to discourse context will generalize to all of the structure-based indices. Any measure that is expressed as a quotient of the number of utterances in a sample is subject to the manner in which discourse context provides opportunity for the use of that structure.

One way to avoid the possibility of bias introduced by differing discourse contexts is to constrain the language elicitation situation in such a way that variation in discourse functions is limited. This can not be achieved with ease, and would require far more than controlling the setting, or the stimulus material, or the topic. Control of discourse context could be achieved only by sacrificing the naturalness of the discourse. This would seem to be exactly the opposite of what is desired for valid measurement of language development. Speaking of the data advanced to support arguments in theoretical linguistics, Labov formulated what he termed the "observer's paradox": "To obtain the data most important for linguistic theory, we have to observe how people talk when they are not being observed" (1972, 113). Exactly the same can be said for measurement of language development in either bilingual or monolingual children. Labov further pointed out that "naive approaches to eliciting speech rely heavily upon questions which superficially force response. Experimental methods used to assess the verbal competence of children also utilize direct questions and obtain systematically misleading data" (1972, 114).

The strong suggestion from Labov and from other sociolinguists would be that the optimal data for assessment of language development would come from the most naturalistic interactions of children. This, however, is only likely to increase the variance found in measures of length of syntax above that which has been found here in a picture-based language elicitation task. The more natural the language elicitation, the greater will be the need to provide some means of accommodating the effects of discourse context.

From the maximum likelihood calculations, it is possible to derive predicted probability distributions for length. These weights can, in turn, replace length as a language development indicator. The resulting weights correlate more highly with judges' holistic ratings of proficiency than does MLU, in both English and Spanish. In Spanish, the correlation of the weights to age is substantially higher than the correlation of MLU; in English, they are roughly comparable, with consideration of number of clauses producing a somewhat lower correlation. A similar pattern results when age and judges' rankings are considered jointly in multiple regression. Thus the relationship of length to either age or judges' rankings can be increased by taking into account the effects of discourse context. Particularly in Spanish, however, the correlation is still not high.

Even when discourse context is controlled, there will, of course, remain considerable variance in length or structure of utterances for any speaker. Some of this variance will relate to the complexity of the information being conveyed in any particular turn, and to any number of other intentional and situational variables. There is also an extensive sociolinguistic literature that points out the sensitivity of conversation to setting, participants, and topic. This literature does not include measures of length, but shows that many other characteristics of interaction, including the willingness of children to participate in conversation, are affected by these nonverbal variables. In some contexts children may appear virtually nonverbal, in others the same children show themselves as adept conversationalists (Labov 1969). Wald (1981) reports that a number of studies demonstrate that language production is sensitive to situation, both qualitatively and quantitatively. In his own study of the language abilities of ten- to twelve–year–old Spanish–English bilinguals, he contrasts characteristics of language elicited using a linguistic proficiency assessment instrument as a speech stimulus with that elicited in a peer group interview which includes a variety of topics of relevance for the speakers.

It would probably be impossible to identify and quantify all of the sources of such variation, much of which may well be idiosyncratic with the individual and the unique circumstances of any particular observation of language use. Nonetheless, distinguishing between opportunity for language use, as defined by discourse context, and the particular way in which a child uses the opportunities discourse provides may well lead to improvement in the measurement of language development, whether for educational applications or for further research in the language development process. Even in this distinction, however, it is important to bear in mind the dynamic nature of discourse, and the fact that to one extent or another participants adjust the opportunities or demands that they place on discourse partners (Rondal 1978). The measurement of language development will be perhaps enhanced most by using discourse context not just as a means of distinguishing utterance-based measures, but also by including a measure of how discourse context itself is used in terms of discourse function.

## REFERENCES

Barlow, M. C., and Miner, L. E. Temporal reliability of Length-Complexity Index. *Journal of Communication Disorders* 2(1969):241–51.

Berdan, R. *On the nature of linguistic variation.* Unpublished doctoral dissertation, University of Texas at Austin, 1975.

Berdan, R. H., and Garcia, M. Discourse-sensitive measurement of language development in bilingual children. Technical Report 07–82. Los Alamitos, CA: National Center for Bilingual Research, 1982.

Brown, R. *A first language. The early stages*. Cambridge, MA: Harvard University Press, 1973.

Buch, K. R. A note on sentence-length as a random variable. In *Statistics and style*, L. Dolezel and R. Bailey, eds. New York: American Elsevier, 1969, pp. 76–79.

Cedergren, H. J., and Sankoff, D. Variable rules: Performance as a statistical reflection of competence. *Language* 50 (1974): 333–55.

Cowan, P. A., Weber, J., Hoddinott, B. A., and Klein, J. Mean length of spoken response as a function of stimulus, experimenter, and subject. *Child Development* 38 (1967): 191–203.

Cox, D. R. *The analysis of binary data*. London: Methuen, 1970.

Darley, F. L., and Moll, K. L. Reliability of language measures and size of language sample. *Journal of Speech and Hearing Research* 3 (1960): 166–73.

Davis, E. A. 1937a. The development of linguistic skill in twins, singletons with siblings, and only children from age five to ten years. Inst. Child Welfare Monogr. Ser., No. 14. Minneapolis: University of Minnesota Press.

Davis, E. A. 1937b. Mean sentence length compared with long and short sentences as a reliable measure of language development. *Child Development* 8: 69–79.

Dore, J. Conversational acts and the acquisition of language. In *Developmental Pragmatics*, E. Ochs and B. B. Schieffelin, eds. New York, NY: Academic Press, 1979.

Erickson, J. G. 1981. Communication assessment of the bilingual bicultural child, an overview, pp. 1–24. In *Communication assessment of the Bilingual bicultural child. Issues and guidelines*, J. G. Erickson and R. Omark (eds.). Baltimore: University Park Press.

Fisher, M. S. Language patterns of preschool children. *Child Development Monographs* No. 15, 1954.

Garcia, E. E., Maez, L., and Gonzalez, G. A national study of Spanish/English bilingualism in young Hispanic children of the United States. *Bilingual Education Paper Series* 4, no. 12 (1981).

Garcia, M., Veyna-Lopez, A., Siguenza, C., and Torres, M. Baseline data report of the Spanish-English longitudinal study. Working paper 82-3W. Los Alamitos, CA: National Center for Bilingual Research, 1982.

Halliday, M., and Hasan, R. *Cohesion in English*. London: Longman, 1976.

Heider, F. K., and Heider, G. M. 1940. A comparison of sentence structure of deaf and hearing children. *Psychol. Monogr.* 52, no. 1: 42–103.

Herbert, C. *Basic inventory of natural language. Instructions manual (Revised ed.)*. San Bernardino, CA: Checpoint Systems, Inc., 1979.

Hunt, K. *Grammatical structures written at three grade levels*. Research Report 3. Urbana, IL: National Council of Teachers of English, 1965.

Hunt, K. Syntactic maturity in school children and adults. Monographs of the Society for Research in Child Development, vol. 35, no. 1, 1970.

Jones, R. H. Probability estimation using a multinomial logistic function. *Journal of Statistical Computation and Simulation* 3 (1975): 315–29.

Kidder, C. L. Using the computer to measure syntactic density and vocabulary intensity in the writing of elementary school children. Unpublished doctoral dissertation, Pennsylvania State University, 1974.

Kramer, C. A., James, S. L., and Saxman, J. H. A comparison of language samples elicited at home and in the clinic. *Journal of Speech and Hearing Disorders* 44 (1979):321–30.

Labov, W. *The social stratification of English in New York City.* Washington, DC: Center for Applied Linguistics, 1966.

Labov, W. The logic of non-standard English. In *Linguistics and the teaching of standard English to speakers of other languages or dialects*, J. Alatis (ed.), Georgetown University Monograph Series on Languages and Linguistics No. 22. Washington, D.C.: Georgetown University Press, 1969, pp. 1–44.

Labov, W. Some principles of linguistic methodology. *Language and Society* 1 (1972): 97–120.

Lindsey, J. K. Likelihood analyses and tests for binary data. *Applied Statistics* 24 (1975):1–16.

Maez, L. F. 1983. The acquisition of noun and verb morphology in 18–24 month old Spanish speaking children. *NABE Journal* 7 (1983):53–68.

McCarthy, D. 1930. The language development of the preschool child. (Inst. Child Welfare Monogr. Ser., No. 4) Minneapolis: University of Minnesota Press.

McCarthy, D. A. Language development in children. In *Manual of Child Psychology* (2nd ed.), L. Carmichael, ed. New York: John Wiley, 1954, pp. 492–630.

Minifie, F. D., Darley, F. L., and Sherman, D. Temporal reliability of seven language measures. *Journal of Speech and Hearing Research* 6 (1963):139–48.

O'Donnell, R. C., Griffin, W. J., and Norris, R. C. *Syntax of kindergarten and elementary school children: A transformational analysis.* Research Report 8. Urbana, IL: National Council of Teachers of English, 1967.

Padilla, A., and Liebman, E. Language acquisition and the bilingual child. In *Bilingual Education for Hispanic Students*, J. Fishman & G. D. Keller, eds. New York, NY: Teacher's College Press, 1982.

Peters, A., Ostman, J., Larsen, T., and O'Connor, M. Manual for computer coding of bilingual data. Unpublished manuscript. Berkeley, CA: School of Education, University of California at Berkeley, 1982.

Rondal, J. A. Maternal speech to normal and Down's Syndrome children matched for mean length of utterance. In *Quality of life in severely and profoundly mentally retarded people: Research foundations for improvement.* C. E. Meyers, ed. Washington, D.C.: American Association for Mental Deficiency, 1978, pp. 193–265.

Rousseau, P., and Sankoff, D. Advances in variable rule methodology. In *Linguistic Variation. Models and Methods*, D. Sankoff, ed. New York, NY: Academic Press, 1976.

Scott, C. M., and Taylor, A. E. A comparison of home and clinic gathered language samples. *Journal of Speech and Hearing Disorders* 43 (1978):482–95.

Shriner, T. H. A comparison of selected measures with psychological scales values of language development. *Journal of Speech and Hearing Research* 10 (1967): 828–35.

Shriner, T. H. A review of mean length of response as a measure of expressive language development in children. *Journal of Speech and Hearing Disorders* 34 (1969):61–68.

Siegel, S. *Nonparemetric statistics for the behavioral sciences.* New York, NY: McGraw-Hill Book Company, Inc., 1956.

Sinclair, J., and Coulthard, R. M. *Towards an analysis of discourse. The English used by teachers and pupils.* London: Oxford University Press, 1975.

Smith, M. E. 1926. An investigation of the development of the sentence and the extent of vocabulary in young children. Univ. Iowa Stud. Child Welfare, 3, No. 5.

Stormzand, M. J., and O'Shea, M. V. *How much English grammar?* Baltimore: Warwick and York, 1924.

Templin, M. C. Certain language skills in children, their development and interrelationships. *Inst. Child Welfare Monograph Series*, no. 26. Minneapolis: University of Minnesota Press, 1957.

Tyack, D., and Gottsleben, R. Language sampling, analysis and training. Palo Alto, CA: Consulting Psychologists Press, 1974.

Wald, B. Topic and situation as factors in language performance. Technical Report 05-81. Los Alamitos, CA: National Center for Bilingual Research, 1981.

Wells, G. Learning through interaction: *The study of language development*. Cambridge, MA: Oxford University Press, 1981.

Williams, C. B. A note on the statistical analysis of sentence-length as a criterion of literary style. In *Statistics and style*, L. Dolezel & R. Bailey, eds., New York: American Elsevier, 1969, 69–79.

Winitz, Harris. "Language Skills of Male and Female Kindergarten Children". *Speech and Hearing Research* 2 (no. 4, 1959):377–86.

Yule, G. U. On sentence-length as a statistical characteristic of style in prose, with application to two cases of disputed authorship. *Biometrika* 30 (1938):363–90.

# 3.
# The Effect of Language Transfer on Bilingual Proficiency

*Dennis Leasher Madrid and Eugene E. Garcia*

WITHIN THE FIELD OF PSYCHOLINGUISTICS a large number of studies address the topic of language acquisition in monolingual children (Brown, 1973; deVilliers and deVilliers, 1973). An equally important aspect of language acquisition is childhood bilingualism and second language acquisition. Three major theoretical positions concerning the areas of bilingualism and second language acquisition in children have surfaced in the research literature. Krashen (1977) has proposed a Monitor Model which attempts to account for the concomitant development of two possibly independent systems for second language performers. One system is *acquired* and develops similarly to children acquiring their first language. The second is *learned* consciously and in most cases arises from formal situations. Burt, Dulay, and Finocchiaro (1977) state that the acquired system may develop through a process of *creative construction* in a sequence of stages universally common, via the application of universal strategies. The Monitor Model predicts that second language learning errors will depend on whether the monitor is in operation. Errors which result from speech guided by the acquired system are seen as those which are similar to all learners, regardless of first language. Errors which result from the operation of the monitor are seen as the learner's conscious mental representation of linguistic regularities in the target language. Krashen, Madden, and Bailey (1975), Larsen-Freeman (1975) and Krashen and Pon (1975) provide evidence that when adult English as a Second Language (ESL) learners are given sufficient time for intrusion of consciously learned material, changes occur in rank ordering of structures in English. Although this model gives additional insight into the issues of adult second language learning, its general applicability to the case of childhood bilingualism and second language learning remains in question. Therefore, the focus of the remaining text will be on the following theoretical positions.

The creative construction hypothesis, a developmental approach proposed by Dulay and Burt (1972: 1974) assumes that children learn a second language in the same way as children learn a first language. That is, children construct hypotheses about the structure (words, syntax, and so forth) of the language they are learning, and then, in using the language, generalize to other aspects of their speech based on their initial hypotheses. The same process is assumed to occur in any language. Therefore, errors in a second language will be similar in kind to those of children learning the same language as their first language. For example, using Klima and Bellugi's (1966) first stage of negation development as a model, one would predict that the *no* + *nucleus* construction would appear in English both as the first language and as the second language, for example, "*no* have candy."

The critical test is one in which bilinguals are required to produce utterances in two languages and monolinguals to produce the same utterances in one of the languages. Then, a comparison is made at a syntactic, phonological and morphological level, noting constructions across the two languages for bilinguals, and across the two language groups. Developmental theory predicts that bilinguals and monolinguals will produce similar errors. For example, the negative preceding the auxiliary (no have money) would be viewed as a developmental error in English, in the instance where English is the first language and in the instance where English is the second language. Research based on developmental theory (Dulay and Burt 1972; 1974) has sought to find evidence of strategies common to all children learning a second language. Some studies, for example, have found that regardless of the first language background, children reconstruct English syntax in similar ways (Dulay and Burt 1974). Dulay and Burt (1973) also examined natural sequences in the acquisition of eight English grammatical structures by three different groups of Chicano children. They found that there was a significant correlation between the acquisition lists of their groups for the eight grammatical structures (e.g., plurals, possessives, articles, etc.).

Dulay and Burt (1974) also hypothesized that if the creative construction process does, in fact, play a major role in second language acquisition, then a common sequence of acquisition of grammatical structures would be found in children who speak different languages but are learning the same second language. To test this hypothesis Dulay and Burt (1974) compared Chinese- and Spanish-speaking children's acquisition order for eleven English functors, with the use of the Bilingual Syntax Measure (BSM) (Burt, Dulay, and Hernandez 1973). The results of their study revealed: (1) the sequences of acquisition of the eleven functors in English obtained for Spanish and Chinese children were the same; (2) the same sequence of acquisition of the eleven functors provides strong evidence that children exposed to natural, second language speech acquire certain structures in a universal order.

One major problem with the above studies, such as Dulay and Burt's (1972, 1973, 1974) investigations of invariant sequences, is that the speech samples were not spontaneous but consisted of elicited speech, using the BSM (Burt, Dulay and Hernandez 1973). There seems to be a question of whether the responses given by subjects to the syntax measure are influenced by the test itself (Hakuta and Cancino 1977). Hakuta's data (1976), concerning the development of English as a second language in native Japanese speakers, did not produce evidence for an invariant order in the acquisition of English morphemes.

Language transfer, an alternative theoretical position with roots in transfer of learning (Lambert and Rawlings 1969), suggests that during the time a child is learning a second language, he/she will use language structures from the native tongue in the new language. For example, adjectives come after nouns in Spanish so that Spanish speakers learning English may say "car red." Within the present context, language transfer refers to the influence of the acquisition and use of one language on the acquisition and use of the other language. This is contrasted to the creative construction hypothesis which assumes that errors in second languages are not due to the influence of the native language on the second language but are developmental in nature and will occur in similar forms across many languages and speakers. Language transfer assumes that second language errors reflect native language forms influencing the structures of the second language.

Garcia (1977) reported that as the use of Spanish prepositional expression was acquired by three- and four-year-old English monolinguals, correct English prepositional use declined. This type of interaction, which was restricted to the expressive level, reflects the changes in one language which occur as a function of changes in a second language. The critical test is one in which bilinguals are required to produce utterances in two languages, and monolinguals produce the same utterances in one of the languages. Then a comparison is made at a syntactic, phonological, and morphological level noting constructions across two languages and across the two language groups (bilingual vs. monolingual). Transfer theory predicts that constructions which differ in their structure across two languages will result in speakers of a second language producing utterances which reflect language constructions of the first language. For example, in Spanish, the negative precedes the verb. Therefore, Spanish speakers learning English may impose this structure on the English auxiliary+negative construction.

In an attempt to provide an instance of hypothesis testing concerning the transfer theory, Madrid and Garcia (1981) carried out an analysis of bilingual acquisition with particular emphasis on the development of negation. Of specific interest was the analysis of errors under forced conditions, requiring the child to use negative syntactic structures; for example, there is *no* penny. The study attempted to isolate qualitative differences in constructions across age level, three, four, five, and six, with a comparison of English constructions for Spanish/English bilinguals and matched monolingual English-speaking children. The three dependent variables of focus were (1) *Negative-agent+* verb sequence; in Spanish the negative precedes the verb; John *no* walking. In English the negative comes after the auxiliary; John is *not* walking. Transfer theory predicts that the former example will be produced by bilinguals. This prediction was supported in the study; (2) *do* inclusion; in English, the transformation of a phrase which does not have a *do* form (I like candy) will utilize the *do* transformation in the negative counterpart and insert a *do* form; I *don't* like candy. Since the *do* transformation is nonexistent in Spanish, transfer theory predicts that bilinguals will not produce *do's* in their negative statements; I like candy, transforming to I *not* like candy. There is no *do* form in this negative statement where one is needed. This hypothesis was also supported by the research; (3) *subject* omission; since it is permissible to omit subjects of sentences in the Spanish language, transfer theory predicts that bilinguals will omit subjects in their English constructions. This prediction was confirmed by the research. Comparisons were made on the three dependent variables with a group of age-matched monolingual English-speaking children. In all groups, the English monolingual children produced significantly more correct English structures than did the bilingual children. The findings suggest the influence of Spanish on English negative constructions. An unanticipated, nevertheless interesting, result was the conspicuous absence of English effect on Spanish constructions. Transfer theory predicts that language interaction is a reciprocal process, but the data revealed only the *incorrect* English reflected Spanish language intrusion. Performance with Spanish negative constructions across the three dependent measures for the bilingual children remained high at 100 percent correct. It seems appropriate to suggest a selective interaction phenomenon since bilinguals *did* produce correct Spanish negative constructions and produced English constructions which reflected Spanish negative syntax structures.

Cummins (1979) has suggested that if a child attains only a low level of competence in a language, then interaction with the environment through that language, both in terms of input and output, is likely to be impoverished. There seems to be an implication for the case of bilingual acquisition: the less proficient a child is in one or the other language, the more probable it is that performance will be influenced by external sources, in this case another language. This may explain why the level of performance in Spanish in the Madrid and Garcia (1981) study remained at 100 percent across the three dependent variables. The bilingual children used in the study were all native Spanish speakers. Also, the intrusion of Spanish structure on the English utterances of the bilingual children may be accounted for by the fact that they were not proficient in English.

It was the purpose of this study to look at the interactive influence of two languages, Spanish and English, in relation to the child's bilingual proficiency. In the present study, a proficient bilingual was one who was fluent in both Spanish and English. A non-proficient bilingual was one who could fluently speak Spanish but was "limited" in the use of English, as defined by the Language Assessment Scales (LAS) (DeAvila and Duncan 1977).

The independent variables, ages three, four, and five and bilingual condition (proficient and nonproficient) were looked at in relation to four dependent variables: (a) *Do* inclusion; the *do* transformation which exists in English, e.g., *I like you*, is transformed to *I do not like you* in the negative form. This transformation does not exist in Spanish; therefore, nonproficients should include fewer *do's* in their English negative statements than do proficients; *I not like you*. (b) *Subject* omission; in Spanish it is correct to omit sentence subjects; therefore, nonproficients should include fewer sentence subjects in their English statements than do proficients; *no has wheels*. (c) *Negative-agent+* verb sequence; in Spanish the negative precedes the verb, *no tengo dinero*, and in English the negative comes after the auxiliary, *I do not eat*. Therefore, nonproficients should have a significantly greater number of English phrases reflecting Spanish syntax in their English phrases; *I no like candy*. (d) *Adjective+*noun sequence; in Spanish the adjective comes after the noun, *muchacho grande*/boy big, and in English the adjective comes before the noun, big boy. Nonproficients should give a larger number of English phrases which reflect the Spanish syntax; boy big.

The first three dependent variables listed above were elicited by having subjects describe complete and incomplete toys, for example, a car with wheels and a car without wheels. The *adjective+*noun sequence was elicited by having subjects name a toy and its color; red car or black pencil. These procedures allowed for the comparison of syntactic structures across two languages. In addition, measuring proficiency in the two languages further allows for the systematic investigation of the relationship between bilingual proficiency and language transfer.

## METHOD

### Subjects

The subjects were sixty children from the Goleta Union School District, Goleta, California. They were divided into two groups, proficient Spanish/English bilinguals and nonproficient Spanish/English bilinguals, with thirty children in each group. Each language group consisted of ten three-year-olds, ten four-year-olds and ten five-year olds.

## Operational Definitions

*Bilingualism*. Children in six classrooms identified initially by their teacher as bilingual were administered the *Circo Language Check*. Admission to the study was determined by scores on the measure. This measure provides sixteen questions administered in Spanish. Since the original form was in Spanish, a direct translation of the original form into English was used to arrive at an English score. The types of questions asked in the *Circo Language Check* were related to name, address, age, number of brothers and/or sisters, what they like about school, etc. Additionally, this measure required children to identify a clown, balloons, a boy, and an elephant within a circus picture presented to them. Bilingual children were defined as those children tested who correctly responded to ten of the sixteen items on both the Spanish and English versions.

*Proficiency*. Proficiency was defined according to the Language Assessment Scales I (DeAvila and Duncan 1977). This measure provides an overall picture of oral linguistic proficiency based on a child's performance across four linguistic subsystems. For purposes of the present study proficient bilinguals scored at 4 or 5 in both Spanish and English. Nonproficient bilinguals scored at 1, 2, or 3 in English and 4 or 5 in Spanish.

## Apparatus

All of the sessions took place in a testing room provided by the school. The experimenter and subject faced each other across a small table. A Sony cassette tape recorder was used to record the negation and *adjective*+noun sequence task responses. All stimuli were placed in a box hidden out of view of the subjects to avoid distraction. The following sixteen stimulus items were used for the experimental task: (a) two baby dolls and removable hats; (b) two cans with removable lids; (c) two small plastic chairs which seat removable dolls; (d) two cars with removable wheels; (e) two small boxes with a penny in each; (f) two small plates with a rock in each; (g) two small plastic bags with candy in each; and (h) two small plastic drinking glasses with plastic flowers in each. The stimulus items were selected such that particular properties of the stimuli could be removed to facilitate the expression of negation. Also, care was taken to select items which seemed to be commonly used by children of the three- to five-year-old age group.

## Negation

The negation was elicited as follows: a complete toy, for example a car, was shown to the child; then his attention was drawn to the part to be removed.

"See this nice car; it has all the wheels." Immediately the child was shown a second car without wheels and asked, "What's wrong with this car?" (The first car was placed on the table in front of the child while the experimenter pointed to the second.) Subjects were presented the items in Spanish and English during the same session with language order randomly determined.

### Adjective + noun Sequence

*Adjective* + noun sequence was elicited as follows: a toy of one entire color was shown to the child, for example a red car, then placed on the table in view of the child. At this point the child was told, "This is something red." Immediately following, the child was shown a different toy, for example, a ball, which was of a contrasting color, perhaps a green ball. The child was asked, "What is this?" (as experimenter pointed to the second object shown). Each subject was presented with eight pair to match the number of negative responses. Subjects were presented the items in Spanish and English during the same session. Order of negative probes and *adjective* + noun probes was randomly presented for each successive session. At the end of the experiment each child was given a small toy for his/her cooperation.

### RESULTS

The analysis of negative constructions and *adjective* + noun sequences by three-, four-, and five-year-olds was conducted by two bilingual transcriber observers. Each observer, $t_1$ and $t_2$, transcribed (wrote from cassette tapes) all sessions *blind* and independently, without any information regarding the purpose of the study. Reliability was calculated by comparing the language scripts of the two transcribers. Although all utterances were transcribed, only negative phrase constructions and *adjective* + noun sequences were used to calculate the reliability. Those phrases which contained words such as *no, not, none, don't, doesn't, didn't, can't, ain't*, and so forth, were included. In addition, all descriptions of the stimulus objects presented were used in the analysis, for example, *red car* or *big car*. Only negative utterances and *adjective* + noun forms which were exact duplications by the transcribers, 100 percent agreed upon, were used for the analysis. This system resulted in eliminating 12 percent of the transcribed utterances. Therefore, interobserver agreement was 88 percent on an utterance by utterance basis, and all utterances which were not agreed upon were eliminated from the analysis.

### Do Inclusion

*Correct responding.* Figure 3.1 presents the mean percentage of correct production of *do* inclusions for proficient and nonproficient Spanish/English bilinguals in English.

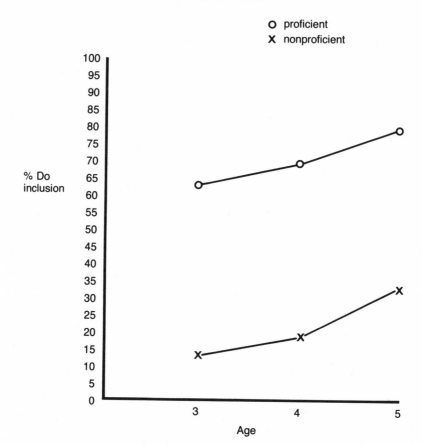

**Figure 3.1** Mean percentage of *do* inclusions for three-, four-, and five-year-old proficient and nonproficient Spanish/English bilinguals in English.

Mean-percent correct *do* inclusions for the proficient and nonproficient groups in Spanish was consistently at 100 percent. Mean percent correct responding in English for proficient bilinguals and nonproficient bilinguals (Figure 3.1) ranged from 58 to 77 percent for proficient bilinguals and 13 to 32 percent for nonproficient bilinguals. A two-way analysis of variance incorporating bilingual condition (proficient and nonproficient) and age (3, 4, and 5) indicated a significant bilingual condition effect, $F$ (1, 54) = 264, $p < .001$. Similarly, a significant age effect, $F$ (2, 54) = 17.7, $p < .001$, was obtained. There was no bilingual condition $x$ age interaction. As indicated in Figure 3.1, mean-percent correct *do* inclusions in English were consistently higher for proficient bilinguals.

*Error analysis.* Of interest to a linguistic interference analysis is the type of errors which these children committed. Errors were classified at those English utterances which demand a *do* form but did not contain that form. For example, "it *doesn't* have wheels" was stated as "*no* have wheels." Three-year-old proficient bilinguals failed to include *do* in about 42 percent of their English constructions which required its use. Three-year-old nonproficient bilinguals incorrectly responded in about 87 percent of their utterances. Four-year-old proficients had approximately 34 percent incorrect responses compared to 83 percent for nonproficients. Five-year-old proficients gave 23 percent incorrect responses compared to 68 percent for nonproficient bilinguals.

*Conclusion.* Proficient three-, four-, and five-year-old Spanish/English bilinguals included a significantly higher percentage of *do* forms in their English negative utterances. Although both groups appear increasingly to include *do* forms in their English utterances over age, nonproficient and proficient Spanish/English bilinguals gave 100 percent *correct* Spanish utterances. There was no age *x* language condition interaction.

### Percent of Subject Inclusion

*Correct responding.* Figure 3.2 presents the mean percentage of *subject* inclusions for proficient and nonproficient Spanish/English bilinguals in English. Mean-percent *subject* omissions in Spanish for both bilingual groups were consistently high, at 100 percent. Mean percent of *subject* inclusions in English for proficient and nonproficient bilinguals (Fig. 3.2) ranged from approximately 60 to 69 percent for proficient bilinguals and 8 to 32 percent of nonproficient bilinguals. A two-way analysis of variance incorporating bilingual condition (proficient and nonproficient) and age (3, 4, and 5) indicated a significant bilingual condition effect, $F(1, 54) = 188.2$, $p < .001$. Similarly, a significant age effect, $F(2, 54) = 8.9$ $p < .01$, was obtained. There was no bilingual *x* age interaction.

*Error analysis.* On this variable, errors were classified as those utterances which reflected Spanish construction. In Spanish it is correct to omit the subject of the sentence. Three-year-old proficient bilinguals omitted 40 percent of their sentence subjects compared to 92 percent omissions for nonproficient bilinguals of the same age. Four-year-old proficient bilinguals omitted 38 percent of the English subjects compared to 84 percent omissions for nonproficient four-year-olds. Five-year-old proficients omitted 31 percent of their English subjects compared to 68 percent omissions for five-year-old nonproficients.

*Conclusion.* Proficient three-, four-, and five-year-old Spanish/English bilinguals included a significantly higher percentage of *sentence* subjects in their English negative utterances. Proficients and nonproficients gave 100 per-

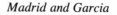

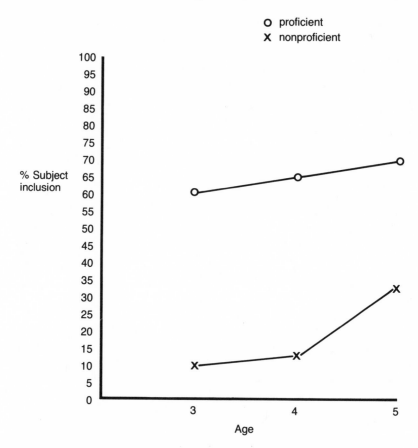

**Figure 3.2** Mean percentage of *subject* inclusions in English for three-, four-, and five-year-old proficient and nonproficient Spanish/English bilinguals.

cent *correct* Spanish utterances which did not contain *sentence* subjects. There was no age *x* language condition interaction.

### Negative agent + verb sequence

*Correct responding.* Figure 3.3 presents the mean percentage of correct production of *negative agent* + verb sequences for proficient and nonproficient bilinguals in English.

Mean percent of correct *negative agent* + verb sequence use for bilinguals in Spanish was consistent at 100 percent. Mean percent correct responding in English for proficient bilinguals and nonproficient bilinguals (Figure 3.3)

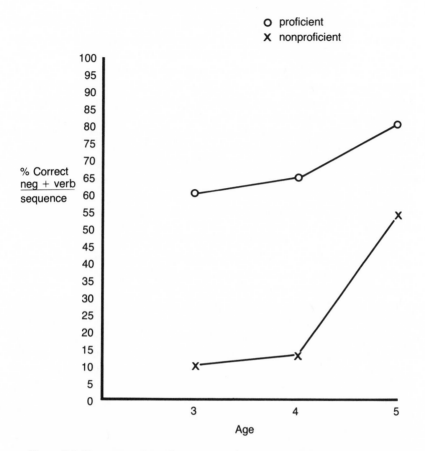

**Figure 3.3** Mean percentage of correct *negative agent*+verb sequence responses in English for three-, four-, and five-year-old proficient and non-proficient Spanish/English bilinguals.

ranged from 59 to 78 percent for proficients and 8 to 54 percent for nonproficients. A two-way analysis of variance incorporating bilingual condition (proficient and nonproficient) and age (3, 4 and 5) indicated a significant bilingual condition effect, $F$ (1, 54) = 186.1, $p$ < .001. Similarly, a significant age effect, $F$ (2, 54) = 43.3, $p$ < .001, was obtained. In addition, a significant interaction effect, $F$ (2, 54) = 9.1, $p$ .01, was obtained.

*Error analysis.* In the present variable, errors were classified as those negative constructions in English which reflected Spanish negative construction, that is, *no* inserted before the verb phrase. Three-year-old proficient bilinguals gave approximately 41 percent incorrect *negative agent*+verb sequences in English, compared to 92 percent for three-year-old nonproficient bilinguals. Four-year-old proficient bilinguals had 36 percent incorrect responses compared to 88 percent for nonproficients of the same age. Five-year-old proficients had 12 percent incorrect responses compared to 46 percent for nonproficient five-year-olds. As can be seen in Figure 3.3, proficient bilinguals consistently made fewer errors across bilingual and age condition.

*Conclusion.* Proficient three-, four-, and five-year-old Spanish/English bilinguals produced a significantly higher percentage of *correct negative agent+* verb sequences in their English negative syntactic constructions than nonproficient three-, four-, and five-year-old Spanish/English bilinguals. Although both proficients and nonproficients increasingly gave correct sequences in English, both groups produced 100 percent correct *negative agent+*verb sequences in Spanish. A significant language $x$ age interaction was obtained.

## Adjective + Noun Sequence

*Correct responding.* Figure 3.4 presents the mean percentage of correct production of *adjective+*noun sequence for proficient and nonproficient bilinguals in English.

Mean percent correct *adjective+*noun sequence for both bilingual groups in Spanish was consistently at 100 percent. In Spanish, as opposed to English, the adjective comes after the noun, for example, casa grande, *house big.* Mean percent correct responses in English for proficient and nonproficient (Figure 3.4) ranged from 35 to 76 percent for proficient bilinguals and 20 to 63 percent for nonproficient bilinguals. A two-way analysis of variance incorporating bilingual condition (proficient and nonproficient) and age (three, four, and five) indicated a significant bilingual condition effect, $F$ (1, 54) = 18.7, $p < .001$. Similarly, a significant age effect, $F$ (2, 54) = 113.5 $p < .001$, was obtained. There was no bilingual condition $x$ age effect interaction. As indicated by Figure 3.4, mean percent correct *adjective+*noun sequence in English was consistently higher for proficients.

*Error analysis.* In the present study, errors were classified as those *adjective+*noun constructions in English which reflected Spanish noun+*adjective* construction, that is, the adjective coming after the noun. Three-year-old proficients gave 65 percent incorrect noun+*adjective* sequences in English compared to 80 percent for three-year-old nonproficients. Four-year-old proficients had approximately 76 percent incorrect responses compared to 86 percent for nonproficients of the same age. Five-year-old proficients had 24 percent incorrect responses compared to 37 percent incorrect responses for five-year-old nonproficient bilinguals.

*Conclusion.* Proficient three-, four-, and five-year-old Spanish/English bilinguals gave a significantly higher percentage of *correct adjective+*noun se-

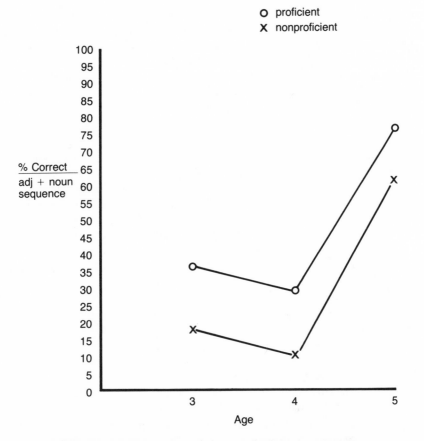

**Figure 3.4** Mean percentage of correct *adjective*+noun sequence responses in English for three-, four-, and five-year-old proficient and nonproficient Spanish/English bilinguals.

quences in their English utterances than nonproficient bilinguals. Both proficients and non-proficients gave 100 percent correct noun+*adjective* sequences in Spanish. There was no language condition *x* age interaction.

## SUMMARY OF RESULTS

It appeared that across the four dependent variables, proficient three-, four-, and five-year-old Spanish/English bilinguals produced a significantly higher percentage of *correct* English utterances than nonproficient three-, four-, five-year-old Spanish/English bilinguals. In addition, Spanish language production remained high at 100 percent correct for both proficients and non-proficients across all ages and across four dependent measures. A language condition *x* age interaction did occur in the *negative agent+*verb analysis. All other measures failed to produce an interaction.

## DISCUSSION

The present study has attempted to evaluate the effect of multiple language constructions on the production of negative syntactic forms and *adjective+* noun sequences in relation to bilingual proficiency. When bilingual subjects were requested to supply negative syntactic forms, the mean percent of correct *negative agent+*verb sequences in Spanish was 100 percent for all age groups. Likewise, omission of sentence subjects was at the 100 percent level for all age groups in Spanish. Additionally, bilinguals did not include *hacer*, or *do*, forms in their negative constructions, as indicated by zero inclusions in their Spanish negative constructions across all age groups. Moreover, when bilingual subjects gave *adjective+*noun sequence forms, the mean percentage of correct noun+*adjective* forms, in Spanish, was 100 percent for all age levels.

However, the performance of nonproficient bilingual subjects, in English, resulted in a significantly higher percent of utterances which reflected Spanish language constructions, than that of proficient bilinguals. That is, all bilinguals *correctly* omitted subjects in Spanish construction but nonproficients tended to *incorrectly* omit a significantly greater number of sentence subjects in English negative constructions than proficients. Also, all bilinguals *correctly* omitted *do's* in their Spanish negative constructions but performance of nonproficient bilinguals with the *do* form in English revealed that they tended to omit a significantly greater number of *do's* in their English negative utterances than proficient bilinguals. In addition, nonproficient bilinguals gave a significantly lower number of correct *negative agent+*verb sequences than proficient bilinguals in their English negative constructions. All of these indices taken together seem to provide partial support for the language transfer view, since the direction of errors across the four dependent variables for both proficient and nonproficient bilinguals reflected Spanish structures as predicted by transfer theory; errors with the *do* form were those of omission, reflective of Spanish structure and also predicted by transfer theory; *negative agent+*verb errors in English consisted of utterances which reversed the auxiliary *negative* English form into the *negative*-verb Spanish form, thus giving such utterances as *no have wheels*; in addition, *adjective+*noun errors consisted of reversing the English form into the Spanish noun+*adjective* form in their English utterance, for example, *house green*.

The present evidence is not supportive of Dulay and Burt's (1974) findings in which they report a very low percentage of transfer errors in children learning English as a second language. Quite the opposite, the present data suggest that in negative syntactic construction and *adjective*+noun construction, the frequency and qualitative nature of errors for nonproficient bilinguals are a possible reflection of previously acquired linguistic strategies. Research with young monolingual English-speaking children (Klima and Bellugi 1966) reports that Stage I in the development of negation consists of: (a) *no + nucleus* and *not + nucleus*; *nucleus + no* forms also frequently occurred. In the present data, the *not* did not appear, nor did the *nucleus + no* form. Klima and Bellugi (1966) report that in Stage II, *can't, won't* and *don't* appear and the negative moves to the inside of the phrase by negative transportation. This did not occur in the present data, nor did *can't, won't* and *don't* appear in the present investigation. Stage III in the monolingual research indicates the realization of the auxiliary through its appearance in declaratives and questions. The implication from the present data is not clear, since bilinguals did not produce declaratives and questions. The evidence seems to indicate that the purported universal order of acquisition in negation syntax and *adjective noun* sequence has not been supported by the present data. Additionally, there is no evidence to suggest that monolinguals learning English as their native language invert the *adjective*+noun sequence as did the bilinguals in the present study, providing further support for a transfer phenomenon. Cancino, Rosansky, and Schumann (1978) provide evidence which is not supportive of Klima and Bellugi's (1966) data. They reported that errors occurred in their subject's responses, which reflected interference from the native language to the second language.

The present data do not reflect a *complete* transfer effect between Spanish and English. A transfer hypothesis predicts that language interaction is a reciprocal process and that constructions of English syntax should be visible in Spanish and Spanish syntax be reflected in English. The present data reveal only that English use reflected Spanish language intrusion. Performance on Spanish negative constructions and *noun*+adjective sequences across four dependent variables remained high, at 100 percent correct. Cummins (1979) has suggested that a low level of competence in the two languages of the bilinguals results in an interaction that is likely to produce impoverished linguistic development. The present data seem to support Cummins' (1979) notion, since nonproficient bilinguals gave a significantly higher percentage of *incorrect* English negative constructions and *adjective*+noun sequences than proficient bilinguals. It seems appropriate to suggest a selective or modified language transfer phenomenon which is mediated by level of competence in a first or second language.

The results of the present study are viewed within the perspective of certain methodological and empirical constraints. A cross-sectional approach, such as was used in the present research, does not give information concerning particular changes that occur at the individual subject level. In effect, data have been averaged, therefore, individual distortion is possible. Additionally, there is the problem of regionality, as well; previous research has pointed out the existence of regional variations for both Spanish and English among bilingual populations of the United States (Laosa 1975). The generalizability of the results of this study to other bilingual populations is unclear. Also, the present study utilized a *forced-task* situation thereby raising concerns about the generalizability of the results to natural situations. In addition, the method of measuring language ability in the present study does not comprehensively describe the exact bilingual character of the subject population.

As Madrid and Garcia (1981) have indicated, bilingual acquisition in childhood is a complex phenomenon, incorporating linguistic as well as cognitive and social language-use dimensions. The present study's failure to consider these interactive dimensions of bilingualism limits its external validity. Yet, the attempt to deal with this complexity will continue to be an experimental dilemma. Keeping in mind the above constraints of the study, certain statements about the relationship between the present findings and previous data seem worthy of consideration. Garcia (1977) reported that the acquisition of Spanish prepositions by three- and four-year-old English monolinguals resulted in an increase in incorrect English prepositional use. This type of interaction, which was restricted to the expressive level, reflects the changes in one language which occur as a function of changes in a second language. Also, Madrid and Garcia (1981) report that Spanish/English bilinguals (three-, four-, five-, and six-year-olds) used Spanish negative constructions in their English negative constructions across three dependent variables. The present findings support a modified transfer theory which is mediated by proficiency in the first and second language.

Of particular interest is the statistically significant interaction that occurred in the *negative agent*+verb sequence. A possible statistical explanation may be that although the group means of the five-year-old proficient and nonproficient bilingual groups came from different populations (11.2 and 7.8, respectively) the variances overlapped at the upper end for the nonproficient group and at the lower end for the proficient group because of extreme scores by five subjects. That is, two proficient subjects scored low and three subjects scored high. It is important to note that although one may interpret the *subject* omission and *do* omission measures as a *simpler* method of communication, that is, just dropping part of the sentence, the *negative agent*+verb sequence and *adjective*+noun sequence measures offer evidence which is directly supportive of a transfer hypothesis.

The implications of this study regarding the potential character of bilingual instruction rests on the direction of future research. That is, the question of how we teach a second language is dependent on findings of more extensive research. Future investigations of language transfer and second language acquisition must focus on additional language parameters, for example, phonology, morphology, and so forth. Language transfer studies should look at other languages as first and second languages to gain additional information about the processes across languages which may give insight into the question of language transfer and proficiency level.

## REFERENCES

Brown, R. *A First Language: The Early Stages.* Cambridge, Mass.: Harvard University Press, 1973.

Burt, M., Dulay, H., and Finacchiaro, M. (eds.). *Viewpoints on English as a Second Language.* New York: Regents, 1977.

Burt, M., Dulay, H., and Hernandez, E. *The Bilingual Syntax Measure.* New York: Harcourt Brace Jovanovich, 1973.

Cancino, H., Rosansky, E. J., and Schumann, J. H. The acquisition of English negatives and interrogatives by native Spanish speakers. In *Second Language Acquisition*, E. M. Hutch, ed. Rowley, Mass.: Newbury House Publishers, 1978.

Cummins, J. Linguistic interdependence and the educational development of bilingual children. *Review of Educational Research* 49 (1979):221–51.

DeAvila, E. A., and Duncan, S. E. *Language Assessment Scales I*, 2nd ed. Corte Madera, Ca.: Linguametrics Group, Inc., 1977.

deVilliers, J. G., and deVilliers, P. A. A cross-sectional study of the acquisition and grammatical morphemes in child speech. *Journal of Psycholinguistic Research* 2 (1973):267–78.

Dulay, H., and Burt, M. Goofing: An indication of children's second language learning strategies. *Language Learning* 22 (1972):235–52.

———. Should we teach children syntax? *Language Learning* 23 (1973):245–58.

———. A new perspective on the creative construction process in child second language acquisition. *Language Learning* 24 (1974):253–78.

Garcia, E. The study of early childhood bilingualism: Strategies for linguistic transfer research. In *Chicano Psychology*, J. L. Martinez, Jr., ed. New York: Academic Press, 1977.

Hakuta, K. Becoming bilingual: A case study of a Japanese child learning English. *Language Learning* 26 (1976):321–51.

Hakuta, R., and Cancino, H. Second language acquisition: A review. *Harvard Educational Review* (Summer 1977):59–72.

Klima, E., and Bellugi, U. Syntactic regularities in the speech of children. In *Psycholinguistic Papers*, J. Lyons and R. Wales, eds. New York: Harper and Row, 1966.

Krashen, S. D. The monitor model for adult second language performance. In *Viewpoints on English as a Second Language*, M. Burt, H. Dulay, and M. Finacchiaro, eds. New York: Regents, 1977.

Krashen, S., Madden, C., and Bailey, N. Theoretical aspects of formal instruction in adult second language learning. *TESOL Quarterly* 9 (1975): 173–83.

Krashen, S., and Pon, P. An error analysis of an advanced ESL learner: The importance of the monitor. *Working Papers on Bilingualism* 7 (1975): 125–29.

Lambert, W., and Rawlings, C. Bilingual processing of mixed language associative networks. *Journal of Verbal Learning and Verbal Behavior* 8 (1969): 604, 609.

Larsen-Freeman, D. The acquisition of grammatical morphemes by adult ESL students, *TESOL Quarterly*, 1975.

Laosa, L. Bilingualism in three United States Hispanic groups: Contextual use of language by children and adults in their families. *Journal of Educational Psychology* 1975, 617–27.

Madrid, D., and Garcia, E. The development of negation in bilingual Spanish/English and monolingual English speakers. *Journal of Educational Psychology* 5 (1981): 624–31.

Padilla, A., and Lindholm, K. Development of interrogative, negative and possessive forms in the speech of young Spanish/English bilinguals. *The Bilingual Review/La Revista Bilinque* 2 (1977): 135–43.

# 4.
# Motivation for Language Choice Behavior of Elementary Mexican American Children

*Benji Wald*

BILINGUAL EDUCATION IS CRUCIALLY CONCERNED with making decisions about language choice as part of the educational process affecting bilinguals of limited English abilities. There is much discussion of varying educational practices in choosing which language teachers and students speak when in the classroom. A useful basic classification of bilingual educational approaches is found in Krashen (1981). Types of programs range from "submersion"—English only—to the use of the first language with only English as a Second Language (ESL) instruction—essentially, subject matter in L1, with English included among the subject matter. In theory, these language choices are controlled in order to meet educational objectives. The minimal objective is parity of academic achievement with monolinguals of equal status, and a growing command of English for academic purposes, especially English literacy.

While language choices made as part of educational policy are consciously planned, unplanned language choices are made outside of the dictates of the school in bilingual communities. The social aspects of language choice have been subject to continuous research. Fishman's (1967) hypotheses concerning the relation of language choice to language maintenance and shift are widely known. According to Fishman, strict separation of languages in some social domains is necessary for language maintenance, and language shift proceeds progressively through the use of the second language in an increasing number of situations. More recent work on spontaneous speech behavior in bilingual communities has revealed the complexity of codeswitching and its motivations. Pedraza, Attinasi, and Hoffman (1980) have proposed on the basis of naturalistic observations of codeswitching among adults in the East Harlem Puerto Rican bilingual community, that some forms of codeswitching are not necessarily signs of language shift or of a transitional stage from all Spanish to all English use. The fact that some members of the community speak both

English and Spanish fluently allows them to rapidly switch from one language to the other and back again without violating the grammatical rules of either language (demonstrated for syntax and morphology by Poplack 1979).

Studies of this type, however, have used data from adults, not preadolescents or younger children. When linguistic and social development has not reached the adult level in either language, conclusions about the meaning of either rigid language choice or codeswitching are more problematic.

While a number of studies have shown social motivations for language choice and codeswitching among adults (e.g., Gumperz and Hernandez-Chavez 1970; Poplack 1979; Valdes 1980), other scholars have suggested that under the condition of imbalance in the command of both languages among nonadults, codeswitching is directional from the weaker to the stronger language. One particular model, proposed by Gonzalez and Maez (1980), suggests that many Chicano children entering school with Spanish as the stronger language often shift toward English preference, after a few years, by predictable stages manifest in their language behavior. According to this model English alone comes to be used in many situations. At the same time, English encroaches on Spanish through codeswitching so that Spanish no longer develops alone, while English does. Gonzalez and Maez label this kind of language mixing *regressive codeswitching*. Like fluent adult codeswitching, it operates within sentences, but unlike the fluent type, it is based on the inability to speak Spanish to meet growing communicative demands, without the support of English. Zentella (1981) has noted in a study of elementary school-age Puerto Rican bilinguals that both social and linguistic motivations are found for codeswitching. Social motivations are evident in the choice of one or the other language for footing, keying, appeal, and control. Linguistic motivations are found in "crutching," the type of motivation suggested by Gonzalez and Maez.

In seeking an informed and rational policy of language choice, educators need information about unplanned language choice patterns already operating among the children they intend to teach. Even more importantly, they need to know what linguistic and social factors motivate preexistent language choice patterns among the students so that they may adapt their teaching strategies accordingly.

In this paper, discussion is devoted to bilingual preadolescents from the Hispanic community of Greater East Los Angeles. The sample of speakers discussed below derives from a study including forty-six preadolescents (aged 10 to 13 years), in the fifth and sixth grades at the time of the study. The speech behavior of the speakers was sampled in four situations in which topic and situation varied. In three situations a peer setting (including three self-selected peers) was kept constant. Two of these situations included a male adult interviewer but differed in that he intervened in the language choice of the peers. In the third peer setting, the peers were alone. The fourth (and sequentially last) situation was an individual session, consisting of each speaker and a female adult test administrator, involving formal testing in both Spanish and English. (Further discussion of the design, purposes, and results of the overall project are found in Wald 1981a.)

Amidst the variety of types of language choice behavior found among the students, very striking language preferences and ordering of speakers according to *grammatical*, *discourse* level (extended speech), and *conversational* level behavior were evident. Although the patterns came from spontaneous speech, they are consistent with the findings of educational research on the test performance of bilingual students from a variety of communities. However, careful inspection of individual students adds detail to the motivations which underlie the statistics based on grosser measurements of aggregated students, and allows practitioners in close and frequent contact with students to recognize, with reasonable accuracy, the stage of development for such students.

In previous discussion, I have examined the predictability of gross language preference according to age of arrival and/or length of residence at the last stage of elementary school (Wald 1981b), and some specific grammatical features which correlate with language preference and/or grade of entry into the local school systems for the same students (Wald 1982a). In the following discussion, attention will focus on the general progression emerging cross-sectionally among individual students in producing extended discourse and managing conversational participation. Consideration of the generality of this progression as it applies to this and other communities, and the implications of the progression for the educational treatment of bilingual students is reserved for the concluding discussion.

The students discussed are all bilingual in Spanish and English, to some degree. The language preference behavior displayed in Table 4.1 is based on discourse behavior in two contrasting peer situations. The role of the interviewer in manipulating language choice in the second situation is crucial to the contrast.

Common to both situations the topics, around which each unit of extended speech is centered, are based on the personal knowledge of the student or group of students. The interviewer does not share this knowledge, nor is it reasonable to argue that he is perceived by the peers as sharing this knowledge until it is given to him by a peer. Under the conditions of greater speaker than addressee knowledge of the topic, speech is classified as *spontaneous*.[1]

1. The term "spontaneous" as used here follows sociolinguistic practice. It contrasts with the use of the same term applied to the task of describing pictures or making stories out of them, as in the method of language elicitation used by Garcia, Maez, and Gonzalez (1981), from which the Gonzalez and Maez (1981) study derives. Under the circumstances of elicitation of language

**TABLE 4.1**
**Language Choice in Producing Discourse Units**

| | Displayed Language Preference | Total No. of | | Percentage Total Discourse Units in | | |
|---|---|---|---|---|---|---|
| | | Speakers | Discourse Units | Spanish | Mixed | English |
| DI-1 | Spanish | 11 | 93 | 86 | 6 | 8 |
| | English | 22 | 220 | 1 | 3 | 96 |
| DI-2 | Spanish | 11 | 66 | 56 | 24 | 20 |
| | English | 22 | 126 | 54 | 13 | 33 |

Note: DI-1, language choice is speaker's; DI-2, language choice is the opposite of DI-1 for each speaker; language preference of each speaker is determined by DI-1.

Examples of these units of extended speech, called *discourse units* (DUs), are narratives of personal experience, house and room descriptions, recipes, directions from school to home, and movie descriptions. DUs are defined as multi-sentence topically coherent units of information. They are interruptible under certain circumstances, either by the speaker or by an addressee, for example, in order to insure attention or understanding, to make a request, digress, or make a correction. For these reasons they are not necessarily restricted to a single turn at speaking. Examples (10), (14), (16), (26) and (27) below illustrate segments of DUs distributed over several turns with interruptions involving difficulties in self-expression or comprehension intervening, on the part of members of the audience (see Wald, 1976, forthcoming, and Linde, 1980 for further discussion of the DU as a linguistic category). In the present study the category DU was further operationalized to consist of a minimum of *three* clauses.

The two situations are referred to as the *preferent* and *counter-preferent* interviews (DI-1 and DI-2 respectively on Table 4.1). In the preferent interview, speakers produced their own language choice dynamics without intervention of the interviewer. Most speakers characteristically showed extreme preference for one language under these conditions. In the counter-preferent interview, the interviewer, IV, a fluent third-generation bilingual member of the community in his early thirties, followed a conscious strategy of trying to counter the language preferences displayed by the speakers in the preferent interview by overtly requesting the other language and maintaining it himself when addressing the target speaker [as in example (8) below]. The results

---

samples from pictures, it is not clear that the speakers perceive that there is no "correct" response, ensuring that the speaker has greater knowledge of the topic than the addressee (tester). Indeed, it is quite likely that speakers perceive the task as a test in which the tester has an advantage in knowledge, since picture description is characteristic of school tests given to preliterates at early school grades.

show that many speakers displayed resistance to the other language, resulting in an increase in mixed discourses, especially for the Spanish-preferent speakers. This resistance took various forms, for both Spanish- and English-preferent speakers.

Table 4.2 displays the language choice behavior of key speakers in each age-on-arrival group, according to the following criteria for categorization of their discourse units.

*Spanish/English*. All clauses in the discourse unit were in one language, excluding reported speech (quotes of other speakers).[2]
*Mixed*. There was at least one full clause in the other language. That is, *clause-level* code-switching (rather than individual lexical items or phrases) was produced at least once in the discourse unit.

The key speakers displayed in Table 4.2 have the richest output among the Spanish-preferent speakers and therefore contribute most to the patterns already displayed in Table 4.1. The ranking by age-on-arrival is intraconvertible with length of residence and grade of entry into the local school system, given the narrow age range of the speakers involved in the study.

In Table 4.2, any category having four or more DUs is in boldface. This criterion is used to recognize mixing or separation of languages as a significant recurring behavior. Language preference is measured by language choice in the preferent interview. All speakers easily meet a preference criterion of 75 percent discourse units in one language.

Note that English preference is only found below age-on-arrival of nine years, with a minimum length of residence of five years. There were no exceptions to this pattern, out of the total of forty-six speakers interviewed in the project. Other English-preferent speakers, not displayed on Table 4.2, conform to one of the types represented below the solid line, especially as represented by (1) AL, with extreme separation of English and Spanish, or (2) JR, with low use of Spanish and a preference for mixing over Spanish alone in

---

2. Switches coinciding with quotations (reported speech) were excluded because scholars have commonly observed that bilinguals have a tendency to report speech in the language in which it was originally spoken, although this tendency is not categorical. Failing to discount this type of switching would have had a confounding effect on the criteria used for characterizing a DU as mixed, and would have complicated the task of defining language preference. On the other hand, quotations were of two types: 1) relatively simple formulaic utterances, e.g., "I'm gonna kill you" (quoted several times by Spanish-preferent CR in describing an English-language horror movie he had seen); 2) relatively complex and extended quotes in the other language. The second type were largely confined to English-preferent speakers quoting Spanish speakers (e.g., parents scolding them as part of a narrative of personal experience) in (otherwise) all-English DUs (by the criteria actually adopted). The ability of English-preferent speakers to quote complex utterances in Spanish is revealing of their Spanish skills and could be used as evidence of the social motivation for their English preference. However, in the interest of limiting complexity, I have not pursued that line of inquiry in this paper.

**TABLE 4.2**
**Progression of Key Speakers for Language Choice Patterns**

| Speaker[n] | Age/Sex | DI-1 | | | DI-2 | | | Total Discourse Units | | | Language Preference | AOA |
|---|---|---|---|---|---|---|---|---|---|---|---|---|
| | | S | M | E | S | M | E | S | M | E | | |
| *SO[1] | 12 f | 10 | — | — | 4 | — | — | 14 | — | — | S | 10 |
| AA[2] | 12 m | 6 | — | — | — | — | 1 | 6 | — | — | S | 11 |
| RM[3] | 13 m | 8 | 1 | — | 5 | 3 | 1 | 13 | 4 | 1 | S | 10 |
| CR[4] | 12 m | | ** | | 7 | 1 | 2 | 7 | 1 | 2 | S | 9 |
| RR[5] | 11 f | 7 | 1 | — | 1 | — | 1 | 8 | 1 | 1 | S | 7 |
| PQ[5] | 12 f | 11 | 2 | — | — | 7 | — | 11 | 9 | — | S | 6 |
| CB[5] | 11 f | 8 | 1 | — | 5 | 3 | 1 | 13 | 4 | 1 | S | 6 |
| AL[6] | 12 f | — | 2 | 9 | 9 | — | — | 9 | — | 9 | E | 7 |
| *CS[7] | 11 m | | ** | | | ** | | — | — | 21 | E | 6 |
| JB[7] | 11 m | — | — | 6 | 2 | 5 | 3 | 2 | 5 | 9 | E | 4 |
| JR[3] | 12 m | — | 2 | 13 | 2 | 7 | 1 | 2 | 9 | 14 | E | 0 |

S = Spanish
M = Mixed
E = English
*Marks an extreme case of suppression of one language.
**Is an irregular interview (CR did not freely choose his first peer group in DI-1, CS only spoke Spanish in a further peer group not chosen by him as discussed at the appropriate point in the text).
[n]Refers to the arbitrarily assigned group number of each speaker's self-selected peer group.

peer-supported conversation (recall discussion of Gonzalez and Maez). Crucial to understanding the more precise meaning of this progression will be the difference between JR and JB at the bottom of Table 4.2. This difference is not reflected in the gross measures displayed here.

Spanish-preference is encountered at all ages on arrival but is very unusual after five years residence for this age group. Six years residence, or arrival before age seven, appears to be the transitional point between Spanish and English preference for the key speakers.

In pursuit of understanding the patterning and differences hidden from this display, language choice behavior of individuals in each preference group is examined on the basis of age on arrival.

In examining the possible linguistic motivations for Spanish-preferent behavior, Spanish-preferent speakers are characterized for frequency of use of English irregular past marking in spontaneous speech, for example, using *ate* (marked) as opposed to *eat* (unmarked) in past contexts. This criterion is common to many language proficiency assessment instruments, as discussed below. Its virtue is its easy elicitability (by story retelling, for example), and

**TABLE 4.3**
**Percentage of Marking of English Strong Past Verbs in**
**Spontaneous Speech for Key Speakers**

| Speaker | % | (N) | Age on Arrival | Group | Language Preference |
|---------|-----|------|------|------|------|
| JR | 100 | 35+ | 0 | 0–5 | E |
| AL | 100 | 35+ | 7 | 6–8 | E |
| CS | 100 | 35+ | 6 | 6–8 | E |
| JB | 82 | 23 | 4 | 0–5 | E |
| RM | 80 | 10 | 10 | 9+ | S |
| CB | 76 | 79 | 6 | 6–8 | S |
| PQ | 71 | 128 | 6 | 6–8 | S |
| CR | 66 | 90 | 9 | 9+ | S |
| RR | 60 | 5 | 7 | 6–8 | S |
| AA | 25 | 8 | 11 | 9+ | S |
| SO | — | 0 | 10 | 9+ | S |

the high degree of objectivity involved in its recognition by analysts (or test scores).

Notice, in particular, that in Table 4.3 RM shows greater development of irregular past morphology than PQ, despite his later age on arrival. Nevertheless, in Table 4.2 he shows greater resistance than PQ to the use of English in discourse, as shown by his maintenance of a large number of Spanish-only discourse units in the counter-preferent interview. This behavior suggests that the overall use of English in extended discourse is not necessarily as quickly developed as the use of particular English grammatical features. Extended use of English involves the coordination of a large number of skills, including competing with other speakers for the floor, information ordering, syntactic framing, and a vocabulary equal to communicative needs.

Table 4.4 shows the correspondence of test to spontaneous speech for irregular past marking. It can be seen that the main problem with the tests is that they do not provide enough possible contexts for accurate measurement of irregular past development. Thus, for example, where the Bilingual Syntax Measure (BSM) succeeds in eliciting a range of from two to four past contexts for verb marking, and averages two past contexts per speaker, the percentage of possible contexts actually marked as past shows a 31 percent difference from spontaneous speech for the group as a whole. The Language Assessment Scales (LAS) English story-retelling succeeds in eliciting a larger number of possible contexts (four to fifteen), and the percentage of possible contexts actually marked differs by only 15 percent from spontaneous speech for the group as a whole (see Wald, in press, for further discussion of the relation of test to spontaneous speech).

**TABLE 4.4**
**Correspondence Between Test and Spontaneous Speech**
**on Strong Past Tense Marking for Speakers Showing**
**Variation Between Marked and Unmarked Verb Forms**

|  | Test | | Spontaneous |
|---|---|---|---|
|  | BSM* | LAS** | |
| Range (N of contexts) | 2–4 | 4–15 | 5–128 |
| Average N of contexts per speaker | 2.0 | 8.2 | 48.6 |
| Average difference in % of past marking compared with spontaneous speech | 31% | 15% | 0 |

\* Bilingual Syntax Measure
\*\* Language Assessment Scales

The most frequent irregular pasts develop relatively quickly, but considered alone they merely gauge the English of bilinguals of any age with English monolinguals under the age of six. In view of the disparity between grammatical development and discourse development, as exemplified by the difference between RM and PQ in Table 4.3, it would not be rational to use the measure of degree of irregular past marking alone as criterial of proficiency in English speech for eleven- to twelve-year-old bilinguals.

## LANGUAGE CHOICE

To discuss, through examples, the progressive linguistic and social effects on the language choice of the key speakers, groups are categorized as follows (in years): 1) *late arrivals*: age of arrival 9+ (length of residence max 3); 2) *middle arrivals*: age of arrival 6–8 (length of residence max 5); 3) *early arrivals*: age of arrival 0–5 (length of residence max 12). Given the narrow age range of the speakers, the same categories could just as easily be labeled short-residence, mid-residence and long-residence, respectively.

### Late Arrivals

All late arrivals are Spanish-preferent. Use of English varies, but is limited. SO and AA are extremely disinclined toward English. They both talk at great length in Spanish. SO fears ridicule in English, although her comprehension is high, and the LAS story-retelling reveals acquisition of many irregular past forms. She explicitly stated, when questioned about her refusal to speak English:

(1) como—cuando yo lo hablo . . . en la mesa donde estoy asentada con—con mis amigas, lo hablo y se burlan de mí . . .

"like when—when I speak it (= English) . . . at the table (i.e., in the classroom) where I sit with—with my friends, I speak it and they make fun of me."

There is no spontaneous English speech data since she refused to speak English in peer sessions, despite the presence of one monolingual English peer chosen by her (cf. Table 4.3).

AA shows limited acquisition of the irregular past. The requirement of English had an extreme suppressive effect on his overall conversation. Example 2 below is typical of his evasive behavior when required to speak English.

(2) IV: So, so do you like doing that or does that bother you (= taking care of younger siblings) or—huh?
  *AA: I don't know.
   IV: You don't know?
  *AR: ¿Te gusta hacerlo?
  *AA: No.
(later)
   IV: Oh the last—yesterday you were talking like crazy, I couldn't stop you. Now you don't wanna talk, now you don't know anything.

(*In all examples containing dialogue, the speaker under discussion will be marked by an asterisk.)

AA's disinclination to speak English is finally overtly expressed in:

(3) IV: Mm, do you feel that way, A? (= that people's views of other people depend on where they were born)
  *AA: Yes.
   IV: Why?
     (long pause)
   AR: ¿No sabes otra palabra, A?
  *AA: No (laughs uncomfortably). Yo no quiero hablar inglés.
   IV: No quieres hablar inglés. So how come you told me yesterday you didn't mind talking in English?
  *AA: Se me olvidó. (All laugh.)
   IV: So what do you do when you need to talk in English at a store or you have to help somebody in—in a situation when they only speak Spanish?
  *AA: I don't want to speak English.

An interesting feature of AA's behavior, which recurs with CB and PQ in example 15, is the *peer-help* pattern. Although AA shuns English for personal expression, he uses English where he may be viewed as helping a peer express himself in English. This is the type of situation which minimizes stress, since the speaker is not the principal focus of attention. It allows the speaker to practice speaking English without fear of embarrassment.

(4)　　IV:　(to PA) So what part of Mexico are you from, PA?  
　*AA:　Chihuahua.  
　　PA:　In Tijuana.  
　　IV:　(to PA) Tijuana, so you were raised in Tijuana?  
　*AA:　Yes.  
　　PA:　Yes.  
　　IV:　(to PA) So what do you think about uhm living here and going to school here. You like it?  
　*AA:　Yes.  
　　PA:　Maybe.  
　　AR:　(to AA) Shut up, all right? (Everyone laughs)  
　　IV:　(to PA) You don't want to talk either, huh?  
　*AA:　No.  
　　AR:　I know. They're lazy.  
　　IV:　They're lazy?  
　*AA:　(to AR) and you too!  
　　AR:　unh unh. I'm talking like a *perico* (pause).  
　*AA:　That's what you say!

RM and CR are more advanced in English than SO or AA in either language choice or irregular past measures. It will be seen that RM shows a behavior intermediate between the speakers, discussed above, and CR.

Example 5 illustrates RM's high comprehension of English, but typical avoidance of English production.

(5)　　JR:　Yeah, last—last time uhm you could tell right away. They (=the fish) start moving their tail and then you see like when the water boils, like that, it looks like that.  
　*RM:　Una de esas que hay—son tumbes—cosas que dice agua así que se ve.  
　　AP:　Like yesterday there was . . .

RM often used a code-switching strategy with his bilingual peers, in which only the beginnings of his discourse might be in English, in response to English speech. Usually before reaching the criterial clause length for mixing, by completing an entire clause (including the verb) in English, he switched to Spanish and maintained that language for all following clause-length segments. For example:

(6) *Me when* ahí junto a mi casa siempre nos ponemos a veces—en *summer* nos ponemos a jugar . . .

Example 7 achieves criteriality for a *mixed* discourse unit.

(7) *Man, I has three years in this school.* Mi hermano llegó de once años y—y el primer año pasó él . . .

His single English DU was produced perfunctorily under stress in example 8.

(8) *RM: m, pues le gustaban las novelas (laughs) y le iba—en—en Sonora esta hacía mucho—a sus amigos.

    IV: a ver, platicanos en inglés, a ver. En Sonora que pasaba? Y luego le preguntó en español (laughs) n what useta happen in Sonora with your brother?

  *RM: Man, he only—he *goes* to his friend's house n *said* to—if he *has* some books, to read. That's it.

CR shows greater accommodation to English. Example 9 is taken from a session with two monolingual English-speaking peers (both third-generation Mexican Americans). This segment shows his persistence in participating in conversation despite his disadvantage in English ability.

(9)   JP: and then you get their other shoe n you get it n tie it together, or you could tie both, one person to another.

    VS: (quickly) or where you could tie both feet together . . .

  *CR: n she's all right come on n she's come

    JP: (interrupting CR) the thing I hate is when—

  *CR: N when—when   remember—remember when we saw in
    VS: (overlap)         (inaudible). . . . . . . .

  *CR: movie, we n go under the table.

    VS: Oh yeah. (They all laugh.)

This persistence is all the more remarkable given the great distortion of community English norms found in his English pronunciation, combined with the social pressure exerted toward him by VS in example 10.

(10) *CR: Yesterday I went—
        VS: You what?
      *CR: I went with my mother. I say my mom Alpha Beta (= name
            of a supermarket chain) and then—
        VS: You what? You forbid her?
        JP: (to VS) Just shut up n listen.
      *CR: (to VS) Yeah, man.
        JP: (to CR) Just ignore him.
      *CR: n then they stop my mother . . .

This is in marked contrast to SO's totally reticent behavior based on fear of
embarrassment. In example 11, CR shows that he is aware of the relativity of
control of language and projected image in his retort to VS.

(11)   IV: (to VS) No, he (=CR) was asking me how to say that in
            English. Do you know what *machucar* means?
       VS: No.
      *CR: (to VS) Dummy!

Example 12 illustrates a similar persistence in claiming the floor in competition with more fluent English speakers in a peer group of his own choosing.

(12)   IV: (to OS) Melted, eh. So    tell me—
      *CR: (overlap)                      I know how to cook
            everything    everything everything!
       IV: (overlap)      Tell me—                          Tell me
            more of the dishes you know how to cook, CR.
                    I know you're a great cook
      OM: (overlap) Can you make a b-boiled steak?
      *CR: (overlap)                          I'm a
            great cook. I—I always make cakes.

       IV:              Hot    cakes?
      *CR: (overlap)           Huh?
      OM: Can you make a boiled steak?
      *CR: *El me ha visto siempre* (inaudible) . . .
       IV: How do you make them. *Platícame cómo se hacen.*
       OS: Oh I know how—awright,   go on
      OM: (overlap)                 Make a boiled steak.
      *CR: (beginning the recipe DU) Put uh first *harina* on—no, the
            butter, butter. Then all we needs like wet—put the *harina*.
            Then do it, do it. When it's all like balls right there you
            put . . .

It can be seen that CR maintains English on the clause-level to a much greater extent than RM, discussed above. However, as he becomes more involved in what he is saying, and the difficulties of maintaining English surmount, he too switches to Spanish. Example 13 shows the point at which he switched to Spanish in the recipe he initiated in example 12 above.

(13)   . . . like and then it's—it's sti—like like *masa. Luego l—masa, luego* sugar, *luego rollarlo, luego pienso de que color* . . .

Characteristic of all the speakers mentioned so far is that when they switch to Spanish, they do not switch back to English, but rather, maintain Spanish for the duration their discourse units. This behavior can be represented schematically as: (English) Spanish. This means that discourse units may begin in English, but when a clause-level switch to Spanish is produced, Spanish is maintained for the duration of the DU. In the case of SO, the option of opening a discourse unit (DU) in English is not exercised at all. RM and CR both exercise the option, but CR maintains English longer before switching to Spanish.

### Middle Arrivals: Spanish-preferent

This group is transitional between Spanish and English preference. Most individuals showed Spanish preference. Exemplary is the peer group consisting of RR, PQ, and CB. These speakers showed relatively high ability to use English grammar and to maintain English over several clauses. However, like CR, as their DUs become more involved, they tended to switch to Spanish. Yet, unlike any of the late arrivals, they switch back to English without the interviewer's intervention. Example 14 is typical of this behavior. As PQ encounters difficulty in English, she switches to Spanish, but without further intervention, she switches back to English at a point where she can do this with ease.

(14)   *PQ: I put some oil on the frying pan n then—uhm *como se dice polvo—polvito ese?*
       IV: . . . Oh, they're like breadcrumbs.
       *PQ: *ay, le pongo de eso* (laughs) and then—and then I put the shick—the chicken . . .

PQ's peer CB showed similar switching behavior. Her other peer RR, however, is more similar to AA. RR's English production shows stress, although she is more accommodating than AA. Both RR and AA avoid mixing, but only because they speak English very slowly and with great effort, with a maximum of conscious attention paid to language choice.

(15) *RR: By m- my mom said that when—when I was little I would—
            I—I was—I want to [u:]—
     PQ: only wash the dishes.
     *RR: only wash the dishes, and then my mom said when you
            grow bigger you not gon' to [u:] uhm
            wa-      to-        to like to-    wash the dishes
     CB: to like    to like                   di-
     PQ:            to-              to wash     dish

The peer help pattern, observed above in example 4, is seen again, this
time with the mixers, CB and PQ, helping and coaching RR. This suggests
that mixing, or clause-level switching, is a more advanced behavior in acquiring English discourse skills. The use of mixing allows the speaker to maintain
discourse coherence when encountering difficulties in English.

The strategy used by speakers like PQ (and CB) in producing discourse
units can be schematized as: English (Spanish) English. This means that these
speakers will start in English, but may use Spanish as they encounter a difficulty in English. However, unlike the later arrivals discussed earlier, they will
switch back to English when they find it possible to do so. Zentella (1981)
labels this strategy "crutching," the use of one language to fill gaps in knowledge of the other. Crutching commonly results in mixed DUs for PQ and CB,
as they tend to form complete clauses in Spanish before switching back to
English.

RR's less advanced behavior can be represented as: English (pause) English. Speakers like RR substitute pause (silence) for Spanish when encountering a difficulty in English. They are then dependent on another speaker to
supply an appropriate English word or longer expression on their behalf. They
do not "crutch" with Spanish, but rather rely on a more fluent English speaker.
Example 15 shows that more advanced speakers are willing to supply help,
and may even anticipate difficulties, given the slow pace at which RR speaks.
However, if help is not forthcoming, the speaker cannot continue without
switching to the Spanish option, lest the whole attempt at producing an English discourse dissolve in frustration. To the extent that the speaker is restricted to a language in which she is weak, she is not free to exercise independent control over her production of the discourse unit and is forced to
share it with more fluent speakers. It seems that loss of control over expression necessarily limits the speaker's involvement in what she is saying by
causing her to concentrate more attention on her form of expression than on
the content. It is important, then, to note that the mixing strategy enables the
learner to develop greater discourse competence in English by allowing maintenance of control and involvement in speaking, despite linguistic difficulties.

## Middle Arrivals: English-preferent

The minority of middle arrivals are English-preferent. They have been in an English-speaking environment for at least five years. This corresponds closely to the length of time many researchers of bilingual education have posed as showing a pay-off in academic achievement in the school language for minority language students (e.g., Cummins 1981).

AL and CS, both English-preferent, provide an important contrast in Spanish behavior at this stage. Both AL and CS show that the mixing found for the middle arrival Spanish-preferent speakers is extremely rare, but switching is still found in a few contexts. In example 16, vocabulary restricted to the home domain is involved.

(16) *AL: it has like seats. Do you know Spanish?
    IV: si.
    *AL: there's *una silla así, y como sillas de fierro . . . no, sí, para de que se usan en de- para* backyard.

In (17), AL has trouble with the complex doubly embedded left-branching possessive construction of English syntax.

(17) This friend of the boyfriend's girl . . . *el* friend *del novio de la muchacha* . . .

In (18), AL automatically, and apparently unconsciously, switches to Spanish in order to compete for the floor with VM, who had already switched to Spanish.

(18) VM: . . . she had barely got something *que le había regalado.* She had it n- n- *cuando cuando* sh- she
    *AL: (overlap)      she hit—*le pegó al muchacho.*

These behaviors, and AL's total switch to Spanish in the counter-preferent interview, indicate great comfort with Spanish underlying great ability in English. She is close to the paradigmatic *coordinate bilingual*, a speaker who can easily maintain separation of both language systems (Weinreich, 1953: 8ff).

Example 19 shows a phenomenon in which a word commonly used in both Spanish and English among the speakers *triggers* further use of Spanish.

(19) the first cholo in the whole wide world is the zootsuit *pero e(l)*—
he was—he wasn't those kind of *cholos* there is right now.

The effect of the trigger on CS in example 20 is even more striking, given his extreme avoidance of Spanish.

(20)  My brother, when we ate—we ate *arroz*, not *arroz pero* y'know—
      can, like, well, soup, not with—not dried, not *arroz* dried . . .
      y'know that gots like water, something like that . . . then he had
      the pancake.

The triggering behavior reveals that Spanish is closer to the surface than usually revealed by the language preferences of these speakers.

Note that AL and CS both monitor themselves to edit out the triggered Spanish words and continue in English. This is evidence of a socially induced English preference which overlies a high degree of ability in both languages. The social motivation for English preference is evident when Spanish is triggered by necessary Spanish vocabulary (e.g., *arroz*, *zootsuit*), but when crutching is rare.[3]

CS is an extreme case of socially induced English preference. In avoidance of Spanish, he is the polar opposite of SO (who avoids English). Example 21 shows the dual language pattern of conversation. CS responds to Spanish with English.

(21)    IV:  (to CS) Cuantos amigos tienes afuera de l'escuela, CS?
        JB:  Mm, dos docenas.
        JF:  Dos (laughs)
      *CS:  *Two.*
        IV:  ¿Nomás dos? (laughs) ¿Es todo, eh?
      *CS:  *Or three. Yeah, three.*
        IV:  ¿Son Chicanos o que?
      *CS:  *No, they're Americans.*
        IV:  *They're Americans, eh.* Te gustan los Americanos?
      *CS:  *Yeah.*

In a further session with monolingual Spanish-speaking classmates, not selected by him, the preference for English was still strong and showed signs of automaticity. At first CS spoke in English, as if to the interviewer alone, for example:

3. At first glance one might be tempted to argue that *arroz* is equivalent to English rice, and that *zootsuit* is an English word. However, according to the speaker's perspective, *arroz* is the family name for food referred to, and *zootsuit* is used in both English and Spanish. Therefore, these are not examples of "crutching." Given the triggering behavior, it is likely that these words are associated with Spanish language contexts. This reveals that the speakers spontaneously use Spanish in contexts which have not been observed, most likely with their parents, as their home language surveys reported.

(22)    IV: ¿Y tu nunca has fumado cigarros? ¿No?
      *CS: *Only a little bit when my grandma tells me to light it up
           or—*
       IV: ¿Para élla?
      *CS: *Yeah.*

Example 23 shows that he eventually accepted the situation, demonstrating his accommodation to the pressure of new peers. As the peers showed interest in what he said, and asked the interviewer for a translation, CS himself began to shift to expressing himself in Spanish. But the need for the switch, here and in other examples, indicates that he is counteracting a more habitual tendency.

(23)    have you seen that little thing that instead of—*pa—para que no
        fumen no mas lo agarras y te lo comes?*

CS's Spanish showed a high degree of grammatical development, although he was relatively untalkative in that language. In this way he differs from SO. Her English does not show a degree of development comparable to CS's Spanish. For example, CS had no problem with Spanish preterits, although SO showed variable behavior in forming English pasts.[4]

CS exemplifies a rule which was widely found among the English-preferent speakers of his age group: Don't speak Spanish unless you have to. For the most part, "have to" refers to the English ability of the *addressee* rather than limitations on the *speaker's* knowledge of spoken English.

It turned out that CS, like AL, is a coordinate bilingual. However, CS's use of Spanish is socially more restricted and less accommodating than AL's.

The major pattern has become simply: English; with only rare occurrences of: English (Spanish) English.

### Early Arrivals

JR and JB present a contrast among English-preferent speakers of early arrival. This contrast is not immediately registered in Table 4.2, due to ambiguity in the type of mixing shown. Each speaker is discussed, in turn.

JR's behavior is a near opposite to the middle-arrival Spanish-preferent speakers. He maintained English (his preferred language) to the exclusion of

---

4. Similarly, SO showed no use of the modals in English proficiency testing, for example, in response to the Bilingual Syntax Measure (BSM) question: *what would the king have done if the dog hadn't eaten his food*, SO replies simply: *the king eat it*, without use of the modal *would*. In response to the Spanish equivalent of the same question she used the conditional (equivalent to the English modal *would* in context): *el rey se la comeria*. CS used both *would* in English and the subjunctive in Spanish. In counterfactual conditions (as in the BSM stimulus question), the subjunctive is the more usual Spanish equivalent to English *would* among the students, regardless of English proficiency.

Spanish in the preferent interview. In the counter-preferent interview, he tended to frequently switch rather than maintain Spanish. However, there is a crucial difference between his switching and that of later arrivals. His switches were most often smooth and without any apparent motivation in terms of difficulty in expressing himself in Spanish, for example, the switches were not preceded by hesitation in either English or Spanish.

(24) *Nos tiene coraje X* (= a teacher). Man, X hates us, man. I hate X too . . . I hate him all around. *Me cae bien gordo*, man. I—man, *yo no me gustaría* . . .

or

(25) Yeah they're something like that but they—they're like Vanns (= brand of sportshoe), but *no tienen eso azúl, y 'it*, man, *estan muy bonitos* . . .

JR's behavior in Spanish can be represented as: Spanish (English) Spanish, where the English option is frequently exercised. This tendency to mix Spanish and English with minimal hesitation contrasts with both the later arrivals and JB.

In contrast to JR, while JB is typical of early arrivals in English preference, he is atypical in the overt difficulty he has with English. Examples 26 and 27 show overt expressions of difficulty in maintaining English, in a narrative and recipe, respectively.

(26) . . . n then the window got broke n—*este*—*¿cómo se dice? el este*—

or

(27) First, I put uh—*en español lo digo porque no se decirlo en inglés* . . . *primero yo pongo casuela, y luego* . . .

Example 28 shows a switch to Spanish on the conversational level, in order to compete for the floor with peers of greater English ability.

(28)    IV: Hey, JB, do you know how to drive?
       *JB: No way!
            (but . . . )
        JF: I have. I've had—I've had to drive a car.
       *JB:                            Yeah, I have.
        CS: So have I.

```
* JB:     Me too. Yeah. I—my dad's
  JF:                    Yeah I—
  CS:  My uncle's.
  JF:                    una—Yeah my uncle's n my dad's.
* JB:  I—I always t- ah mi papá siempre me dije va aprender
  JF:                              when my uncle—
```

JB serves as a warning that rate of development of English skills on the discourse and conversational levels is not the same for all speakers. However, he is decidedly exceptional given his age of arrival and length of residence. His performance is transitional between the middle arrival Spanish-preferent speakers and middle arrival English-preferent speakers such as AL. His English skills have not kept pace with the increasing social pressures to speak English according to length of residence.

Undoubtedly, the social pressure toward English among the students of this age group in this community has historical bases in a general elevation of English above Spanish in the society at large, and especially in the schools (see, for example, Penalosa's (1980) discussion of the notorious discipline cards for speaking Spanish on school grounds in many Southwestern communities, including East Los Angeles, as recently as the late 1950s). While these pressures may not affect all students, they certainly represent a major trend. It is likely that the same trend can be found in most urban lower Socio Economic Status (SES) Hispanic communities. Similarly, trends in language preference for this age group are observed in comparably segregated Puerto Rican communities in New York City, although with slightly more accommodation to Spanish (Pedraza 1982).[5]

It cannot be claimed that Hispanic children resist English. On the contrary, the norm of the community is to value English highly, but to be reticent about speaking it before one can speak it well.

Until five years of residence, speakers cannot be expected to prefer English to Spanish. The later arrivals, especially, may show rapid development in core grammatical skills, but may be reticent about practicing discourse and conversational skills in public—among peers or in the classroom—because of their relative lack of skill and the inadequate public image projected. However, this depends on individual personality factors, as the contrast between SO and CR among the late arrivals has illustrated.

The middle arrivals are more secure in English. This corresponds to longer

5. The same trend is perceivable in Rodriguez-Brown and Elias-Olivares' (1981) study of six Waukegan Hispanic children. The three children with longest residence showed an extreme preference for English in the classroom, and a trend toward favoring English among friends and siblings at home.

exposure and greater acquisition of English skills on all levels—grammar, discourse, and conversation. It is important to note that these speakers started to speak English at an earlier age than the late arrivals. EG, a middle arrival bilingual member of SO's peer group, provided the key to social factors influencing willingness to speak English among limited students, when she pointed out that when she started speaking English in second grade there were many other peers in her situation. This provided a larger base of group support than available to the later arrivals. It is a demographic fact that with increasing age the number of speakers at early stages of English acquisition diminishes. At the same time, the students' social roles and concern with public image become more complex and demanding. Mexican Americans, as distinct from new arrivals from Mexico, are expected, by the community itself, to have competent English social roles.[6]

The general pressure toward English, along with concern for projected image, propels speakers toward more English, but not for speaking until they have achieved a certain status and self-confidence among peers. Those speakers who have achieved extensive comprehension of English and internalized much English grammar of the local vernacular variety display their competence in English speech. As we have seen, this is sometimes done at the expense of Spanish, according to language preference in peer situations. Less competent English speakers also conform to this norm, but by avoiding English. The norm is: It is better to avoid speaking English when public image is at stake, until one can speak it well. An incompetent image in English is worse than no projected image at all. Only a *competent* image in English is more highly valued by the community, as by the society at large.

JB's behavior suggests that at the higher levels of development, social pressure toward English overrides English language resources. It is evident that he is affected by the social norm requiring English-speaking roles as he integrates himself into the local Mexican American urban society. CS's extreme behavior shows an overreaction to the English norm felt by all, but may turn out to be a nonfinal stage in the development of bilingual behavior. That is, this may be a type of "hypercorrection" in language choice, based on the same learning mechanism by which a learner exaggerates a newly learned linguistic feature, overextending its use to inappropriate contexts, for example, *whom is it?* for *who is it?*. A Spanish example might be the use of $/\theta/$ instead of $/s/$ with words like '*s*eis' as well as '*c*inco' by American Spanish speakers affect-

---

6. This assertion is discussed at length in Wald (1982b), particularly in terms of the territoriality expressed by adolescent and adults native to the community and by fluent English-speaking preadolescents in their bilingual humor. Among adult Mexican Americans in Los Angeles, competence in English counterbalances a widespread self-perception of inferiority in Spanish abilities in comparison with Mexican nationals.

ing the Castillian model. Another type of hypercorrection might be overly frequent use of consonantal constriction with syllable-final /r/ in reading among
the upwardly mobile lower-middle-class in New York City (Labov, 1972).

In sum, for communities like East Los Angeles, where pressures toward
English are great, even outside of the school context, at least in part directly
due to peer values, the following points should be considered in integrating
language choices into instructional strategies.

Pressure toward competence in *spoken* English already exists at large without additional aggravation from the school. Students are receptive to English
input from the outset of schooling. This is seen in the relatively high comprehension of extended conversational speech by the late arrivals with two to
three years of residence. This suggests that measured introduction of English,
alongside Spanish, need not be delayed until Spanish literacy skills are mastered, but rather that the delay, if any, should be short.

The usual morphological measures of English used by language proficiency tests have a low monolingual age ceiling, only useful between kindergarten and first grade. They do not predict language preference for English
among eleven- to twelve-year-old bilinguals until virtually 100 percent performance level in English is reached. In other words, the acquisition of morphology is *easier* than talking extendedly in a particular language, or than
actively participating in a conversation, especially one in which one must compete for attention with speakers more skilled in the same language. Students
of less than five years residence generally need Spanish as a public medium of
communication while they are acquiring extensive speech skills in English.
Although they will generally understand most of what is said to them in English after two to three years, they will prefer to answer in Spanish with or
without mixing with English for two or three more years, both according to
concern with public image and involvement in what they themselves want to
say. Students of non-early ages of arrival vary according to self-confidence in
English, expressed in willingness to speak English in public, but can learn
English along with Spanish in private or semiprivate encounters.

Peers of greater ability in English have a spontaneous peer-help pattern to
aid students in communicating in English. This needs to be explored and encouraged in terms of school friendship networks of students with different
degrees-of-English-spoken and literacy skills.

Mixing and codeswitching break down into various categories according to
motivation and to indication of development and preference. Spanish tends to
show a fluent pattern for all first-generation and many second-generation
speakers. Avoidance of Spanish appears to be socially motivated rather than
due to limitations in basic language abilities. However, one must not stereo-
type all Hispanics, especially second generation, as fluent in Spanish, even if

they are of a local vernacular. By the end of elementary school, the degree of extensive English discourse and hesitation before switching to Spanish varies with length of residence more than any other easily observable factor. However, cases like JB illustrate that other factors are involved and underlie the length-of-residence measure. JB's involvement in English is predictable at his age, but may have started more recently than for the others, due to a rapid change in peer group accompanying moving from another neighborhood. Early arrivals tend to show the same facility in vernacular Spanish as the late arrivals, but they tend to prefer English. They tend to switch smoothly between languages in Spanish contexts. Clause-level codeswitching of any type is a sign of more advanced acquisition of English skills than the painstakingly slow and audibly stressful maintenance of English found in early stages of acquisition. Therefore, codeswitching should not be discouraged in the development of high level English skills, such as extended speech or participation in conversational exchanges.

Translating the cross-sectional data into a longitudinal progression, an anticipated trend is as follows:

1. Spanish is spoken exclusively while English is being acquired. English speech is avoided. In all contexts, extended discourse units take the shape: Spanish.
2. English is used when necessary and with effort. English utterances are short, rarely as long as a clause. In counter-preferent contexts, discourse takes the shape: English (pause) English, where recurrences of English may depend on help from other speakers.
3. English is used as a concession to the situation, but under duress. When difficulty is encountered, the speaker switches to Spanish and maintains that language as long as possible. Essentially, English becomes an optional opener to step (1) above, a strategy for participating in conversation with English-preferent bilinguals, acknowledging their preference, but initially only in a token manner. In counter-preferent contexts discourse units take the shape: (English) Spanish.
4. English can be used more extensively with switching in and out of Spanish, according to involvement in what the speaker is saying, playing against self-monitoring to maintain English. In counter-preferent contexts discourse units take the shape: English (Spanish) English.
5. Preference, especially in public and peer situations, shifts toward English, according to the preferences and abilities of the perceived majority in the situation. For an increasing variety of situations, English has preferred status. In preferent contexts, discourse units take the shape: English.

6. Overreaction may set in with suppression of Spanish except when Spanish is absolutely necessary. Dual-lingual behavior may occur [recall CS's behavior in (21) above]. If this is automatized, speakers now tend to switch to English in Spanish discourse, but without the signs of hesitation characteristic of English-to-Spanish switches of speakers at earlier stages of English acquisition. In counter-preferent contexts, discourse units take the shape: English (Spanish).

Even if step (6) is reached, as it is for many early-arrival speakers in the community, it is not evident that Spanish discourse and conversational skills do not continue to develop surreptitiously. However, they will no longer be evident in school performance in Spanish as long as the school momentum is toward transition to *English-only* situations. This momentum simply reinforces the historical pattern of devaluing Spanish, a much stronger force before the advent of bilingual education, but still felt by effects that have filtered down to late elementary school age children. This devaluation and its effects have been internalized and used as community norms by apparently large segments of the lower SES population, especially of non-first generations. It is most likely that the same norm will be found operating among bilinguals of this age group in virtually any urban community in the United States. This is the age and stage at which historical repression of Spanish appears to be keenly felt by the students.

It is important to note that although this major trend appears to add up to shift in language choice by the age of twelve for early and some middle arrivals, research on adolescents may show an expansion of repertoire, including a comeback of Spanish at a later stage for some speakers. The meaning and differential influence of this expansion among individuals and networks in Hispanic bilingual communities remains for further investigation. Here, the future of late arrivals is most in need of investigation.

It is beyond the scope of this paper to discuss the work and proposals of Garcia, Maez, and Gonzalez (1981) and Gonzalez and Maez (1980) in the detail that they deserve. Those studies are addressed specifically to the performances of a younger age group (four-to-six years of age) on the tasks mentioned in an earlier note. There are many problems in comparing those data with the data presented here. The methods are different. In their study, data were obtained in only one language (half of their sample were tested only in English, the other half only in Spanish). There is no indication in that study how many and which speakers came from bilingual vs. monolingual Spanish-speaking homes, or how ages-on-arrival (or generation) are distributed among the samples. Consequently, it is not clear that selection (ten speakers per language, per site) insures comparable samples across languages. Nevertheless, the result of that study—that among early arrivals (before the age of six years), switching to English in Spanish contexts is much more frequent than switching to Spanish in English contexts—is a familiar phenomenon among second generation speakers. However, as mentioned earlier, there were also *early arrivals* (many second generation) who exhibited the behavior represented by AL, of coordinate bilingualism. In any case, the type of switching behavior displayed showed that JR is fluent, without hesitation, and is not analogous to the hesitant switching behavior in the opposite direction (English to Spanish) exhibited by the later arrivals of limited linguistic ability. Gonzalez and Maez may concede that avoidance of Spanish, even among their younger sample, is socially motivated (especially given their test instruments, associated with the English-dominant school environment), but still argue that avoidance of Spanish leads to limitations in linguistic abilities in Spanish. This argument is all the more powerful given the fact that these younger speakers may have become English-preferent before reaching a *threshold* level of competence in Spanish. This must remain a moot point in certain respects until linguistic characteristics of the threshold are identified, if they indeed exist. The use of Mean Length of Utterance measures in their study leaves many questions unanswered. It seems probable that the observed decrease in Spanish Mean Length of Utterance with increasing grade simply reflects socially induced avoidance of Spanish, since no decrease in morphology is reported. In a further study of the data base used in the present study, it would be feasible to review each of the early arrivals (0 to 5 years of age) individually in order to determine to what extent and for what reasons they conform to either the coordinate or "JR" type. However, in this paper the analysis has been restricted to identification of types. The focus is on acquisition of English rather than on the possible attrition of Spanish. That is a separate issue about which this paper can only say that avoidance of Spanish is not necessarily a sign of attrition of linguistic abilities. That issue is of sufficient linguistic and social importance to merit a paper of its own. As in this paper, it would be advisable to trace social and linguistic motivations in language choice from preschool through adolescence, for members of the community.

## REFERENCES

Cummins, James. 1981. The role of primary language development in promoting educational success for language minority students. In *Schooling and Language Minority Students: A Theoretical Framework*. Evaluation, Dissemination and Assessment Center. California State University, Los Angeles, California, 3–50.

Fishman, Joshua. 1967. Bilingualism with and without diglossia: diglossia with and without bilingualism. *Journal of Social Issues* 23:29–38.

Garcia, E. E., L. Maez, and G. Gonzalez. 1981. A national study of Spanish/English bilingualism in young Hispanic children in the United States. *Bilingual Education Paper Series*, vol. 4, no. 12. Los Angeles: National Dissemination and Assessment Center, California State University, Los Angeles.

Gonzalez, Gustavo, and Lento F. Maez. 1980. To switch or not to switch: the role of code-switching in the elementary bilingual classroom. In Raymond V. Padilla, ed. *Theory in Bilingual Education. Ethnoperspectives in Bilingual Education*, vol. 11, 125–35.

Gumperz, John, and E. Hernandez-Chavez. 1970. Cognitive aspects of bilingual communication. In *Language Use and Social Change*, H. Whiteley, ed. London: Oxford University Press, pp. 111–25.

Krashen, Stephen D. 1981. Bilingual education and second language acquisition theory. In *Schooling and Language Minority Students: A Theoretical Framework*. Evaluation, Dissemination and Assessment Center. California State University, Los Angeles, pp. 51–82.

Labov, William. 1972. *Sociolinguistic patterns*. Philadelphia: University of Pennsylvania Press.

Pedraza, Pedro, J. Attinasi, and G. Hoffman. 1980. Rethinking diglossia. In *Theory in Bilingual Education: Ethnoperspectives in Bilingual Education*, Raymond V. Padilla, ed., vol. 11, pp. 75–97.

Penalosa, F. 1980. Chicano sociolinguistics. Rowley, Mass.: Newbury House.

Poplack, Shana. 1979. Sometimes I'll start a sentence in English y termino en español: toward a typology of code-switching. New York: Centro de estudios puertorriquenos, City University of New York.

Valdes, Guadalupe. 1980. Code-switching as a deliberate verbal strategy: a microanalysis of direct and indirect requests among bilingual Chicano speakers. In *Latino Language and Communicative Behavior*, R. Duran, ed. New Jersey: Ablex, pp. 95–105.

Wald, Benji. 1976. The discourse unit: a study in the segmentation and form of spoken discourse. Unpublished ms. Los Angeles: University of California.

———. 1981a. The relation of topic/situation sensitivity to the study of language proficiency. In *Bilingual Education Technology. Ethnoperspectives in Bilingual Education*, Raymond V. Padilla, ed. vol. 3, pp. 281–306.

———. 1981b. On assessing the oral language abilities of limited English proficient students. In *Issues of language assessment: Foundations and research*, S. Seidner, ed. Evanston, Ill.: Illinois State Board of Education, National College of Education, pp. 117–26.

———. 1982a. Test and spontaneous language behavior of late preadolescent bilinguals: morphology vs. syntax. Paper presented at the Hispanic Research SIG of the AERA in New York City. March 20, 1982. To appear in Stan Seidner, ed. *Issues of Language Assessment: Language Assessment and Curriculum Planning*. National College of Education. Evanston, Illinois.

———. 1982b. Sociolinguistic aspects of the Mexican American community in Los Angeles. Paper presented at the Xth World Congress of Sociology. August 19, 1982. Mexico City.

Weinreich, Uriel. 1953. *Languages in contact*. Reprinted in 1966. The Hague: Mouton and Co.

Zentella, Ana Celia. 1981. "Hablamos los dos. We speak both": growing up bilingual in El Barrio. University of Pennsylvania Ph.D. dissertation. Order No. 8127100.

# 5.
# Bicultural Personality Development: A Process Model

*Fernando Jose Gutiérrez*

THE PURPOSE OF THIS STUDY is to integrate acculturation/assimilation and identity theory in order to formulate a theoretical process model of bicultural personality development. This model will be useful to psychologists, educators, and other helping professionals as a way of gaining increasing understanding of the process of personality integration that immigrants and ethnic minority groups go through as they experience a dual cultural membership.

Before proceeding, it will be useful to define several terms in order to provide a common base of understanding.

*Acculturation*: ways in which some cultural aspect is taken into a culture, adjusted and fitted to it (Herskovitz 1936).

*Assimilation*: transfer of membership from one group to another whose norms are different from those of the first (Taft 1957).

*Biculturalism*: two types have been identified: 1) behavioral biculturalism, and 2) attitudinal biculturalism. Behavioral biculturalism refers to a person's ability to participate in more than one culture depending on what the situation demands. This type involves proxemics and kinemics. The person must be able to adapt gestures, tones, and inflections to the particular culture in which he is communicating. Attitudinal biculturalism is present when persons are able to evaluate their behavior in comparison to culturally distinct reference groups. In this type, persons must be able to relate emotionally, and their values must be similar to those of the reference group (Oliver 1975).

*Culture*: K. Young defined culture as "these folkways, these continuous methods of handling problems and social situations . . . the whole mass of learned behavior or patterns of any group as they are received from a previous group or generation and as they are added to by this group and then passed on to other groups or to the next generation" (in Kroeber and Kluckhohn 1952).

*Identity*: the "ability to experience one's self as something that has continuity and sameness" (Erikson 1963).

*Process Model*: a representation of a dynamic natural phenomenon marked by changes that lead to a particular result (adapted from *Webster's Seventh Collegiate Dictionary*, 1966).

## RATIONALE FOR STUDY

The analysis of human behavior can be approached from three systems: psychological, social, and cultural. The personality system includes traits, feelings, attitudes, and needs, as well as processes such as learning and perception. The social system focuses on how people relate to one another and on their positions in these relations. How a person thinks, acts, and feels in each position held is considered. In the cultural system, beliefs and values related to activities of members of society are examined.

Historically, the personality domain has been the responsibility of the psychologist. The answer that is most generally sought by psychologists, according to Kaplan (1961), is the relationship between the person's personality development and the influence of the social environment on this development. They are only interested in socio-cultural systems as they relate to personality development. The social domain has been the responsibility of the sociologist, and the cultural that of the anthropologist. Kaplan (1961) identified the sociologists' and anthropologists' interests as the problems of social cohesion and functioning, social order, and social change. Their focus of inquiry centers around the relationship between personality processes and their effects on the way societies function. Kaplan states that societal functioning depends on the existence of a congruent personality or motivational structure in its members. This personality or structure is also referred to as a national character.

In the past, there have been major differences among these three groups of social scientists. However, as the fields advance and gain recognition in their own right, social scientists are moving toward an interdisciplinary approach. Diaz-Guerrero (1977) stated that next to genetics, culture is the other major determinant of human behavior; therefore, socio-cultural psychology must be able to relate culture to the psychological processes of perception, learning, and thinking. Holtzman, Diaz-Guerrero, and Swartz (1978) identify several environmental factors that require a cross-cultural approach in order to study them under realistic life conditions: variations in family lifestyle, patterns of child rearing, sociolinguistic variations, social orders, and their political and economic systems. An example of this new perspective is reported by Edgerton (1974) in his reference to the *Biennial Review of Anthropology*

(Siegel 1972). "It contains not its usual chapter entitled 'culture and personality' or 'Psychological Anthropology' by an anthropologist, but a chapter called 'Cross-cultural Psychology' by psychologists Triandis, Malpass, and Davidson."

Before a satisfactory model combining all three disciplines can be effectively implemented, divergent methodology must be recognized and integrated. A major difference between psychology and anthropology, identified by Price-Williams (1974), is that the anthropologist does not separate an item from its context, whereas the psychologist typically does. According to Edgerton (1974), while cultural psychologists apply experimental procedure as their method of verification, anthropologists prefer the naturalistic method. Edgerton further states that if anthropology and psychology are to converge, there will need to be a combination of experimental and naturalistic methodology.

Olmedo (1979) points out that psychologists have become involved in the study of acculturation only in the last decade. What body of knowledge has existed concerning acculturation has yet to be integrated within the total body of psychology. According to Chance (1975), psychologists and psychiatrists tend to view acculturation in terms of intra-psychic mechanisms, that is, a change in the perceptions, attitudes, and cognitions of the individual. Anthropologists and sociologists, on the other hand, have, in general, chosen an interpsychic or interpersonal approach which has led to an emphasis on acculturation as a group process, in terms of its relationship to socialization, social interaction, and mobility.

An integration of the psychological, social, and cultural domains is extremely important in the study of ethnicity. Isajiw (1974) defines the concept of ethnicity as "an involuntary group of people who share the same culture . . . who identify themselves and/or are identified by others as belonging to the same involuntary group." This definition incorporates three domains. It takes into account the traits, feelings, attitudes, and perceptions of individuals and how they identify themselves, which is part of the psychological domain. The definition also includes the social domain in its focus on people's relationships to one another, and the cultural domain in its focus on shared beliefs and values.

The study of ethnicity is aiding the evolution of this new, interdisciplinary approach, since scientists involved in these studies view the person in a psychological, sociological, and cultural context, and often use a combination of naturalistic as well as experimental methods in their research design.

To examine acculturation/assimilation more thoroughly, an interdisciplinary approach is required. Flexner (1979) states that the interdisciplinary approach "permits both instructors and students to draw upon one or several disciplines when and as they are pertinent to the solution of a specific problem, however broad or narrow it may be." The interdisciplinary approach, according to Kockelmans (1979), aids the validation of generalizations and findings made by scientists in one social science by measuring them against another social science. As a result of this venture, new ground in research is broken, and the disciplines involved can be extended beyond their boundaries. Mouly (1963) states that ". . . a major task of science seems to be that of building bridges from one discipline to another in order to integrate this specialized knowledge into a single conceptual structure."

## METHODOLOGY

In this study, the present author utilized psychological, sociological, and anthropological empirical as well as observational data to develop the theoretical model.

A theory can be defined as an "analysis of a set of facts in their relation to one another . . . a plausible or scientifically acceptable general principle or body of principles offered to explain phenomena, a hypothesis assumed for the sake of argument or investigation" (*Webster's* 1966).

Marx (1976) proposes that a theory serves two main functions: (1) as a tool, in order to refine and solidify facts, through guided observation, and (2) as a goal in science, to stimulate comprehension of the natural world. More succinctly stated by Marx, a theory describes, explains, and summarizes. It is in this context that the model for this paper was constructed.

The research from which this model is drawn is representative of isolated incidents in different cultures. This research was selected following a review of the literature on acculturation/assimilation in the fields of psychology, sociology, and anthropology. Incidents of acculturation/assimilation of immigrants to the United States, ethnic minorities within the United States, as well as ethnic minorities and immigrants of other countries were cited and certain patterns emerged. Personal observation was made of some of these same patterns in the author's acculturation/assimilation process, as well as that of clients and students, in a mental health setting and in institutions of higher education. The synthesis of these isolated incidents may provide a more sophisticated framework from which to continue investigative baseline studies on bicultural personality development. (See Gutierrez 1981 for a more complete review.)

The formulation of the model is based on the assumption that culture is not a static phenomenon, but is in constant stages of evolution. Stonequist (1937) suggests that only a small part of culture is invented by any one group. The remainder is borrowed from other groups with different cultures; the evolution takes place at a slow pace, to allow for accommodation to these changes. Current and future models of bicultural personality development must allow for the interaction between the cultures.

This model, depicted in Table 5.1, draws from Erikson's (1980) identity theory; Atkinson, Morten, and Sue's (1980) model of minority identity development; and Greeley's (1971) and Taft's (1957) models of acculturation/assimilation.

Before proceeding to the examination of the model itself, it will be helpful to summarize the theories and models on which the present model is based.

## MODELS OF IDENTITY AND ACCULTURATION/ASSIMILATION

### Erikson's Identity Theory

The most noted contemporary authority on identity formation is Erik Erikson. Erikson was influential in developing a model of personality development which accounted not only for the biological predetermined attributes which contributed to a person's growth, but also the social and cultural influences on this growth. Erikson stated that "personality can be said to develop according to steps predetermined in the human organism's readiness to be driven toward, to be aware of, and to interact with, a widening social radius, beginning with the dim image of a mother and ending with mankind, or at any rate, that segment of mankind which 'counts' in the particular individual's life." Erikson attempts to bridge infantile sexuality theory with "our knowledge of the child's physical and social  growth within his family and social structure" (Erikson 1980, p. 54). The stages depicted in column I, Table 5.1, p. 105, represent essentially *nuclear conflicts* or *crises* which persons must resolve in their life span. Havighurst (1953), who was influenced by Erikson's conceptualizations of these stages, refers to them as the developmental tasks of life— "those things that constitute healthy and satisfactory growth in our society. They are the things a person must learn if he is to be judged and judges himself to be a reasonably happy and successful person. A developmental task is a task which arises at or about a certain period in the life of the individual, successful achievement of which leads to his happiness and to success with later tasks, while failure leads to unhappiness in the individual, disapproval by the society, and difficulty with later tasks" (p. 21).

Adolescence is a very important period in personality development according to Erikson, since it is during this period that a person plans for the future; consolidation of one's personal identity takes place. During this period, Erikson believes that a moratorium or delay of adult obligations takes place so that a person can make a decision about who and what he/she will become in the future (Enker 1971).

*Moratorium*. Arredondo-Dowd (1978) explains that in this period, adolescents experiment with different roles and identities outside the family, in order to make choices about these identities and incorporate them into their personalities. Adolescents can emerge from this moratorium stage either confused about their identity, or with a sense of formed identity. Successful attainment of an identity will result in self-esteem (Erikson 1980). This self-esteem is confirmed at the end of a successful resolution of each crisis which helps adolescents perceive that they are learning effective steps toward the future. Erikson warns that the development of an ego identity depends on "whole-hearted and consistent recognition of real accomplishment, that is, achievement that has real meaning in their culture" (p. 95). This step is essential in personality development, for if adolescents are deprived of the expression of their ego identity, they will react very violently, according to Erikson, as though they were forced to defend their lives. Failure at this stage will cause identity diffusion, with adolescents unable to make up their minds about who they are and what they believe. Erikson states that such doubt, as doubt about ethnic identity would be, may bring about delinquency, psychotic episodes in an individual, or a negative identity.

The negative identity occurs when adolescents choose those roles which are considered improper or undesirable by significant others in their lives (Erikson, 1968). Examples of this negative identity are: "images of the violated (castrated) body, the ethnic out-group, and the exploited minority. . . . In any system based on suppression, exclusion, and exploitation, the suppressed, excluded, and exploited unconsciously believe in the evil image which they are made to represent by those who are dominant" (Erikson 1980, p. 30). Erikson (1968) suggests that persons who live in environments of economic, ethnic, and religious marginality are more susceptible to acquiring negative identities.

For Erikson, the ego ideal represents those qualities for which people strive. These qualities undergo revision to coincide with the historical era in which the person lives. The values which the family, a race, a nation hold influence the ego ideal; therefore, the ego ideal is flexible enough to incorporate these cultural changes. Developing a bicultural personality could be an ego ideal which can prevent a person from developing a negative identity or a sense of marginality.

### Atkinson, Morten, and Sue

Atkinson, Morten, and Sue (1980) have proposed a five-stage process of minority identity development based on a person's reactions to oppression. These stages include: conformity, dissonance, resistance and immersion, introspection, and synergetic articulation and awareness. Each stage marks the beginning of a new process for ethnic minorities.

*Stage 1.* During the conformity stage, minorities develop a clear preference for dominant (or host group) cultural values, roles, and lifestyles. Ethnic members become self-deprecating, as well as deprecating of their native group.

*Stage 2.* During the dissonance stage, they become confused when they experience inconsistencies in previously accepted values and beliefs. They hold both appreciating and deprecating attitudes toward self and group.

*Stage 3.* Minorities explore their ethnic history and culture and continue to develop self- and group-appreciating attitudes, and reject the dominant group.

*Stage 4.* Minorities introspect about their basis for self and group appreciation. They explore a balance between responsibility and allegiance to their minority group versus personal autonomy. There is greater concern for *group-usurped individuality*. In addition, they question their blanket distrust of the dominant society and begin to selectively trust and distrust certain individuals of the dominant group.

*Stage 5.* Minorities develop a feeling of resolution of conflict which allows them to become more flexible, with a feeling of individual control. There is a strong feeling of appreciation of self and group, and obliteration of oppression becomes a goal. There is also selective appreciation for the dominant group.

### Milton Gordon

Gordon (1964) identified seven basic subprocesses of assimilation: 1) The first step is for people to change their cultural patterns to those of the host culture; 2) they form primary group relationships in increasing numbers with members of their host culture; 3) they eventually intermarry with members of the host culture; 4) once intermarriage has taken place, these immigrants develop a host culture sense of ethnicity; 5) they eventually get to the point where they will not encounter any prejudicial attitudes; and, as a consequence, 6) they do not encounter any discriminatory behavior; 7) therefore, they do not feel the need to raise any issues with the host society concerning power conflicts between their original ethnic affiliation and their new host culture affiliation.

### Andrew Greeley

Greeley (1971) presents a six-step process of assimilation. According to Greeley, the first step in the process of assimilation is a person's experience of culture shock. Having left the familiar surroundings and the necessary support systems, a person experiences a tremendous feeling of isolation. The second step is that of organization and self-consciousness, strengthening a sense of nationalism for the native country (or ethnic group). Greeley sees an inward focus where immigrants or members of ethnic groups recuperate from the shock of culture change and begin to regain pride for who they are as members of their native country or group. Once having regained a feeling of self-pride, they have the strength to begin the process of assimilation, the third stage. The fourth stage is the militancy stage, where the elite of the native country (or ethnic group), who have successfully assimilated, gain power and use it to better the status of their people. As a result of their militancy, however, immigrants may encounter further prejudice and discriminatory behavior from the host culture, and the feeling of loyalty to their ethnic group or compatriots precipitates a second crisis in the evolution of adjustment to life. Thus, Greeley proposes the fifth stage of self-hatred and anti-militancy. This stage is very crucial because a great deal of introspection occurs. Immigrants and ethnic group members have experienced both worlds and have been successful in both, separately, yet they can neither remain militant and antagonize the host culture nor betray the native group. Following this period of introspection and examination of alternatives, immigrants reach the sixth and final step of adjustment when they accept their identities as members of the host culture as well as their ethnic group. These identities are seen as compatible.

One of the weaknesses of Greeley's explanations of adjustment is that it emphasizes compatible identities alone. There is no consideration of the person's ability to function in both cultures simultaneously. While identification with both cultures takes place, there is no guarantee that people will be able to relate culturally to newcomers from their native country, because *identifying* oneself with a particular group does not necessarily imply that the cultural material or values which enhance understanding between a person and another of the same ethnic group or culture of origin are shared.

### Ronald Taft

Taft (1957) provides a model which incorporates psychological, social, and cultural processes. He bases his model on the following assumptions (p. 102): "Membership in a new group implies a number of things, including: a mutual willingness on the part of the new and old members to communicate with each other with some degree of social intimacy, consensus between the members on norms and values, the allocation and acceptance by the members of certain role requirements, and some degree of identification with the group."

Taft presents seven stages of assimilation, which he further breaks down into processes which are internal and external to the immigrant.

In Taft's model, the first stage of assimilation requires knowledge of the host culture on the part of the immigrant or ethnic group member. The second stage involves the development of a favorable attitude on the part of the immigrant/ethnic member toward the members and norms of the host group. The third stage involves the immigrant's or ethnic minority's perceptions of an unfavorable attitude of their native group toward the host culture and the immigrant's decisions not to withdraw from their own native group. Stage four involves the ethnic minority's and immigrant's conformity toward the roles of the host group. Stage five evolves when the ethnic minorities and immigrants are accepted by the host group. Stage six involves identification with the host group. And finally, stage seven is achieved when there is congruence between a person's own norms and those of the host group.

After examining the various theories and models, several observations can be made. Erikson's theory provides a good explanation of identity development; however, it needs to be interpreted in the context of culturally different individuals and in the context of culture change as this change affects the experiencing of Erikson's developmental stages.

Atkinson provides an excellent description of the process of minority identity development; however, this model does not present the relationship between minority identity development and identity formation in general.

Greeley's and Taft's models of acculturation/assimilation present a situation which requires the immigrants or ethnic minority group members to reject their native culture and adopt the dominant culture. Thus, there is a need for a model which can incorporate the process of acculturation/assimilation with the psychosocial stages of identity development and the stages of minority identity development.

### Process Model of Bicultural Personality Development

Table 5.1 depicts the proposed model of bicultural personality development. Column I depicts the stages of identity development proposed by Erikson (1980). Column II depicts periods of disequilibrium experienced by immigrants or ethnic minorities. These periods of disequilibrium represent crises in the natural process of culture change that individuals must resolve as they are becoming bicultural. Column III depicts levels of acculturation/assimilation that lead to bicultural personality formation. This last set of stages results from the interaction between the stages of Column I and Column II. Many of the stages in Columns II and III are derived from Atkinson's model of minority identity development and Greeley's and Taft's models of acculturation/assimilation.

Table 5.1 is broken down into rows which follow horizontally. The rows, which have been numbered from 1 to 8, represent each set of stages. The reader is asked to follow the rows from left to right and continue to the next row in the same direction. The order of the stages represents the sequence at

**TABLE 5.1**
**Stages of Bicultural Personality Development**

| I<br><br>Psychosocial<br>Stages | II<br><br>Stages of<br>Disequilibrium | III<br>Stages of<br>Acculturation/<br>Assimilation |
|---|---|---|
| 1 Trust<br>vs.<br>Mistrust | Lack of<br>Knowledge of<br>Host Culture | Culture Shock<br>vs.<br>Conformity |
| 2 Autonomy<br>vs.<br>Shame and Doubt | Sense of<br>Nationalism<br>for Native<br>Country | Alienation<br>vs.<br>Role Accommodation |
| 3 Initiative<br>vs.<br>Guilt | Assimilation | Marginality<br>vs.<br>Role Accommodation |
| 4 Industry<br>vs.<br>Inferiority | Militancy | Immigrant Group<br>Appreciation<br>vs.<br>Host Group<br>Appreciation |
| 5 Identity<br>vs.<br>Identity Diffusion<br>Part Conflicts | Introspection | Rejection of<br>Host Culture<br>vs.<br>Bicultural Sense<br>of Peoplehood |
| 6 Intimacy<br>vs.<br>Isolation | Selective<br>Appreciation | Self-Hatred<br>vs.<br>Bicultural<br>Adjustment |
| 7 Generativity<br>vs.<br>Self-Absorption | | |
| 8 Integrity<br>vs.<br>Despair | | |

which the stages normally appear. However, the interactions that occur among the stages do not necessarily follow in one direction (see Figure 5.1).

### Interaction Among Stages

The proposed model is process dominated. Each of these stages depicts a process which interacts with another, and together they form yet another process that can impact on earlier as well as later interactions. These processes are evolutionary. One builds upon the other, as though each interaction has a

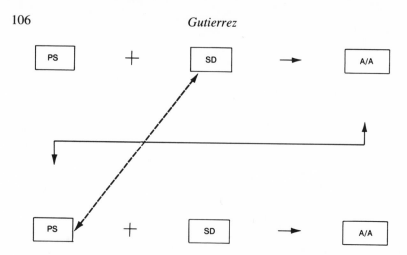

**Figure 5.1** Chain reaction among psychosocial stages (PS), stages of disequilibrium (SD), and acculturation/assimilation stages (A/A).

resulting outcome that can become the catalyst for the next set of interactions, as presented in the following formula:

$$PS + SD - A/A + PS + SD - A/A$$

where PS stands for psychosocial stages, SD for stages of disequilibrium, and A/A for acculturation/assimilation.

The creation of this new stage of A/A leading to bicultural personality development results in an interaction with the next psychosocial stage, creating the next chain reaction (solid arrow, Fig. 5.1).

These interactions create a dynamic process which acts as a homeostatic mechanism for immigrants/ethnic minorities in their adjustment to a dual cultural membership. They are triggered by a range of stimuli from the immigrant's or ethnic member's past as well as those of the new environment. These stimuli include: the state of the immigrant's mental health prior to immigration (Weinberg 1961); the successful resolution of nuclear and part conflicts of the psychosocial stages, prior to entering the United States and after; similarities and differences between the immigrants, members of the host group, and members of the immigrant's ethnic group in the United States; and the differences in the rate of acculturation within the individual's family unit (Szapocznik and Kurtines, 1980).

The resulting fluidity of personality, as represented by the two-directional solid arrow in Figure 5.1, is necessary in order to maintain flexibility in adaptation to life's changing conditions, as suggested by Ackerman (1958) and

Ramirez (1977). This arrow represents a person's attempt to draw from past as well as present experiences from both cultures, a process which allows the person to maintain the two cultures. This concept differs from Greeley's, Gordon's, and Taft's models that resulted in a unidirectional process of acculturation, whereby the immigrants or ethnic members gave up their native culture and adopted that of the host culture. The two-directional arrow implies that a person can go back to a prior stage and tap into the information obtained from the recapitulation of that stage and accommodate this information into the present experience.

Fluidity is an important concept in this model. The flow can take place as the person grows through each level, as implied by the solid arrow, or the process of a later stage can interact with an earlier one, out of sequence, as represented by the two-directional broken arrow. The nonsequential interaction does not imply that a person bypasses a stage; however, a person may not have completely resolved a stage conflict and through maturation or later experiences is then able to return to a prior stage and resolve it.

As immigrants become exposed to another culture, they may experience the stages of disequilibrium identified in Table 5.1. These become the buffers that slow down the pace of change, as though creating periods of moratorium, similar to the moratorium proposed by Erikson (1968). During these periods, a person can examine where he has been and where he wants to go in the process of cultural maintenance or change. They are slowing down the process of acculturation/assimilation so they can accommodate the changes that are taking place during that particular phase of development.

There seems to be an alternating pattern among the rows in the model. For example, people move from conformity to a renewed sense of nationalism. From there, they continue their role accommodation, and as their identity unfolds, they develop a militancy toward their native culture and eventually they can balance their appreciation for both cultures. It seems that each step toward acculturation is balanced by another step toward an appreciation of the native culture and a rejection of the conformity toward the host culture which has taken place. Eventually, a resolution of these conflicting pulls toward either culture takes place, resulting in bicultural adjustment.

The preceding paragraph is a simplified explanation of what is taking place in the process of developing a bicultural personality. In order to gain a better understanding of this process, an explanation of each of the stages will follow. In doing so, a composite fictitious case study will be introduced to aid in the explanation.

The proposed model consists of eight stages to coincide with Erikson's (1963) eight developmental stages of identity, which he termed the *eight stages of man*. Let us examine these stages:

*Stage 1*. The first stage toward bicultural personality development involves the dichotomy of trust versus mistrust, a lack of knowledge of the host culture, and the dichotomy of culture shock versus conformity.

Erikson (1980) explains that a sense of trust is achieved when people learn to trust others as well as themselves. The general sense of trust, according to Erikson, "implies not only that one has learned to rely on the sameness and continuity of the outer providers but also that one may trust oneself and the capacity of one's own organs to cope with urges; that one is able to consider oneself trustworthy enough so that the providers will not need to be on guard or to leave" (p. 63). A child develops "a sense of personal trustworthiness within the trusted framework of their community's life style" (p. 65). Basic mistrust can be characterized in the adult personality by withdrawal into the self when adults are at odds with either themselves or other people.

When individuals leave their country of origin, the messages, values, and beliefs which they have learned are not always applicable or easily transferable to the new culture. These differences may feel like a wall that thwarts communication with the host environment, as well as a person's self-assuredness in dealing with new situations. Furthermore, lack of knowledge of the new culture, when interacting with an unresolved nuclear conflict of trust versus mistrust, may cause confusion, often referred to as culture shock. The concept of culture shock is defined as the "anxiety experienced when one senses a loss of where to do what and how" (Arredondo-Dowd 1981, p. 376). If people have developed a sense of basic trust, they develop high self-esteem, which, according to Mischel (1971) is one of the most critical aspects of the self-concept. Mischel states that people tend to develop their self-concept according to the feedback these persons receive from their experiences.

If people, whether they are immigrants or members of ethnic groups, are operating in two different cultures, they may find it more difficult to react to situations and people in predictable ways. They may not be able to trust that others will react to them in ways that they have expected in the past, due to these cultural differences. Manifestations of culture shock in these situations can be experienced in the form of shyness, withdrawal, and irritability. Families may adapt to the shock simply by staying at home, and going only to school, work, or the grocery store. Behavior breaks down because no best action can be identified, or because a person may lose confidence in being able to judge what will be the best action. At this point, immigrants may begin to experience grief, defined by Marris (1975, p. 35) as: "the expression of a profound conflict between contradictory impulses to consolidate all that is still valuable and important in the past, and preserve it from loss, and at the same time, to re-establish a meaningful pattern of relationships, in which the loss is accepted."

More severe manifestations of culture shock can be seen in the results of Trautman's (1961) findings, which indicated a high risk of suicide potential during the first six months to two years since arrival in the new country.

A specific case study will serve to clarify ideas about assimilation/acculturation. Maria is a twenty-two-year-old college student. She was born in Colombia and at age 12 she immigrated to the United States with her family, where she and her two brothers and sister grew up in a predominantly Anglo neighborhood.

The initial adjustment to the new country was very difficult for Maria's parents. This difficulty created a great deal of turmoil at home. Being the oldest of four children, Maria was given many responsibilities. Sometimes these overwhelmed her, but she tried to meet them as best she could. Having to perform difficult tasks and not knowing how well she was doing, Maria became unsure of herself, developing a mistrustful view of the world and of significant others.

When she arrived in the United States, Maria learned English very quickly. As she became proficient, she had to interpret for her parents whenever they needed to speak with a social service agency or take care of personal business. In this respect, family roles were reversed.

At school, the children teased Maria because she was perceived as being different. The accent, complexion, and style of clothing were unlike those of the children in her class. She began to dislike who she was and was faced with the inability to predict situations and relationships. She became angry when teased and began to fight with her classmates to defend herself. She was literally defending against her loss of self.

Maria's parents became very protective of her. Living in an Anglo neighborhood, they felt like outsiders, so they isolated themselves from the community. Because both parents worked, they left Maria in charge of the children. For a time, Maria played and associated only with her brothers and sister. After a while, however, she began to be accepted by her classmates and established some friendships with them. Now that her parents were at work, she was also able to go out and explore the neighborhood. She found that there were some Latino families living in the area and quickly made friends with the children. She was able to find a support system for herself while she was going through the shock of not knowing the culture in which she was now immersed.

To reduce culture shock, the unity and support of the family is important, for it is the family who transmits and shares the cultural values that will help a person maintain his/her native culture. The family can act as a homeostatic mechanism through which a person can find a balance between conformity and alienation. Ackerman (1958) addresses this issue when he states that: "effective adaptation requires, therefore, a favorable balance between the need to protect sameness and continuity and the need to accommodate to change" (p. 85).

The family, according to Ackerman, expands a person's concept of psychological identity. The family shares values, actions, strivings, expectations, fears, and problems of adaptation. These are complicated by the role behaviors of individual members of the family. Ackerman further states that it is this family psychological identity that will determine the way in which aspects of sameness and differences among the personalities of each family member are held in certain balance.

To this end, the immigrant's family, ethnic group, and host group influence his/her homeostatic state. They provide pressure on an individual to maintain a sense of sameness and continuity and control to a certain extent a person's experience of new situations. Ackerman identifies positive and negative family role relations which affect this homeostatic state. Positive role relations exist, according to Ackerman, when there is mutual fulfillment among family members that allows positive emotional growth in each individual. Negative family relationships neutralize the effects of conflict and anxiety for the individual involved, but do not allow that person to resolve the conflict. At this point, immigrants or ethnic group members may feel a sense of loss of autonomy. They may then be reenacting the second nuclear conflict of autonomy versus shame and doubt.

*Stage 2.* Erikson (1980) states that as children master the first stage of developing basic trust, they can then move on to the second stage, where they begin to perceive themselves as separate from their parents. Children learn the concepts of *I* and *you*. Children also learn to have self-control without a loss of self-esteem or independence. Ackerman warns that autonomy can be healthy only as a satisfactory union is also maintained. Autonomy does not imply rejection of others but rather implies living in complementarity with them.

As immigrants or ethnic group members conform to the host culture, they may realize that the reason for conforming is a sense of shame for being culturally different. As they experience the new culture, the homeostatic mechanism is such that the power shifts toward the host culture. If people are immersed into an environment where the host culture is the most dominant, immigrants or ethnic group members may find little support for their identity, values, and fears. In their wish to become accepted, they may reject their immigrant or ethnic identity for their new-found culture. At the same time, they are also feeling shame for having conformed, since this is viewed by the ethnic group and family members, usually the parents, as betrayal. These contradicting feelings of shame may create a strong feeling of doubt among immigrants. How can they establish their autonomy without appearing disloyal to either group?

Some immigrants may react by giving up their loyalty to their native group and continuing to conform. At this point, they begin to reject their sense of nationalism, yet as we will see in Maria's case, she later had to come to terms with it. Child (1943) refers to this group as the *Rebel Group*. In a study of Italian-Americans in New Haven, Child found that the *Rebel Group* accommodated to the Anglo culture. Other immigrants, however, maintained or renewed their loyalties to their ethnic group. Child referred to this group as the *In-group*. Others remained somewhat marginal. He referred to this group as the *apathetic group*.

Loyalty to a country, cause, revolutionary movement, or occupation is an important aspect of ethnic identity, for it provides a sense of similarity of emotional experience with the group (De Vos 1975). Padilla (1980) conducted a study on ethnic loyalty and found that ethnic loyalty was much stronger among first generation Mexican Americans, supporting Morawska's (1976) findings in her study with Polish Americans in Boston. This loyalty allows immigrants or ethnic group members to maintain a sense of sameness and continuity.

The sense of nationalism which immigrants and ethnic group members feel helps immigrants to place their conformity in perspective. It forces them to examine where this conformity is leading and to what degree they will give up some of their native traits.

The methods of adaptation that immigrants choose depend on the perceptions and attitudes toward the receiving group by the immigrant or ethnic group member, as well as the perceptions and attitudes of the receiving group toward the immigrant (Taft). If the new members are accepted by the dominant group in an open and positive manner, they will not have to feel ashamed of their culture. They then can perform the accommodation of roles without having to give up as much of their native culture in the process. In this way, immigrants can develop a healthy sense of autonomy. The loyalty and sense of nationalism which has been used as a defensive reaction can be transformed into a positive sense of sameness and continuity that also allows mutual fulfillment and a satisfying union to take place. To recapitulate, autonomy does not imply rejection of others or a part of oneself, but living in complementarity with them. Those who rejected their native culture for the host culture also need to reevaluate this rejection so that a satisfying union can take place. It would be ideal if this role accommodation were reciprocal between the host and immigrant or ethnic groups; however, this is not usually the case.

As the reader will recall, Maria, the subject in the case study, had been making friends in the neighborhood with children of both her ethnic group and the host group. Since she spent a great deal of time in school with Anglo teachers and classmates, she began to identify herself from an Anglo perspective. Her father, on the other hand, did not feel accepted by the host society. Because he experienced hostile attitudes from his co-workers, he developed a sense of nationalism in order to defend his integrity as a member of the ethnic group which his co-workers were putting down. Maria's father noticed that she was starting to identify with the Anglo culture and her values were shifting from those of her family. Maria found herself in a dilemma. When she was with her family, she was shunned for behaving in a manner conforming to the host culture. The converse was true with her friends from the host culture. Angry with his daughter for anglicizing, Maria's father began to set restrictions, triggering in her the recapitulation of the third psychosocial stage, initiative versus guilt.

*Stage 3.* When people immigrate or move to a neighborhood composed of members outside of their ethnic group, their experience is similar to the third stage of psychosocial development that children experience as they are developing. During this third stage, children learn to move around; they also learn a new language, new roles, and behaviors. They must accommodate these new roles and behaviors so that they will not conflict with their personality. The end result of this accommodation is presented differently by Greeley, Gordon, and Taft. Gordon suggests a complete immersion into the host culture. Greeley sees immersion as a temporary state after which people learn to accept their ethnic group as well as the dominant society. However, in accepting one's ethnic group, Greeley does not include the preservation of the cultural materials and symbols of that ethnic group. Taft does not see immersion taking place, but rather a conformity on the part of the immigrants to the roles they must play, without necessarily integrating these behaviors into the personality. This type of conformity is akin to that discussed in Stage 1 of the present model.

During this assimilation stage, people may experience a different sense of nationalism. This identification is transformed into a feeling of pride in one's culture of origin, while at the same time feeling a reduction or termination of the sense of rejection toward the host group. Role accommodation allows immigrants and ethnic group members to assimilate into the host culture. At this stage, immigrants are continuing to receive pressures from different sources: family members, ethnic group, dominant society, and themselves.

As individuals continue to adopt behaviors of the host culture, family members and ethnic compatriots may find this offensive and may react by squelching the immigrant's sense of initiative. This reaction may generate feelings of insecurity and guilt, as well as resentment. It may cause the immigrant to become marginal, feeling as though he/she doesn't belong to either culture, thus escaping the conflicting expectations of the host group and the native group.

Sommers (1964) reports that during World War II Ichiro, a Japanese-American, experienced feelings of marginality. Prior to the incident at Pearl Harbor, Ichiro had identified almost totally with American values and ideals. When the United States went to war with Japan, Ichiro felt rejected by Americans. Suddenly, Ichiro was left without a support group. In attempting to expand his social environment, he had neglected his group of origin. When the host group rejected him, he seemed paralyzed, unable to initiate contact with either group. Ichiro's case is representative of the experience of many Japanese-Americans during the war era, as well as that of many immigrants in the United States.

Hickman and Brown (1971) pointed out that marginality need not necessarily result in stress, insecurity, and frustrated hopes. In their study of Aymara and Quechua Indians' adaptation to a bicultural context in Bolivia, Hickman and Brown found that Indian full-time workers who moved with their families to the mining town were able to adapt in order to fulfill the expectations of the employer, but retained their original attitudes and values. Hickman and Brown stated that this form of adaptation represents a "well-known and historically stable kind of adaptation to non-Indian society," even though it was experienced by this group as a state of marginality.

Polgar (1960), however, studied twenty male members of the Mesquakie Indian community of Tama, Iowa. Polgar found that the Mesquakie boys underwent concurrent socialization into two or more cultures, although exposure to the white culture did not occur directly until age five. This concurrent socialization allowed the Mesquakie boys to identify with both cultures without experiencing the masking or marginality process.

The interrelationship between role accommodation and the psychosocial stages is evident in Ichiro's case. According to Ackerman (1958, p. 61), the identity of an individual can be either weakened or strengthened by group participation:

> In mature, well-integrated personalities, a social role can reflect the strength of the individual expressed positively in participant group action. Here, there is no conflict between the individual and the social component of self . . . the weaker the person's sense of individual identity, the greater the need for support from the group. The deeper the anxiety about self, the more intense is the dependence on group belongingness. In this context, social role signifies a compensatory, defensive, and negative function.

In order to grow from a sense of marginality to a well-integrated personality with little conflict between the individual and the social component of the self, immigrants and ethnic group members learn to accommodate to the roles of each of the groups to which they belong. This accommodation may be superficial, as in the group studied by Hickman and Brown, or well integrated as in the groups studied by Fitzgerald (1974), McFee (1968), Polgar, and Szapocznik and Kurtines.

When Maria's father scolded her for adopting new ways, she began to feel guilty. She resolved her guilt, at least temporarily, by rebelling even more against her father. As she rebelled, her brothers and sister sided with her, since they were experiencing similar loyalties to the host group. Because their parents isolated themselves, the children were not provided a supportive reference group that would help to promote their ethnic heritage. Therefore, the children were more easily swayed by the host culture. Maria's mother also began to side with the children. She had been having marital difficulties with her husband prior to coming to the United States. Once in the United States, her role began to change; she had more freedom in the host culture. Economic opportunity also allowed her the possibility of supporting herself and her children, so she began to consider divorce from her husband. As the family assimilated, they were leaving the father behind. Maria's mother assimilated enough to get by at work, but she remained withdrawn in her personal life from both the ethnic group and the host group. She resigned herself to her role as mother, making her children her whole focus in life. She did maintain contact with some friends from her native culture.

Immigrants defend against becoming totally absorbed by the host culture as they accommodate to these new roles. They may react by becoming militant about who they are and where they came from, thus moving to the next stage of bicultural personality development.

*Stage 4.* During the fourth stage of identity development, Erikson (1980, p. 93) states that children must resolve the conflict between industry versus inferiority. It is at this stage that they learn cooperation and the planning and mastering of things. Erikson believes this stage to be a very decisive stage, when children begin to do things "beside and with" others. They develop a sense of "division of labor and equality of opportunity." Failure at this stage, according to Erikson, results in a sense of inadequacy and inferiority.

In spite of the fact that immigrants may have gone through all the stages of immersion described by Gordon, they may still have difficulty becoming accepted by the host society. Their accents, skin color, degree of expression of emotion, values, or ways of viewing the world may still be consciously or unconsciously a part of who they are.

Graves (1967) studied acculturation, economic access, and alcohol consumption in a tri-ethnic community. He found that the lack of expression of new-found values and goals created a feeling of alienation and deprivation which led the members of these groups to a greater abuse of alcohol and a disrespect for the social controls provided by their native culture. This lack of expression of new-found values and goals was the result of prejudice encountered by the ethnic groups because of their identification, as well as the physical and cultural characteristics which separated them from the American mainstream. Even though the ethnic group members had adapted their goals and values to those of the host culture, they were prevented from *participating* in the same activities which would fulfill their aspirations.

Rodriguez (1982) discusses how his sister became very self-conscious about her dark complexion, wishing that her children be born light-skinned, and he relates his feelings of shame because of his family's lack of education. He compensated for this by attending Stanford, Columbia University, the Warburg Institute of London, and the University of California at Berkeley. On several occasions, he repeatedly makes reference to his studies inside the British Museum, as though communicating to the reader that he has made it; he has been accepted and is able to mingle with the elite. However, he has written several essays about the feelings of alienation from his family. He closes his book by recollecting a Christmas scene at his family home where his mother asked him to bring a coat to his father, who was standing out on the porch. He went to his father and placed the coat on his shoulders. His father asked him if he was leaving. Rodriguez then realized that he and his father had said almost nothing to one another all evening. The dramatic impact of this closing shows how Rodriguez was able to resolve his sense of industry versus inferiority but felt inferior in the context of his family and his native culture.

The militancy stage, as proposed in Greeley's model, can help immigrants and ethnic group members to deal with the feelings of inferiority. This militancy can take several forms: refusing to be called by one's anglicized name, living in one's own ethnic neighborhood, or working against discrimination by the dominant society. This militancy allows people to master their environment and actively work toward equality of opportunity.

In the fourth stage of the case study, Maria's mother started to become aware of her new freedoms and change of role as a woman in the United States. When Maria entered high school, she also began her role as a young woman. She went to a high school where she was the only Latina. Up to this point, she had maintained friendships with children from her native group as well as Anglo children. Now, in a new school, Maria felt the peer pressure that is normally experienced by most adolescents in high school. She wanted to date and attend school activities; however, her father objected because he did not approve of the American custom of boys and girls dating without a chaperon. This caused further division between the father and the family. Maria had grown up thinking of herself as a good daughter. She had helped the family through many situations, despite her youth. She also studied hard and received good grades. Now, when she wanted to date, her father *laid down the law* and did not allow her to date. Many arguments ensued between Maria and her father. Maria's mother sided with Maria, since she trusted that Maria would not do anything to dishonor the·family name. Her husband began to accuse her of immorality. This difficulty created a great deal of stress within the family.

At this stage, Maria was rejecting her native culture's values and norms about dating. She attempted to express her militancy in favor of the host culture so that she could have some say in the school activities and dating that she wanted to pursue. However, this militancy was causing a great deal of turmoil at home. Maria changed her goals in mastering her sense of industry and concentrated on doing well in school so she could go to college and leave home. She felt very bitter about her home situation. Her next task was to get over the hurdle of the identity versus identity diffusion stage, stage five.

*Stage 5.* By the end of adolescence, people are expected to have resolved many of the nuclear conflicts already discussed, but a change in cultural environment can affect a person's sense of identity.

During the identity versus identity diffusion stage, adolescents experiment with different roles. Gordon maintains that immigrants acculturate by developing a sense of peoplehood exclusively from the point of view of the host society. If this is true, adolescents have no choice but to adopt the roles of the host group. The assumption that Gordon makes is that the host group is accepting the immigrants in their new roles. However, Erikson (1968) states that if immigrants are rejected by the host society, they develop what he refers to as an evil identity, where they become the exploited minority, or the ethnic outgroup. The evil identity can also be exemplified by marginality. By being labeled marginal, people can, in fact, identify with that particular stage of identity development and remain fixated at that stage, as though they are identifying with no identity, so to speak. To avoid this situation, Linton (1945) proposed that the status of the cultures to which a person is exposed should be equal so that the sense of worth of the cultures involved remains balanced. Erikson (1968) makes a strong argument to support the importance of the equal status of the native and host culture proposed by Linton. According to Erikson, if the status of both cultures were equal, there would be less likelihood for adolescents to develop an evil identity. However, people may be able to come to grips with a loss of status as they experience the *part conflicts* which lead to identity development.

The part conflicts "mirror one of the four nuclear conflicts of adulthood" (Gallatin 1975, p. 196). They aid people in consolidating their personal identities. Two of the part conflicts will be elaborated upon in this section: apprenticeship versus work paralysis and leadership and followership versus authority confusion.

If immigrants experience pressures from different sources and feel discriminated against for being different, they may interpret the environment as demanding omnipotence as an ego ideal, as suggested by Erikson (1968). This ideal is obviously very difficult to live up to, so they may develop a disdain for work, or more subtly, a fear of success. Graves' study shows an example of the demand for omnipotence as an ego ideal. In spite of the fact that some ethnic group members conformed to the Anglo cultural norms and values, they were not allowed the economic access to express these values. As a result, a higher incidence of alcohol abuse was present.

The societal demands for omnipotence may also affect a person's reaction to authority. For example, a study on bicultural adjustment of Cuban families, done by Scopetta, King, and Szapocznik (1977), revealed a high incidence of drug abuse by overacculturated adolescent males. It was suggested that lack of involvement in a bicultural context, a rejection of native culture, is the influential factor leading to drug use. This acting out can be a result of the adolescents' reaction to authority confusion; not knowing which culture to follow, they rebel or try to escape. Racism, social pressures, and the lack of equal status of the cultures can cause people to experience an internal tug-of-war concerning which culture to follow.

As immigrants and ethnic group members pass through these stages, some may adopt a militant stance, either toward the host culture or the native culture. It is possible to embrace the militant attitude to such a degree that immigrants and ethnic group members can lose their sense of identity to that of the militant group just as easily as they could lose it to the opposing group. At this stage, even though immigrants are continuing to feel conflict, they become better able to deal with it more effectively. They learn to internalize their sense of dual cultural identity and begin to move toward less dependency on a reference group and choose a lifestyle that will be more representative of this dual cultural membership.

Maria's parents divorced during her senior year in high school. Since her mother was not as strict in the family's adherence to the native culture as her father, Maria further developed her personality strictly from a host society perspective. However, she did not lose sight of her culture and was able to relate to her mother and her traditions when called upon to do so.

When Maria went to college, she began to meet students from other states as well as other countries. She joined the International Club where she interacted with students from her native country. She came to realize that she had changed. The university also had an organization of Latino students born in the United States. This student organization was militant about Latino issues on campus, in the community, and the nation. Maria did not understand their reasons for this militancy, since she had been protected from negative experiences that Latinos had to face on a day-to-day basis. As a result, she viewed this group as having a *chip on their shoulder*. One day, a member from the Latino organization spoke in her class. As she listened, she began to identify with some of the issues he presented. After class, her American classmates began to talk defensively about the speaker and the group he represented. This angered Maria, yet at the same time, because she feared rejection, she felt the need to deny her identification with the speaker. She became confused about her ideology and began to feel marginal. She took Spanish literature and ethnic studies courses in order to feel connected with her native culture without having to become emotionally committed to any group. As she learned more about herself and her culture through these classes, she became more confused, without understanding why. She was going through culture shock, again. In order to adapt more comfortably, she stopped going to the International Club.

During her sophomore year, Maria began to do volunteer work for credit in her psychology course. In this job she was exposed to Latino families and their living conditions. These were not necessarily different from Maria's experience, but because of upward mobility, she was no longer experiencing them. In working with these families, she was able to see what was happening to Latinos living in this country and the issues became more clear. At this point, Maria came in touch with her sense of nationalism. Maria began to seek out Latinos with whom she could develop friendships. Through her volunteer work, she was able to express her feelings of militancy, which made her feel closer to her parents and family. However, her mother began to disapprove of her militancy. Maria's political views were now beginning to crystallize and they were more liberal than her mother's. Her mother viewed herself as powerless against the government and did not believe in questioning authority. She feared for her daughter's future and any retaliation that Maria might experience.

Maria expected to be more accepted by her family, now that she had found her roots again, but, in fact, was meeting disapproval. She went back to the Latino organization seeking support; however, as she got more involved, she began to feel as though she was losing her identity to the group. Some of the members of the organization felt that she was not being militant enough. She was unable to concentrate on her studies, lost her self-confidence, and no longer volunteered to do projects for the organization. It seemed that the more she attempted to get in touch with her Latina background, the less support she got from her family or members of the organization. She could not accept the support of her American friends, whom she now viewed as the outgroup.

During her junior year in college, Maria finally decided to go to the campus counseling center for some help with her identity confusion. Exclusive membership in either culture would have meant a loss of identity for Maria. Fortunately, she was able to talk with a Latino counselor who helped her to sort out some of the issues that were preventing her from resolving the identity conflicts. This was a year of introspection for Maria. She examined her relationship to both cultures. She also realized that some of the issues with her family did not have to do with where she stood culturally in relationship to them. These issues would have come up in her native country as well. Once she was able to separate these issues, she was able to accept her family and her culture, and her dual cultural membership. This did not mean that she was able to accept everything about each. As will be seen in the next stage, she was able to make choices in order to accommodate the roles of both cultures without feeling guilty.

*Stage 6.* This stage marks the first stage of adulthood, according to Erikson (1980). It is characterized by a dichotomy between intimacy and isolation. The task is to develop intimacy with oneself as well as with others. Failure to do so can result in isolation and self-absorption. In performing this task, we need to look at what we appreciate about ourselves and what we want to change. At the same time, we are also looking at what we appreciate about others and what we do not like in them.

The task of selective appreciation is the final stage of minority identity development proposed by Atkinson. The end result is a bicultural sense of personhood.

As immigrants and ethnic group members begin to develop a bicultural sense of peoplehood, they will begin to question the basis for appreciation of the native culture and for rejection of the host culture. The militancy that was experienced in the prior stage may be questioned and, in fact, be rejected. Greeley suggests that some immigrants may go as far as to develop an unconscious self-hatred and antimilitancy as a reaction to this militancy stage. This is reflected in some of the reactions of minority students who refuse to take ethnic studies courses because they are reminders of the struggles of the sixties. They want to forget that period and want to feel more accepted and assimilated. The fear is of isolation; they want to be accepted by the dominant society and are afraid of becoming isolated if they maintain a militant stance.

The resolution of this conflict can be aided by the resolution of the part conflict of ideological commitment versus confusion of values in the prior stage. Erikson states that it is the lack of commitment that creates a feeling of marginality in people. Ideological commitment to a group's values allows individuals to better appreciate similarities and differences among the groups to which they belong. Commitment to ideals prevents one from feeling threatened when a value contrary to one's own is expressed or introduced by someone else. The end result can be that a person becomes bicultural. This implies more than just identification with groups, or becoming tolerant of them. It implies a sharing and continued transmission of both cultures by the same person.

The phrase "shared and transmitted," according to Linton, helps to limit the conceptualization of culture. He explains that a shared culture implies that behaviors, attitudes, or knowledge are common to two or more members of a particular society. Transmitted culture is referred to by Linton as social heredity. This transmission serves the purpose of providing individuals with information that will help them adapt to the environment in order to save the individual from having to go through the same painful experiences that their ancestors went through in order to adapt. This transmitted culture, according to Linton, includes material objects such as tools, utensils, clothing, kinetics, or movement, as well as psychology, which he defines as "the knowledge, attitudes, and values shared by the members of society" (p. 38). In a bicultural society, elements of the two cultures must be expressed.

Bicultural personality development can thus enhance people's sense of intimacy with members of both cultures, as opposed to isolating themselves from one culture or the other, either through complete acculturation or withdrawal from the host culture, or even marginality. The parents and adults in the society play a very important role in the transmission of these cultures. According to Erikson (1980), this role makes up the next stage of identity development.

*Stage 7.* The next task in the process of identity development is the resolution of the conflict of generativity versus stagnation. Generativity is expressed genitally, resulting in procreation and continuation of the society, or through an interest in establishing and guiding the generation to follow. Failure at this stage, according to Erikson, results in a sense of interpersonal impoverishment.

During the last stage, people begin to shift the focus of personal growth from a focus on self to an inclusion of others. During this stage, people continue their focus on others. By this time, people have resolved most of their issues about who they want to become. Immersion into another culture, however, can disrupt the gains that have been made by persons who have reached this stage prior to immersion. Exposure to different ways of viewing the world can create doubts within the person and may affect the way in which people relate to one another. This confusion will affect how one generation guides another.

At stage three, Maria's parents were disagreeing about how to raise Maria in relationship to dating. Maria's mother began to acculturate in this area while her father maintained the values of the native culture. The parents could not resolve the disagreement. This was one of the factors contributing to the divorce. After the divorce, Maria was able to date freely; however, she maintained her parents' values by refraining from sexual activity in her dating relationships.

Some of the confusion and disagreements between generations is inevitable, as is evidenced in each generation's experience of the *generation gap*. Some of this confusion can be resolved by rejecting the element in the culture which is causing the confusion. It may also be eliminated by the succeeding generation's acceptance of that element, or through a transformation of the element into a form that is an acceptable compromise. This process of modifying cultural material is referred to as syncretism.

It is important at this stage for the persons transmitting the culture to do so in a bicultural context. Successful resolution of this stage will allow the person to move on to the next stage, which involves the resolution of the conflict of integrity versus despair.

*Stage 8.* According to Erikson, the resolution of the conflict of integrity versus despair is the last stage in the attainment of a healthy personality. At this time, adults learn to accept their own life cycle and the significant others in their lives. Satisfied adults do not preoccupy themselves with the wish to have been different. Failure at this stage results in despair, which may be expressed in a fear of death, or a contempt for oneself, or for particular people or institutions.

In order to protect themselves from an identity crisis, people may develop a *past* time perspective, as suggested by Kluckhohn and Strodtbeck (1961). This perspective may manifest itself in gatherings with other members of their ethnic groups where the main topic of conversation centers around the old days. These conversations may remind one of the *Iliad* of Homer, where the storytellers review past events and characters in great detail and hand this information down to the next generations. It is this emphasis on the past that not only preserves their integrity, but also serves the purpose of the transmission of culture. Protection of loss of integrity may be promoted by adopting a sense of nationalism for their native country. This emphasis on the past prevents the person from experiencing despair.

A process model of bicultural personality development has been described and the stages through which immigrants may pass as they are exposed to two cultures have been examined. The process of personality integration develops very slowly. During this time, a person may become fixated at a particular stage, disrupting the flow of events that may result in the development of a sense of biculturalism. A synthesis of the two cultures can result in the development of a flexible personality (Ramirez, 1977), which can aid in the resolution of conflicts which immigrants experience because of their dual cultural membership.

Further studies of immigrants are needed in order to identify stimuli which have a positive or negative impact on the process of bicultural personality development. These studies should measure the degree of psychological adjustment at different stages of acculturation, as a means of determining the impact of bicultural development on personality.

The proposed model of bicultural personality development has implications for the field of bilingual education. One of the most important networks used by society to establish cultural values is the community school system. American education, at the present time, does not take into account the effects that cultural disruption has on students and their families. It was not until 1974 that cultural issues in education began to be addressed with the mandate for bilingual education programs. These programs have made a substantial impact on the education of immigrants and ethnic minorities and have helped them in their transition to the host culture. Yet, many multicultural communities have not implemented these programs due to lack of funding and insufficient political pressures.

The field of bilingual education is young and in the process of development. At this time, the emphasis of many of these programs is on transition from the native to the host culture. As bilingual education grows, it should serve the purpose of bridging the two cultures, so that children are able to function in an Anglo society without losing their cultural connection with their parents and community. This issue goes beyond being able to communicate. It includes the perpetuation of values and beliefs, as well as moral development within a bicultural context.

Havighurst (1953, p. 330) defined the purpose of education as helping "the young person achieve his developmental tasks in a personally and socially satisfactory way. . . ."

Being able to function in both cultures is not something innate, but is learned through a long and sometimes painstaking process. Living in a pluralistic society requires that the different ethnic groups learn to understand one another. One way to do this can be familiarizing ourselves with another culture sufficiently to be able to interact comfortably in both cultures.

## REFERENCES

Ackerman, N. *The psychodynamics of family life*. New York: Basic Books, Inc., 1958.
Arredondo-Dowd, P. Personal loss and grief as a result of immigration. *Personnel and Guidance Journal* 59 (1981): 376–78.

Arredondo-Dowd, P. Psychological education of the foreign born adolescent. Unpublished doctoral dissertation, Boston University, 1978.

Atkinson, D., Morten, G., and Sue, D. *Counseling American Minorities: A cross-cultural perspective*. Los Angeles: University of California Press, 1980.

Chance, N. Acculturation, self-identification, and personality adjustment. *American Anthropologist* 67(1975):372–93.

Child, I. *Italian or American? The second generation in conflict*. New Haven: Yale University Press, 1943.

De Vos, C., and Romannucci-Ross, L. *Ethnic identity: Cultural continuation and change*. Palo Alto: Mayfield Publishing Co., 1975.

Diaz-Guerrero, R. A sociocultural Psychology? In *Chicano Psychology*, J. Martinez, Jr., ed. New York: Academic Press, 1977.

Edgerton, R. Cross-cultural psychology and psychological anthropology: One paradigm or two? *Reviews of Anthropology* 1(1974):52–65.

Enker, M. The process of identity: Two views. *Mental Hygiene* 55(1971):369–75.

Erikson, E. *Identity and the life cycle*. New York: W. W. Norton & Co., Inc. 1980.

———. *Identity: Youth and crisis*. New York: W. W. Norton & Co., Inc., 1968.

———. *Childhood and society*. New York: W. W. Norton & Co., Inc., 1963.

Fitzgerald, T. *Social and cultural identity: problems of persistence and change*. Athens, Ga.: University of Georgia Press, 1974.

Flexner, H. The curriculum, the disciplines, and interdisciplinarity in higher education: Historical perspective. In *Interdisciplinarity and higher education*. J. Kockelmans, ed. University Park, Pa.: Pennsylvania State University Press, 1979.

Gallatin, J. *Adolescence and individuality: A conceptual approach to adolescent psychology*. New York: Harper and Row, 1975.

Gordon, M. *Assimilation in American life*. New York: Oxford University Press, 1964.

Graves, T. Acculturation, access, and alcohol in a tri-ethnic community, *American Anthropologist* 69(1967):306–21.

Greeley, A. *Why can't they be like us?* New York: Institute of Human Relations Press, 1971.

Havighurst, R. *Human development and education*. New York: Longmans, Green, and Co., 1953.

Herskovitz, M. *Acculturation: The study of culture in contact*. New York: J. J. Augustin, Publisher, 1936.

Hickman, J., and Brown, J. Adaptation of Aymara and Quechua to the bicultural and social context of Bolivian mines. *Human Organization* 30(1971):359–66.

Isajiw, W. Definition of ethnicity. *Ethnicity* (October 1974):109–121.

Kaplan, B. *Studying personality cross-culturally*. Evanston, Il.: Row Peterson, 1961.

Kluckhohn, F., and Strodtbeck, F. *Variations in value orientation*. Evanston, Il.: Row Peterson, 1961.

Kockelmans, J. (ed.). *Interdisciplinarity and higher education*. University Park, Pa.: Pennsylvania State University Press, 1979.

Kroeber, A., and Kluckhohn, C. *Culture: A critical review of concepts and definitions*. Cambridge, Ma.: Peabody Museum of American Archaeology and Ethnology, Harvard University, 1952.

Linton, R. *The cultural background of personality*. New York: Appleton-Century-Crofts, Inc., 1945.

Marris, P. *Loss and Change*. Garden City, N.Y.: Anchor Books, 1975.

Marx, M. Formal theory. In Marx, M., and Goodson, F. *Theories in contemporary psychology*. New York: Macmillan Publishing Co., 1976.

McFee, M. The 150% man, a product of Blackfeet acculturation. *American Anthropologist* 70(1968):1096–1107.

Mischel, W. *Introduction to personality*. New York: Holt, Rinehart and Winston, Inc., 1971.

Morawska, E. The maintenance of ethnicity: The case of the Polish-Americans in Boston. Unpublished dissertation, Boston University, 1976.

Mouly, G. *The science of educational research*. New York: American Book Co., 1963.

Oliver, J. Los Ojos: A study of bilingual behavior. San Francisco: R. & E. Research Associates, 1975.

Olmedo, E. Acculturation: A psychometric perspective. *American Anthropologist* 34(1979):1061–70.

Padilla, A. (ed.). *Acculturation: Theory, models, and some new findings*. Boulder, Co.: Westview Press, 1980.

Polgar, S. Biculturation of Mesquakie teenage boys. *American Anthropologist* 62 (1960):217–35.

Price-Williams, D. Psychological experiment and anthropology: The problem of categories. *Ethos* 2(1974):95–114.

Ramirez, M. Recognizing and understanding diversity: Multiculturalism and the Chicano movement in psychology. In *Chicano psychology*. J. Martinez, Jr., ed. New York: Academic Press, 1977.

Rodriguez, R. *Hunger of memory: An autobiography*. Boston: David Godine, Publisher, 1982.

Scopetta, M., King, O., and Szapocznik, J. *Relationship of acculturation, incidence of drug abuse, and effective treatment for Cuban Americans*. National Institute on Drug Abuse. Final Report of Research Contract No. 271-75-4136, 1977.

Sommers, V. The impact of dual cultural membership on identity. *Psychiatry* 27(1964): 332–44.

Stonequist, E. *The marginal man*. New York: Charles Scribner's Sons, 1937.

Szapocznik, J., and Kurtines, W. Acculturation, biculturalism, and adjustment among Cuban Americans. In *Acculturation: Theories, models, and some new findings*. A. Padilla, ed. Boulder, Co.: Westview Press, 1980.

Taft, R. A psychological model for the study of social assimilation. *Human Relations* 10(1957):141–56.

Trautman, E. Suicide attempts of Puerto Rican immigrants. *Psychiatric Quarterly* 35(1961):544–54.

Weinberg, A. *Migration and belonging*. The Hague: Martinus Mijhoff, 1961.

*Webster's Seventh Collegiate Dictionary*. Springfield, Ma.: Merriam Co., 1966.

**PART TWO**

**Educational Perspectives**

# 6.
# Ethnographic Pedagogy: Promoting Effective Bilingual Instruction

*Luis C. Moll and Stephen Diaz*

MICROETHNOGRAPHIC STUDIES OF ETHNICALLY MIXED and bilingual classrooms have suggested that the organization of classroom interactions has important consequences for students in such settings (e.g., McDermott 1976; Mehan 1978, 1979; Erickson and Mohatt 1982; Carrasco, Acosta, de la Torre-Spencer 1981; Moll 1981). Each study has pointed out ways in which schooling, as a social process, mediates students' academic experiences and outcomes.

As important as these detailed investigations of the daily life of schooling have been for understanding bilingual instruction and education in general as a socially organized phenomenon, it has become clear to us that an explicit theory of learning, that is, a theory that helps specify the academic consequences of the interactions that microethnography so aptly describes, has been missing from such studies. To complement the microethnographers' interactional theory of social relations, we have turned to the theory of learning which was developed by Vygotsky and other participants in the socio-historical school of psychology. These ideas are a powerful supplement to microethnography because they emphasize how interactions between people are central to the way in which individual learning and development occur. From this perspective, learning is a process that involves social as well as cognitive transformations.

The research that led to the adoption of this theoretical formulation included two distinct but interrelated studies. In the first study (Moll, Diaz, Estrada, and Lopes, in press), reading lessons in a bilingual elementary school program were analyzed. The program contained an instructional arrangement that allowed the study of the *same* bilingual (Spanish dominant) students participating in reading lessons in separate Spanish and English language classrooms. Analysis of videotapes of these lessons generated detailed microethnographic descriptions of the interactional work of the teachers and students who

127

assembled the lessons. This, in turn, led to the specification of variations in the organization of reading instruction that created differentially effective learning conditions for the students.

Generally, students, even when they came from the top reading group in the Spanish-language classroom, were relegated to relatively low levels of reading in English. A reason given by teachers for this discrepancy in instructional level was the students' weak *oral* English development. Thus, students were placed at *reading* levels in the English language classroom where their *oral* language deficiencies were addressed, but where the levels did not allow them to make full use of higher order reading skills acquired in the more advanced Spanish language classroom. For example, students reading at third grade levels or higher in Spanish were placed in reading lessons at a first grade level or lower in English (Moll et al., in press).

Analysis of lessons suggested that this discrepancy in reading level across language and instructional setting could be prevented. Observations strongly suggested that most of the Spanish readers were capable of comprehending more English than they were able to express in the English reading lessons. On the basis of these results, a second study, reported here, was initiated to develop ways to systematically take full advantage of the students' reading skills in Spanish in order to place them at higher English reading levels, while using the content of the English reading lessons to expand oral language proficiency in that language. This was accomplished by implementing a series of *ethnographic experiments* designed to shape the way the children cope intellectually with bilingual reading tasks. Analysis of these experimental sessions indicates that many current practices make it very difficult to organize effective bilingual instruction because of complex misunderstandings created by procedures used to select students and curricular activities. We believe that the strongest warrant for our claims was our ability to intervene effectively in a theory-driven way in the reading instruction of the children with whom we worked.

## THEORETICAL FRAMEWORK

This research has been influenced by two theoretical approaches which study teaching and learning as a system of interactions. These two theoretical approaches are the microethnographic study of schooling and the sociohistorical approach to the study of learning and development. Together they provide us with ways to systematically study the content and organization of lessons, identify areas of difficulty, and suggest interventions for beneficial change.

## The Microethnographic Approach

Microethnographers (e.g., McDermott and Roth 1979; Mehan 1979; Erickson and Shultz 1977; Griffin and Shuy 1978) study people's actions and the circumstances under which these actions take place. A basic premise of microethnographic studies is that social events such as classroom lessons are interactional accomplishments (McDermott and Roth 1979). The unit of study in microethnography is always organism-environment interaction. Persons are viewed as active, creating parts of their environments. That is, the focus is on concerted activity (behaving) rather than on the individual as an agent of action apart from the environment. Hence, a primary goal of microethnographic study is to describe lessons or other important educational activities by characterizing the interactions of the participants who *assemble* these activities (Mehan 1979; Shultz, Florio and Erickson 1980; Au 1980).

Microethnography seeks to study participants' activities as part of the contexts in which they occur. However, from this perspective, context is not limited to a physical location or the characteristics of the participants, although these are clearly influential; context is constituted by what the participants are doing, which is only partly conditioned by where and when they are doing it (Erickson and Shultz 1977; McDermott and Roth 1979). This interactional approach to context is particularly attractive in the study of classrooms where students and teachers differ ethnically or speak two or more languages with various degrees of fluency (Moll 1981). It provides a systematic way to analyze the *communication exchanges* that make up classroom lessons, while also taking into account that whatever the students do influences the teacher and that they are both largely influenced by, and in turn construct, the context in which their interaction takes place (Watzlavick, Beavin and Jackson 1967).

## The Socio-historical Approach

Like microethnographers, the socio-historical school of psychology (e.g., Laboratory of Comparative Human Cognition 1982; Vygotsky 1978; Wertsch 1981) emphasizes how interactions between people are central to how learning and development occur (for a review, see Wertsch 1979). At the heart of this approach is the analysis of learning in terms of the forms of interaction embodied in distinct, socially organized activities. Thus, in the study of any learning activity, the unit of analysis is the act or system of acts by which learning is composed (Leont'ev 1973; Talyzina 1978, 1981).

We have been particularly influenced by the instructional implications that Vygotsky drew from his theory. Vygotsky (1978) argued that children internalize the kind of help they receive from others and eventually come to use the *means of guidance* initially provided by the others to direct their own problem solving behaviors. That is, children must first perform the appropriate behaviors to complete a task under someone else's guidance and direction, for example, the teacher, before they are able to complete the task competently and independently. This shift in task control from teacher to student constitutes learning. To say that a child is working independently is equivalent, roughly, to saying that the child is carrying on an interaction, which had been previously carried out with others, *in his head*.

Vygotsky called systems of interactions like those embodied in many classroom tasks, *zones of proximal development*. He defined this zone as

> . . . the distance between the actual developmental level as determined by independent problem solving and the level of potential development as determined through problem solving under adult guidance or in collaboration with more capable peers (1978, p. 86).

Applied to the study of formal learning environments (e.g., reading lessons), the student's entering skills, as perceived by the teacher, and the instructional materials present for use combine to set the *lower* boundary of the zone. The kinds of skills that the teacher wants the child to master and the embodiment of those skills in the instructional materials used in a lesson constrain the *upper* end of the zone. The way the teacher organizes interactions between children and text to move them from lower to higher levels of the zone, *reading level*, is *teaching-learning*, and is the focus of our attention.

Soviet researchers have identified other characteristics of zones of proximal development that are important for the study of bilingual classrooms. The first comes from Vygotsky's view of the relation between learning and development. Vygotsky insisted that learning and development are part of a single, interactive process in which learning is transformed into development, and development produces the foundation for further learning. Zones of proximal development should be constructed precisely so that learning can precede development. Teaching which is oriented toward developmental levels that have already been reached is likely to be ineffective (Vygotsky 1978). Good teaching provides students with learning experiences which are in advance of development. From this perspective, the temporal parameters of teaching-learning are essential. That is, instruction should be *prospective*, it should create a zone of *proximal* development. If instruction trails behind development rather than coaxing it along, it becomes ineffective. Likewise, if instruction runs too far ahead, very little learning will result (Siegler and Richards 1983).

Talyzina (1978, 1981) reminds us that instruction assumes its leading role through the *content* to be acquired. The content, however, does not produce its developmental effect directly. It is always mediated through the teacher who distributes tasks and regulates student communicative/learning activities. Hence, the teacher's organization of learning activities that are appropriate in terms of content and student developmental level creates the proximal learning conditions. But it is the actual teacher-student interaction within these conditions which gives instruction its developmental effect. The complexity of teacher/student roles is apparent because each school subject has its own specific relationship to the child's level of development (Vygotsky, 1978). The relationship changes as the child goes from one level of achievement to another. In the case of bilingual instruction, these relationship changes include the shift from one linguistic context to another. The teacher-student interactions must be adjusted, depending on the conditions these relationships create.

The use of this socio-historical/interactional approach influences observations of schooling in at least three ways: (1) Do not look for the origins of intellectual skills inside the teacher or the child; instead, focus on the child-adult interactional system (Dowley, 1979). (2) Study child-adult interactions in relation to the content and the objectives of the specific lessons. It is the relationship between social organization, content, and the child's entering skill level which creates *effective* zones of proximal development. (3) Look for evidence that particular zones (e.g., particular lessons) provide the kinds of interactions that should, theoretically, be the basis of learning.

## RESEARCH PROCEDURES

Work was conducted in two fourth grade classrooms in southern California. This school, the site of the first study, implements a *maintenance* program aimed at promoting academic development in Spanish and English. Two *sister* classrooms were involved in the study, one with a Spanish and one with an English curriculum. During the course of the day the children received reading instruction in Spanish, their native language, and later in the day they went to the English-language classroom for reading lessons in their second language. This arrangement allowed us to observe and videotape the same students in separate language and instructional settings.

Our plan first called for replicating in these classrooms the findings of our previous study (Moll, et al., in press) which indicated that regardless of reading ability in Spanish, children are usually subjected to English reading lessons that feature primarily lower-level skills. Classroom observations confirmed the existence of a similar discrepancy of instruction.

We then focused our instructional interventions on the children assigned to the *lowest* reading group in English. These children represent a good sample of a group of students which greatly concern educators. They are students usually designated as limited- and non-English-proficient (LEP and NEP). In many cases, they have entered the United States with some academic skills in their native language or have a dominance in their native language that justifies being taught in Spanish, prior to English instruction. Three girls made up this group—we'll call them Sylvia, Delfina, and Carla. The teacher in the English-language classroom is an Anglo female and monolingual; her Spanish-language counterpart is female, Mexican-American, and a fluent bilingual. All of our instructional manipulations were videotaped for analysis.

## The First Intervention: Instruction Before Assessment

Our first intervention consisted of two parts. First, we asked the English-language teacher to teach a typical lesson to the lowest group. The transcripts presented below illustrate the types of difficulties the children had as they participated in the English reading lesson. Immediately after the lesson, one of the researchers (Stephen Diaz) replaced the teacher and asked the children comprehension questions in Spanish about what they had just read in English. This was done to obtain evidence regarding earlier observations that these children understood more about what they were reading in English than they could display in the lessons.

*A typical reading lesson.* The lesson began with a brief prereading discussion about field trips, the topic of the story. Reading aloud followed.

T (Teacher): Let's start reading the first page. We are going to meet a lot of new people in this book. (Carla and Sylvia have their hands up.)

D (Delfina): Can I read first?

T (Teacher): (To Delfina only) I'm going to let Sylvia read first. She has her hand up. (Delfina immediately puts her hand up—more like a joke; Sylvia starts reading.)

S (Sylvia): "You can't guess where we are going, said David."

T: OK, just a minute, please, Carla. We need you to follow with us. (Carla was not glancing at the book.)

C (Carla): OK.

T: Delfina, we need you to follow right along. (To Sylvia) Would you start all over again?

S: OK, I'll start over again. "You can't guess."

T: OK, what is this? (Points to a word)

S: Can't?

T: Can't. What does that mean? (Pause)

D: Um . . .

T: OK, Carla, if I say you can guess or you can't guess.

D: (With hand raised) Oh! Can't is like no . . .

C: Don't do that.

T: Uh, yeah, uh huh. Read the sentence, the whole sentence again and let's see if it says . . .

S: "You can't guess where we are going, sayd David Lee."

T: Good.

S: "It's going to be a . . ." (Looks at teacher)

C: Surprise.

T: Surprise.

S: "Surprise. I like surprises, sayd Isabel. You bet, I'll bet you guess where we are all going, sayd David." (Carla and Delfina raise their hands to read next; teacher selects Delfina.)

Note that the children were unfamiliar with some of the English words, such as the contraction "can't." Sylvia was unable to pronounce the word "surprise" without help from the teacher, and she mispronounces "said" as "sayd." This brief excerpt is characteristic of the entire lesson. There were frequent teacher interruptions to help the children's pronunciation and to define unfamiliar words.

The following transcript illustrates the difficulty the children had with verbal expression. This was apparent especially when they needed to participate actively to display reading comprehension.

D: "Are we going to the zoo? asked Pet, Petty?"

T: Pete.

D: "Pete. We went to the zoo, said Penny." "That is not where we are going, said David. Are we going to the art" . . .

T: Airport.

D: "Airport, said Ken."

S: Asked.

D: "Asked Ken. We can went, no went to the airport, said David. I want to go up in the building, sayd Isabel. That is not where we are going, sayd David."

T: Any idea where they're going?

D: I know where.

C: To the park.

T: Which one is Isabel? Which one do you think? (Delfina and Sylvia point to something in their book.) The girl? How could you tell that?

S: Because she said, "I want to go up in the building, said Isabel."

D: Go up in the building.

T: And in the picture, what's she doing?

S: She raises her hand . . . (points up as if at a building.)

T: She's pointing up, isn't she, that's called pointing. OK, let's go and read the next one. Carla, would you read this one for us?

The difficulties in verbal expression are evident. However, this transcript also illustrates that, even in the context of this low group lesson, the children may be better readers than expected. Note that in answering the teacher's questions about the identity of Isabel, Sylvia went immediately to the text and extracted the necessary information, thus revealing skills in text analysis that seem to be beyond what one would expect from a child in a low-level reading group.

*Assessing English reading comprehension in Spanish.* After the lesson ended, a brief session was conducted in Spanish by Stephen Diaz. He asked comprehension questions similar to those that the teacher had asked in English. During this session, the children showed that they understood much more than they could express in English. Three brief examples with Sylvia, one in English and two in Spanish, make this point emphatically. First, during the English lesson:

T: . . . Why don't we just close our book now for a second? (To Delfina) Yeah, leave your bookmark in. (To everyone) *Was Isabel lost?*

All: Yes. No.

T: Was she really lost?

S: She was in the, uh . . .

D: Fire truck.

S: Uh huh, fire truck, and

T: Why did they think she was lost?

D: Because, the boys and girls, um, looked, (Sylvia raises her hand)

T: Sylvia.

S: Uh, because the boys and girls, uh (pause, laughs) the . . . um,

D: Had to go home.

S: Because the boys and girls go—

T: Mhm . . .

S: —out in the first place . . . (Delfina has her hand raised) and the girls not say "I am here."

Now, Sylvia's response to virtually the same probe in Spanish was as follows:

SD: ¿Cómo sabían los muchachos, que se había perdido la muchacha. ¿Cómo se llama?

C: Isabel.

S: Um, um, David, y

SD: Pero, ¿cómo sabía? (Delfina raises her hand)

S: Um, porque, (gestures to Delfina that she can answer).

SD: Que me diga Sylvia, porque no la oí.

S: Porque el, ella, ellos le, le gritaban, y, y, la buscaban, por donde todo el edificio donde viven los bomberos y ella no les contestaba (is nervously shaking paper around) ni (ellos) la miraban.

Sylvia later elaborates.

SD: Digo, ¿cómo supieron que estaba, que se había perdido Isabel?

S: Por que David dijo que ya se tenían que ir. Entonces dijo, ¿quien falta? No falta nadie, entonces dijeron, Isabel. Entonces empezaron a buscar, y no la encontraban y decían está perdida ella, señor. El bombero dijo, No, no, no puede estar perdida. Pues andaban buscandola, y llegaron al troque y el señor dijo que allí estaba Isabel.

In examples IV and V Sylvia answered in Spanish the same question posed initially in English. Obviously, her Spanish fluency facilitated the more elaborate answer, but our point goes beyond this observation. The details provided in her answer reveal that she understood the story without difficulty. Sylvia's oral language limitations in English are masking her comprehension.

A final excerpt may be even more revealing. During the Spanish session, Diaz also asked Sylvia to read in English, but to explain the passage in Spanish. Here is what happened.

SD: OK. Quiero que me leas tu (to Sylvia) y también que me digas, esta (points to two pages).

S: ¿Todo?

SD: Mhm.

S: "There she is, the fire fighter said, and here's my hat." "Came, come down now Isabel," said David. "It's time to go."

SD: ¿Que pasó?

S: El señor, um el fireman, dijo "aquí está, aquí está ella," ¿verdad? "está ella, dijo el señor," entonces, y, "aquí, también está mi gorro," y luego, y, David dijo, "ven para abajo ahorita, Isabel, que ya nos tenemos que ir."

Sylvia gave a sophisticated and accurate translation of the passage. Note that she made syntactic adjustments in Spanish to accurately translate the English sense across languages.

Thus, the analysis of the English reading lesson and the brief bilingual intervention provided the following information: (1) the most obvious deficiencies displayed by the students (at least those that are explicitly addressed in the lesson) are English decoding, vocabulary, and verbal expression; (2) the children, when allowed to use Spanish, understood a great deal more about the story than they could display in the context of the English reading lesson. To supplement this information we turned to the gathered data on the same students in the Spanish-language classroom.

### Reading in Spanish

The lessons videotaped in the *Spanish-language* classroom provide additional information for analyzing the English lessons. An important finding of the Spanish classroom was that the same three children who were placed in the low English-reading group were in three different Spanish reading levels (see Table 6.1). Briefly put, Sylvia belonged to the most advanced Spanish reading group, Delfina to the middle group, and Carla to the lower group. Although these three students are receiving practically the same instruction in English reading, the skills which they brought to the English lessons are very different.

This information about their reading placement in *Spanish* is very important in analyzing *English* instruction as well as in guiding beneficial interventions. As mentioned earlier, the English reading groups were formed primarily on the basis of the children's perceived oral language competence. Since all three girls had difficulties in decoding and engaging in English language discussions about the lessons, they were placed in the same low English-reading group. As the transcripts show, the behaviors that they displayed during the English-language lessons seem to affirm the appropriateness of such a placement. It follows that the teacher, *who is not bilingual*, would make decisions about the organization and focus of instruction based on the children's English oral competence. It also follows that lessons are directed at remediating the children's difficulties. If a child has difficulty in decoding, time is provided to practice decoding skills; similarly, if a child has difficulty with verbal expression, practice is provided in oral English. This is a reasonable approach, given what we have seen on the tapes.

Our analysis indicates, however, that such an organization of lessons relegates the children to reading levels far below those they had reached in *Spanish*. What is not taken into consideration or taken advantage of is that at least two of the children have relatively well developed *reading* skills. Why weren't the English lessons organized to take advantage of students' Spanish reading skills? Our subsequent experiments were designed to address this question and the following questions, as well: What factors are important to consider in assessing student reading? What types of reading and oral language experi-

**TABLE 6.1**
**Reading Group Assignments**

|  | English | Spanish |
|---|---|---|
| Sylvia | Low | High |
| Delfina | Low | Middle |
| Carla | Low | Low |

ences should be organized for children who perform at differential reading levels? To answer these we turned to our theoretical propositions for help.

### A Vygotskian Interpretation of the Lesson

To recapitulate what was stated earlier, Vygotsky applied the idea of a zone of proximal development in his discussions of assessment and instruction. In general, this concept is an extension of the basic principle underlying his socio-historical approach; social interactions are central to how learning and development occur. He expressed this relationship between social interaction and individual cognitive development in what he called the general law of cultural development, where Vygotsky proposed that any higher psychological function appears

> . . . twice, or on two planes. First it appears on the social plane and then on the psychological plane. First it appears between people as an interpsychological category and then within the individual child as an intrapsychological category (Vygotsky 1978, p. 57).

This movement from the social to the individual characterizes learning activities in the zone of proximal development.

An important instructional implication that Vygotsky drew from his approach is that for instruction to be optimally effective it must be aimed at the students' *proximal* level: at those behaviors that are maturing, developing, and as such, go beyond the child's level of independent problem solving. Instruction aimed prospectively provides the students with the help to perform at the most advanced level possible and with the time to practice and appropriate this help to eventually direct their own behaviors. Therefore, lessons must be socially organized so that shifts in control of the task can occur.

In our bilingual situation, the students have at least *two entry levels* for reading; one in English, plagued by difficulties in verbal expressions, vocabulary, and so on, and a more advanced level as manifested in their Spanish reading lessons. For reading instruction to be proximal in *English* it has to be aimed at those levels manifested in *Spanish*. That is, English reading must be taught in the context of what the children can do in Spanish. What the children are doing in Spanish reading creates the *proximal* conditions for learning in English. As our data suggest, failure to relate Spanish reading to how reading is taught in English leads to lessons aimed at reading levels *beneath* the students' performance capabilities; levels that do not facilitate development.

As we have described, the students in the low reading group in English were assigned to their group primarily on the basis of their English-oral-language difficulties. Usually their level of English oral proficiency is taken as indicative of where instruction should be directed. That is, the demands of reading are simplified to match the students' low level of English proficiency. However, information about these students' reading performance in Spanish shows that they can perform beyond the level of competence they can display in English. Although the children are performing in English at the *first grade* level they are performing in Spanish, especially Sylvia and Delfina, at a *fourth grade* level. Can they perform in English at levels that approximate their Spanish reading performance? Can reading instruction in English be organized in ways that bridge their considerable gap? How can their English performance be *stretched* to their most advanced reading level?

### The Second Intervention: Creating a Proximal Reading Lesson

Our observations of classroom lessons show that the lower reading group's instructions are organized to promote fast and accurate decoding. The children that form the low group take turns reading aloud from the text. This enables the teacher to evaluate decoding proficiency. Not only is reading aloud characterized by turn-taking but by frequent interruptions in which the teacher helps the reader define or pronounce unfamiliar words. When children are not fluent in English, this process is slow and time consuming. Invariably, decoding becomes the dominant activity of the lesson, usually at the expense of comprehension. Comprehension activities which do occur are constrained by the children's inability to produce enough discourse to facilitate text discussion. Furthermore, an English monolingual teacher has difficulty, despite continuous efforts, differentiating a lack of understanding from a lack of verbal fluency.

For the teacher, a reasonable strategy was to provide the children with help in decoding, vocabulary, and oral language development. Thus, the reading lessons performed a double duty: teaching the children to read and increasing their fluency in English. This becomes necessarily so because the children's verbal difficulties were seen as serious impediments to reading development. In fact, overcoming these oral English difficulties was viewed as a necessary precursor to reading comprehension. The tendency was to simplify the level of reading to match the children's level of oral language development and to provide plenty of practice in those skill areas in which the children were weakest.

Our approach called for us to modify this process. As the lesson began, we assumed the *initial* responsibility for decoding the text. We read the story (*Sr. Coyote and Sr. Fox*) to the students and asked them to concentrate on listening and understanding what it was about, thus capitalizing on the comprehension skills they had developed in Spanish. Throughout the lesson we emphasized that "reading for meaning" was the goal of the lesson. Accordingly, any help provided explicitly facilitated text comprehension, so that the students never lost sight that understanding what is being read is the primary goal of reading. What follows is a sequential description of how these procedures were implemented.

*Session 1: Facilitating comprehension.* We began by reading the story to the students in a deliberate and clear fashion. This took approximately eight minutes. We then reviewed the plot. Both the reading and the review were done in English. We knew that, given their English language proficiency, we would also have to assume most of the initial responsibility for text discussion. However, it was essential for the students to *participate* in the discussion at some level, even if only to respond minimally to our questions. We established a question-answer pattern usually known in the literature as *scaffolding* (see Moll et al., in press). Scaffolding consists of adjusting the difficulty level of the questions until a response is prompted from the students. The idea is that, as the students become better able to answer more difficult or abstract *text-free* questions, the help the adult provides is removed; that is, the *scaffold* progressively disappears. The following is an example of an early attempt at *scaffolding*.

First, we established that the Coyote wanted to eat the Fox, as described in the opening lines of the story. Notice the students' hesitance to participate and our attempts to elicit some response. This *control* of the interaction by the adults and the skewed division of labor it represents characterized the first lesson.

Stephen: What was Señor Coyote going to do to Señor Fox?
Luis:    Mhm.
SD: What?
 L: Mhm.
SD: (To Sylvia) Speak up.
 L: Yeah, that's right.
SD: What did she say? I didn't hear her.
 L: I think she said he was going to eat him.

S: Mhm.

SD: Oh, OK.

L: She was going to eat, he was going to eat Señor Fox when he saw him. At first . . .

SD: And then what did Señor Fox do?

C: Oh. (Pause)

S: He said that (pause) Señor Fox say to, um, Señor, ah, Coyote that he'll help to—

L: To help him do what? Hm? Here's the picture.

SD: To help him do what? Where is it? OK.

S: To hold.

L: Right. To hold up.

SD: Hold up.

S: The rock.

E: Right.

L: Right. He said, he said, look, this big cliff, this big mountain, it's falling down. I'm holding it up. See? Why don't you help me hold it up? The fox told Señor Coyote. Did Señor Coyote?

SD: I need a book here.

L: You need a book—Señor Coyote looked up at the mountain and he saw this big mountain. And he said, maybe the mountain is falling down (Luis gives book to Esteban). But did he, did Señor Coyote believe him right away?

S: Uh uh . . .

L: That the mountain is falling down? Hm? You say no, Sylvia. What do you think, Carla?

SD: When, when, when Señor Fox pushed against the cliff, what did Señor Coyote do? Do you remember? Did he just stay there? And just stand there?

C: No.

SD: What did he do?

S: Um . . . (pause)

SD: Why did he, why did Señor Coyote decide to help him? (pause)

C: Um, because then the . . .

SD: Take your time.

L: Mhm?

C: The, the rock, um, gonna fell in him. The coyote.

L: OK.

This transcription illustrates how we attempt to facilitate student *entry* into the discussion. Although we controlled most of the talking, as the students *entered* the discussion, we immediately built on the students' responses and filled in missing elements to present the *whole picture*. Soon thereafter, we found the appropriate level of difficulty to elicit more student participation. We pick up the transcript after the Fox gets the Coyote to help him hold up the cliff.

L: So what did the fox do? At that point. Sylvia.

S: He said that he would bring food, food.

SD: Mhm?

L: Right, that he was going to go, he says wait a minute, I'm going, I'm going to go.

SD: All right. Wait a minute. He said he was going to do what? I'm in the wrong spot.

L: Mhm. Where are you reading that, Sylvia?

SD: Oh, OK.

S: Chicken and tortillas.

L: Mhm.

SD: And bring help.

S: Mhm.

L: He says you, right, you're right. You see, Carla, the, the fo, the, the, the co, the fox said to the coyote, "You stay here and you hold up this wall, and I'll be right back. I'm going to go get some help." Right?

C: Mhm.

L: He's explaining, "I'm going to go," and also, I'm going to bring you some chicken and I'm going to bring you some tortillas. So don't move. Stay right there holding up this big wall. I'm going to go get all those things and I'll be right back," he says. "Don't worry, I'll be right back, ah, I'm just going to be gone half an hour." Right? Do you think the fox was serious about returning?

C: No.

S: No.

D: He was lying.

L: He was lying, right.

SD: How long did Señor Coyote stay there?

D: Half an hour.

S: Two hours.

SD: How long? Do you remember how long he stayed there, Carla?

C: No, like . . .

SD: (To Delfina) How long do you think he stayed there?

D: Um, all the night.

L: Right.
SD: That's right.
L: He stayed all night long.

Once again, we stepped in and elaborated the children's answers in the context of the story. As such, the discussion of the story became a *mutually accomplished* interaction between adult and students.

After we had some certainty that the students had a cursory understanding of the story, we reviewed unfamiliar, difficult, or unknown vocabulary items. Again, the idea was to define the words, to facilitate a better understanding of the story. We concluded this session by asking the students to reread the story as homework, and identify new words that we could define in class. We also explained that we would continue to help them discuss the story.

*Session 2: Building vocabulary through comprehension.* As we concluded the first session, we had a good sense (*in situ*, before reviewing the tapes) that the students understood the story generally and that this understanding would provide a base by which to move them forward. We also felt that their English vocabulary needed improvement, since clearly it inhibited more adept comprehension. Yet, we wanted to first facilitate a better understanding of the story and then use this knowledge to clarify unfamiliar words.

The session described below is one of the key moments in the investigation. It contains incidents which established that the children could perform at the fourth grade reading level in English. As part of the session, we asked comprehension questions from the text. These were the same questions that regular English-speaking students also had to answer and, as we learned from the teacher, had difficulty answering. This is a key point, because when the students make what we have called the *jump* to fourth grade level reading, their problems are similar to what any fourth grade English-speaking student would have when dealing with the more abstract, subtle information these questions elicited.

The actual transcripts provide concrete examples of what we mean. In contrast to the session already described, we allowed a selective use of Spanish in expressing what the story was about. We did this purposely because we did not want the children's difficulties in oral English to constrain unnecessarily their participation and practice in lessons at this proximal level. It worked. Within the first minute of the lesson, Sylvia provided a fair summary of the plot in Spanish, once again showing a grasp of the literal meaning of the story she had read in English.

L: (To Carla) Huh? Should we do it in Spanish first, and then switch to English afterwards?

C: Yes. (laughs)

L: OK. Bien, este, cuenta un poquito de, de que se trata la historia, el Señor Coyote y el Señor Fox.

C: Um, es que el Señor Coyote se quería comer a, al, um, al Señor Fox, en, de, entonces,

L: Mhm. Ese es el principio. El Señor Coyote vió al Señor Fox y da la casualidad que el Señor Coyote tenía hambre.

C: Mhm.

L: Y dijo "Mmm. Este Señor Fox, me lo voy a comer." Bien, y entonces, ¿que? Delfina. (Delfina laughs and looks in book)

L: ¿Mhm? Ayúdala, Sylvia. Ayúdala, Sylvia.

SD: ¿Que estaba haciendo el Señor Coyote? En el principio.

S: ¿El Señor Coyote? Estaba caminando.

SD: Mhm. ¿Y luego, que paso?

S: Se encontro al Señor Fox.

L: Mhm.

SD: OK.

S: Y el Señor Fox supo que le se lo quería comer.

L: Mhm.

S: Entonces, entonces, este, le, el dijo que, que le ayudara a detener la piedra grande. Que porque si no le ayudaba, la piedra les iba a caer encima de los dos. Entonces el Señor Coyote dijo que, el pe, el miró para arriba y pensó y dijo que, que le iba a ayudar. Entonces, le ayuda y el ese el, el Señor Fox dijo, el pensó que, que hay, no es una mentira de que iba a ir a, a pe a pedir ayuda y que le iba sa traer comida.

The session continued and Delfina haltingly summarized what happened next as the Fox left the Coyote *holding up* the hill. We then arrived at the key to the story; the Coyote's realization that he has been fooled by the Fox. Note that Carla was able to answer although she was the poorest reader in the group.

SD: Mhm, OK, y, y mientras, OK, what happened, after cal, when, when the fox said, "OK."—foolish. When the fox said, um, "OK, I'm going to go get some chicken and tortillas." What happened after

D: He went around, ahi, he was lying, lying, and he was, el Señor Coyote was holding every time up all the time the, the hill.

E: All right, and what was he thinking?

D: That he, he, he, um, the . . .

L: Hm? What was el coyote thinking? When he was holding, as, as he was holding up the hill.

SD: Mhm.

L: What do you think?

SD: —en el español o en inglés.

L: ¿Sylvia o Carla?

C: Que . . .

L: —a Carla.

C: Que le ha echado mentira.

Also, note how Sylvia followed up, without much adult help, with a more coherent description of the ending of the story.

S: Y si luego no le cayó nada en, porque el, el Señor Fox le había dicho que, que es, que si es y luego si suelta cuando el Señor Fox se iba, le dijo que no la soltara porque si la soltaba no va a alcanzar a correr y le iba a caer encima.

SD: Mhm.

S: Y luego, por eso, el, el agarraba y agarraba.

L: Exacto—exacto.

S: Entonces, el dijo que iba a intentar a ver si no le caía. Cuando el, y, a, el Señor Coyote cuando el se iba allá. El, um, dijo que iba a ver si no se le caia y ya cuando corrió muy recio y miró que la, la piedra, um, no se le caía, el dijo que le estaba echando mentiras el Señor Fox y entonces se enojó.

L: Entonces—se dio cuenta, mhm.—

S: Aja, que, que era mentira lo que estaba cayendo la piedra.

L: Exacto. Exacto. Este, muy listo Señor Fox, ¿verdad?

S: Uh huh.

L: Pensó muy rápido. ¿Y si no piensa rápido?

S: Se lo come el coyote.

This recreation of the story was followed by a discussion of unfamiliar terms. Again, we tried to discuss these items as they related to the story. A brief example should suffice; Carla was reading from the text.

C: "If he, if I held it up for I will by myself."

L: Sí.

C: "Then surely you with your great s . . ."

L: Strength.

C: "strength can hold it up for the short time it will take me to, to return and, and bring help and chicken and tortillas. I will bring other with me and they will carry . . ."

L: Poles.

C: "poles to . . ."

S: Brace.

C: "brace this thing . . ."

S: "up with."

L: OK.

SD: It's a long, and what is that, what, what is that, what is he saying there? Can somebody tell me? (Pause) OK. I will, I will, I, "if I held it up for a while by myself then surely you, with your great strength can hold it up." What is it, what is he saying there? If I held it up for a while by myself, then surely you, with your great strength can hold it up for the short time it will take . . .

S: Fuerza.

D: Oh!

L: All right!

SD: Aha. Very good. Strength quiere decir.

C: Fuerza. Si, yo le aguanté por un rato, ah, dijo Señor Fox, entonces, entonces usted, Señor Coyote con su gran fuerza puede aguantar, aguantarlo un rato. Todavía más tiempo.

Finally, we turned to the questions included in the text. The first question is typical of the type of inference expected of children at this reading level. It asked why the Fox changed the way he addressed the Coyote from "Mr. Coyote" to "Brother Coyote." The answer to this question had to come from the students' understanding of the story. Simple recall would not suffice. Note that Delfina attempted to provide an explanation in English and, in fact, gives a hint that she can answer. Before we could extend what she was saying in English, she clarified her answer in Spanish; we then expanded what she said and Sylvia then succinctly gave an appropriate answer to the question.

L: Um, why do you think, what do you guys think that the fox started calling Señor Coyote "brother coyote?" He says here, "How about it, brother coyote?"

S: ¿En qué página?

L: En la página, en las dos, en la dos, dos noventa y nueve.

C: —

L: He says, " 'Why do you say?' asked Señor Fox. 'How about it, brother coyote?' "

D: Oh!

L: " 'I won't be gone more than half an hour.' " Why did he start calling him brother coyote?

D: Oh, because he, only said to try lying because he wanted to . . .

L: Right.

SD: Mhm.

  L: You know he, he was

  D: Ay, para que el crea que nada más que haya venido aquí.

  L: Claro, cambio de señor a, a, a, a brother coyote para hacerse
     más el amigo de la, si como si fuera amigo.

  S: Mhm.

  D: Mhm.

SD: El, hermano.

  L: —

  S: Para que le creyera lo que iba a hacer.

  L: Exacto. Very good. Excellent. That is why. Good point.

We continued by asking other comprehension questions from the text. The students were able to answer with varying success. In general, however, they needed considerable help before approximating reasonable answers. Nevertheless, at the conclusion of the session, we were confident that the students could perform at the more advanced level.

The next day we again briefly reviewed the children's understanding of the story. Although there was some variation, they understood the story. For example, Carla willingly provided a reason why the Fox was able to trick the Coyote. She explained that maybe the Coyote had overestimated his own intelligence and underestimated the intelligence of the Fox. further, she was able to give the explanation with minimal help. Shortly afterward, Carla and Sylvia jointly clarified a point that Delfina had misunderstood. In response to our questions, the group established that the cleverness of the Fox was reflected in the use of his mind to avoid a physical confrontation that he could not win.

## DISCUSSION

In describing the lesson interventions, we attempted to clarify the logic of our strategies for the reorganization of reading into effective zones of proximal development. We started by using the available information about the students' level of reading in Spanish to adjust the level of reading in English. This represents not only a change in the content of the lesson, but a change in the type of interactions that the students are asked to manifest, from the text-specific recall characteristic of the lower levels of reading to inferences based on a good understanding of the story.

We also changed the structure of the reading activities to focus on, and emphasize from the beginning, reading for meaning. In so doing, we established comprehension as the higher order goal of the lesson; the other interventions, as shown, were implemented to sustain this goal. It should be clear that we did not do anything very different from the way the regular English teacher had been teaching. After all, the children still had the same difficulties in oral expression, decoding, and vocabulary development which needed immediate help. What we did was implement similar teaching interventions, but as part of a different teaching-learning system. Our help repackaged and applied interventions in a theoretically different way.

It is clear from our results how easy it is to underassess the Spanish dominant student's reading abilities in English. The source of difficulty, in our opinion, derives from the teacher's use of the students' *English-oral-language* proficiency assessment to make placement decisions. This immediately confounds the problems for the teacher, because it addresses an oral language problem with a reading curriculum. This, in fact, is not a bad idea, but it lacks two critical ingredients: a bilingual *teacher* and a reorganization of lessons which recognizes that *two* problems are being addressed, namely, reading and oral language skills development.

Two important policy implications derived from our study. First was the importance of the advanced level of reading skills that the students had acquired in the course of participation in the Spanish-language classroom. We believe that our interventions were successful because of this strong student preparation in their native language. Our research, therefore, provides strong support for programs which develop strong reading skills in the native language. Conversely, our research also shows the English half of the program is working less well or at a lower level than it has to, but that, as we demonstrated, it can be readily modified to take maximum advantage of extant student skills and resources. We believe the latter to be an important contribution, in light of decreasing resources for new curricula.

A second and related point deals with bilingual staffing. Our interventions require, or at least strongly suggest, bilingual facility on the part of the person taking the teaching role in the reading lessons. Because we were not trained elementary teachers, and yet, successfully intervened, it could be construed that almost anyone can assume the teaching role. This is not the case; it is best for all concerned if trained bilingual teachers are in charge of the reading. But bilingual aides, assisted by the teacher, could also function in this capacity. That is what we mean by taking advantage of existing school resources. Many school districts with student population such as was the focus of this study, employ bilingual aides to assist in classrooms (many states require the presence of bilingual staff, by law). In addition, textbooks and other resources we employed are already part of the existing curriculum. Again, we must stress the importance of bilingual staff in such an enterprise.

Many school districts are presently abandoning bilingual programs in favor of English as a second language (ESL) programs that accelerate more rapid acquisition of oral English skills but de-emphasize the development of a strong academic skills base in the native language. Such an approach may be justified in the case of students who are on the borderline of Spanish-English proficiency, but may not be the most beneficial approach for those students whose dominant language is not English. These students already have the strong oral proficiency that is needed for the development of academic skills, via that language. In fact, the school district's reading consultant made similar recommendations for a strong oral English base before beginning English reading instructions with this group of students. This is not an ill-founded suggestion; our research does not counter the logic of such a recommendation. Rather, our research qualifies the consultant's recommendation. It appears that if students already have a moderately strong background in reading skills in their first (dominant) language, then one can begin to teach them reading in the second language (English). The reason for this is that the students (at least those at their grade level) have mastered the advanced skills required for reading, reading for comprehension, and are merely behind in the lower order English phonics skills. We reorganized lessons to permit the students to read in English at grade level while using the reading content to promote the more slowly acquired oral language skills. This arrangement, as our theory posits, more validly reflects an optimal organization of lessons because it is aimed at the children's higher order level of skills.

## REFERENCES

Au, K. H. On participation structures in reading lessons. *Anthropology and Education Quarterly* 11, no. 2 (1980):91–115.

Carrasco, R., C. Acosta, and S. De La Torre-Spencer. *Language use, lesson engagement and participation structures*. Paper presented at the American Educational Research Association, Los Angeles, April 1981.

Dowley, M. G. The social interaction origins of narrative skills. *The Quarterly Newsletter of the Laboratory of Comparative Human Cognition* 1, no. 4 (1979):63–68.

Erickson, F., and G. Mohatt. Cultural organization of participant structures in two classrooms of Indian students. In G. D. Spindler (Ed.), *Doing the ethnography of schooling*. New York: Holt, Rinehart & Winston, 1982.

Erickson, F., and J. Shultz. When is a context? *The Quarterly Newsletter of the Institute for Comparative Human Development*, 1977, *1*(2), 5–10.

Griffin, P., and R. Shuy (Eds.). *Children's functional language and education in the early years*. Report to the Carnegie Corporation of New York. Arlington, Virginia: Center for Applied Linguistics, 1978.

Leontév, A. Some problems in learning Russian as a foreign language (Essays on Psycholinguistics). *Soviet Psychology* 11, no. 4 (Summer 1973).

McDermott, R. P. *Kids make sense: An ethnographic account of the interactional management of success and failure in one first grade classroom*. Unpublished doctoral dissertation, Department of Anthropology, Stanford University, 1976.

McDermott, R. P., and D. R. Roth. The social organization of behavior: Interactional approaches. *Annual Review of Anthropology* 7 (1979): 321–45.

Mehan, H. Structuring school structures. *Harvard Educational Review* 45, no. 1 (Feb. 1978): 311–38.

Mehan, H. *Learning lessons*. Cambridge, Massachusetts: Harvard University Press, 1979.

Moll, L., E. Diaz, E. Estrada, and L. M. Lopes. Making contexts: The social construction of lessons in two languages. In S. Arvizu and M. Saravia-Shore (eds.), *Cross-cultural and communicative competencies*. New York: Horizons Press, in press.

Moll, L. C. The microethnographic study of bilingual schooling. In R. Padilla (Ed.), *Ethnoperspectives in bilingual education research*, vol. 3. Eastern Michigan University, Ypsilanti, Michigan, 1981.

Shultz, J., S. Florio, and F. Erickson. Where's the floor?: Aspects of the cultural organization of social relationships in communication at home and at school. In P. Gilmore and A. Glatthorn, (eds.), *Ethnography and education: Children in and out of school*. Georgetown: Center for Applied Linguistics, 1980.

Siegler, R. S., and D. D. Richards. The development of intelligence. In R. Sternberg (ed.), *Handbook of human intelligence*. New York: Cambridge University Press, 1982.

Talyzina, N. F. One of the paths of development of Soviet learning theory. *Soviet Education* 20, no. 11 (1978).

Talyzina, N. F. *The psychology of learning*. Moscow: Progress Publishers, 1981.

Vygotsky, L. S. *Mind in society*. Cambridge, Massachusetts: Harvard University Press, 1978.

Watzlavick, P., J. Beavin, and D. Jackson. *Pragmatics of human communication: A study of interactional patterns, pathologies and paradoxes*. New York: W. W. Norton & Co., Inc., 1967.

Wertsch, J. V. (ed.). *The concept of activity in Soviet psychology*. White Plains: Sharpe, 1981.

# 7.
# Uncovering the Covert Bilingual: How to Retrieve the Hidden Home Language

*Rodolfo Jacobson*

THE IMPLEMENTATION OF a Title VII Demonstration Project in San Antonio has revealed some interesting facts concerning the language choice of bilingual children. Some bilingual students may pretend to have lost their home language and, regardless of their proficiency in the mainstream language, prefer using the latter, as if it were a status symbol. The Project in Bilingual Instructional Methodology, conducted jointly by The University of Texas at San Antonio and the Southwest Independent School District, has attempted, as one of its multiple objectives, to create a psychological climate that would be conducive to uncovering the native language of those children who are reluctant to use it at school. It is the objective of this paper to report on a group of twelve Mexican American children from the project and the degree of their home language retrieval.

## A TITLE VII DEMONSTRATION PROJECT IN
## BILINGUAL INSTRUCTIONAL METHODOLOGY

The debate over bilingual education has largely ignored the methodological focus and concentrated on its political implications. Where educational issues have been stressed, its supporters have, at best, argued in favor of bilingual education because two languages are used or developed and bilinguality is held to be an asset for any individual in a multicultural environment like ours. More recently, we have encountered support for bilingual education mainly as a bridge to mainstreaming, but obviously without the frank admission that monolingualism, not bilingualism, should be the actual goal. This issue of transitional rather than maintenance bilingual education has contributed little, if anything, to the outcome of the debate, since it does not deal with the issues from a strict educational viewpoint. Tne maintenance of a language or its attrition is not determined in the classroom: issues much broader than school language use are at stake.

The question to ask, then, is not whether a maintenance or a transitional bilingual program should be implemented but, given the fact that bilingual education is found to be appropriate for a group of minority students, what a teacher must do to teach bilingually. Since the content of a math, science, or even social studies class is relatively uniform regardless of the language used as a means of instruction, it is obviously the use and distribution of two languages rather than a single one that distinguishes bilingual from monolingual education. Conventional bilingual educators would insist that the two languages should be strictly separated from one another, whereas some educators have now come to believe that the concurrent use of the two languages is viable under certain conditions.

The dichotomy of *language separation* as opposed to *concurrent use*, however, still describes these language options quite imperfectly. Obviously, the two languages can be separated on the basis of time or content. Some bilingual programs have used the morning-afternoon as well as the alternate day approaches, whereas others have attempted to teach every subject twice, in $L_1$, then $L_2$, or assigned one language to certain subjects and the other language to the remaining subjects. The two languages can also be allowed to concur in the teaching of a subject. Some bilingual programs have incorporated in their design the random alternation between $L_1$ and $L_2$, whereas others have found it useful to translate to $L_1$ whatever was taught in $L_2$. A more recent version of the concurrent instruction incorporates a highly structured alternation strategy, whereby the teacher switches back and forth between the two languages but only in response to certain cues in the classroom. The various options open to the bilingual teacher can be summarized in the following diagram:

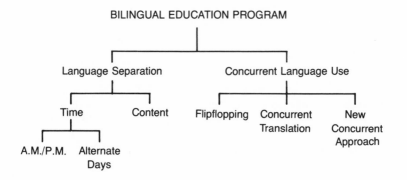

In view of the great variety of language distribution options from which the bilingual teacher can draw, it hardly makes any sense to discuss the merits of an educational program only in terms of its bilinguality. There is certainly a need for greater methodological specificity, not only in defining or describing the various methods of dual language distribution, but also in empirically testing the efficacy of a bilingual education program, in light of the language strategy chosen for instructional purposes. The two methods of dual language distribution discussed in this paper are the New Concurrent Approach (NCA) and the Language Separation Approach (LSA). In the NCA method, the bilingual teacher concurrently uses the two languages when teaching content, whereas in the LSA method, the two languages are separated according to some set criterion. The question now posed is whether it is to the child's advantage to have the teacher alternate between the two languages when teaching, say, science or social studies, or to separate them, such as, science in one language and social studies in the other. A project that gathers data concerning the relative effectiveness of these two approaches would help bilingual educators assess each more effectively and also help them to select one in preference to the other. If, in turn, the data supported the fact that both approaches were equally sound, a study of this nature would allow educators to select confidently either approach, whichever appeared more appropriate in a given setting.

A project of this nature is currently implemented in San Antonio, Texas. The University of Texas at San Antonio and the Southwest Independent School District have been funded by the U.S. Department of Education to conduct a Title VII Demonstration Project that would gather data on children instructed by the NCA and the LSA. The project operates in two schools, Indian Creek Elementary and Sky Harbour Elementary. In the first, English and Spanish are strictly separated in that math, science, and health are taught in English and social studies, art, music, and physical education, in Spanish. In the other school, English and Spanish are used concurrently, such that the teacher would switch from English to Spanish or vice versa when such alternation could be justified on educational, linguistic, or attitudinal grounds.

Basic for the success of the project is the extent to which its crucial variables are controlled. *The students* selected for the project are LEP children who were assigned to grades K and 1 with the understanding that they would continue in the same project for three years, so that their progress could be monitored as they moved up to grades 1 and 2 in 1982–83 and to grades 2 and 3 in 1983–84. The attrition rate during the first two years has been extremely low—much lower than what is customary for the other grades—so that there is reasonable assurance that meaningful test data can be gathered during the time that the project is in operation. *The schools* identified at the beginning of the project are continuing to be involved, so that by now, an excellent working relationship has been established between the project staff and the school personnel. Initial tensions were easily overcome and the presence of university staff on the elementary school campuses is not seen as a disruption of school activities. *The teaching staff* has undergone one change. A teacher from the school where the LSA method is implemented withdrew from the project and was therefore replaced by another bilingual teacher. The remaining three project teachers as well as the four aides are still participating in the program, but with slight changes in their grade assignments. This staffing stability has greatly contributed to producing a psychologically well balanced and relaxed atmosphere for all the children involved. *Equipment and materials* are above average and distributed in equivalent quantities throughout the grades. Orders are placed with the consensus of teacher, aides, and program coordinator and federal as well as local funds have provided what the children might need in order to receive superior bilingual instruction.

Except for a short time prior to selecting a coordinator, the program coordination has been the responsibility of the current program coordinator who, in conjunction with the director, implements the overall design in the two participating schools. Therefore, no changes in direction have occurred and the program as a whole appears to be functioning harmoniously, as a result of excellent public relations, a very important asset. By controlling the cited variables in the indicated way, the project director has the assurance that the incoming data will shed significant light on the relative effectiveness of the two methods.

A second significant objective of the project is of particular interest to the student of first and second language development. Jacobson (1982a, 1982b) shares the argument presented by James Cummins (1979, 1980) that a child must reach the threshold level in the first language in order to develop his/her cognitive and academic skills, which may then be transferred to the second language as he/she acquires that language to function in a second language environment. Cummins (1982) and Jacobson (1982c), however, hold that the acquisition of $L_2$ does not have to await the *full* attainment of the $L_1$ threshold level, as both objectives go hand in hand: the $L_1$ threshold level is pursued while $L_2$ learning takes place concurrently. With this reasoning in mind, Jacobson (1981) proposed a language distributional pattern, whereby children would be exposed to 90 percent Spanish and only 10 percent English as ESL. The kindergarten sections of the two schools, however, would differ in that at the treatment school (Sky Harbour) this ratio of distribution was held constant, whereas, at the comparison school (Indian Creek), the percentage of Spanish language use would be decreased (75% at the end of grade K) and that of English language use increased (25% at the end of grade K), thus simulating the conventional trend in bilingual education pattern where the amount of exposure to the home language is reduced, as the mainstream language is allegedly acquired. This constancy, as opposed to the variability (decrease-increase) pattern, is a characteristic feature throughout, distinguishing the treatment from the comparison school, and it holds significance because of its psychological implications.[1]

The use of the home language and its use in the classroom presupposes a favorable attitude toward the vernacular. The notion of, say, Spanish being as valuable a tool of communication as English is by no means shared by all members of the Hispanic minority because of the attitudes, stereotypes, and socio-economic pressures to which they may have been exposed. Hence, the concept of the prestige of the code, whether English or Spanish, becomes an unusually important element in the project. The *prestige of a code* is emphasized in the treatment school as it is in the comparison school. A favorable psychological climate must be promoted, so that children feel comfortable with the use at school of the language of the home. Against their and their parents' anticipation, Spanish is not restricted to home and hearth, but becomes a most welcome means of communication in the classroom.

The presence of the vernacular in the teaching of content fulfills not only an attitudinal objective, but also one that, in the professional literature, has been referred to as the "comprehensible input hypothesis" (Krashen, 1981: especially, 119–37). Krashen stresses the importance of the three simple codes, that is, teacher-talk, interlanguage-talk, and foreigner-talk, as prerequisites for second language acquisition (ibid.: 128). All these codes are incorporated into the approach discussed in this study, as teachers and aides in this project seek to reach the children in either language at a level that is comprehensible to them, allow peer conversation and facilitate the communication with outside personnel, such as project director, coordinator, and parents. The level of the teacher/aide-pupil interaction is comparable to Krashen's i + 1 structure (ibid.: 132) as both teachers and aides *shoot* for a level slightly above the children's language ability in order to encourage language growth in the mainstream and the vernacular language. The project teachers (NCA and LSA) are particularly well qualified to *hit* the desirable structure level because, through their language alternation training, they have become conscious of language manipulations and controls, a strategy with which average teachers have a great deal of difficulty. The NCA method, however, goes beyond Krashen's requirement of simple codes and comprehensible input in the target language, as it uses the source *and* the target language to carry out the task of dual language development. Simple codes, even in their most effective forms, still leave a residue of incomprehensible inputs that the NCA method can dissolve,

---

1. For a more detailed report on the overall design of the project refer to R. Jacobson, "The Implementation of a Bilingual Instruction Model, the *New Concurrent Approach*," in Raymond Y. Padilla, ed., *Bilingual Education Technology*, 1982, Ypsilanti, MI: Eastern Michigan University.

in order to achieve total comprehensibility. Jacobson (1983) gave the following example to illustrate NCA:

> T: This is a seed. We plant it in the soil to develop roots. To make it grow fast, we water it. Después que la planta ha echado sus raices y la hemos regado bastante, produce un tallo y las hojas. ¿Qué más tiene la planta?
> ST: Tiene hojas y una flor.
> T: Muy bien, tiene hojas y a veces tiene también flores. Have you ever actually seen plants with leaves and flowers?
> ST: Yes, in my backyard (Jacobson 1983:3).

Here, the dual language acquirer accomplishes several tasks simultaneously:

> Learns in two languages the concept of "the plant," from planting the seed to growing leaves and flowers;
> Expands the specialized vocabulary needed for the understanding of the lesson by acquiring new words or merely affirming insecure knowledge of these in the source language, in the target language or in both;
> Is exposed to simple utterances in both languages using the present or present perfect tense of some very common verbs of general as well as specialized use;
> Learns to answer in complete or partially deleted responses;
> Practices sound language choice criteria in responding in Spanish to a Spanish question and in English to an English question.

If this lesson is taught using visual media (charts, transparencies, blackboard designs), no residue of noncomprehension can possibly stall appropriate language growth.

Children vary, however, in the degree to which they are willing to use the vernacular in school, as this requires that they reconsider their preconceptions, attitudinal or other, and speak both languages freely in class. They also vary in the time that they need to make such readjustment. After one-and-a-half years of project implementation it may be worthwhile to examine more closely what actually constitutes the favorable vernacular climate provided for them and how children are reacting to it in terms of language choice. In other words, does the instructional method used carry any implication for the language choice observed in the classroom?

## COVERT AND PASSIVE BILINGUALISM

In an attempt to identify college students with potential to become bilingual teachers, Janet B. Sawyer (1977) began to explore the degree of Spanish-

English bilingualism which she encountered in her introductory linguistics classes. This led her to recognize three different types of bilinguals. She describes these bilinguals succinctly as follows:

> Some frankly admitted that they spoke *Spanish* at home and with friends, and *English* at school. Others, however, claimed that although their parents and relatives spoke Spanish in the home, they themselves never did. They explained that they *understood* the language, but couldn't speak it. . . . We labeled these informants *Passive* Bilinguals, and decided to concentrate our first investigation upon them, in an attempt to determine the extent of their first-language ability. Inadvertently, during the course of the investigation, we stumble[d] upon a third type of bilingual, representing the extreme in *suppression* of the mother tongue. To our surprise, we discovered some bilinguals, at least some bilingual students in the college classes, who had deliberately chosen to deny their bilingual skills altogether, preferring to pass as monolingual English speakers. . . . These informants we decided to call *Covert* Bilinguals (Hoffer and Dubois 1977:59).

The proposed typology of covert bilinguals, passive bilinguals, and code-switchers (ibid.:60) can be expanded further if we examine more closely the kind of language alternation in which code-switchers may engage.

Recent research has provided much new information in this respect; switching of codes may be lexical or syntactic in nature, involve intra-sentential or inter-sentential alternations and, finally, display psychological or sociological conditioning (Jacobson 1978). Sawyer explains passive bilingualism as a sign of linguistic insecurity and quotes Saville and Troike (1971) in this respect who argue that "the teacher may interpret the child's use of his native language as a rejection of the majority culture, and may react with hostility toward the child" (Hoffer and Dubois 1977:62). They continue, writing that "it is not uncommon to find children from Spanish-speaking homes *denying that they know any Spanish*, since the repression of the language in school and the generally subordinate status of Spanish speakers have made them ashamed of their linguistic and cultural heritage. . . ." It appears, however, that the feeling of linguistic insecurity develops, even before the child comes to school. Many of the children entering kindergarten and first grade carry a very distinct notion of the nonadmissibility of Spanish in the classroom, even when, in a bilingual program, they are encouraged to use the home language at will. The parents at home and the peers on neighborhood streets seem to have pressured the child, much before the first day of classes, into believing the superior value of the majority language.

Most revealing in this regard was the attitude of a young Mexican American girl who approached the author during a preliminary taping session of an NCA class at one San Antonio school. As the videocamera was about to capture the beginning of the lesson she approached him and said, after categorizing him as a non-Hispanic, "I don't speak any Spanish." He, however, brushed aside the remark by saying in nativelike Spanish, "Claro que hablas español. Aquí todos hablamos español, ¿verdad?" [Of course, you do speak Spanish. All of us here speak Spanish, don't we?] She went back to her seat and performed beautifully in Spanish or in English, as expected. By denying Spanish, the Mexican-American second-grader had given a social, not a linguistic message, to the effect that she was a fully assimilated individual. The response in Spanish, on the other hand, made it unnecessary for her to insist further on her ignorance of Spanish. Obviously, this was an easy way of changing the child from a covert to an active bilingual. Other similar cases have been more complex and may require deeper insight. In a classroom situation, they require the promotion of a psychological climate conducive to the use of the home language in spite of pressures external to the classroom.

How can such a climate be promoted in the classroom? Which considerations can be expected to produce the relaxed bilingual atmosphere that is crucial for learning through two languages? The author's earlier experiences as an external evaluator of the Title VII Bilingual Program of the Laredo United I.S.D. may provide some information in this respect. During the spring semester of 1975, he evaluated the bilingual program at Clark Elementary School with overall findings concerning the role of Spanish in the program summarized as follows:

> Children, when asked questions in Spanish, would respond in English most of the time.
> The use of Spanish, even though not avoided entirely, was extremely limited and could be observed only during a 30-minute period of time devoted to bilingual education.
> There seemed to be little future for the use of Spanish at school, as it only served very few as a means of communication while they had not yet learned sufficient English to make themselves understood.
> The teacher's limited use of Spanish lacked all cultural connotations; it was mainly "mainstream culture but rendered in Spanish."

How could changes be brought about to make Spanish worth remembering, retaining, and even developing further? The following four years of continued consultant services have provided the opportunity, among other objectives, to identify the elements needed to enhance the role of Spanish in the primary grades. Table 7.1 is an analysis of the eight evaluation reports submitted between fall 1975 and spring 1979.

A brief commentary on categories and their ingredients is an aid in recognizing the multiplicity of elements that must be considered.

**TABLE 7.1**
**The Psychological Climate for Minority Language Retrieval**

| Time | Vernacular and its use | Value Judgment | Strategies |
|---|---|---|---|
| Time Factor | Regional Spanish | Equal Prestige | Flexibility |
| Ratio for Use | Proficiency | Freedom of Social Connotations | Purposefulness |
| | Equally Valid for Teaching/Learning | | Consciousness of Choice |
| | Loss of Reluctance | | Overuse of Majority Language |
| | Self-assessment of Use | | |

| Child Performance | Affective Factors | Environment | Community |
|---|---|---|---|
| Emphasis on Child Performance | Self-Image | Decorations | Norms |
| Opportunity to Respond | Rapport | | Parental Approval |
| Bilingual Balance (length) | Relaxed Atmosphere | | Culture Sharing |
| Control of Language Distribution | | | |
| Modeling | | | |

*Time*: The time allotted to each language is crucial. The excessive use of one language over the other will lend itself to the interpretation that one language is more important (or better) than the other. The ideal ratio of distribution is 50:50.

*Vernacular and its use*: Regional Spanish must be accepted although standard forms should be gradually introduced as *other ways of saying the same*. The native or nativelike proficiency of teachers and teacher aides is important. Spanish shall be recognized as an equally valid medium of instruction. One can teach/learn any subject in either language; it is the content that counts. Gradually, children will become less reluctant to speak Spanish. On the other hand, teachers may deceive themselves regarding the amount of time they stay in either language. Self-assessment must be trained.

*Value judgment*: The two languages hold equal prestige. This concept is best acquired when teachers and/or aides alternate languages, also in out-of-class interactions. Eventually both languages will be free of social connotations, at least in school.

*Strategies*: The flexibility of using either language will be valued. From the teacher's viewpoint, there must be a purpose in shifting from one language to the other. In other words, he/she must be conscious of his/her language choice. An overuse of the majority language has either psychological or methodological reasons. Psychologically, the teacher may attribute a greater value to the majority language. Methodologically, he/she may not have learned to detach him/herself from the teaching task and self-monitor his/her language behavior.

*Child performance*: The emphasis must be on the child and his/her language performance. The teacher's use of the two languages without providing the child with the opportunity for a response in one as well as the other language is unsatisfactory. If bilingual balance is achieved, child and teacher/aide must stay within the same language a certain period of time because continuous switching tends to be confusing. The teacher must control the language distribution by initiating the switch and having the child follow his/her initiative. The teacher or aide is the model that children will mimic.

*Affective factors*:[2] The teacher or aide's self-image is crucial in developing the child's self-image. The rapport between teacher/aide and the child must be

---

2. The resemblance of *affective factors* with Krashen's *Affective Filter* is more apparent than real as Krashen focuses on the ESL learner, and his data are mainly based on the research with secondary students or adults.

"Secondly language attitude," Krashen argues, refers to acquirers' orientations toward speakers of the target language, as well as personality factors. The (second) hypothesis is that such factors relate directly to acquisition and only indirectly to conscious learning. Briefly, the "right" attitudinal factors produce two effects: they encourage useful input for language acquisition and they allow the acquirer to be "open" to this input so it can be utilized for acquisition (1981:5).

such that it produces a positive working relationship as well as mutual respect. All this will lead to the relaxed atmosphere that children need to function bilingually; without it, they will not use at school the language they have learned at home.

*Environment*: Classroom decorations must tell the bicultural and bilingual story. Words in two languages, phrases, and pictures which remind children of the two worlds must brighten the atmosphere of the classroom.

*Community*: There must be an understanding and a knowledge of the norms of the community. Parents should be involved and approve of the language development of the children. They should be instrumental in helping school personnel share their culture and, in particular, realize the expectations they have for their children.

These early lessons on how to retrieve the home language at school have been instrumental in promoting, also in the schools of the San Antonio Title VII Demonstration Project, the aforementioned psychological climate that has enabled almost all children to feel comfortable in their use of Spanish.

The preceding discussion is likely to evoke in the reader the concept of linguistic and cultural maintenance which, during the first decade of federally sponsored programs, identified bilingual programs that stressed the retention of vernacular language and culture over a gradual transition to monolingualism and monoculturalism as practiced by the middle-class majority in the United States. Despite some similarity between the cited psychosociological factors and those of earlier maintenance programs, the rationale, as well as the ultimate objective, of these programs is different, which can be appreciated in the following analysis of the two types of bilingual programs:

| **Maintenance Programs** | **NCA Program** |
|---|---|
| The home language is retained to allow the child to identify him/herself as a member of the ethnic group. | The home language is retained to allow the child to first reach the threshold level in the native language. |

---

Even where Krashen refers to younger children, the setting is different from the one described in this study and he admits that "there has been little work in this area" (ibid: 36). In his reference to Fillmore's 1976 work, Krashen describes it as a "case study of five children acquiring English as a second language in an *American* [Italics, mine] kindergarten, implying hereby that the children were not Americans. Krashen's other reference to small children described Swain and Burnaby's 1976 study of an *immersion* kindergarten whose English-speaking children acquired French very successfully (ibid.). Anglophones, in the Canadian setting, are middle or upper middle class families and are not socio-economically comparable to the low income minority children of the cited Title VII Demonstration Project.

The *affective factors* of the present study, then, refer to the teaching of low-income Hispanic children who are already bilinguals but in need of developing further both languages in order to acquire and/or transfer the cognitive skills (CALP) that are prerequisites to academic achievement in school. To enable the teacher to do so, the manipulation of adequate affective factors is crucial and requires an expertise quite different from the *Affective Filter* described in Krashen's book.

The home culture is retained to keep the child's cultural traditions alive.

The home culture, in conjunction with the majority culture, is appreciated in order to develop sound bicultural identity.

Home language/culture is stressed over majority language/culture to neutralize the linguistic/cultural impact of the broader environment.

Home language/culture and majority language/culture are fully balanced in the school environment, neither surpassing the other in prestige.

Dual language use is expected to continue throughout the entire school career.

Dual language use in school is limited to primary grades, although extracurricular activities at school or parent/neighborhood activities may want to continue the use of Spanish to avoid home language attrition.

English and the home language are expected to be media of instruction during the entire school career.

Primary years to serve as adjustment period for the child to accept the fact that English is the school language from grade four on.

Prevention of alienation from home language and culture despite external influences.

Acquisition of sociolinguistic flexibility to alternate culturally and linguistically between vernacular and non-vernacular domains.

Whereas the psycho-sociological factors underlying the NCA program do not differ substantially from those used in the earlier maintenance programs, NCA strives for transition as far as the school language is concerned. However, because of intensive home language development, the vernacular is not forgotten and continues to be available to the child, whenever culturally and/or socially appropriate. This program represents, therefore, a viable compromise between maintenance and transition, focusing however, on educational rather than societal goals. A positive attitude of this kind is expected to create within the classroom an atmosphere conducive to maximizing the learning efforts of bilingual children at school, regardless of any political or interethnic conflict that may prevail in the broader setting. A different approach is, however, taken by some foreign scholars who seem to blame the political arena for a state of affairs that can be remedied by resourceful educators. Tove Skutnabb-Kangas (1978) believes that schools offering bilingual programs can have an impact on the society at large. She sees *bilingualism as an instrument to achieving broader societal goals.* Bilingualism can be used to pacify or try to pacify (or repacify) groups who otherwise might be more difficult to keep down. Bilingualism can be a well-meant bone which you throw to hungry dogs who otherwise would attack you. Bilingualism can be used to prevent equality—or to help to create equality. And of course it is important to note again, that the official goals of bilingual education do not necessarily reflect the real goals, which can better be seen in the measures taken to realize the officially agreed-upon goals (241).

It is unlikely that societal goals can be achieved in the classroom nor that bilingual programs should be built on such grounds. Also, guided by her concern about the power conflict between majority and minority groups, Skutnabb-Kangas assesses the language situation of the minority child in ways that are linguistically questionable. This author has found no evidence for the so-called presence of semi-lingualism among minority children in the Southwest. "Semilingualism," argues Skutnabb-Kangas (1978:222),

means not knowing any language properly at the same level as monolingual native speakers (Paneldiskussion om dubbel halospråkighet, 1977), or, put more precisely, a situation where a child does not acquire the linguistic skill appropriate to her/his original linguistic capacity in any language (Skutnabb-Kangas and Toukomaa, 1976).

The anecdotal description of a five-year-old Finnish immigrant child in Sweden is obviously only a case study and not a general phenomenon, unless the European migrant situation differs fundamentally from everything we know about minority children in the United States, a fact that Skutnabb-Kangas is not suggesting. By the same token, her quote from Karin Aronsson's (1978) study stresses a view that is hardly convincing when she joins Aronsson in supporting that "exposure (whether in small or great amounts) cannot be equated with learning" (Skutnabb-Kangas 1978:227). Quite to the contrary, it is often surprising how much language is learned by the child by only being exposed to it from children of her/his own age group. Semilingualism or its counterpart among monolingual children, averbality, cannot be justified on grounds of linguistic competence (or incompetence) as, by the age of, say, four or five years, he/she has acquired *a* linguistic system, the one to which she/he was exposed. As for the child's linguistic performance, a number of questions arise which William Labov (1969) has addressed. Labov was one of the first to point out that a child interview demanded rapport, ingenuity, ethnic *savoir faire*, and so forth, in order to bring to the open the kind of language performance to which one expects a child to be capable. Instead of averbality and monosyllables, Labov's interviewer elicited quite sophisticated language structures. Hence, instead of semilingualism, active bilingualism tends to emerge, as long as the appropriate bilingual climate referred to above is generated, so that the child's home language may be fully retrieved.

During the first semester of the demonstration project implementation (fall 1981), most children were found to be covert or passive bilinguals. Responses to questions in Spanish were given in English; student-initiated comments were in English; and even in one-to-one informal conversations, Spanish was usually avoided. On the other hand, the results of the Language Assessment Scales, or Linguametrics (LAS), showed, in the English version, that the children's proficiency level in English classified them as being Limited English Proficiency children (LEPs), thus corroborating the information obtained in the parents' questionnaires that Spanish and not English was the language of the home. The second year of implementation, 1982–1983, provided a completely different picture. The number of covert and passive bilinguals was almost negligible and children in either group (treatment as well as comparison) were most willing to follow the teacher's lead in terms of language choice. Where the home language had not been fully recovered, children would switch to English intrasententially, but many had acquired the expertise of shifting from one to the other language without engaging in mixed language constructions. An assessment of their progress in dual language use was, therefore, called for. The findings of the language choice experiment are briefly described below.

## THE LANGUAGE CHOICE EXPERIMENT

The objective of the Language Choice Experiment has been to assess the degree of bilinguality and the extent of sociolinguistic sophistication of a randomly selected group of students from both the comparison and the treatment schools. Depending on the children's ability to perform in the two languages, the subjects have been categorized on the basis of their bilingual performance and some tentative judgments have been made concerning whether the instructional method used in the school would have any bearing on the bilingual category to which these children have been assigned.

### Methodology

Twelve children were selected from participating grades in consultation with the teachers and aides serving in the project. Of these, eight subjects had been instructed in the LSA Method and four in NCA. There was no special reason for selecting more comparison than treatment students, other than that all the children recommended by their teachers were accepted. Only grades 1 and 2 were part of the project during the 1982–83 year. As a result, the following was the distribution of the subjects according to grade level and instructional method:

| Grade Level | Teaching Method | Number of Selectees |
|:-----------:|:---------------:|:-------------------:|
| 1 | LSA | 5 |
| 1 | NCA | 2 |
| 2 | LSA | 3 |
| 2 | NCA | 2 |

The subjects were interviewed individually and only by the author. He conversed with them in English and Spanish, eliciting responses in home-related, neighborhood-related, and school-related topics. More Spanish than English was spoken, as the interviewer hoped to determine the extent to which the home language was being retrieved and/or developed. The interview began with questions in English; however, the conversation soon shifted to Spanish. Further alternations occurred as the dialog demanded, in order to obtain natural and smooth responses. The interview structure was kept uniform, allowing for some variations depending on the subjects' answers and/or language ability. In general, all the questions elicited the child's reactions to the following topics: home; family; school; classroom; teacher and/or aide; school subject; peers; television; Spanish vs. English; project.

As sole interviewer, the author provided uniformity in the elicitation process and promoted a relaxed atmosphere during the interview. He knew all the project children well, because he had visited their classrooms regularly for almost two years and also had taught demonstration classes. The children showed no fear at any time during the interview. Quite to the contrary, they were pleased to be selected for the experiment. The rapport between interviewer and interviewees was also due to the fact that the interviewer had eaten lunch with the children in the school cafeteria, talked with them at parent meetings and on the playground, and organized school programs in which they had participated. Because of this favorable climate of the interview, the subjects' responses were believed to be truthful, natural and reflective of everyday language behavior.

The setting of the interview, the school library, was chosen carefully in order not to interfere with the interviewing process. Each student was interviewed individually, and the recording was done as unobtrusively as possible; no separate microphone was used and a cassette recorder with in-built microphone was placed on a chair where it would be least visible. With these precautions taken, the children's responses during the interview reflected their typical language choice.

The recordings of each subject were transcribed fully and evaluated on the basis of several language performance criteria that would allow a tentative assessment of the children's degree of binguality. The following criteria were used:

> Comprehension and/or willingness to comprehend questions asked in the home language;
> Response and/or willingness to respond in the majority language to questions asked in the home language;
> Ability to respond in the home language to questions in that language but with intra-sentential switches to the majority language;
> Ability to respond in either language but avoiding intrasentential switches;
> Flexibility in language alternation following the interviewer's switching patterns.

No rigorous quantitative assessment was used in this preliminary evaluation, but the interviewer's ability to judge student performances and conduct and/or rate language interviews made it possible to arrive at a valid tentative judgment of the subjects' binguality.

The following dialog transcription illustrates the language choice performance of an LSA second grader who can be considered average. MV's speech reflects some mixing but also some intrasentential and intersentential switching. When referring to individuals, MV's use of English seems to suggest that she interacts with them in English, and her use of Spanish, that she speaks Spanish with the others. Her father's work also seems to favor MV's switch to English. Altogether, she speaks Spanish well, understands it when it is spoken to her, and is secure in her language behavior. MV's teacher and also her aide had this to say about her:

> MV seems to have made an improvement in understanding the Spanish language. She was able to speak *some* Spanish last year but she was very *shy*.

Using Sawyer's categories, one might say that last year MV was basically a passive bilingual, but had advanced to that of a codeswitcher within a year's time. Her switching ability, however, was still somewhat crude, in particular when one compares it to some of the other interviewees. The complete conversation is transcribed below:

RJ: Do you walk to school or do you come by bus? Do you take a bus or does your mommy bring you?

MV: My *tia* brings me.

RJ: Very good. ¿Y tú tienes hermanitos? ¿Cómo se llama él?

MV: Tengo dos.

RJ: Ah, dos, ¿Cómo se llama él?—llaman ellos?

MV: Uno se llama . . . y uno se llama Rudy.

RJ: Qué bien. Yo también tengo un hijo que se llama Rudy. ¿Y tienes alguna hermanita?

MV: Si, tres. Dos.

RJ: Dos mas tú.

MV: Jennifer, that is my sister, and Cathy, that is my mother's sister, *y nada más*.

RJ: Aha, bastante. Así que son cuatro mujeres y dos hombres. ¿Sí? ¿Seis en total, no?

MV: Ocho.

RJ: ¿Ocho? Vamos a ver otra vez. Tu tienes tres hermanas, uno, dos, tres y tu eres la cuarta mujercita, ¿verdad? Son cuatro. Después tienes el hermano Rudy son cinco. Y ¿Cuál es el otro hermano?

MV: . . . . . .

RJ: Van seis. Así que son seis y después está tu mamá. ¿Está en la casa también?

MV: Y mi Papá.

RJ: Y tu papá. Ocho en la casa. ¿Qué hace tu papa?

MV: . . .

RJ: ¿Pero el trabaja?

MV: Trabaja.

RJ: ¿A donde trabaja? ¿El que hace?

MV: Se va para otra *city* a trabajar.

RJ: Aha.

MV: He goes out of town.

RJ: Aha, muy bien. ¿Te gusta la escuela?

MV: Sí.

RJ: Sí. Y ¿te gusta hablar en español?

MV: Sí.

RJ: Y tu hablas más español que antes, ¿verdad? ¿Tu has aprendido bastante español aquí en el programa, no? Muy bien. ¿Cómo se llama tu maestra?

MV: Ms. Ramos.

RJ: ¿Y la otra? La asistente a la . . .

MV: Ms. Garza.

RJ: Muy bien. ¿Y a tí qué te gusta aprender en la escuela? ¿Hay algo que te gusta aprender?

MV: Aprender a escribir, aprender a contar, y aprender a . . . (?)

RJ: ¿Te gusta la matemática?

MV: Si, muy bien, me gusta a . . .

RJ: La matemática.

MV: Me gusta hablar en español.

RJ: Muy bien y dime una cosa ¿Tu tienes muchos amiguitos o amiguitas en el salón?

MV: Sí.

RJ: Una.

MV: (cinco no seis)

RJ: Cinco, seis. Esto es bastante. Seis amiguitas. ¡Qué bien! ¿Cuál es la mejor de tus amiguitas? ¿Cómo se llama?

MV: Se llama Ema. Es la mayor. [!]

RJ: Aha, Ema. ¿Y ella se sienta en la misma mesa que tú?

MV: Sí.

RJ: ¿Y tu platicas en español o en inglés?

MV: En español.

RJ: Tu entiendes bastante ya. ¿Te gusta la televisión?

MV: Sí.

RJ: ¿Tu ves muchos programas en la casa?

MV: Sí.

RJ: ¿Qué programas te gustan?

MV: Cartoon.

RJ: Ah, las caricaturas. Y ¿cuándo tu las ves?

MV: A las ocho.

RJ: ¿A las ocho por la noche?

MV: Aha, a las ocho.

RJ: Y cuando te acuestas, ¿cuándo vas a dormir?

MV: A las seis.

RJ: ¿A las seis? Entonces tu no puedes verlas a las ocho si te vas a dormir a las seis.

MV: A las diez.

RJ: Ah, te acuestas a las diez.

MV: A las diez.

RJ: Aha, y ¿Qué más ves en la televisión?

MV: . . . .

RJ:   ¿Ves los Muppets?
MV:  Hmmmmm.
RJ:   ¿Te gusta? ¿Quién te gusta allí?
MV:  . . . . Miss Piggy and Kermit
RJ:   O.K. Ya tu hablas bastante español. Y en tu casa ¿qué
        hablan, español o inglés?
MV:  Inglés y español.
RJ:   Las dos cosas. Muy bien.


Not all children have appeared to be as comfortable in Spanish as was MV.
Another LSA second-grader, DD, not only avoided Spanish altogether but
pretended that she did not understand the language at all.

RJ:   How long does it take you to come from your house to the
        school? How many minutes?
DD:   Two.
RJ:   Two minutes? Oh, that's very close. O.K., very good. ¿Y tu
        tienes alguna hermanita? [and do you have a little sister?]
DD:   ¿Eh?
RJ:   ¿Tienes hermanita? [Do you have a little sister?]
DD:   I don't know any Spanish.
RJ:   You don't understand Spanish! How come? What is *her-
        manito*? [little brother]
DD:   . . . . . ?
RJ:   A little brother. Don't you have a little brother?
DD:   My mother has . . . (pause)
RJ:   Asi que tienes hermanitas entonces . . . [So, you do have
        little sisters . . . . then.] And what do you do when the
        teacher speaks in Spanish? You don't understand what she
        says?
DD:   (gestures no)


A second attempt to elicit her Spanish is made later in the interview. DD does
not answer in Spanish but once she responds to a Spanish question in English:

RJ:   ¿Te gusta la televisión? [Do you like TV?] ¿Qué programa
        ves en la televisión? [Which program do you see on TV?]
        The Muppets? ¿Te gustan The Muppets? [Do you like . . .]
DD:   Annie.
RJ:   Which one,
DD:   Annie.

When asked about DD, the classroom aide made the following comment:

> DD is very nervous. I feel that she has some understanding of Spanish but it is very limited. Last year she had not developed an ability to speak Spanish at all but this year she does well in group responses.

At lunch time the aide showed the author what she had meant when referring to DD's Spanish comprehension. The aide asked her in Spanish to give her milk carton to a little boy whose milk was frozen. DD understood the request at once and handed over the milk that she did not want. She did not pretend this time not to understand Spanish. DD is probably a good example for the covert bilingual who is almost ready to become a passive bilingual, which is the first step in the direction of active bilingualism.

At the other extreme there is DR, an NCA second-grader, who exhibits, in his responses, excellent language choice behavior. He is secure in Spanish; he will occasionally switch to English, but never within the same sentence. It is as if he can anticipate when the need to speak English will arise. He also displays an excellent feeling for the appropriateness of the switch by following the interviewer's language alternation pattern:

RJ: Do you know how long it takes you to walk?

DR: About 3 minutes.

RJ: Oh, that's not too far, not too bad. Now, did you get wet today?

DR: No.

RJ: It wasn't raining when you came to school?

DR: No.

RJ: That's good. Dime, David, ¿quién vive en tu casa? [Tell me, David, who lives at your home?]

DR: Mi mama, papa, mi hermanita y yo. [My mother, father, my little sister and I.]

RJ: ¿Y tu hermanita cómo se llama? [And your little sister, what is her name?]

DR: Stephanie.

RJ: ¿Stephanie? ¿Y habla español también? [And she speaks Spanish, too?]

DR: Sí [yes]

RJ: ¿Sí? [Yes?] ¿Ustedes hablan bastante español en casa o poquito? [Do you speak a lot of Spanish at home or a little bit?]

DR: Mucho. [A lot.]

RJ: Mucho, bien. [A lot, good] ¿Y cuántos años tiene Stephanie? [And how old is Stephanie?]

DR: Dos. [Two years]

Once DR stumbles over a word and recasts it in English to make himself understood:

> RJ:  ¿Mecánico, troquero? [A mechanic, a truck driver?] ¿Qué
>      hace? [What does he do?] ¿O trabaja en construcción? [or
>      does he work on a construction?] ¿O es chofer? [or is he a
>      chauffeur?] ¿O qué hace? [Or what does he do?]
>
> DR:  En aire condi . . . (pause) *air condition.*
>
> RJ:  Ah, en aire acondicionado, entonces él es como mecánico.
>      [Ah, in air conditioning; then, he is sort of a mechanic.] El
>      sabe de máquinas y de aire acondicionado y todo eso. [He
>      knows about motors and air conditioning and all that.] Ah,
>      éso está muy bien. [Ah, that's very good.] Muy bien. [Very
>      well.]

An interesting switch occurs upon the interviewer's question *¿y sabias ya bastante inglés cuando venías a la escuela?* [And did you know already a lot of English when you came to the school?]. DR's response, "Yes, sir," is obviously intended to be a demonstration of his English language ability but, when the interviewer continues in Spanish, he has no difficulty in following the former's lead:

> DR:  Yes, sir.
>
> RJ:  ¿Poquito o bastante? [A little or a lot?]
>
> DR:  Bastante. [A lot.]
>
> RJ:  ¿Como se llama tu maestra? [What is you teacher's name?]
>
> DR:  Miss Ramos.
>
> RJ:  ¿Y la otra señora? [And the other lady?]
>
> DR:  Mrs. Vasquez.

At a later point, DR demonstrates the same language choice flexibility. After thirteen lines in English only, the interviewer continues as follows:

> RJ:  Do you have a nice bike?
>
> DR:  Uh-huh.
>
> RJ:  When did you get it? Christmas? La última, ahora las úl-
>      timas navidades? [the last one, now, this last Christmas?]
>
> DR:  La última. [the last one]
>
> RJ:  Uh-huh, es muy buen regalo. ¿Y tú eres cuidadoso en la
>      calle para que no te vaya a pasar nada? ¿Tu miras bien
>      cuando vienen las coches, sí? [It is a very good present. And
>      you are careful on the street so that you won't have an acci-
>      dent? Do you watch out for the cars, yes?] ¿Carros? [Cars?]
>
> DR:  Si. [Yes.]

RJ: Muy bien. [Very well.] ¿Y dime, tú tienes abuelito y abue-
   lita? [And tell me, do you have a grandpa and a
   grandmama?]
DR: Si. [Yes.]

## Bilingual Continuum

The other interviews reflect different degrees of bilingualism that can be
accommodated between DD and MV or between MV and DR, a continuum of
sorts that shows the transition from covert to active bilingualism. By ar-
ranging the interviewees in their proper sequence, one obtains the following
distribution:

DD→FR→MT, EP, MV, AM, DV→CS, SB, C, PU→DR,

where DD represents the most covert and DR the most overt type of bilingual.
The middle section of the continuum contains five interviewees listed in the
order of increasing overtness and decreasing intrasentential switching. It is
followed by a group of interviewees who display almost identical abilities (1)
to respond to the interviewer's cue (English, Spanish) appropriately, and (2)
to only engage in intersentential switching when language alternation seems
to be unavoidable. The proposed continuum could, therefore, be rearranged to
show not only the relative language choice ability of the child, but also the
feasibility of breaking the continuum down, first into two major categories
and then five minor subcategories.

| INACTIVE | | ACTIVE | | |
|---|---|---|---|---|
| COVERT | PASSIVE | INTRA | INTER | SUPERIOR |
| | | DV | | |
| DD | FR | AM | CS<br>SB<br>CV<br>PU | DR |
| | | MV | | |
| | | EP | | |
| | | MT | | |

This illustrates the language choice development that the bilingual child un-
dergoes at his/her own pace as he/she is immersed in a favorable bilingual
setting.

These observations seem to suggest that it is feasible to categorize bilingual children in light of their degree of bilinguality in order to monitor their dual language development as they move from inactive to active bilingualism. The child who comprehends the home language but cannot bring him/herself to actually use it, that is, the *passive* bilingual, is one step ahead of the *covert* bilingual, who rejects the home language by pretending not to speak it. They resemble one another, however, in that they do not actually use the language despite the basic, shared familiarity with it. Hence, *inactive bilingualism* seems to be an appropriate term to describe this state of affairs. The transition from *covert* to *passive* bilingualism is, therefore, only a minor step forward, mostly attitudinal in nature, for it never reaches the point of vernacular language use. *Active bilingualism*, in turn, shows a strong desire on the part of the child to communicate in the home language in spite of certain limitations, such as a limited lexicon or immature grammatical structures. *Intrasentential* codeswitching helps him/her to overcome these shortcomings. The advance to the *intra* category from inactive bilingualism represents a major step in dual language development. It is upgraded further when the child succeeds in staying in one language for at least one sentence. As one reads the interview transcriptions of MT, EP, MV, AM, and DV, the gradual decrease of *intra*sentential switching is apparent and, by definition, the increase of intersentential switching. From there it is only a small step to the *superior* category. The greater expertise in bilingual flexibility observed in DR's speech was evidenced not only in the intersententiality of his switching but also in the greater capability in following the lead of the interviewer in alternating between the two languages.

## Bilingual Typologies

The professional literature makes almost no reference to a typology of this nature. Sawyer is the exception, but has not pursued the topic further since 1977. Other bilingual typologies have been discussed, but only in regard to strictly linguistic or semantic criteria. The discussion of the relative dominance of one language among bilinguals has yielded a wide range of views about the nature of bilinguality. The introduction of such terms as *balanced bilingualism*, *bilingual dominance*, *domain*, *diglossia*, and *semi-lingualism* all show the concern of scholars in determining how much knowledge of either language is actually needed for a person to be considered bilingual (Alatis 1970:1–12; Cohen 1975; Fishman 1970:73–90; Dil 1972:307–339).

Scholars have also proposed a bilingual typology that would conceptualize the presence of only one semantic system underlying the bilinguals' two languages. This typological distinction between *coordinate* and *compound* bilinguals has been justified on the basis of when and/or where the two languages were first acquired (Alatis 1970:25–45; Hernández-Chávez 1975: 165–66; Jacobson 1975, ERIC ED 115112; Jakobovits 1968; Dil 1972:300–30; Ewton and Ornstein 1970:138–39; Shaffer 1974; Weinreich 1968). Neither typology captures what is here proposed, that is, the retrieval and/or identification of a language of low prestige and the simultaneous development of that language in conjunction with the mainstream code in order to assist the teacher in his/her effort to upgrade the child's dual language development.

### Deviations From School Language

It is not within the scope of this paper to deal in detail with the child's actual language development and, in particular, with the extent to which his/her structures deviate from *school English* and Spanish grammar, but a brief reference to the standardness of their grammar may be in order. No flagrant violations of standard grammar, either in English or in Spanish, were detected in the dialog excerpts above. There is a remarkable difference between the language data gathered here and those discussed by Andrew D. Cohen (1975: 167–218) in his description of the Redwood City Project. Some instances of child language are found and some interference can be traced to the occurrences of a few intrasentential switches. Nonstandard dialect of the kind reported in Cohen, black vernacular English, is virtually nonexistent, because the student population in the project is 100 percent Mexican American.

The importance of assessing deviations from the school language in greater detail has been recognized and reported.[3] Not attitudinal, but linguistic criteria are applied to a number of recorded samples of student talk. This new corpus included "five class segments consisting of a total of 3,844 words . . . recorded on audio-tapes. The recordings represent two Math classes, two Social Studies classes, and one Science class" (1983:9). The analysis of the recorded student talk revealed only five minimally deviant responses, four in Spanish and one in English, with deviations apparently "attributable to child language rather than lack of language proficiency due to other-language dominance" (ibid.:13). It is therefore concluded in the cited study that the children's responses, in spite of their brevity, conform to school standards and do not reflect grammatical deviations of importance. The mentioned *deviant* structures in Spanish found in the cited corpus are the following:

[7]    Sumar el 3 y [el] 2 [To add three and two] (II, A:8).
[13]  Trabaja en [cosas de] guerra. [He works in (matters of) war.] (III, E:9).

---

3. Rodolfo Jacobson, "Intersentential Codeswitching: An Educationally Justifiable Strategy." American Education Research Association Conference, Montreal, Canada, 1983.

[20] Le habla y le dice que como que [necesita que le traigan] una
tierra. [He talks to him and tells him that (he needs to bring him)
dirt] (III, G:14).

[22] Cuando estan mal(os). [When they are ill] (III, G:33).

Therefore, on the basis of the data gathered here, as well as for the cited
Montreal study, it appears that the language is being retrieved almost in its
complete form.

### Fluency

The decrease in Spanish fluency reported by González and Maez (1980)
has not been observed among the children of the project, probably due to the
fact that, at the kindergarten level, Spanish was the medium of instruction 90
percent of the time and, in the first two primary grades, Spanish continued to
be used roughly half of the time. Hence, the phenomenon observed was one
of increased proficiency and not of loss. The degree of fluency, in turn, has
not been measured, since that would have required the comparison of pre- and
post-data of Spanish language fluency that was not a part of the actual evaluation design. Each child, however, appeared to have increased his/her entry
level fluency, and lack of fluency in Spanish was only observed among the
covert and the passive. As for the active bilinguals, a distinction between the
fluent and the nonfluent seems to lack importance for the purpose of the present
study. The covert and the passive bilinguals are, by definition, nonfluent as
neither, for whatever reason, will speak the language. The *intra, inter* and
*superior* bilinguals all exhibit native or nativelike fluency although not necessarily with equal grammatical and/or lexical insights into the language. *Fluency* and *proficiency* differ in the sense that a speaker with a high level of
language proficiency is not necessarily a fluent speaker and a fluent speaker is
not necessarily proficient in all phonological, structural, and semantic aspects
of the language. González and Maez seem to view fluency and proficiency as
identical when they argue that

> as he/she [the learner] is exposed to English formally and through in-
> creased contact with English-speaking peers, he/she begins to gain *flu-
> ency* in English and because of reduced opportunities to communicate
> ·in Spanish, begins to lose proficiency in Spanish (1980:132; italics
> mine).

Furthermore, the target population in González and Maez' study "because of
reduced opportunities to communicate in Spanish" evidently differs from the
one in this study where *increased* opportunities to communicate in Spanish
are provided and fluency as well as proficiency are developed concurrently.

To what extent has the instructional method used had an impact on the child's bilingual achievement? The following diagram identifies the methodological approaches, LSA and NCA, through which the interviewees have learned:

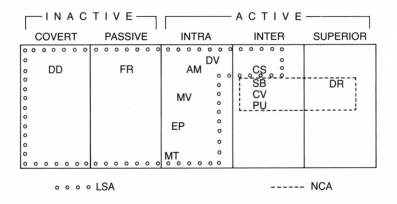

The children who separated the two languages in their school subjects are spread out over four subtypes with heavy concentration in *intra*. Only one child has been evaluated as an *active inter* bilingual. On the other hand, those who used the two languages concurrently, switching according to the pre-established pattern, are all concentrated in the sections *inter* and *superior*. If future studies arrive at similar findings, it might be possible to argue much more strongly in favor of the NCA method.

## OPTIMUM CLIMATE FOR LEARNING THROUGH TWO LANGUAGES

The importance of providing a favorable psychological climate for the student to retrieve or recover the home language, so that language can be used in the classroom and assists the bilingual teacher in developing it further has been stressed. The development of the home language, say, Spanish, is crucial for cognitive/conceptual growth and this, in turn, will facilitate the academic achievement in English. In reference to work in Laredo, special emphasis was placed on the retrieval of the home language where children were first reluctant to use it in class. Finally, an analysis of a series of interviews with children was included to show that the proper climate promotes bilinguality among children who otherwise might lose the language whose further development is crucial for academic achievement in the mainstream setting. A number of additional issues discussed in the professional literature (Cohen 1975; González and Maez 1980; Krashen 1981) were reviewed which shed further light on the unique character of the cited Title VII Project. It now remains to show, in light of the previous discussion, which basic elements should be emphasized in a bilingual program to optimize the psychological climate, so that inactive bilinguals may become active and their bilingual overtness can be instrumental to improved academic achievement.

The basic elements in need of constant attention are:

(1) the time factor, because of its psychological impact;
(2) language distribution with regard to school subjects;
(3) parallel language development;
(4) sociolinguistic sensitivity;
(5) teacher's/aide's proficiency in home language, including the knowledge of regional *and* standard forms;
(6) teacher's/aide's bilingual performance;
(7) acceptance of either language as a medium of instruction;
(8) good use of equipment and materials;
(9) proper physical appearance of the classroom; and
(10) parental support.

Since several of these elements are somewhat repetitive and have been discussed in the survey of Laredo, a few brief statements should suffice. The *time* element requires careful consideration to avoid assessments, on the part of the students, concerning the relative value of either language. The excessive use of English may suggest to the child that Spanish is worth little and may as well be forgotten. The decrease-increase pattern tells the child a similar story and may encourage underestimation of the importance of the home language for academic achievement in the upper grades. Therefore, *balance* and *constancy* seem to be crucial notions to consider when the amount of time to be devoted to each language is decided.

The *language distribution* factor is resolved most naturally in NCA, because every school subject, excluding language arts, is taught in both languages, allowing equal time to each. LSA, on the other hand, faces the problem of requiring a decision as to which subjects will be taught in the home language and which in the majority language. It is difficult to make a convincing case for Spanish as a medium of instruction in social studies, and English for math and science, as was done in the comparison school. Does Spanish lack the preciseness of a language appropriate for the work in the sciences? Is English a foreign medium when local or regional events are explored? Even if one agrees that the choice is entirely random and that neither impreciseness nor foreignness is the rationale for it, the child is acquiring the linguistic tools to do the sciences *only* in English and the social studies *only* in Spanish. In any event, it is no easy decision to split the curriculum to accommodate two languages. On the other hand, to teach everything in the two languages is also an impossibility. The day is not long enough to do everything twice and such redundancy is undesirable.

*Parallel language development* is a valuable objective, because it pursues the growth of the home language in conjunction with the acquisition of the majority language. As Spanish is developed further, important concepts are learned effectively and can be transferred to the second language to provide the child with the academic tools for later years. Knowing both languages well and using them freely in the classroom will make the child feel good about him/herself. As a matter of fact, it will develop in the child the *sociolinguistic sensitivity* that everybody needs to use language properly in social context. The child thus learns to make socially appropriate decisions as to what to say, to whom, when, where, and in which language. No bilingual can afford not to learn such a lesson. *The teacher and aide's proficiency* in the home language is a prerequisite for vernacular language use. Lack of fluency in the child's home language, in turn, promotes the shift to the majority language, since neither the child feels at ease in listening to, nor the teacher feels comfortable in speaking, a language that does not flow naturally. *The teacher and the aide's bilingual performance* in class and outside of class serve as models for the child. By observing them alternate meaningfully between the two languages, the child comes to appreciate linguistic versatility and mimic it whenever he/she can. The influential role of the adult in the classroom can be put to no better use, and language attitudes are thus modified almost unconsciously. *The acceptance of either language as a medium of instruction* emphasizes the importance of knowledge over form. What is said, not how it is said, convinces the child that he/she can learn math and science, as well as social studies, through either language and, by the same token, also retrieve the knowledge in either language without penalty.

The *good use of equipment and materials* enhances any class. In view of the recent concern for bilingual methodology, however, the use of video cameras, audio-tape recorders, film and filmstrip projectors, record players, and so forth has come to play a very crucial role. At the same time, it is necessary for the teacher and the aide to utilize materials that will allow the children, at their individual pace, to advance in Spanish as well as English. The *physical appearance* of a classroom should reveal to children, teachers, aides, school personnel, parents, and the community that two languages are the adopted media of instruction. Colorful decorations utilizing both Spanish and English have a surprising effect on the child and can set the mood for redefining the language situation in class. In other words, the diglossic separation between home and school may thus be reconsidered and language choice viewed on the basis of social interaction criteria. Finally, *parental support* holds a strong guarantee that the work accomplished in school is not destroyed as the child returns home. Thus, parental approval strengthens the program, as this is the school's only way to elicit support from the immediate community with respect to the educational, linguistic, and social development of the children.

These ten variables have emerged significantly during the implementation of the Title VII Demonstration Project. The degree of success in dealing with them has been found to be crucial for the establishment of the psychological climate in which bilingualism can thrive. The mere presence of two languages in a bilingual program does not suffice unless the affective portion of such a program is also controlled in order to allow for the child's total growth.

The success of home language retrieval and the further development of the recovered vernacular which will enable the child to reach the threshold level in that language is crucial for the full acquisition of English as needed for academic achievement. Far too little attention has been paid to the affective side of first language recovery of those students who are reluctant to speak it in public. The analysis of a random sample of interviews with children has shown that, not three, but five bilingual types can be identified in tracing the child's route from inactive to active bilingualism when the psychological climate is found to be favorable. The variables controlling such a climate were recognized as the Title VII Demonstration Project in Bilingual Instructional Methodology was conducted. More studies of this nature should be undertaken to better understand how inactive bilinguals may become active ones and how their recovered vernacular can serve as a better foundation for a second language acquisition.

## REFERENCES

Alatis, James E., ed. *Bilingualism and Language Contact: Anthropological, Linguistic, Psychological and Sociological Aspects* 21st. Annual Round Table, Washington, D.C.: Georgetown University Press, 1970.

Aronsson, Karin. 1978 Language concepts and children's classification strategies in *Dissertation Series*, Lund University, Lund, Sweden.

Cohen, Andrew D. 1975 *A Sociolinguistic Approach to Bilingual Education*. Rowley, MA: Newbury House.

Cummins, James. 1979 Cognitive/Academic language proficiency, linguistic interdependence, the optimal age question and some other matters. *Working Papers in Bilingualism*, No. 19.

―――. 1980 The entry and exit fallacy in bilingual education. NABE Journal, 4.25–29.

————. 1982 Conceptual and linguistic foundations of language assessment. Paper presented at the Second Annual Language Assessment Institute, Chicago, IL, June 28–30.

Dil, Anwar S., ed. 1972 *The Ecology of Language* Stanford University Press.

Ewton, Jr., Ralph W. and Jacob Ornstein, eds. 1970 *Studies in Language and Linguistics* 1969–70. El Paso, TX.: The University of Texas.

Fishman, Joshua 1970 *Sociolinguistics, a brief introduction* Rowley, MA: Newbury House Publishers.

Giglioli, Pier 1972 *Language and Social Context* Penguin, New York, N.Y.

González, Gustavo and Lento F. Maez. "To Switch or not to Switch: the role of code-switching in the elementary bilingual classroom" in R. Padilla, ed., 1980.

Hoffer, Bates and Betty Lou Dubois, eds. 1977 *Southwest Areal Linguistics Then and Now*, San Antonio, TX.: Trinity University.

Jacobson, Rodolfo. 1975 Semantic Compounding in the Speech of Mexican-American Bilinguals: A reexamination of the compound-coordinate distinction ERIC ED115112.

————. 1978 The social implications of intra-sentential code-switching in Romo and Paredes, eds. *New Directions in Chicano Scholarship*, University of California, San Diego, CA.

————. 1982a The implementation of a bilingual instruction model *The New Concurrent Approach* in Padilla, ed. *Bilingual Education Technology*, Eastern Michigan University, Ypsilanti, MI.

————. 1982b The role of the vernacular in transitional bilingual education in Hartford, Valdman and Foster, eds. *Issues in International Bilingual Education: the Role of the Vernacular*, New York: Plenum.

————. 1982c Promoting concept and language development in the classroom. Paper presented at the Second Annual Language Assessment Institute, Chicago, IL, June 28–30.

————. 1983 "Intersentential Codeswitching—an educationally justifiable strategy." Paper presented at the AERA Conference, April 14, 1983, Montreal, Canada.

Jakobovits, Leon A. 1968 "Dimensionality of Compound-coordinate Bilingualism." *Language Learning*, Special Issue 3 (August).

Krashen, Stephen 1981 *Second Language Acquisition and Second Language Learning* Oxford, England: Pergamon Press.

Labov, William 1969 The Logic of non-standard English *Georgetown Monograph on Language and Linguistics*, Vol. 22, Georgetown University, Washington, D.C.

Saville, Muriel R., and Rudolph C. Troike 1971 *A Handbook of Bilingual Education* Revised edition, TESOL, Washington, D.C.

Sawyer, Janet B. 1977 The implications of passive and covert bilingualism for bilingual education, in Hoffer and Dubois, eds. *Southwest Areal Linguistics Then and Now*, Trinity University, San Antonio, TX.

Shaffer, Douglas 1974 "Is Bilingualism Compound or Coordinate?" (Unpublished manuscript)

Skutnabb-Kangas, Tove 1978 Semilingualism and the education of migrant children as a means of reproducing the caste of assembly line workers, in Dittmar, Harberland, Skutnabb-Kangas and Teleman, eds. *Papers from the First Scandinavian-German Symposium on the Language of Immigrant Workers and their Children* Universitets Center, Roskilde, Denmark.

————. and P. Toukomaa 1976 "Teaching migrant children's mother tongue and learning the language of the host country in the context of the socio-cultural situation of the migrant family." Research Report 19 Tampere, Finland: University of Tampere.

University of Texas at San Antonio 1981 *A Title VII Demonstration Programs Proposal in Bilingual Teaching Methodology* (mimeo)

Weinreich, Uriel 1968 *Languages in Contact*. The Hague, Netherlands: Mouton & Co.

# 8.
# A Holistic Supervisory Model for Bilingual Programs

*Josefina Villamil Tinajero and Maria Gonzalez-Baker*

RESEARCH IN THE AREA OF instructional supervision within the context of bilingual education is sorely needed. While a recent review of bilingual education research revealed an increase in the number of studies dealing with teaching methodology, curriculum, and language acquisition theory, supervision of teaching in bilingual programs was mentioned only occasionally in studies related to teacher training.

In a report to the American Psychological Association (APA) on the "Effectiveness of Bilingual Education: Policy Implementations of Recent Research," during its 90th Annual Convention in Washington, D.C., Hilliard (1982) argued that what is needed in the improvement of education—particularly bilingual education—is increased research which deals with leadership in the improvement of instruction. He suggested that too much faith has been placed in the capacity of current bilingual education research to effectively assess programs and methods. Policies which can affect the future of bilingual education are being formulated on the basis of research which is too limited in scope to truly judge its effectiveness (Baker and de Kanter 1981; Hilliard 1982).

One particularly significant study which supports these same arguments and pointedly deals with the need for supervision of bilingual programs was conducted by Leonard Valverde (1979). In a three-month survey of bilingual programs in three states—California, Arizona, and Texas—where most bilingual programs exist, Valverde attempted to determine the extent of instructional supervision in bilingual education. He discovered that supervision of instruction is, in fact, one of the most neglected aspects in the process of implementing dual-language programs in the public schools. The same study also concluded that current practices in supervision of bilingual teaching were random, unsystematic, and in most cases virtually nonexistent. Valverde proposed that major deficiencies in the supervision of these programs could be removed by more clearly defining the roles, relationships, and responsibilities of supervisory staff and by providing relevant formal training and guided field experience.

A recent interview with Valverde indicated that since the date of his publication, "Instructional Supervision in Bilingual Education: A New Focus for the 1980's," little progress or follow-up research has been made in the supervision of bilingual teachers. Valverde emphasized that the importance of high quality instructional supervision in all educational programs is unquestionable. He believes that those interested in quality bilingual education should also direct more time and effort to the leadership sector through instructional supervision. Through quality instructional supervision, many of the major problems facing bilingual education could begin to be resolved. Supervision, when properly practiced, can provide a mechanism to promote the growth of instructional staff members, improve the instructional program for bilingual learners, and foster improved curriculum development.

Many aspects of bilingual programs supervision are in need of attention. Observations of bilingual teachers and supervisors, made prior to and during the present study, support some of the same contentions which surround general instructional supervision in regular programs: teachers and supervisors need to develop a more productive relationship.

Research studies have indicated that supervisors and teachers hold different views regarding supervisory effectiveness. Comments and observations frequently made by bilingual teachers parallel those criticisms expressed by regular program teachers in a study by Blumberg (1974). In this study, teachers stated that supervisors seem to be out of touch with the classroom; much of what is communicated involves procedural trivia; supervisors avoid teachers, which makes teachers think that supervisors are insecure; and supervisors particularly lack interpersonal communication skills.

A more recent study by Blumberg (1980) indicated that supervisors generally lack training to fulfill most of their duties and responsibilities. If supervisors are not technically competent in the performance of those tasks most directly related to teacher's work and to the improvement of it, then teachers and supervisors tend to avoid one another (Alfonso and Goldsberry 1982). Studies by Ritz and Cashell (1980) attribute problems in supervision to the process through which supervisors are selected. Their studies revealed that very few school systems selected instructional supervisors on the basis of their human relations skills; most acquire their new positions as a result of demonstrated success in the classroom, which does not assure success as a supervisor. Ritz and Cashell contend that *success* in the educational sense is more closely related to the formal responsibilities of supervision than to successful teaching experience. They also noted that only the rare school district rewarded a supervisor for his or her emphasis on interpersonal/communication activities. Valverde (1979) made similar observations in his study of supervision in bilingual education. The problems in supervision of bilingual education programs arising from lack of training are further compounded by the fact that there are not enough supervisors available to provide the necessary support to the classroom teacher.

While much is made of the importance of instructional supervision in the field of education, in bilingual programs the teacher sees little of it. In Texas, for example, the study by Valverde (1979) showed the ratio between bilingual classroom teachers and supervisors to be approximately 50:1. It was also found that only 5 percent of the instructional staff were certified by the Texas Education Agency as having successfully completed an academic program in supervision, and that, in fact, many of the Texas school districts circumvent the requirement for supervisor credentials by appointing instructional support staff as *resource teachers*.

Bilingual education involves many complex, difficult issues that have been little, or insufficiently, studied; the need for additional research is great. Educators involved in bilingual program implementation have faced numerous problems beyond the realm of instructional supervision. Many of the original problems and pressures which challenged the concept of bilingual education from the onset are still present today. Although the need for the development of leadership and supervisory competencies in bilingual education has not been sufficiently expressed in the literature, those who work closely with bilingual teachers agree that the time has come to place instructional leadership, through proper supervision, high on the list of priorities if bilingual education is to gain credibility with school administrators, teachers, and the community as a whole. Bilingual educators and researchers must now look beyond the importance of competencies solely for classroom teachers and realize the importance of competent supervisors and instructional leaders.

It has been a number of years since the publication of Valverde's (1979) study and the state of the art of instructional supervision of dual-language programs is still unstable and relatively undefined. However, conditions for focusing on the field of supervision are far better today than they were five years ago. The additional years of research and field experience have improved services to bilingual classroom teachers and paraprofessionals in terms of materials, inservice training, teaching methodology, teacher competencies, and student language assessment. The fact that these areas have been strengthened has paved the way for a clearer delineation of the role of supervision within the bilingual context.

This work does not attempt to deal with large numbers of socio-political factors and community cross-pressures which often affect the supervision of bilingual programs, nor does it focus on the entire scope of general instructional supervisory competencies required to fulfill other supervisory tasks.[1] Instead, this work proposes a framework from which theories, concepts, and skills can be defined for improving bilingual instruction in the *clinic* or classroom setting. The proposed framework will draw on the basic principles of clinical and developmental supervision, since supervision in this approach is field-based and can be specifically directed to supervisors, bilingual classroom teachers, and student teachers. This type of framework can offer practical solutions to those programs in the local school districts which have bilingual supervisors and to institutions of higher education that are involved in the training and certification of bilingual student teachers. Ultimately, the goal of this work is to encourage bilingual researchers and educators alike, to use enlightened forms of human interaction for the purpose of developing instructional leadership.

The principles and procedures of clinical supervision inherent in the proposed framework can provide clarity and specificity of competencies, roles, and responsibilities needed for direct, in-class supervision of the bilingual teacher or student teacher. If clinical supervision is practiced in light of what is currently known regarding teacher concerns and teacher stages of development, it has the potential of improving the quality of instruction which is currently being provided to children of limited English proficiency.

## CLINICAL AND DEVELOPMENTAL SUPERVISION IN BILINGUAL EDUCATION

Clinical supervision in bilingual education was first suggested by Valverde (1978a) as a possible mode for providing staff development within the classroom. The clinical approach for supervising teachers was developed in the 1960s by Morris Cogan and a group of colleagues at Harvard University. Later, Goldhammer *et al.* modified the clinical cycle. According to Goldhammer, clinical supervision involves a five-step process designed to help the teacher identify and clarify problems, receive feedback from the supervisor, and develop solutions, with the help of the teacher. The major theory and principles underlying clinical supervision are described in detail in two books: Morris Cogan's *Clinical Supervision* (1973) and Robert Goldhammer's *Clinical Supervision: Special Methods for Supervision of Teachers* (1980).

Goldhammer defined clinical supervision as that phase of instructional su-

---

1. For a more comprehensive list of supervisory competencies needed in bilingual programs refer to Leonard A. Valverde, "Supervision of Instruction in Bilingual Programs," in *Bilingual Education for Latinos*, Washington, D.C.: Association for Supervision and Curriculum Development, 1978, pp. 74–77.

pervision which draws its data from firsthand observation of actual teaching events and recurring teaching patterns. It involves face-to-face interaction between the supervisor and teacher in the analysis of teaching behaviors and activities for instructional improvement.

Clinical supervision more clearly defines, as well as prescribes, the role of the teacher and supervisor. According to Goldhammer the following nine characteristics or notions are generally associated with clinical supervision; it

> is a technology for improving instruction;
> is a deliberate intervention into the instructional process;
> is goal-oriented, combining school and personal growth needs;
> assumes a working relationship between teacher and supervisor;
> requires mutual trust, as reflected in understanding support and commitment for growth;
> is systematic, yet requires a flexible and continuously changing methodology;
> creates productive tension for bridging the *real/ideal* gap;
> assumes the supervisor knows more about instruction and learning than the teacher; and
> requires training for the supervisor.

The basic clinical sequence of supervision model described by Goldhammer is comprised of five stages. By applying this sequence to various mutually identified instructional problems the teacher and supervisor are involved in the *cycle of supervision*. The sequence consists of the following five stages: (1) preobservation conference; (2) observation; (3) analysis and strategy; (4) supervision conference; and (5) post-conference analysis.[2]

Cogan (1973) advised that any one of the steps in the cycle may be altered or omitted, or new procedures instituted depending on the nature of the situation or on the successful development of working relationships between the supervisor and the teacher. Garman (1982) warns that care must be taken to ensure that the method of clinical supervision and the spirit with which it is practiced does not become ritualistic or mechanical in nature. Most educators realize that no single approach to supervision can address the myriad problems that teachers face in their day-to-day responsibilities. If supervision is to be effective, the approach must be flexible and sensitive to the ever-changing conditions in the classroom.

Recent studies by educators interested in supervision of adult learners (Loucks 1979; Glickman 1980) have suggested adding the developmental

2. For a summary of each stage of the cycle, refer to Robert Goldhammer *et al.* "The Clinical Supervision Cycle: An Overview," in *Clinical Supervision: Special Methods for the Supervision of Teachers*. New York: Holt, Rinehart, and Winston, 1980, pp. 208–11.

**TABLE 8.1**
**Simplified Stages of Teacher Development**

| Thought | Egocentric ———————————————————— Altruistic | | |
|---------|-----------|-----------|-----------|
| Concern | Self Adequacy | Classroom | Other students & teachers |
| Stage   | I | II | III |

dimension to clinical supervision. Glickman, for example, believes that it is necessary to consider specific stages of teacher development before defining supervisory behavior. This view is supported by the pilot research studies done by Frances Fuller (1969) with beginning teachers and successful experienced teachers. These studies parallel Piaget's studies of development in children. The Fuller research shows that the child development progression from egocentric to altruistic thinking recapitulates itself when adults enter a new career. Glickman illustrates in Table 8.1 how teacher levels of concern shift as they progress through the three stages of development along the Piagetian continuum—from self-adequacy, to the classroom, and finally to other students and teachers. Fuller noted that student teachers tended to always remain at the lower level of the developmental continuum, while the developmental stage of inservice teachers tended to range from one extreme to the other. Glickman is careful to note that the stages illustrated here are not all-inclusive and that there is often some overlap from one to the next, as well as a possibility of regression when obstacles become too great.

According to Glickman, classroom supervision can be more effective when it is practiced with a developmental approach. He proposes that supervisory behavior should match the developmental stage of the teacher. The nature of the activities that occur within each of the stages of clinical supervision have a set of purposes and possibilities which encourage the supervisor to incorporate strategies for matching supervisory behavior with the appropriate stages of development of the teacher. As the supervisor progresses through the stages in the clinical supervision cycle, the supervisory behavior is tailored to the individual teacher. Generally, supervisory behavior can be grouped into three somewhat simplified models, categorized as directive, collaborative, or nondirective. The directive model proposes supervisory behaviors that are almost exclusively asserted by the supervisor, such as enforcing standards of teacher competency by modeling, directing, and measuring proficiency levels. The collaborative model advocates that the roles and responsibilities in the supervisor/teacher relationship be based on equality. Any change in the classroom environment is mutually planned and both teacher and supervisor share in presenting, interacting, and evaluating the outcomes. The nondirective model suggests that the supervisory behavior be of minimal influence—a listener, nonjudgmental clarifier, and encourager of teacher decisions. Thus the super-

**TABLE 8.2**
**Stages of Concern:**
**Typical Expressions of Concern About the Innovation**

| Stages of Concern | Expressions of Concern |
| --- | --- |
| 6 Refocusing | I have some ideas about something that would work even better. |
| 5 Collaboration | I am concerned about relating what I am doing with what other teachers are doing. |
| 4 Consequence | How is my use of time affecting students? |
| 3 Management | I seem to be spending all my time getting material ready. |
| 2 Personal | How will using it affect me? |
| 1 Informational | I would like to know more about it. |
| 0 Awareness | I am not concerned about it (the innovation). |

visor decreases or increases the degree of influence based on the teacher's own perception, thoughts, and concerns of his or her own competency.

Hall, Wallace, and Dossett (1973) applied the concept of teacher development and level of concern based on Fuller's earlier work with teachers involved in instructional innovations. Hall, Wallace, and Dossett developed the Concerns Based Adoption Model which identified seven stages of concern about the innovations (Table 8.2). Dominguez et al. (1980) and Acosta (1981) utilized these concepts with bilingual teachers. They administered the stages of concern questionnaire[3] to bilingual teachers in various school districts in Texas. The purpose of their study was to determine the level of concern about bilingual education and to determine the relationship of selected variables to the type of concern expressed. The researchers wanted to establish the extent of the commitment of bilingual program participants. This kind of information is helpful in identifying the type of staff development activities needed for bilingual program improvement.

By understanding and analyzing the stages of teacher or student teacher development, a bilingual supervisor or cooperating teacher can identify the nature and degree of supervisory responsibility needed to better serve individual needs of bilingual teachers or teachers-to-be, instead of using a single uniform approach regardless of the level of development.

The bilingual teacher's and practice teacher's stage of development can be determined by using the Concerns Questionnaire used by Acosta (1981) or by closely analyzing their own statements of concern. Generally, at the beginning stages, the developing bilingual teacher is characterized by concerns for his or

3. A copy of the questionnaire is contained in the Appendix of the doctoral dissertation of Sylvia Acosta, available from Texas A&I University in Kingsville, Texas.

her own adequacy. The most typical questions asked at this stage are largely, "What should I teach?" "Can I face the classroom tomorrow?" "What language do I use to teach what subject?" As bilingual teachers become more secure in their competence, the question might shift to, "How can my teaching in the native language and the target language be of increased benefit to limited English proficiency students?" At this stage the bilingual teacher would want to seek better bilingual materials and utilize other dual-language teaching strategies which could enhance the educational opportunities of students with limited English proficiency. In the final stage of development, the bilingual teacher would be more concerned with the school or profession as a whole and would look for answers to questions which would benefit the field of bilingual education.

Thus far, we have set the context for clinical-developmental supervision of inservice bilingual teachers and to some degree reference has been made to clinical preservice bilingual teacher education. Maxine Greene (1982) describes practice teaching as a cornerstone of education and believes that the nature of student teaching must be further researched since it has possibilities for affecting all of schooling. In a report to a recent conference on student teaching, Robert Hughes, Jr., (1982) stressed that one cannot discuss the education of teachers without giving some consideration to the place and purpose of student teaching or practice teaching. In that report Hughes stated that "the task that emerges in student teaching seems to be one of establishing a theoretical and empirical basis for making decisions about what practice, evaluation, and strategies for supervision lead to the most competent teachers."

A study by Sprinthall and Thies-Sprinthall (1982) describes supervision of student teaching as the most troublesome aspect of programs in teacher education. The study concluded that part of the difficulty in practice teaching seems to derive from an inability to specify the supervisor's role. Either the role is so global, that is, general instructional supervision, or too specific, such as supervision as individualized instruction, that it is most difficult to create, either theoretically or empirically, a systematic supervisory mode. The study further pointed out a need for careful work with inservice cooperating teachers. This is perhaps one of the most significant findings of the study. Sprinthall is currently conducting a first attempt to systematically instruct cooperating teachers through a method designed to raise the developmental stage of teachers. More solid research is needed in defining the responsibilities and behavioral roles of cooperating teachers as they assume supervisory functions in the development of the teacher-to-be. Cooperating teachers must realize that the student teacher also develops in stages from a dependent observer, to a guided apprentice and ultimately to the practitioner who begins to initiate instructional change.

The research studies which have been reviewed in this work amply support the belief that the clinical-developmental approach to supervision is appropriate for preservice and inservice teachers alike. Likewise, in defining an approach or a model of instructional supervision for bilingual programs, a dual model, the clinical developmental model, appears to be the most appropriate since it provides a more holistic approach to supervisor/teacher interaction. The dual model incorporates all of those specific features which are sensitive to the developing teacher. Bilingual teachers and student teachers, like all teachers, are at various stages of development in their career in bilingual education. In Texas, for example, the extent of training which bilingual teachers have received can vary from the thirty-clock-hour institute for endorsment, to a twenty-four-hour university program where bilingual education has been selected as the area of specialization. Experience often varies from teachers just beginning to teachers with twenty-five years or more in the classroom. The perceived level of competence, concerns, and security that bilingual teachers possess is largely dependent on program and experience (Acosta, 1981). A supervisory model for bilingual education programs must be flexible, yet sufficiently structured so as to be comprehensive. A flexible model must provide for all levels of teacher competency. In addition, a supervisory model for bilingual programs must be particularly directed toward the development of a bilingual teacher's competencies in relation to those competencies not mutually exclusive to bilingual education. In some cases these competencies may have been previously acquired by individual teachers. In the State of Texas, for example, the Texas Education Agency has designated thirty-nine specific teacher competencies within the following five areas: (1) language, linguistics, and content; (2) culture; (3) testing methods; (4) instructional methods; and (5) instructional material use.[4] Teachers and supervisors in bilingual programs in Texas must use this list as criteria for improving teacher performance, since they are considered crucial to effective instruction within a bilingual setting. The monitoring of bilingual program implementation by the Texas Education Agency is conducted using a monitoring checklist which includes items from the list of competencies.[5] This checklist can be adapted and utilized by the local school district to help the bilingual teacher and supervisor evaluate teacher performance and mutually define areas for improvement identified during the pre-observation conference of the clinical supervision cycle. A series of competency checklists for developing bilingual competencies in the classroom was also developed and utilized by Golub (1980).

4. See the *Texas State Plan for Bilingual Education*. Texas Education Agency. Austin, Texas, 1978.
5. See "Program Monitoring Report." Texas Education Agency. Austin, Texas, 1981. Items 15A-E.

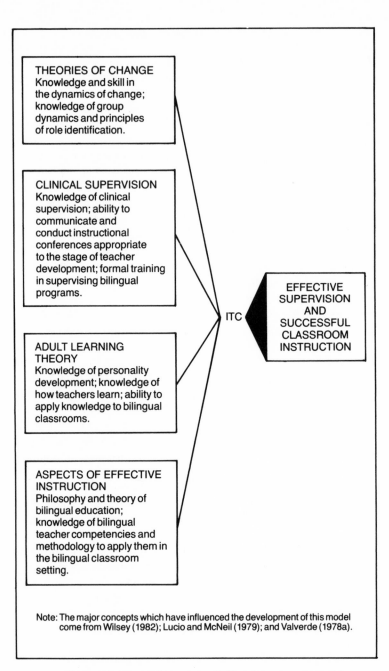

**Figure 8.1** Essential elements of bilingual-program supervision.

In summary, we believe the literature thus far reviewed, and our own experience with the problems of bilingual program implementation, make a compelling case for designing a comprehensive framework for developing field-based bilingual supervisory competencies. This framework must contain essential elements from (1) theories of change for increasing skills in the dynamics of instructional improvement, for increasing skills in group dynamics, and for understanding the principles of role identification; (2) clinical supervision for increasing the ability to communicate and conduct instructional conferences between teacher or student teacher and supervisor; (3) adult learning theory for increasing the supervisor's understanding of how teachers and prospective teachers learn and how they apply their knowledge to the bilingual instructional setting; and finally, (4) major aspects of effective instruction for increasing the bilingual teacher or student teacher's competency based on performance criteria. Conceptualization and application of these four areas through the instructional team concept (ITC) with clearly defined roles, relationships, and responsibilities would undoubtedly yield successful classroom instruction (Figure 8.1).

## ROLES, RELATIONSHIPS, AND RESPONSIBILITIES

The success of an educational innovation is largely dependent on programmatic design and direction for its implementation. Valverde (1978) noted that although these two functions are traditionally vested in the persons occupying the leadership positions in bilingual programs, the competencies of these individuals have never been clearly delineated. Valverde responded to the challenge by defining the responsibilities of two individuals with key leadership roles, the school principal and the district bilingual program director. Gonzalez-Baker and Tinajero (1983) discussed in detail the major roles, relationships, and responsibilities of these and five other key individuals involved in supervising the *clinical* aspects of bilingual teachers and student teachers within a clinical-developmental model of supervision.

Conceptualization of the supervisory role in bilingual education may be aided by understanding some of the basic tenets of role theory. Briefly, such theory postulates that a school system is a miniature society in which administrators, supervisors, teachers, and pupils represent positions or offices within the system. Certain rights, duties, and responsibilities are associated with each position. The actions appropriate to the positions are defined as roles. Lucio and McNeil emphasized that a role is linked with the position, not with the person who is temporarily occupying the position. According to them, supervision is itself a distributive function which holders of various positions discharge in different ways. They further explain that at a general level there is

**TABLE 8.3**
**Bilingual Supervision:**
**A Dimension of Behavior in Many Positions**

1. To propose desirable ends or results to be attained.
2. To develop a dual language program and define strategies, methods and procedures that promise to produce the results desired in the academic achievement of limited English proficiency students.
3. To see whether the desired and desirable results actually are obtained from the procedures followed.

| Teacher/ Student Teacher | Cooperating Teacher | Bilingual Supervisor | IHE Supervisor | Bilingual Director | Principal |
|---|---|---|---|---|---|

Source: Adapted from Lucio and McNeil 1979.

a common dimension in the expected role behavior of those who are supervisors, regardless of their position in the school system's organization chart. This common element is what defines the nature of supervision within a school.

In the context of bilingual program implementation, bilingual classroom supervision involves the determination of ends to be sought, the design of dual language instructional methods, procedures, and strategies for effecting the ends, and the assessment of results. Therefore, the major responsibilities of persons involved in bilingual supervision would be to predict what consequences will follow from the introduction of the innovation and to check results to see if predictions are realized. Table 8.3 illustrates the common dimension of bilingual program supervision regardless of who holds that position.

Lucio and McNeil also noted that defining the relationships among persons filling the supervisory roles or functions is perhaps more important than searching for a common supervisory role. It *is not* expected that all of the persons involved in the supervision of bilingual teachers should perform the same supervisory job; instead, it *is* expected that they understand that for the purpose of meeting the educational needs of students with limited English proficiency they must share common goals and objectives and relate to one another within an instructional team concept.

Since the development of teachers ultimately involves both local school districts and institutions of higher education, the responsibilities of personnel in both of these sectors must be examined. Among those examined here are the responsibilities of the principal, the bilingual supervisor from the institution of higher education, the bilingual director, the district bilingual supervisor, the cooperating teacher, the teacher, and the student teacher.

Traditionally, universities and school districts have not worked cooperatively in developing systematic strategies for effecting instructional innovations. The polarization between university academicians and public school practitioners has kept emergent programs, such as bilingual education, from being effectively implemented. In spite of divergent viewpoints, the public schools have historically sought leadership and consultative services from universities in the area of staff development. Perhaps this is largely due to the fact that universities hold the power for recommending the certification of teachers. Nonetheless, both the institution of higher education and the local district have convergent interests in the preparation of teachers and they must join together in the development of instructional leadership for directing effective bilingual classroom practices. The need for a valid and lasting partnership is evident and should be sought by leaders from both institutions.

Valverde (1978) suggests that individuals within the local district establish an instructional team concept (ITC) among staff members working with innovative programs. We suggest that in schools where bilingual student teachers are being trained, the instructional team concept be expanded to include personnel from the institution of higher education. Most educators will agree that the roles, relationships, and responsibilities for the network of individuals involved in training bilingual student teachers, likewise, have never been clearly established. These persons must also perceive and work from the ITC which structures role relations on a functional basis rather than on the traditional decision by decree which is typically practiced with organization charts and traditional job descriptions. The ITC allows program and non-program staff to use their creative thinking power and expertise to make pedagogically sound decisions through quality involvement.

Valverde's ITC model stipulates that decision-making and responsibilities should be designated according to student needs, rather than through the authority bestowed by hierarchical positions. People operating within the ITC would not perceive decisions as flowing from the top down, since there is no top. Communication in the ITC flows within and across those individuals involved in the team. The interaction among team members would require them at times "to be leaders, other times followers, sometimes influentials, and at other occasions minor players."[6]

## Institution of Higher Education Supervisor

In situations where universities have the opportunity to work with the local school districts in training bilingual teachers, the university supervisor

---

6. Additional information on the rationale and benefits of ITC can be found in Leonard A. Valverde "Supervision of Instruction in Bilingual Programs" in *Bilingual Education for Latinos*. Washington, D.C.: ASCD, 1978, pp. 65–80.

should make every effort to provide the leadership for initiating a clinical-developmental model of supervision. The major principles of this model can be introduced to the cooperating teacher by the supervisor at the institution of higher education and shared with the campus supervisor and the building principal. For school districts that are not involved with a university in training student teachers, the principles of clinical-developmental supervision could be introduced by a qualified administrator, supervisor, or consultant who has knowledge and training in this realm of instructional supervision.

The notion that the classroom teacher is the most influential person in the determination of the kind of teacher that the student teacher will become is supported by various educators (Blanco 1977; Golub 1980; Bennie 1972). These educators advocate that the college supervisor may well devote more time working with the cooperating teacher than with the student teacher. Since more than one person is responsible for guiding the student teacher, problems often arise in the area of student teacher evaluation. These problems stem from the differing status relationships within local school districts and institutions of higher education. The best way to resolve these role conflicts is for the supervisor at the institution of higher education and the cooperating teacher to function as a team. In the team approach, they can work out procedures and standards of evaluation and share expertise to introduce a younger colleague-to-be into the profession. While the university bears the legal and institutional responsibility for evaluating and grading the student teaching experience, there must be a clear understanding that the cooperating teacher will have an influential voice in determining the evaluation and grading of the student teacher.

## Cooperating Teacher

This year more bilingual teachers throughout the country will be called on to perform major roles in the professional education of the new generation of teachers of students with limited English proficiency, as well as to help other inservice teachers. Known by such names as cooperating, supervisory, or master bilingual teachers, they supply novices with the background knowledge and benefit of the experience necessary for a beginning proficiency in dual-language teaching.

Heitzmann (1977) states that the cooperating teacher continues to play the key role in the development of the student teacher. It is the cooperating teacher who provides the day-to-day assistance and supervision of the clinical experiences of the prospective teacher as he or she progresses within the pre-teaching and early training stages.

In the context of bilingual classrooms, the cooperating teacher, in addition to being an experienced person who possesses the competencies required for effective bilingual instruction, must also be trained in the dynamics of super-vision. The functions involved in this supervisory role are intensive, personal, and highly individualized; they demand skill, motivation, intelligence, and emotional stability. All competent teachers are not automatically good super-vising teachers. The skills necessary for teaching elementary or even second-ary school students are not identical with those needed in teaching a prospec-tive teacher, or those needed in providing demonstrations, analysis, and evaluation of the teaching act itself. In order to provide proper training for a teacher-to-be, the bilingual cooperating teacher needs to be functioning in a higher stage of development. The concern level of the cooperating bilingual teacher should be well beyond all the vague uncertainties of managing oneself in the classroom. The cooperating teacher should be secure in his or her own professional role, or it will weaken the relationship which must exist during the critical stages when the student teacher begins to acquire the teacher role.

Bennie (1972) states that colleges and universities prefer cooperating teachers who are altruistic enough to want to work with student teachers, who feel a professional duty involved, and who thoroughly enjoy such assignments as cooperating teachers.

When a student teacher is placed in a designated bilingual classroom and is asked to participate as a member of an instructional team practicing the prin-ciples of clinical-developmental supervision, the quality of the practice teach-ing is increased. It is through this unique cooperative effort of training bi-lingual teachers that the goals of bilingual education and the improvement of bilingual programs may be further realized. The presence of an apprentice in a classroom results in an indirect self-evaluation and self-improvement of all the members of the instructional team. Indeed, the cooperating teacher must be a competent bilingual individual, practitioner, and field researcher with skills in supervision as well as in public relations.

### Bilingual Student Teacher

The student teaching experience is the culmination of education and training for the prospective bilingual teacher. The potential value of the practice teaching experience has seldom been questioned. Within a clinical-developmental approach for supervising bilingual student teachers, the expe-rience appears to be even more valuable as the developmental stages of the student teacher and the corresponding supervisory behavior within the clinical cycle are combined to create a harmonious interaction among personnel from both the institution of higher education and the local education agency inter-ested in improving the student teaching program.

Regardless of the time required by the institution of higher education for the student teaching experience, the student teaching program is usually divided into three major stages which provide for gradually experiencing greater responsibility and increasing the complexity of the bilingual teaching tasks. These phases define the role of the student teacher as one of an observer (role identification phase); apprentice (role induction phase); and practitioner (role assumption phase).[7]

As the student teacher progresses through the student teaching experience, he or she also passes through a series of developmental stages of teaching effectiveness which also parallel the student's stages of concern. An awareness of the developmental stages and concerns is helpful to team members from the institution of higher education and the local education agency who have supervisory responsibilities. This awareness enables the instructional team to establish a program which facilitates the student teacher's development.

No aspect of the student teaching experience is more critical for success than that of establishing a special team relationship among the supervisor from the institution of higher education, the bilingual cooperating teacher, and the student teacher. Cooperative planning, feedback, and encouragement are necessary elements which foster this relationship. These elements are inherent in the clinical-developmental approach to supervision. By following the principles of this type of supervision, members of the instructional team are able to share in the responsibility of assisting the student teacher in acquiring, maintaining, and improving the matrix of competencies needed to function effectively as a bilingual teacher. This unique opportunity for interaction between personnel from the institution of higher education and the local education agency has the potential for improving supervisory practices and effectively institutionalizing bilingual programs.

### Local Education Agency Bilingual Program Director

The bilingual program director is involved in the overall administration of the bilingual program in the local school district. The major responsibilities of this role require a variety of administrative duties. However, instructional supervision is also a major responsibility of the bilingual director. The bilingual director must structure and monitor the entire organization of the bilingual program using input from principals, teachers, and supervisors so that information and procedures are specified and made concrete prior to implementation.

In larger districts, the director may have a staff of supervisors, while in smaller districts the director may also need to function as a clinical supervisor of classroom teachers. Informal interviews with program directors in over

---

7. For more details, see *Elementary Student Teaching Handbook*, The University of Texas at El Paso.

forty school districts in South Texas revealed that it creates a severe hardship on the bilingual program when the bilingual director also supervises the classroom teacher.

In schools which participate in student teaching programs, the bilingual director would also need to be involved in coordinating student teacher activities. The opportunity to participate in a student teaching program where the supervisor from the institution of higher education uses the clinical-developmental approach could be of great benefit to the bilingual director. By acquiring the knowledge and skills of a clinical supervisor, the quality of the instructional program would be greatly enhanced. Many school districts, however, do not enjoy the opportunity of student teacher training. Consequently, the bilingual director might not be involved with personnel from the institution of higher education trained in clinical-developmental supervision and, therefore, would need to employ a consultant or an administrator trained to provide assistance in implementing this approach. Valverde (1978b) cites other supervisory duties of the bilingual director which extend beyond clinical supervision.

### Bilingual Supervisor

Perhaps the most complex role in a school is that of supervisor. Supervisors are responsible for so many areas of service that the title is hardly descriptive. It might be wiser not to consider *supervisor* as a title, but as a specialized job that requires specialized training, inasmuch as supervisors must contribute to any area of the school program or to any service required to keep the school running.

In the field of bilingual education, the supervisor is primarily responsible for providing in-class support to classroom teachers. The bilingual supervisor's role is basically as a resource leader. The supervisor must provide expertise to support program development, along with needed information and practical experiences for professional improvement of the teachers he or she supervises. In addition to supervisory functions, the supervisor is also involved in general administrative functions. Lucio and McNeil noted that conditions in school situations do not always permit the operation of the logic-tight compartments of line and staff or authority and influence. In the implementation of bilingual programs, supervisors are sometimes delegated authority and held responsible for results. They must, therefore, hold others responsible for carrying out instructions.

The bilingual supervisor must establish a special professional relationship with the classroom teacher. Cogan describes a variety of relationship patterns between supervisors and teachers. The major ones are as follows: the superior–subordinate relationship; the teacher–student relationship; the counselor–

client relationship; the supervisor as evaluator and rater; the *helping relationship* in supervision; and the clinical supervision, as colleagueship.

In the clinical-developmental mode, the colleague relationship predominates. Instructional change is determined through mutual agreement and mutual trust between professionals. Communication between the teacher and supervisor is privileged and confidential. It is recommended that no reports of the teacher's performance be given to the administration unless it is feared that the teacher poses a threat to the welfare of the students and all the resources have been exhausted by the supervisor to remove the problems. Adherence to confidentiality and the ideals of professionalism will reduce teacher-supervisor anxiety, and energies can be focused on the learning needs of students through their mutual professional development.

### Bilingual Teacher

The major role of the bilingual teacher is that of developer, practitioner, and field researcher. The teacher must provide input and feedback about the bilingual program, the students, and his or her own performance at every step of implementing the innovation.

The continued development and refinement of teacher competencies is crucial to the implementation and institutionalization of emerging programs such as bilingual education. In addition to basic teaching competencies, bilingual teachers must receive special training to meet the linguistic, cultural, and pedagogical needs of the student with limited English proficiency. Cogan (1973) noted that in the implementation of innovative programs, teachers must also be given enough expert help to make such innovations *stick*. He suggests that clinical supervision can facilitate innovative program implementation, and that the competencies required can be systematically and mutually developed and evaluated through the cycle of clinical supervision. Clinical supervision can also provide a relationship of continuing support from his or her colleagues, particularly the bilingual supervisor and the principal, that the bilingual teacher needs.

Ultimately, the role of the bilingual teacher, in responding to the unique needs of limited English-speaking students, is to interact effectively with each component of the educational setting. Additionally, this interaction takes place within the framework of the philosophy and objectives established by board policy, consistent with statutes and standards of regulatory agencies and in accordance with administrative regulations and procedures, to create an educational environment which is conducive to learning and which provides opportunities, strengthens areas of weakness, and extends positive values to each facet of life.

## Principal

An important function of the principal is to exert dynamic leadership to improve the quality of life of each individual within the school (Roe and Drake 1980). Basic to this improvement is the development, implementation, and institutionalization of emerging instructional programs, such as bilingual education, which have the potential for improving instruction of the child with limited English proficiency. As the instructional leader of the school, the principal plays a key leadership role in coordinating the knowledge and abilities of all personnel within the school, as well as reviewing the evidence about how well each individual is or is not succeeding with pupils.

In addition to leadership skills and being knowledgeable in the dynamics of change, Valverde (1978a) states that for a principal to be effective in implementing and institutionalizing emerging programs, a principal must also possess some basic qualities and skills similar to those required of a bilingual teacher. Among the qualities identified by Valverde are a genuine sensitivity toward the culture(s) carried by the students, a thorough knowledge of the philosophy and theory concerning bicultural education and its application, and formal training in administering and supervising bilingual programs. A knowledge of clinical-developmental supervision is also necessary for a principal attempting to implement this type of supervision. The principal must also be willing to practice his or her leadership role within the instructional team concept (ITC). As a member of the ITC, the principal interacts with a group of people who may facilitate the principal's opportunity to build a knowledge base about bilingual education and its supervision. Information on the legal, theoretical, psychological, and conceptual foundations of bilingual education, for example, may be provided by the college supervisor or by the bilingual cooperating teacher. Information on program implementation, scheduling, and supervision of bilingual programs may be provided by the school district supervisor or the program director. The principal, in turn, may share administrative knowledge and leadership skills with other members of the instructional team.

In school districts with student teacher training programs, the principal is also in a strategically important position to influence directly the bilingual student teaching program. He or she can assist the team in setting up criteria to select the cooperating bilingual teachers. Together with other team members, the principal can also evaluate the student teaching program. Through visitations and conferences he or she is able to exercise the same relationship with bilingual teachers that exist with regular faculty members.

The major role, however, of the principal in the implementation of the bilingual program within the school is to serve as liaison, and function as a clarifier and supporter. The principal must monitor communication channels among program personnel and must also be the primary school agent for having materials available in bilingual classrooms when they are needed.

### Specific Roles and Duties of Bilingual Personnel

Specific roles and duties for the network of personnel involved in teaching and in training bilingual teachers and student teachers have never been clearly established. Role conflict and role ambiguity among and between bilingual personnel have been major problems which have prevented the effective implementation of many bilingual programs. The tables of specific roles and duties of ITC members contained in the appendix to this paper were formulated to address this lack of direction and may be used as guidelines in writing job descriptions for bilingual personnel. The lists were developed by analyzing and synthesizing suggestions and recommendations from various sources (Bennie 1972; Valverde 1979; Valverde 1978a; Dull 1981; Cogan 1973; Goldhammer 1980; Lucio and McNeil 1979), as well as from the experiences of the authors.

### THE FRAMEWORK OF CLINICAL-DEVELOPMENTAL SUPERVISION AS A SYSTEM FOR BUILDING INSTRUCTIONAL LEADERSHIP COMPETENCIES

Few educators have advocated the exploration and development of the leadership sector of bilingual programs. Consequently, the leadership component has lagged behind as the instructional component moved ahead in the development of teaching competencies. A system for building instructional leadership and supervisory competencies must be established if bilingual programs are to be effectively implemented. Establishing such a system requires:

> a collaborative effort among a network of people within the institution of higher education and the local education agency;
> a redefinition of the existing approaches to supervision of both preservice and inservice bilingual teacher training;
> that the initiative for making the system operational be forthcoming from both institutions;
> that the roles, relationships, and responsibilities of principals, supervisors, and other personnel from both the institution of higher education and the local education agencies be translated into specific leadership (supervisory) competencies; and
> that procedures for monitoring and evaluating the performance of bilingual supervisors and teachers be specified.

Once systematic procedures are installed for defining supervisory competencies, it is necessary to set a climate which fosters collaboration, coordination, and cooperation among individuals involved.

### Instructional Team Concept: Cooperative Action

The instructional team concept is the mechanism for instructional change
through cooperative effort. Innovations such as bilingual education require
that all of the individuals involved in the training of bilingual personnel possess a common understanding of bilingual program goals. The ITC serves as a
forum within which team members from the institution of higher education
and the local education agencies who are responsible for instruction and
supervision of preservice and inservice bilingual teacher training programs
can work cooperatively toward these goals.

The ITC replaces the traditional leadership roles practiced by administrators
and supervisors alike. It requires that roles, relationships, and responsibilities
be clearly delineated on a functional basis rather than on administrative hier-
archies. Cooperative effort, joint decision-making, mutual support, and communication are the basic principles which undergird the instructional team
concept (Valverde 1979).

Most educators realize that no single approach to supervision can address
the myriad problems that teachers face in their day-to-day responsibilities. If
supervision is to be effective in bilingual education, the approach must be
flexible and sensitive to the ever-changing conditions in the classroom. Our
experience with the problems of bilingual program implementation makes a
compelling case for defining a framework for developing field-based bilingual
supervisory competencies.

### The Framework: Clinical-Developmental Supervision

The existing traditional approaches to supervision of student teachers and
inservice bilingual teachers are unsystematic and generally dysfunctional. Bilingual educators must seek to define alternative modes of supervision which
are change-focused and directed at promoting the development of supervisory
leadership competencies as well as teacher competencies. The supervision of
emergent programs requires procedures for assessment and direct feedback
evaluation of those aspects of instruction that are of concern to teachers,
rather than procedures that concentrate on items on an evaluation form or on
items that are of major concern to the supervisor only.

Clinical and developmental supervision can provide a more direct and
functional approach for improving the performance of bilingual supervisors
and teachers alike. Clinical supervision offers a systematic process that helps

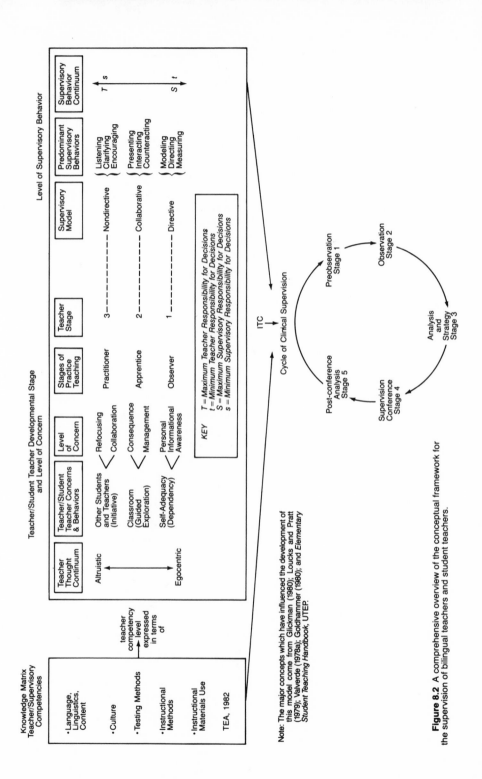

**Figure 8.2** A comprehensive overview of the conceptual framework for the supervision of bilingual teachers and student teachers.

teachers identify and clarify problems, and receive feedback data and mutual support for developing solutions to those problems. Clinical supervision focuses on *what* and *how* teachers teach *as* they teach. The basic method of clinical supervision is systematic rational study and analysis of teaching. The major concepts which clinical supervision provides are planned change, colleagueship, mutuality, direct contact, and skilled service in the laboratory of the teacher's own classroom (Cogan 1973; Goldhammer 1980).

Developmental supervision, on the other hand, is derived from an educational philosophy of progressivism and is premised on stage theory. Developmental supervision offers a framework of concepts from humanist, cognitivist, and behaviorist views of how adults learn. It suggests that there are methods and orientations to learning that are more appropriate than others when determined by purpose, situation, and needs of individuals. Humans learn through self-exploration, collaboration, and conditioning. Research has not (nor will it likely ever) unequivocally established one orientation towards learning as the proven way (Glickman 1981).

The principles of clinical and developmental supervision can be practiced simultaneously to create a dual-supervisory model. In this eclectic model, systematic procedures can be executed in terms of the developmental stage of the bilingual teacher or student teacher. The clinical-developmental approach to supervision is appropriate for preservice and inservice teachers alike. Clinical-developmental supervision is a field-based approach which allows bilingual teachers, student teachers, and supervisors to move through a series of stages to higher degrees of competency. Figure 8.2 provides a comprehensive overview of the proposed conceptual framework for a more systematic approach to the development of supervisory and instructional competencies in the context of bilingual programs.

### Initiating the Process: A Challenge

The initiating responsibility for making clinical-developmental supervision operational in the context of bilingual education needs to be felt by both university and public school educators. Bilingual educators in both institutions need to be more supportive of quality instruction for the limited English proficiency learner. Leaders in the field need to demand improvement of instruction through accountability, competency, and renewed commitment to bilingual program goals. Bilingual teachers, supervisors, and parents, together with university educators, need to look at current practices with a sense of constructive dissatisfaction. Our society must risk disrupting the status quo for the purpose of quality bilingual education. We must hold to the strong opinion that faulty bilingual programs cannot be remedied, satisfactorily, from a distance. We must accept the challenge and the opportunity that intense clinical interaction between teachers and supervisors incorporates more possibilities for yielding higher levels of student achievement. The times call for strong leadership. We must learn to do more with less. As Valverde (1979) so explicitly remarked, "individuals placed in a new structure and required to perform complex behaviors must be given rigorous formal, academic, and on-the-job training." We must choose to use our best talent and invest the next generation of bilingual educators with skills to meet the emerging problems with confidence.

### Process Evaluation in the Clinical-Developmental Model

Bilingual programs have faced numerous problems with traditional approaches to evaluation. Bilingual education has not been evaluated in equitable terms and with pertinent standards of judgment. Typically, evaluation designs focus on product and ignore process evaluation. This limited analysis damages the opportunities for quality programming for minority children.

Bilingual researchers and educators have argued that innovative programs require innovative evaluation procedures. In bilingual-teacher-training programs, educators must attempt to evaluate various other dimensions of the program, which are also directly related to the achievement of bilingual learners, such as the effects of supervision on teaching and the quality of supervisory practices (Gonzalez and Baumanis 1981). Evaluation is perhaps the most salient feature of the proposed clinical-developmental model. Formative or process evaluation is inherent in the clinical supervisory model. The face-to-face analysis of teaching-learning behaviors are unlike the traditional *form* evaluations. The strength of clinical evaluation is vested in the notion that analysis is for the purpose of providing assistance in developing teaching skills and not for the mere arbitrary rating of performance. This removes suspicion, fear, and mistrust and creates a problem-solving atmosphere. Data obtained in a climate of mutual trust will provide measures which will ultimately prove to be more equitable and true.

### A Dual Model

This paper proposed the utilization of two types of supervision—clinical and developmental—for application within a bilingual education context. Whereas each independent model has numerous merits, it is proposed that for bilingual education programs, a dual model would prove more effective. Efforts to develop a delivery mechanism for supervision of bilingual teachers and student teachers could yield multiple benefits to bilingual education personnel—with teacher training programs—and to school districts. We believe that through a network of university field-test programs, utilizing a more holistic approach to supervision, a clearer definition of the role of supervision in bilingual education programs can be realized. The opinion of other educators on the feasibility of collaborating efforts between universities for field testing this endeavor is welcomed. Ultimately, the design of clinical-developmental supervision in the context of bilingual education must be examined more thoroughly for adequacy through research and through critical analysis.

## APPENDIX

### Roles and Duties of the Supervisor at the Institution of Higher Education

Work with personnel from the local education agency on establishing goals for administration of the student teaching program.

Cooperate with the local education agency in formulating roles and responsibilities of the instructional team members.

Participate in the decision making process during the review of selection process for cooperating teachers and assignments of student teachers and ensure that specific criteria are followed.

Assist district personnel in administering questionnaires to determine student teacher and cooperating teacher competence, developmental stage, level of teacher concern, and personality.

Appraise student teacher and cooperating teacher characteristics at entry level.

Introduce the concept of clinical–developmental supervision to campus principal, campus supervisor, cooperating teachers, and student teachers.

Model the use of clinical-developmental supervisory steps and allow the cooperating teacher to observe the clinical cycle while working with the bilingual student teacher to develop a particular competence.

Confer with other school personnel, such as principal, director of instruction, supervisors, etc.

Confer with the cooperating teacher to develop shared procedures and standards for evaluating teacher competence.

Provide consultation services through regular inservice training.

Assess the performance of the student teaching training program and plan experience with school district personnel which will lead to greater understanding and improvement of teaching.

Coordinate university and public school efforts through the director of student teaching at the institution of higher education.

### Roles and Duties of the Cooperating Teacher

Understand the characteristics of bilingual instruction and seek to improve personal competence while working with the student teacher.

Work with the members of the instructional team to establish goals for the administration, operation, and evaluation of the student teaching program.

Confer with the university supervisor regarding the observation and evaluation of the student teacher.

Assist the student teacher to plan activities which will provide the opportunities for the prospective teacher to gradually experience greater responsibility for and complexity in the teaching task.

Serve as a model for the student teacher.

Provide the student teacher with basic information for adjustment to the class and school.

Implement principles of clinical–developmental supervision.

Supervise all clinical experiences of the student teacher.

Confer with the student teacher regarding the progress being made.

Meet periodically with other teachers in the school or school system to openly discuss problems and strategies for solutions.

### Roles and Duties of the Bilingual Student Teacher

Recognize and respect the position of the cooperating teacher and assume responsibilities mutually agreed upon with the cooperating teacher.

Maintain an active interest in the support of the policies and activities of the whole school in order to be a constructive force for the growth and betterment of the limited English proficiency child, the school, and himself or herself.

Work on a day–to–day basis with the cooperating teacher to discuss and plan the instructional program.

Plan and teach lessons incorporating feedback received during the conference cycle of clinical supervision.

Meet with the university supervisor and principal to discuss the student teaching objectives.

Attend university seminars.

Attend meetings which the cooperating teacher attends, according to building policy.

Demonstrate mastery of the competence matrix for bilingual instruction.

Hold conferences with the cooperating teacher and college supervisor.

Discuss the final evaluation with the cooperating teacher and the college supervisor.

Practice the principles of clinical–developmental supervision.

### Roles and Duties of the Bilingual Program Director

Work with personnel from the institution of higher education and the local education agency to establish goals for administration, operation, and evaluation of the student teaching program.

Assist in committee selection of program teachers, teacher aides, and assignment of student teachers to cooperating teachers, when applicable.

Provide training or hire consultants to provide training for improving clinical–developmental supervisory competence of teaching personnel, particularly to the bilingual supervisor and, if applicable, to the cooperating teacher.

Require evidence from supervisors in charge of the bilingual program that observation, feedback, and analysis of teaching are being systematically conducted.

Identify program evaluation procedures and evaluate supervisory and instructional personnel.

Require supervisors and teachers to evaluate the quality and effectiveness of bilingual materials.

Provide timely disbursement of program money to purchase materials and equipment.

Coordinate meetings with supervisors, teachers, and subject matter specialists to discuss teacher training requirements and procedures.

Provide for the teachers' release time from instructional duties for inservice training.

Develop procedures to involve teachers in the decision making process during the implementation of the bilingual program.

Plan, schedule, and document meetings for principals, teachers and supervisors to review program progress and to identify and solve problems.

If no supervisors are available, provide clinical supervision to teachers.

Periodically distribute a newsletter throughout the school system describing the progress of the bilingual program.

### Roles and Duties of the Bilingual Supervisor

Provide evidence of the innovation's appropriateness to the school's goals.

Provide activities designed to deal with existing attitudes and values that are obstacles to the change.

Work within the instructional team for proper selection of program teachers, teacher aides, and assignment of student teachers to cooperating teachers, when applicable.

Assist the staff at the local campus level in planning and implementing the bilingual program.

Cooperate with the principal and staff in identifying and solving instructional problems related to coordination of regular and bilingual programs.

Provide leadership over procedures for bilingual program evaluation.

Develop a well–organized inservice education program concerning the innovation for participating staff.

Assist the school staff in diagnosing the needs of limited English proficiency children, interpreting assessment instruments, and utilizing results for identification and placement.

Assist in the evaluation and selection of instructional programs, materials, and equipment with regard to supporting the bilingual program.

Review any hardware and software carefully with teachers during inservice programs so that teacher acceptance is not jeopardized by ambiguities in how to use various parts of the program.

Focus interaction with teachers on specific instructional strategies, demonstration teaching, content questions, etc., using principles of clinical–developmental supervision.

Provide sound estimates of financial and staffing requirements and reasonable projections of future program costs.

Cooperate with administrators and teachers in formulating roles and responsibilities for team members, as well as for any outside consultant.

Promote positive community relations through effective dissemination of information.

## Roles and Duties of the Bilingual Teacher

Understand the characteristics, theory, and philosophy of bilingual education.

Make ideas known on how to develop and strengthen the communication process and on how to smoothly install the innovation; describe preferences and attitudes toward the proposed innovation in an open, direct, and honest manner.

Communicate questions and concerns to the appropriate members of the instructional team.

Use administrators and supervisors as resources in meeting needs resulting from the innovation.

Work with the principal and supervisory staff to identify and solve problems related to limited English proficiency students.

Administer and analyze oral language proficiency tests to identify limited English proficiency students and group them according to language proficiency and level of cognitive development.

Utilize teaching techniques and classroom strategies to accommodate the various learning styles and modes of the limited English proficiency students.

Teach subject matter in the student's first and second language.

Assist in the selection of programs, equipment, and materials to meet student needs.

Supervise paraprofessionals, aides, and volunteers assigned to the classroom.

Promote positive community relations through effective communication and involvement with parents and community members.

Meet periodically with other teachers in the school system to openly discuss role problems and strategies for solutions.

Visit teachers in other schools using bilingual education strategies to learn what new roles and responsibilities are required for effective implementation.

Use feedback gained through the clinical supervisory cycle for continued improvement in the process of developing the required bilingual teaching competence.

## Roles and Duties of the Principal

Understand the characteristics, theory and philosophy of bilingual education and attend training sessions in order to better support the teachers.

Assess teachers' attitudes, morale, and preferences before implementing the bilingual program.

Design a system by which differing views of teachers, specialists, etc., may be communicated and reconciled prior to implementation.

Develop, with teachers, proposed procedures for gathering evaluative data and for obtaining periodic feedback on the innovation.

Design procedures to obtain teacher input on the tasks to be performed by consultants.

Make sure necessary materials and supplies are available in the classroom before implementation.

Develop plans for teacher training about what to do and expect during the early stages of the program.

Assure that parents are knowledgeable concerning the program.

Assure that teachers receive the recognition they deserve for work in the bilingual program.

Assist in screening potential cooperating teachers who meet the criteria set forth by the university and school district, and assist in setting up procedures for their continued selection.

Participate in the orientation of the student teachers and cooperating teachers assigned to the building.

Act as an advisor to the cooperating teacher and student teacher and in some cases, if problems arise, serve as mediator.

Occasionally analyze strategies being used in clinical–developmental supervision.

Evaluate the quality of conferences which take place between cooperating teacher and student teacher, and at times, become part of that process to make sure it is taking place.

Assist in arrangements for any exchange of ideas among public school personnel and college faculty to ensure that the student teaching program will be continuously improved.

## REFERENCES

Acosta, Sylvia. 1981. *An Investigation of the Stages of Concern Toward Bilingual Education in Selected South Texas Independent School Districts*. Doctoral Dissertation. University Microfilms International. Ann Arbor, Michigan.

Alfonso, Robert J., and Lee Goldsberry. 1982. "Colleagueship in Supervision." In *Supervision of Teaching*, Thomas J. Sergiovanni, ed. Alexandria, Virginia: ASCD, pp. 90–107.

Baker, Keith A., and Adriana A. de Kanter. 1981. *Effectiveness of Bilingual Education: A Review of the Literature*. Final Draft Report. Office of Planning, Budget and Evaluation, U.S. Department of Education.

Bennie, William A. 1972. *Supervising Clinical Experience in the Classroom*. New York: Harper and Row Publishers.

Blanco, George. 1977. *Bilingual Education: Current Perspectives in Education*. Arlington, Virginia: Center for Applied Linguistics.

Blumberg, Arthur. 1974. *Supervisors and Teachers: A Private Cold War*. Berkeley, California: McCutchan Publishing Corporation, pp. 15–16.

Blumberg, Arthur. 1980. *Supervisors and Teachers: A Private Cold War*. Second Edition. Berkeley, California: McCutchan Publishing Corporation.

Cogan, Morris L. *Clinical Supervision*. 1973. Boston: Houghton Mifflin Company.

Dominguez, Domingo, et al. 1980. "Measuring Degree of Implementation of Bilingual Education Programs: Implications for Staff Development and Program Evaluation." *Bilingual Education Paper Series*. Monograph. Evaluation, Dissemination and Assessment Center. California State University of Los Angeles. Volume 4, No. 5, (December).

Dull, Lloyd W. 1981. *Supervision: School Leadership Handbook*. Columbus, Ohio: Charles E. Merill Publishing Company.

*Elementary Student Teaching Handbook*. College of Education. The University of Texas at El Paso. El Paso, Texas.

Fuller, Frances F. 1969. "Concerns of Teachers: A Developmental Conceptualization." *American Educational Research Journal* 6 (March): pp. 207–26.

Garman, Noreen B. 1982. "The Clinical Approach to Supervision," in *Supervision of Teaching* by Thomas J. Sergiovanni. Alexandria, Virginia: ASCD., pp. 35–52.

Glickman, Carl D. 1980. "The Developmental Approach to Supervision." *Educational Leadership*, pp. 178–80.

Glickman, Carl D. 1981. *Developmental Supervision: Alternative Practices for Helping Teachers Improve Instruction*. Alexandria, Virginia. ASCD.

Goldhammer, Robert, et al. 1980. *Clinical Supervision: Special Methods for the Supervision of Teachers*. New York: Holt, Rinehart, and Winston.

Golub, Lester S. 1980. "Teacher Preparation in Bilingual Education," in *Ethnoperspectives in Bilingual Education Research, Volume II: Theory in Bilingual Education*. Edited by Raymond V. Padilla, pp. 388–409. Ypsilanti, Michigan: Eastern Michigan State University, Department of Foreign Languages and Bilingual Studies.

Gonzalez-Baker, Maria and Josefina V. Tinajero. 1983. "A Conceptual Framework for Developing Instructional Leadership Competencies." *Bilingual Education Paper Series*, Monograph. Evaluation, Dissemination and Assessment Center. California State University of Los Angeles. Volume 6, No. 11 (June).

Gonzalez, Juan C. and Dace I. Baumanis. 1981. "Ethics Involved in the Evaluation of Bilingual Education," in *Ethnoperspectives in Bilingual Education Research, Volume II: Theory in Bilingual Education*. Edited by Raymond V. Padilla, pp. 381–95. Ypsilanti, Michigan: Eastern Michigan State University, Department of Foreign Languages and Bilingual Studies.

Greene, Maxine. 1982. "Student Teaching a Human Project: Pursuing Possibilities in Schools," in *Student Teaching: Problems and Promising Practices*. Edited by Gary A. Griffin and Sarah Edwards. Report No. 9015. Austin, Texas: Research and Development Center for Teacher Education. The University of Texas at Austin.

Hall, G. E., R. D. Wallace, and W. A. Dossett. 1973. *A Developmental Conceptualization of the Adoption Process Within Educational Institutions*. Austin, Texas: Research and Development Center for Teacher Education. The University of Texas at Austin.

Heitzmann, William Ray. 1977. *What Research Says to the Teacher: The Classroom Teacher and the Student Teacher*. Washington, D.C.: National Education Association.

Hilliard, Asa. 1982. Remarks made at the American Psychological Association (APA) Seminar on "Effectiveness of Bilingual Education," Washington, D.C. Report entitled "Psychological Association Discusses Effectiveness of Bilingual Education." In *FORUM*. National Clearinghouse for Bilingual Education. Volume 5, No. 9 (October): 1, 3.

Hughes, Robert Jr. 1982. "Student Teaching: The Past as a Window to the Future," *Student Teaching: Problems and Promising Practices*. Edited by Gary A. Griffin and Sara Edwards. Report No. 9015. Austin, Texas: Research and Development Center for Teacher Education. The University of Texas at Austin.

Loucks, Susan and Harold Pratt. 1979. "A Concerns-Based Approach to Curriculum Change." *Educational Leadership* 37 (December), pp. 34–37.

Lucio, William H. and John D. McNeil. 1979. *Supervision in Thought and Action*. New York: McGraw-Hill Book Company.

Ritz, William C. and Jane G. Cashell. 1980. " 'Cold War' Between Supervisors and Teachers?" *Educational Leadership* (October), pp. 77–78.

Roe, William and Thelbert L. Drake. 1980. *The Principalship*. New York: Macmillan Publishing Co.

Sprinthall, Norman and Lois Thies-Sprinthall. 1982. "Educating for Teacher Growth: A Cognitive, Developmental Perspective," in *Alternate Perspective for Research and Program Development in Teacher Education*. Edited by Gary A. Griffin and Hobart Hukill. Summary of Proceedings. Austin, Texas: Research and Development Center for Teacher Education. The University of Texas at Austin.

Texas Education Agency. 1981. "Program Monitoring Report." Austin, Texas.

Texas Education Agency. 1978. *Texas State Plan for Bilingual Education*. Austin, Texas.

Valverde, Leonard A. 1978. "Instructional Leadership for Bicultural Programs: Role Responsibilities and Relationships." *Education and Urban Society* 10 (3): 337–46.

Valverde, Leonard A. 1979. "Instructional Supervision in Bilingual Education: A New Focus for the 1980's." *NABE Journal* 3 (3): 49–60.

Valverde, Leonard A. 1980. "Supervision of Instruction in Bilingual Programs," in *Bilingual Education for Latinos*. Edited by Leonard A. Valverde. Washington, D.C.: Association for Supervision and Curriculum Development, pp. 65–80.

Wilsey, Cathy and Joellen Killion. 1982. "Making Staff Development Programs Work." *Educational Leadership* (October), pp. 36–43.

# 9.
# Opinions of Parents, Teachers, and Principals on Select Features of Bilingual Education

*Adalberto Aguirre, Jr.*

FROM ITS BEGINNING, bilingual education was embedded in controversy. Where some questioned its role within an educational enterprise that was primarily oriented toward a mass audience (Epstein 1980; Edwards 1980), others praised its innovativeness within a constraining, one-dimensional educational environment (Troike 1978; Margulies 1981). But like so many other educational experiments before it, bilingual education has not been able to function apart from controversy long enough to demonstrate what it is capable of accomplishing.

One feature that clearly sets bilingual education apart from general educational practice is the inclusion of parent advisory groups in the school district's formulation of a bilingual education plan (Rodriguez 1979). The inclusion of parent advisory groups in a school district's decision-making activities regarding bilingual education was initially assumed by government bureaucrats, not necessarily educational bureaucrats, as a necessary ingredient for increasing the level of success that a bilingual education program could achieve. While this strategy may have convinced parents of the limited scope of educational decisions by exposing them to the bureaucratic apparatus in educational activity, it failed to: (a) extend the meaning of bilingual education into the social consciousness of parents (Rodriguez 1981); (b) communicate the need to question existing patterns of educational inequality that were rooted in social problems and not in linguistic problems (Adelman 1981); and (c) encourage a collaborative effort between parents and school personnel in the development of bilingual education programs that reflect the concerns of the surrounding language-minority community (Aguirre and Bixler-Marquez 1979).

The purpose of this essay is to explore one facet of a complex process involved in the transition from program definition to program development for bilingual education programs. One implication in the preceding paragraph is that inconsistency in the transition from definition to development can result in competing sets of conceptual images for the same phenomenon. In this essay, then, we will compare the level of consistency among parents, teachers, and principals in the perception of selected features in bilingual education by studying their opinions. This examination will contribute to an area of study that examines competing interpretations of bilingual education (Macias 1976; Aguirre 1980).

## THE STUDY

Since 1981, we have been studying parents', teachers', and principals' opinions of bilingual education in selected school districts within southern California. The study reported in this essay was conducted between October and December 1982 at twenty schools in the cities of Riverside and San Bernardino, which readily identifies these schools as urban in their general social composition.

The participants in the study were: (1) two-hundred Mexican American parents with children enrolled in bilingual classrooms; (2) twenty Mexican American teachers assigned to bilingual classrooms and who have taught continuously in a bilingual program for at least three years; and (3) twenty *non*-Mexican American principals of schools with a bilingual program. Each teacher was randomly selected from a pool of Mexican American teachers assigned to bilingual classrooms at each target school. Ten Mexican American students in the bilingual classroom assigned to the teacher selected for this study were randomly selected in order to generate our sample of Mexican American parents.

The interview format employed with participants in the study was divided into two sections. The first section elicited general information regarding educational, occupational, and social background. The second section was a series of fifteen items concerning features of bilingual education. Each item was read to the participant. To obtain the participant's response to the item, he or she was provided with a three-by-five card on which was printed a five-point scale ranging from *strongly agree* to *strongly disagree*. Each participant was asked to rate each item on the basis of this scale. For this analysis responses have been recorded into three categories: Agree, Disagree, Unsure. By limiting the number of categories, the number of empty cells is reduced, thus enhancing the comparability of the data.

The fifteen items presented to participants in this study were derived from field-testing a set of general observations frequently encountered in the bilingual education literature. For instance, some of the more prominent observations in the literature revolve around the issues of: (a) the school's responsibility in educating the language minority child (Fitzpatrick and Rees 1980; Foster 1976; Fong 1978; Sugerman and Widers 1974); (b) the role of language and culture in the bilingual classroom (Ulibarri 1972; Ramirez 1980; Saville-Troike 1978; Cummins 1980); and (c) the role of the teacher in the bilingual classroom (Cohen 1980; Bernabe 1975; Ringawa 1980). The importance of these three areas to bilingual education research can be assessed by noting the frequency with which they appear as parameters in the description of bilingual education models (Paz 1980; Aguirre 1982).

An initial set of forty-five items was field-tested. The resultant fifteen items were those that tended to cluster together on the basis of participant responses. That is, these are the items with the least amount of difference in their frequency of response. The field-testing took place between March and May 1982 with a group of participants that satisfied the same set of scope conditions developed for participants in this study. The fifteen items employed in this study are listed below:

### Educational Features

Item A:  The purpose of American schools is to Americanize the culturally different and linguistically different child.

Item B:  The purpose of the school is to meet the individual needs of children.

Item C:  It is the child's responsibility to change in order to fit the expectations of the school.

### Bilingual Education Features

Item D:  Bilingual education is not acceptable because it meets only the needs of a small select group.

Item E:  The maintenance of bilingual education programs is too expensive for a school district.

Item F:  Bilingual education is acceptable in the school because it is the best means for meeting the educational needs of the limited English-speaking child.

### Role of Culture in Education

Item G:  Mexican American children suffer educational disadvantages because of their culture.

Item H:  Children from different cultures are different and must be treated differently in the classroom.

Item I:  The Mexican American child will have a more positive self-image if the Mexican culture is presented in the bilingual classroom.

*Role of Bilingualism in Education*

Item J: Teaching the Mexican American child in both English and Spanish results in confusion for the child.

Item K: Using both English and Spanish to teach the Mexican American child is a time-consuming activity for the teacher.

Item L: The use of Spanish in the bilingual classroom should stop as soon as the Spanish-speaking child learns English.

*The Teacher's Role in the Bilingual Classroom*

Item M: The teacher in the bilingual classroom should emphasize group cooperation rather than individualized competition between students.

Item N: The teacher-student relationship in the bilingual classroom should be close and personal, and not objective and impartial.

Item O: The teacher in the bilingual classroom should tell the Mexican American student when he or she speaks improper or incorrect English.

Interviewers were bilingual Spanish/English graduate students who were indigenous to the areas they were assigned to work in, and who were familiar with the general literature of bilingual education, survey research methods, and the sociolinguistic nuances of conducting a bilingual interview. For example, since the interviewer was instructed to conduct the interview in the language preferred by the study participant, and to avoid interference with the content validity of the items, interviewers were instructed not to translate.

### INTERVIEW RESULTS

Some of the more salient characteristics of our participants are the following: (a) parents—a mean annual income of $11,500, a mean age of thirty-three years, an average household size of six, and an average completion of eight years of education; (b) teachers—a mean age of twenty-nine years and an average of two years beyond the baccalaureate; and (c) principals—a mean age of forty-five years and an average of three years beyond the master's. The distribution of participants by sex is: parents—52 percent females and 48 percent males; teachers—100 percent female; and principals—100 percent male. Regarding their native language, 80 percent of the parents, 50 percent of the teachers, and none of the principals listed Spanish.

To determine whether there were significant differences among the three participant categories for each of the fifteen interview items, chi-square tests were computed for each of the fifteen three by three (Participant $x$ Response) frequency tables (Willemsen 1974). Individual post-hoc comparisons between each possible pair of participant categories were conducted separately for each interview item, eliciting significant differences among the three participant categories by means of chi-square tests on each of the corresponding two by three ($P_i x R$) tables (McNemar 1969:254–65).

### Educational Features

Participants' responses to items concerned with general educational features are summarized in Table 9.1. The majority of participants disagreed, parents less than either teachers or principals, that it is the school's purpose to Americanize the linguistically and culturally different student. While the majority of participants agree that it is the purpose of the school to meet the individual needs of children, when compared to teachers and principals, only a majority of parents agree that it is the child's responsibility to change in order to fit the expectations of the school. The post-hoc comparisons for items A and C also show that parents' responses tend to differ significantly from the responses by either teachers or principals.

Regarding the general socialization features of the public school, the results suggest that the majority of parents appear to agree that education is both an individual and institutional process with distinct responsibilities for each component. By contrast, school personnel appear to agree that education is not an activity designed to make children meet its needs, but to meet individual needs in children. What these results also suggest is that while there is general agreement among participants regarding general features in education, there is some disagreement between parents and school personnel regarding the child's responsibility to *fit* the school. In a sense, these results are reflective of a dilemma in public education: it is unclear to both parents and school personnel what role children play as contributing members to an educational enterprise. To a certain degree, participants appear to regard children as passive actors in the school.

### Bilingual Education Features

Participants' responses for items concerned with general features in bilingual education are summarized in Table 9.2. The majority of the participants agree that bilingual education is the best means for meeting the educational needs of the limited-English speaking child. The majority of respondents disagree with the observation that bilingual education is unacceptable because it meets only the needs of a small select group. However, only a majority of teachers and principals disagree with the observation that the maintenance of

**TABLE 9.1**
**Participant Responses to Educational Features**

| ITEM | (R) RESPONSE | PARTICIPANTS (P) | | | $X^2(4)$ (P × R) | POST-HOC $X^2(2)$ COMPARISONS | | |
| | | (P$_1$) PARENTS | (P$_2$) TEACHERS | (P$_3$) PRINCIPALS | | (P$_1$×P$_2$×R) | (P$_1$×P$_3$×R) | (P$_2$×P$_3$×R) |
|---|---|---|---|---|---|---|---|---|
| A | Agree | 30% | 0 | 20% | 12.0* | 9.5* | 2.7** | 4.4** |
| | Disagree | 65% | 100% | 80% | | | | |
| | Unsure | 5% | 0 | 0 | | | | |
| B | Agree | 80% | 100% | 100% | 8.8** | | | |
| | Disagree | 20% | 0 | 0 | | | | |
| | Unsure | 0 | 0 | 0 | | | | |
| C | Agree | 60% | 20% | 40% | 43.0* | 43.5* | 20.1* | 2.2** |
| | Disagree | 40% | 60% | 50% | | | | |
| | Unsure | 0 | 20% | 10% | | | | |

*p > .05
**p < .05

**TABLE 9.2**
**Participant Responses to Bilingual Education Features**

| ITEM | (R) RESPONSE | PARTICIPANTS (P) | | | $X^2(4)$ (P × R) | POST-HOC $X^2(2)$ COMPARISONS | | |
| | | (P$_1$) PARENTS | (P$_2$) TEACHERS | (P$_3$) PRINCIPALS | | (P$_1$×P$_2$×R) | (P$_1$×P$_3$×R) | (P$_2$×P$_3$×R) |
|---|---|---|---|---|---|---|---|---|
| D | Agree | 15% | 0 | 0 | 26.1* | 3.9** | 21.6* | 2.2** |
| | Disagree | 85% | 100% | 90% | | | | |
| | Unsure | 0 | 0 | 10% | | | | |
| E | Agree | 45% | 0 | 30% | 22.7* | 17.6* | 6.1* | 7.2* |
| | Disagree | 35% | 80% | 60% | | | | |
| | Unsure | 20% | 20% | 10% | | | | |
| F | Agree | 80% | 80% | 60% | 31.7* | 13.0* | 24.7* | 2.0** |
| | Disagree | 15% | 0 | 0 | | | | |
| | Unsure | 5% | 20% | 40% | | | | |

*p > .05
**p < .05

bilingual education programs is too expensive for a school district. Comparatively speaking, principals appear to be more unsure regarding each of the general features in bilingual education than either parents or teachers.

There is disagreement among parents and school personnel regarding these features in bilingual education. The divergence of opinion can be interpreted as an indication that while parents may be willing to accept the general precepts in bilingual education, they may not be as willing to accept the financial obligation for its maintenance. On the other hand, its ultimate educational benefit for language-minority children may overshadow the concern with its financial obligation for school personnel. However, this is not a clear-cut distinction because, when compared with parents, more school personnel are unsure whether bilingual education is the best means for meeting the needs of language-minority children.

The post-hoc comparisons in Table 9.2 are also in accordance with the post-hoc comparisons in Table 9.1: parent responses are significantly different from responses by either teachers or principals. The post-hoc comparisons in Table 9.2 also show that while teachers and principals tend to have similar responses to the pedagogical concerns in bilingual education, item $D$ and item $F$, their responses differ significantly from each other regarding the cost for maintaining bilingual education programs, item $E$. Comparatively speaking, there appears to be a greater difference between teacher and principal responses than between parent and principal responses for the observation that the maintenance of bilingual education programs is too expensive for a school district.

### Role of Culture in Education

The majority of participants agree, according to Table 9.3, that culture is neither a disadvantage for the Mexican American child nor a general basis for treating children differently. The majority also agree that the incorporation of the Mexican culture in the bilingual classroom will improve the self-image of the Mexican American child. While more principals than teachers agree that culture is a disadvantage for the Mexican American child, more teachers than principals agree that culture is a general basis for treating children differently. Parents, on the other hand, are evenly divided on the issue of whether culture is a general basis for treating children differently, but agree that culture is not a disadvantage for the Mexican American child.

There appears to be general agreement regarding the role of culture in the bilingual classroom. The majority of participants view culture as not having any disadvantageous effects for the Mexican American child, and that its incorporation in the bilingual classroom will have positive effects on the Mexican American child's self-image. On the one hand, parents who agree that cul-

**TABLE 9.3**
**Participant Responses to the Role of Culture in Education**

| | | PARTICIPANTS (P) | | | | POST-HOC $X^2(2)$ COMPARISONS | | |
|---|---|---|---|---|---|---|---|---|
| ITEM | (R) RESPONSE | (P$_1$) PARENTS | (P$_2$) TEACHERS | (P$_3$) PRINCIPALS | $X^2(4)$ (P × R) | (P$_1$ × P$_2$ × R) | (P$_1$ × P$_3$ × R) | (P$_2$ × P$_3$ × R) |
| G | Agree | 40% | 30% | 40% | 0.94** | | | |
| | Disagree | 60% | 70% | 60% | | | | |
| | Unsure | 0 | 0 | 0 | | | | |
| H | Agree | 50% | 30% | 10% | 33.7* | 38.2* | 44.1* | 2.6** |
| | Disagree | 50% | 50% | 70% | | | | |
| | Unsure | 0 | 20% | 20% | | | | |
| I | Agree | 90% | 90% | 80% | 4.5** | | | |
| | Disagree | 5% | 0 | 10% | | | | |
| | Unsure | 5% | 10% | 10% | | | | |

*p > .05
**p < .05

ture is a basis for treating children differently may regard this as a prerequisite for having their children understood as individuals by school personnel. On the other hand, parents who disagree that culture is a basis for treating children differently may regard this as a basis for differentiating students into other activities that may not have educational rationales behind them. That school personnel regard culture as a differentiating variable which is not a disadvantage for the Mexican American child, but which has positive effects on the Mexican American child's self-image, is reflective of their role within the public school: student differentiation on the basis of behavioral variables fulfills institutional requirements regarding the practice of teaching.

### Role of Bilingualism in Education

From Table 9.4, the majority of participants disagree with the observation that teaching the Mexican American child in both Spanish and English results in psychological confusion for the child. The majority of teachers and principals disagree that using both English and Spanish to teach the Mexican American child is a time-consuming activity for the teacher, whereas parents appear to be evenly divided on whether it is. While the majority of parents and teachers disagree that the use of Spanish in the bilingual classroom should stop as soon as the Spanish-speaking student learns some English, the majority of principals agree that this is the appropriate time at which the use of Spanish should stop. In general, there again appears to be greater agreement between parents and teachers regarding the actual use of both languages in the bilingual classroom than between teachers and principals.

As was the case with responses for the role of culture in the bilingual classroom in Table 9.3, parents were evenly divided on whether the use of both languages in the bilingual classroom is a time-consuming activity for the teacher. It may be that parents are uncertain regarding the actual use of language and culture in the bilingual classroom. In other words, they may support their presence in the bilingual classroom, but be uncertain of the demands they may place on the educational activity of the classroom. Teachers and principals, on the other hand, appear to be quite certain that bilingualism and biculturalism are appropriate elements in the bilingual classroom. The fact that parents and school personnel have differing views regarding the role of language and culture in the bilingual classroom may be indicative of the different level of knowledge each group possesses about the use of behavioral variables in the educational technology of the school classroom.

### Teacher's Role in the Bilingual Classroom

Table 9.5 shows that the majority of participants: (a) agree that the teacher in the bilingual classroom should emphasize group cooperation among stu-

## TABLE 9.4
### Participant Responses to the Role of Bilingualism in Education

| ITEM | (R) RESPONSE | PARTICIPANTS (P) | | | $X^2(4)$ $(P \times R)$ | POST-HOC $X^2(2)$ COMPARISONS | | |
| | | $(P_1)$ PARENTS | $(P_2)$ TEACHERS | $(P_3)$ PRINCIPALS | | $(P_1 \times P_2 \times R)$ | $(P_1 \times P_3 \times R)$ | $(P_2 \times P_3 \times R)$ |
|---|---|---|---|---|---|---|---|---|
| J | Agree | 25% | 10% | 20% | 5.6** | | | |
| | Disagree | 70% | 90% | 80% | | | | |
| | Unsure | 5% | 0 | 0 | | | | |
| K | Agree | 50% | 10% | 20% | 35.7* | 26.6* | 23.1* | 0.86** |
| | Disagree | 50% | 80% | 70% | | | | |
| | Unsure | 0 | 10% | 10% | | | | |
| L | Agree | 15% | 0 | 60% | 26.9* | 4.0** | 22.8* | 17.8* |
| | Disagree | 75% | 90% | 40% | | | | |
| | Unsure | 10% | 10% | 0 | | | | |

*p > .05
**p < .05

## TABLE 9.5
### Participant Responses to the Teacher's Role in the Bilingual Classroom

| ITEM | (R) RESPONSE | PARTICIPANTS (P) | | | $X^2(4)$ $(P \times R)$ | POST-HOC $X^2(2)$ COMPARISONS | | |
| | | $(P_1)$ PARENTS | $(P_2)$ TEACHERS | $(P_3)$ PRINCIPALS | | $(P_1 \times P_2 \times R)$ | $(P_1 \times P_3 \times R)$ | $(P_2 \times P_3 \times R)$ |
|---|---|---|---|---|---|---|---|---|
| M | Agree | 80% | 95% | 85% | 4.1** | | | |
| | Disagree | 10% | 0 | 5% | | | | |
| | Unsure | 10% | 5% | 10% | | | | |
| N | Agree | 90% | 95% | 80% | 19.3* | 0.72** | 18.4* | 2.8** |
| | Disagree | 0 | 0 | 10% | | | | |
| | Unsure | 10% | 5% | 10% | | | | |
| O | Agree | 60% | 0 | 55% | 27.3* | 27.0* | 0.24** | 14.8* |
| | Disagree | 35% | 90% | 40% | | | | |
| | Unsure | 5% | 10% | 5% | | | | |

*p > .05
**p < .05

dents rather than individual competition, and (b) agree that the teacher-student relationship in a bilingual classroom should be very close and personal, and not objective and impartial. While the majority of parents and principals agree that the teacher should correct the improper use of English by the Mexican American child, the majority of teachers disagree that this is something a teacher should do. In general, there is little disagreement between participants regarding the teacher's role in the bilingual classroom, and the promotion of a cooperative and warm educational environment. However, when contrasted with teachers' responses, parents and principals appear to regard the teacher in the bilingual classroom as responsible for monitoring proper or acceptable behavior. It could also be that while parents and principals accept the notion of a warm and cooperative educational environment, they may still prefer that the teacher function within the classroom in a symbolic and distinct role.

### SUMMARY AND CONCLUSIONS

Generally, parents and school personnel tend to have similar opinions regarding education and bilingual education. If their responses are indicative of how they perceive education to operate, then the participants appear to share the same conceptualization of those educational activities presented as part of the interview. In instances where differences in response were present between parents and school personnel, they could be due to the different levels of technical knowledge each group has access to regarding educational concerns.

For instance, when the items presented to participants in the interview dealt with the human problem in education (items, *D, I, N*), parents and teachers tended to agree with each other. In comparison, when the items dealt with the institutional functions of persons (items *C, H, K*) teachers and principals tended to agree with each other. These results suggest that it is only when the interview items were focused on what may be considered *insider* knowledge that parents are seen as the *outsiders*. One may suspect that, in general, parents may be supportive of bilingual education, but may not understand its actual working phases because this information may not be adequately communicated to them by school personnel. While the data limit the amount of interpretation regarding this concern, they do indicate that parents have not assumed a more active role in bilingual education vis-à-vis parent advisory groups because the educational technology aspect of bilingual education is not being communicated to them by school personnel.

While the overall results reveal a high level of similarity in participants' opinions, the post-hoc comparisons highlighted areas in which there were differences of opinion. The usefulness of this type of research methodology to bilingual education rests in its ability to locate disjunctions in a social process that are regarded by educators as uniform. As a research strategy capable of monitoring the range of cumulative growth in bilingual education as a social process, it provides the appropriate context for developing meta-perspectives for a social activity; bilingual education may be nothing more than an epiphenomenon of a much larger social issue—a social issue that may lie completely outside the scope of education.

Comparative studies of this type must be encouraged in order to increase our understanding of general educational principles. The paucity of structured comparisons in bilingual education research needs to be addressed effectively. For example, a series of case studies that are part of a comparative research strategy could be developed to study the process features in bilingual education (Lewis 1977). Studies such as this one are, by themselves, at best a particularistic description of a social process. However, by linking studies on a shared set of parameters, the cumulative results obtainable by such a research strategy would enhance our understanding of what bilingual education actually does.

In a classic study of the Renaissance as an educational achievement, Durkheim (1969) argues that in order for people to feel the need to change their educational system they must first become conscious of ideas and needs that have emerged for which the old system of education is no longer adequate. Bilingual education may have appeared on the American scene as a paradigmatic response to a social problem defined by linguistic needs. However, bilingual education has not lived up to the expectations of a paradigm in education. In short, it neither reflects nor manipulates change. One may suspect that bilingual education has had limited success within the American educational environment because it has not drawn significant support from an audience that could elevate it to paradigmatic proportions. By examining the level of consistency of opinion for a given audience, the research strategy employed in this study is useful in understanding what is and what is not a shared feature among members in an audience's social perception of a given social phenomenon. Thus, to follow Durkheim's observation of educational change during the Renaissance, the incorporation of a consistent image of bilingual education in an audience's social perception may be the much needed catalyst for portraying bilingual education as social change.

## REFERENCES

Adelman, C. 1981. "Language, Culture, and Bilingual Schooling: Reflections After A Case Study Of A School." *Journal of Multilingual and Multicultural Development* 2(4):259–68.

Aguirre, Jr., A. 1982. In Search Of A Paradigm For Bilingual Education. Bilingual Education Paper Series, vol. 12, no. 5.

Aguirre, Jr., A. 1980. "The Sociolinguistic Survey in Bilingual Education: A Case Study Of A Bilingual Community." In *Theory in Bilingual Education: Ethnoperspectives in Bilingual Education Research*, vol. 2, pp. 47–61. R. V. Padilla, ed. Ypsilanti, Michigan: Eastern Michigan University, Bilingual-Bicultural Programs.

Aguirre, Jr., A., and D. Bixler-Marquez (1979). "A Sociolinguistic Assessment Model For A Bilingual Community." *NABE Journal* 4(2):1–17.

Bernabe, L. V. 1975. "La Relacion Entre Meastros y Alumnos Como Factor De La Educacion Bilingue." Proceedings Of The First Inter-American Conference On Bilingual Education. R. C. Troike and N. Modiano, eds. Arlington, Virginia: Center for Applied Linguistics, pp. 311–25.

Cohen, A. D. 1980. *Describing Bilingual Education Classrooms*. Rosslyn, Virginia: National Clearinghouse For Bilingual Education.

Cummins, J. 1980. "The Language And Culture Issue In The Education of Minority Language Children." *Interchange* 10:72–88.

Durkheim, E. 1969. *L'evolution pedagogique en France*. Paris: Presses Universitaires de France.

Edwards, J. R. 1980. "Critics And Criticism Of Bilingual Education." *Modern Language Journal* 64:409–15.

Epstein, N. 1980. "Bilingual Education in the United States: The 'Either/Or' Mistake." In *Politics and Language: Spanish and English in the United States*, 85–109, D. J. Bruckner, ed. University of Chicago: Center for Policy Study.

Fitzpatrick, F., and O. A. Rees. 1980. "The Education Of Bilingual Children: A Framework For Discussion." University of Bradford, Mother Tongue and English Teaching Project, Working Paper No. 3.

Fong, K. M. 1978. "Cultural Pluralism." *Harvard Civil Rights—Civil Liberties Law Review* 13:133–73.

Foster, W. P. 1976. "Bilingual Education: An Educational And Legal Survey." *Journal of Law and Education* 5:149–71.

Lewis, E. G. 1977. "Bilingualism In Education: Cross–National Research." *Linguistics* 198:5–30.

Macias, R. F. 1976. "Opinions Of Chicano Community Parents On Bilingual Preschool Education." In *Language in Sociology*, pp. 135–66. A. Verdoot and R. Kjolseth, eds. Louvain: Editions Peeters.

Margulies, P. 1981. "Bilingual Education, Remedial Language Instruction, Title VI, and Proof of Discriminatory Practice." *Columbia Journal of Law and Social Problems* 17(1):99–162.

McNemar, Q. 1969. *Psychological Statistics*. New York: Wiley.

Paz, E. Y. 1980. The Development Of Bilingual Education Models. Bilingual Education Paper Series, vol. 3, no. 10. Rosslyn, Va.: National Clearinghouse for Bilingual Education.

Ramirez, A. G. 1980. "Language in Bilingual Classrooms." *NABE Journal* 4:61–79.

Ringawa, M. 1980. "Cultural Pedagogy: The Effects Of Teacher Attitudes and Needs in Selected Bilingual Bicultural Education Environments." In *Theory in Bilingual Education: Ethnoperspectives in Bilingual Education Research*, 2:347–71. R. V. Padilla, ed. Ypsilanti, Michigan: Eastern Michigan University, Bilingual-Bicultural Programs.

Rodriguez, R. 1981. "Citizen Participation In Selected Bilingual Education Advisory Committees." *NABE Journal* 5:1–21.

Rodriguez, R. 1979. "Citizen Participation in ESEA Title VII Programs." In *Bilingual Education and Public Policy in the United States: Ethnoperspectives in Bilingual Education Research* 1:260–80. R. V. Padilla, ed. Ypsilanti, Michigan: Eastern Michigan University, Bilingual-Bicultural Programs.

Saville–Troike, M. 1978. *A Guide to Culture in The Classroom.* Rosslyn, Virginia: National Clearinghouse for Bilingual Education.

Sugerman, S. D., and E. G. Widers. 1974. "Equal Protection of Non-English-Speaking School Children: Lau v. Nichols." *California Law Review* 62:157–82.

Troike, R. C. 1978. *Research Evidence for the Effectiveness of Bilingual Education.* Bilingual Education Paper Series, vol. 2, no. 5. Rosslyn, Va.: National Clearinghouse for Bilingual Education.

Ulibarri, H. 1972. "The Bicultural Myth and The Education of the Mexican American." *Journal of Comparative Cultures* 1:83–95.

Willemsen, E. W. 1974. *Understanding Statistical Reasoning.* San Francisco: W. H. Freeman.

# 10.
# Family and Offspring Language Maintenance and Their Effects on Chicano College Students' Confidence and Grades

*Homer D. C. Garcia*

THE NATION-STATE HAS TRADITIONALLY been viewed by social scientists as an ideal type of society for many reasons. Among them, it has been thought that when a single language is spoken and a single culture exists in a society, the socioeconomic productivity of the average individual is maximized (Gordon 1964). Culturally plural societies are believed to establish reinforcement systems in order to coerce ethnically dissimilar individuals into acculturating and becoming socioeconomically integrated (Barth and Noel 1980). It is thought that the amount of status, prestige, and overall power which is awarded is proportional to the degree to which an ethnic minority individual is acculturated into the dominant cultural community (Derbyshire 1968).

Linguistic acculturation, the learning of a society's dominant language, is usually only one aspect of the overall acculturation process. Typically, the immigrant also adopts some or all of a dominant community's other cultural characteristics: ethical values, sense of common past history, religio-social beliefs and practices, musical styles, and various other traits (Gordon 1964). Further, the acculturation process is only one of seven types of assimilation usually expected of the immigrant. The other changes include structural, marital, identificational, attitudinal-receptive, behavioral-receptive, and civic assimilation (Gordon 1964). Linguistic acculturation does not occur alone, but is one of many changes which a newcomer is required to undertake simultaneously (H. Garcia 1980).

Nevertheless, the importance of linguistic acculturation should not be underestimated. The learning of English has been and continues to be a crucial determiner of the educational success of Spanish-dominant children (Carter and Segura 1979). Some have argued that it is a rough indicator of the extent of other acculturative changes (H. Garcia 1980). Milton Gordon (1964) has also argued that linguistic acculturation is an essential precursor to all other forms of assimilation. Thus, it is not surprising that foreign language maintenance in the United States has traditionally been seen as an aberrant social phenomenon and a central cause of the psychological alienation and socioeconomic deprivation of linguistically unacculturated immigrant groups (Novack 1973).

For example, Chicanos, the second largest minority group in the United States, have maintained their linguistic and other cultural characteristics (Grebler et al. 1970) to a greater extent than most other minority groups. Rogers (1971) and Coleman et al. (1966) have found Spanish language maintenance among Chicanos to be positively associated with less confident psychological characteristics: lower self-esteem, locus of control, and aspirations. It has also been linked with lower educational success (Carter and Segura 1979). Some researchers have concluded that language maintenance results in such negative effects because individuals who resist the learning of English usually realize the socioeconomically immobile position they are in.

In contrast, other researchers have argued that the type of acculturation which is expected of immigrants to the United States may have adverse effects or outcomes, particularly for nonwhite and/or territorial groups. H. Garcia (1980) has submitted that it is erroneous to believe that capitalistic societies offer equal opportunities to all ethnic groups to acculturate, assimilate, and achieve socioeconomic success. The educational system, which has historically served as this society's major institution of acculturation (Gordon 1964), has treated nonwhite and/or non-English-speaking groups in a more critical, hostile, and educationally inferior manner (Carter and Segura 1979).

In particular, Chicanos have endured intense pressure to devalue and eradicate their native language and other cultural traits and to idealize and adopt the characteristics of the dominant community (H. Garcia 1980). When minority individuals reject their ethnic/racial characteristics and identity, the denial of self can also result (Poussaint and Atkinson 1972). These acculturative pressures have contributed to the relative lack of socioeconomic success of Chicanos, aroused further rejection by the dominant society, and alienated acculturationists from their own community.

Some investigators have proposed that bilingualism is a more desirable alternative than is total acculturation in terms of promoting the self-esteem and socioeconomic success of the ethnic individual. Cognitive consistency theory has told us that there is a basic need for people to find meaning and value in life (Shaw and Costanzo 1970). Faced with never-ending attacks on the culture and unreasonable acculturative demands, minority individuals often respond by finding value in some of their cultural characteristics and by maintaining them (Barth 1969).

Barth and H. Garcia have argued that foreign language maintenance is one type of counter-reaction and that it is an integral characteristic of the ethnic nationalist. Retention of the native tongue is often correlated with the resistance or redefinition of other acculturative and assimilative demands; nevertheless, the desire for upward socioeconomic mobility is likely to remain high (H. Garcia 1980). Although separatist goals are sometimes espoused, greater participation and some accommodation within the mainstream are usually sought.

The family is an important determiner of the language maintenance and ethnic politicization of offspring (Hirsch and Gutierrez 1977). Nevertheless, socialization beyond the home is also important. Peer groups and nationalist organizations help to maintain the linguistic and political characteristics of ethnically aware individuals (Kenniston 1973; Hirsch and Gutierrez 1977).

Because so many Chicano students come from segregated neighborhoods and schools (Grebler 1970), college often provides Chicanos with their first extensive exposure to Anglos and their greatest challenge to their ethnic identity. Bilingual communication serves to reinforce the ethnic pride of students and helps to extend the protection of the barrio into the college campus.

The maintenance of the Spanish language, whether done so through active usage or covertly maintained through continued fluency, is often an express act of power and defiance. To college ethnic activists, bilingualism can be a decree that acculturation and educational success will be sought on their own terms. For these reasons, language maintenance can be seen as an act of self-assertion and confidence on a college campus, perhaps more than in any other setting. Since neither sociocultural community is totally rejected, successful social and competitive endeavors in both worlds are more likely.

Studies have begun to demonstrate bilingualism's positive short- and long-term effects among Chicanos. Elementary school pupils enrolled in bilingual programs have revealed higher levels of self-esteem (Firme 1969; Del Buono 1971; Troike 1979), and academic success (R. Garcia 1974; Troike 1979) than nonparticipants. Ramirez III (1973) has shown that, in contrast to acculturationists, bilingual-bicultural adolescents have more ethnically proud attitudes, higher levels of self-esteem, and they can better cope with integrated settings. Greater confidence and achievement have also been found among Chicano college students who come from Spanish-speaking homes (Long and Padilla 1970) and who are bilingual (H. Garcia 1980).

The findings of these studies appear to be totally inconsistent with those of investigations cited earlier on the negative effects of Spanish language maintenance. It is possible, however, that the apparent conflict is due to definitional problems in contemporary research. There are many possible responses to linguistic acculturation pressures, which can be placed on a continuum as follows:

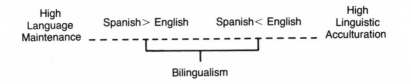

Individuals placed on the left side of the continuum are more Spanish dominant (i.e., they speak more Spanish and they are more fluent in this language
than in English), while individuals on the other side are more English dominant. Further, some people may be placed about in the middle, with roughly
equal levels of Spanish and English usage and fluency. It is possible that adverse effects occur for individuals at the extremes on the continuum. At the
same time, affirmative outcomes may result from an intermediary route:
bilingualism.

   In light of the possible affirmative effects of bilingualism, it is necessary to
question those studies which have argued that only negative outcomes result
from Spanish language maintenance. Indeed, such investigations have not
considered bilingualism as a type of foreign language maintenance. This study
examines the relative effects of high family Spanish language maintenance
and offspring bilingualism on the psychological and academic achievement
characteristics of Chicano college students. Further, high Spanish usage
homes which produce bilingual children cannot be predicted to affect children
in a totally positive manner, because family members are more likely to experience greater societal rejection, and such feelings of alienation can affect offspring. It is also questionable whether bilingualism can be expected to affect
students at all at the college level. This study attempts to clarify these issues.

## METHOD

### Sample

   An exploratory mail survey was conducted to study the nationalist, psychological, and academic characteristics of Chicano college students of
Texas. The sampling procedure was designed to compare types and levels of
ethnic activism between types of colleges for another study (not yet published). A number of criteria were used in the selection of colleges and universities in an effort to collect a stratified random sample of subjects. Institutions were selected which had varying levels of Chicano activism on campus.
Also, schools were selected on the basis of their public/private status, two-
year or four-year nature, level of prestige, and distance from the Mexican

**TABLE 10.1**
**The Number of Chicano College Students Who Received**
**Questionnaires and Returned Them at**
**Each Participating Institution, Spring 1977.**

| College or University | No. Sent | No. Returned | Percent Returned |
|---|---|---|---|
| Juarez-Lincoln University Several south Texas branches | 116 | 65 | 55 |
| Our Lady of the Lake College San Antonio, Texas | 175 | 101 | 58 |
| Pan American University Edinburg, Texas | 175 | 103 | 58 |
| San Antonio College San Antonio, Texas | 400 | 179 | 45 |
| Southwest Texas Junior College Uvalde, Texas | 454 | 236 | 52 |
| South West Texas State University San Marcos, Texas | 175 | 80 | 46 |
| St. Mary's University San Antonio, Texas | 175 | 104 | 59 |
| Texas A & I University Kingsville, Texas | 250 | 130 | 52 |
| Texas Southmost College Brownsville, Texas | 175 | 71 | 40 |
| Trinity University San Antonio, Texas | 200 | 118 | 59 |
| University of Texas at Austin Austin, Texas | 405 | 185 | 46 |
| University of Texas at San Antonio San Antonio, Texas | 250 | 140 | 56 |
| Yale University* New Haven, Connecticut | 50 | 34 | 68 |
| Returned anonymously | | 27 | |
| Total | 3,000 | 1,573 | 52 |

*Only Chicano college students from Texas were sent questionnaires at this out-of-state institution. Yale University was selected as a participating school for two reasons. First, students from prestigious schools were desired. Second, and most importantly, there was much Chicano student activism on this campus and such students tended to be bilingual.

border (see H. Garcia 1980). Of the fifteen institutions contacted, thirteen agreed to participate in the survey.

Participating schools submitted either an official administrative list of students or a commercially sold student directory. Spanish-surnamed pupils on each directory were first assigned unique consecutive identification numbers. After deciding on the size of the sample to be derived from each institution, random numbers were drawn from a book of random numbers (RAND Corporation, 1955) in order to select students (with matching identification numbers) to receive questionnaires at each school. A total of 3,000 Chicano college students were contacted.

As many as five follow-up mail contacts (including a second questionnaire) were made in order to encourage participation. Table 10.1 demonstrates that 1,573 Chicano college students (or 52 percent) responded to the spring 1977 survey, a reasonable response rate for a mail survey (Weisberg and Bowen 1977). Although the sample of this study is probably not representative of the total Chicano college student population of Texas, it can serve as a useful sample in an exploratory survey of a new topic in research and help guide more rigorous subsequent theory development and empirical investigation.

The sample of respondents was composed of roughly equal numbers of males and females, and the median age was 22. About 42 percent came from home communities of less than 50,000 people, 53 percent from hometowns of 50,000 or more, and 5 percent did not report the size of their communities. The median years of education for mothers of respondents was 6.5 years, and 7.0 years for fathers. The median range of respondents' parents' yearly income was $6,000 to $7,999. About 50 percent of respondents were freshmen and sophomores; 35 percent were juniors and seniors; 8 percent were graduate-professional students; and the rest were of an unidentified status. Sixty-eight percent were full-time and 32 percent were part-time students.

### Measures

The self-administered questionnaire, which required about an hour to complete, included the following measures used in this study:

> *The home's income (Income).* A question asked subjects (S) to select an income range category from the sixteen categories offered describing the total yearly income of their families when they, the respondents, were sixteen years of age. A high score (15) indicates high income.
>
> *The home's Spanish usage (Usage).* A measurement scale containing three items (each with six response categories) asked subjects to assess the percentage range of the time Spanish was spoken by particular family members—mother, father, and siblings. A high score (18) indicates high usage in the home.
>
> *Spanish fluency (Fluency).* A single question, with seven response categories, was used to evaluate their own Spanish fluency. A high score (7) indicates high fluency.
>
> *Self-esteem (Esteem).* A scale containing six Likert-type items (each with seven response categories) asked subjects about their self-worth. A high score (42) indicates high self-esteem.
>
> *Educational and income plans (Plans).* A scale containing

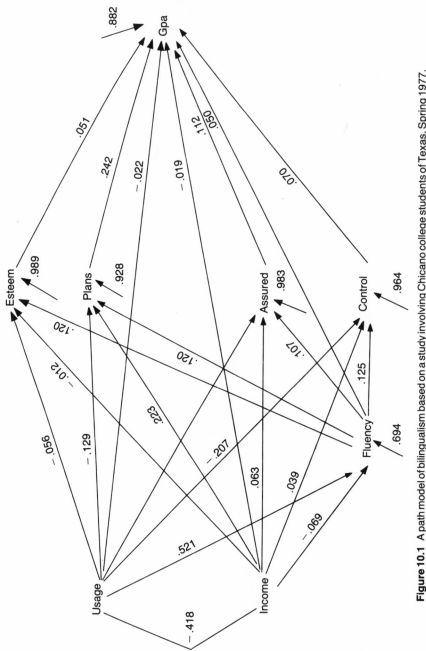

**Figure 10.1** A path model of bilingualism based on a study involving Chicano college students of Texas, Spring 1977.

three items (each item having a different number of responses) asked subjects to describe their educational and income plans. A socioeconomic-plans scale was desired but the occupation question failed tests for internal consistency (described in the statistical analysis section), and so it was excluded. Because each item was equally weighted, scale totals ranged from 0.966 to 3.000 with the latter representing more ambitious plans.

*Assuredness of achieving plans (Assured).* On a scale containing three items (each with six response categories) respondents described how sure they were that they could achieve their educational, occupational, and income plans. A high score (18) indicates high assuredness.

*Locus of control (Control).* A scale containing three items (each with seven response categories) asked subjects to assess how much control they felt they had over their lives. A high score (21) indicates high locus of control (or nonfatalism).

*College grade point average (GPA).* Respondents were asked to report their grade point average from 12 categories ranging from "1.00 GPA or lower" to "4.00." A high score (12) indicates a high grade point average.

Two clarifications are necessary. First, with regard to the home Spanish usage measure, it was assumed that families which communicate largely in Spanish have striven toward high language maintenance. Second, the offspring Spanish fluency variable is also used as a rough measure of bilingualism. There was very little response variation to a question which asked subjects to evaluate their English fluency. That question had a response scale identical to that used in the *fluency* item described above, although a high score (7) represented high English fluency. As might be expected of a Chicano college student sample, most felt that they were very fluent in English (mean = 6.5 and standard deviation = 0.969). Table 10.2 demonstrates that responses to the *fluency* question were more varied. Thus, these findings demonstrate that there was probably variation in the level of bilingualism among respondents.

## Statistical Analysis

An earlier version of the questionnaire was pretested on a mail survey of 124 Chicano college students nine months prior to the final study; the viability of measurement scales was a primary concern. Items with insufficient response variance were dropped and, in accordance with the guidelines set forth by Zeller and Carmines (1980), only those items loading at least at the .4 level with other same-scale items in factor analyses tests were retained in a scale. Factor analyses continued until it was no longer possible to separate same-scale items into distinct factors. Cluster analyses were then conducted using Pearson product-moment correlation coefficients to make certain that the final scale items were highly correlated with each other and that they were related with nonscale items in the same direction and at roughly a similar level, as suggested by Selltiz et al. (1976). Final scales were created by equally weighting items and by employing mean substitution for missing data prior to summation. The above procedures were repeated with the final survey data.

Multiple regression data were generated employing the technique proposed by Duncan (1975) and Alwin and Hauser (1975), so that the total, direct, and indirect effects of family Spanish usage and offspring Spanish fluency on offspring psychology and/or academic success could be studied. However, the approach was modified so that both individual-variable indirect effects (typically analyzed in path analysis) and item-set indirect effects could be calculated, as described by Alexander (1976) and H. Garcia (1980).

Item-set indirect effects are useful here in that they measure whether antecedent variables produce indirect effects on GPA via the set of psychological variables, that is, via *esteem*, *plans*, and *assured*, and on *control* as an aggregate mediating variable. Finally, even though there are no established methods for ascertaining the significance levels of indirect effects, it was decided that indirect effects greater than or equal to .04 would be given closer attention. The calculation of varied forms of effects is particularly crucial to this study because it is anticipated that the Spanish dominant home will yield differential effects depending on whether the Spanish fluency, and therefore the bilingualism, of offspring is enhanced. Only when it does so are positive effects expected.

### Hypotheses

It is predicted that, while holding family income constant throughout, high family Spanish usage will yield negative direct effects on offspring characteristics, such that lower levels of self-esteem, educational and income aspirations, assuredness of achieving such plans, locus of control, and grades in college will result. High Spanish usage homes will produce affirmative impacts (i.e., indirect effects) only if they enhance the Spanish fluency and, therefore, the bilingualism of offspring. Finally, it is predicted that, regardless of the homes of origin, high Spanish fluency will result in positive direct effects.

### RESULTS AND DISCUSSION

Table 10.2 shows that some multicollinearity was present between variables, but it was not significant. Thus, high Spanish usage families tended to have lower yearly incomes and they also produced children who were more fluent in Spanish. However, the magnitude of these correlations was far below

**TABLE 10.2**
**Intercorrelations, Explained Variation ($R^2$'s), Means,**
**Standard Deviations, and Reliabilities for the**
**Variables Entered into the Bilingualism Model,**
**Chicano College Students of Texas, N = 1,573, Spring 1977.**

|  | 1 | 2 | 3 | 4 | 5 | 6 | 7 | 8 |
|---|---|---|---|---|---|---|---|---|
| 1. USAGE |  |  |  |  |  |  |  |  |
| 2. INCOME | −.418 |  |  |  |  |  |  |  |
| 3. FLUENCY | .549 | −.286 |  |  |  |  |  |  |
| 4. ESTEEM | .018 | −.023 | .093 |  |  |  |  |  |
| 5. PLANS | −.156 | .242 | −.014 | .135 |  |  |  |  |
| 6. ASSURED | −.079 | .079 | .028 | .235 | .281 |  |  |  |
| 7. CONTROL | −.154 | .090 | .000 | .202 | .303 | .193 |  |  |
| 8. GPA | −.034 | .042 | .058 | .141 | .291 | .215 | .171 | — |
| $R^2$ | — | — | .306 | .011 | .072 | .017 | .036 | .118 |
| Mean | 12.600 | 4.789 | 5.410 | 35.240 | 2.032 | 15.400 | 12.825 | 10.062 |
| Std. Dev. | 4.193 | 2.854 | 1.744 | 6.378 | .345 | 2.450 | 4.988 | 2.772 |
| Reliability | .856** | .964* | .939* | .745** | .696** | .786** | .656** | .940 |

*This is a test-retest reliability estimate (a Pearson product-moment correlation coefficient) derived from a pilot study in which 31 Chicano College students participated.
**This is an estimate of the internal reliability of this measurement scale (Cronbach's alpha) derived not from the test-retest pilot study, but from the survey data analyzed in this investigation.

unity. Variables in each correlated independent variable pair tended to be correlated differently in terms of their magnitude and/or direction with other common variables. In other tests each independent variable tended to yield path coefficients in the same direction and roughly similar intensity, whether they were placed in the regression equation by themselves or with one or both of the other independent variables.

The R2's reveal that very little variation was explained in most of the subject characteristics included in the model. Thus the antecedent variables had little to do with the determination of a student's levels of self-esteem, educational and income aspirations, certainty of achieving such plans, and locus of control. It is possible, however, that the unreliability of these dependent variables contributed to the low amount of variation accounted for in each case. On the other hand, more variation was explained in the grade point average and, especially, in the Spanish fluency dependent variables.

Despite the low general specification of the model, it is still possible to get a rough idea of the causal roles of home Spanish usage and offspring Spanish fluency. Not surprisingly, Table 10.3 shows that the largest effect yielded in the model was that made on *fluency* by *usage*; families which spoke more Spanish produced children who were more fluent in Spanish.

There are undoubtedly many influences which promote the Spanish language maintenance of children (*fluency*'s R2 was still far below unity). How-

**TABLE 10.3**
**Interpretations of Effects in a Model of Bilingualism:**
**Chicano College Students of Texas, Spring, 1977.**

| Dependent Variable | Independent Variables | Total Effect | Direct Effect | Indirect Effect via FLUENCY | Indirect Effect via Psychology |
|---|---|---|---|---|---|
| FLUENCY | USAGE | | .521*** | — | — |
| | INCOME | | −.069*** | — | — |
| ESTEEM | USAGE | .007 | −.056* | .063 | — |
| | INCOME | −.020 | .012 | −.032 | — |
| | FLUENCY | | .120*** | — | — |
| PLANS | USAGE | −.066** | −.129*** | .063 | — |
| | INCOME | .215*** | .223*** | −.008 | — |
| | FLUENCY | | .120*** | — | — |
| ASSURED | USAGE | −.056* | −.112*** | .056 | — |
| | INCOME | .055* | .063** | −.008 | — |
| | FLUENCY | | .107*** | — | — |
| CONTROL | USAGE | −.142*** | −.207*** | .065 | — |
| | INCOME | .031 | .039 | −.008 | — |
| | FLUENCY | | .125*** | — | — |
| GPA | USAGE | −.019 | −.022 | .059 | −.056 |
| | INCOME | .034 | −.019 | .000 | .053 |
| | FLUENCY | .113*** | .050* | — | .063 |
| | ESTEEM | | .051*** | — | — |
| | PLANS | | .242*** | — | — |
| | ASSURED | | .112*** | — | — |
| | CONTROL | | .070*** | — | — |

*p < .05
**p < .01
***p < .001

ever, these data underscore the importance of the family as one of the primary agents of socialization in the linguistic development of children. Greater fluency was achieved by offspring because they used Spanish more in the home. Family members may have also pressured subjects to achieve better oral Spanish skills.

The major interest of this study is the examination of the effects of home Spanish usage and offspring Spanish fluency on a student's psychological characteristics and success in school. Let us now discuss the effects of each of these variables in turn.

### Effects of Usage

As predicted, home Spanish usage yielded consistently negative direct effects and positive indirect effects on the remaining dependent variables. The negative direct effects demonstrate that families communicating more in Spanish adversely affected an offspring's level of self-esteem, socioeconomic plans, assuredness of achieving such plans, and locus of control. These negative impacts may have occurred because families who spoke more Spanish were not highly bilingual but largely Spanish monolingual. Even with *fluency* controlled, it is likely that such effects were also found when highly Spanish fluent or bilingual children were present in the home (keep in mind that controlling for *fluency* does not eliminate bilinguals in the calculation of these relationships; such coefficients are generated over all levels of offspring bilingualism).

Future research may, in fact, demonstrate that high Spanish usage homes produce these effects because of forces originating both from outside and within the home. Families who maintain their native tongue probably face greater acculturative pressure, social rejection, and socioeconomic discrimination from the dominant society. Further, those promoting high Spanish language maintenance within the barrio, separatist nationalists, for example, are sometimes critical of Spanish-dominant families who have children who are fluent in English, because this is seen as an indication of cultural disloyalty.

In response to such sociolinguistic pressures, such families may, in turn, question the English and/or Spanish skills of their own children. In particular, parents may transmit to their children feelings of disenchantment, uncertainty about what linguistic course of action ought to be taken, and at least some questions about their cultural identity. Even generally confident adult bilingual children may have to deal with such feelings during much of their lives. However, at this point, *these explanations are highly speculative and they await verification.*

Although a significant negative direct effect was predicted, no relationship was found between family Spanish usage and offspring grade point average. This is probably because, at such a high level of education, the school work students complete for college courses is largely independent of family influence.

*Usage* yielded significant positive indirect effects via *fluency* on all of the dependent variables, as predicted. These effects reveal that when high Spanish usage homes enhanced the Spanish fluency of children, the latter developed higher levels of self-esteem, more ambitious educational and income aspirations, greater assuredness of achieving such plans, greater locus of control, and better grades.

In light of the negative direct effects analyzed above, it is clear that the Spanish dominant home can have differential effects on children. The key to understanding these varied impacts lies in comprehending the role of the intervening event, that is, whether or not a family promoted Spanish fluency, and therefore, the bilingualism of offspring. Some negative effects are probably going to be yielded whenever a high Spanish usage home is involved, even when bilingual children are present. However, so long as a family's Spanish usage enhances the Spanish fluency of children who are proficient in English, then the resultant bilingualism and concomitant ability to function in both linguistic settings are going to enhance the confidence of offspring. Such effects are not likely when a Spanish dominant home does not promote Spanish fluency and general bilingualism of their children.

The importance of offspring Spanish fluency as an intervening event is particularly evident when one compares the two ways in which the high Spanish usage home affected an offspring's college grade point average. The significant *positive* indirect effect via *fluency* suggests that if the family enhanced the Spanish fluency of offspring, then higher grades resulted. The significant *negative* indirect effect via the item-set of psychological characteristics suggests that such a home could not enhance the overall confidence or, therefore, the achievement of offspring, without first promoting Spanish fluency of offspring.

Nevertheless, the total effects yielded by *usage* reveal that the overall impact on four out of five of the dependent variables was negative. Such effects occurred because the absolute value of a given negative direct effect was greater than that of the positive indirect effect in each case. Thus, high Spanish usage homes had a negative effect on offspring in the long run, because the indirect positive effects of being bilingual as a result of such a family language socialization could not overcome the direct negative effects of such a home experience. Of course, this does not mean that an offspring's bilingualism cannot have important effects, independent of those caused by the home; this is considered below.

### Effects of Fluency

Table 10.3 shows that in contrast to *usage*, *fluency* yielded consistently positive and usually significant total, direct, and/or indirect effects on the dependent variables. Specifically, the positive direct effects demonstrate that subjects who were more fluent in Spanish developed higher levels of self-esteem, more ambitious socioeconomic plans, greater assuredness of accomplishing such plans, greater locus of control, and higher grades in college.

The results suggest that high Spanish fluency and general bilingualism enhanced the levels of confidence and academic achievement of students. These effects occurred even in light of the problematic character of the homes from which they came. The linguistically reinforcing practices of the family were not in vain. As long as offspring achieved Spanish fluency and general bilingualism, whether through the influence of the home or some other childhood or current socializing agents, affirmative outcomes resulted.

Bilingualism may promote more successful interaction and competition in *both worlds*. Greater respect for the cultural identity and self-confidence are understandable outcomes. And as alluded to earlier, the greater magnitude and consistency of the effects of offspring Spanish fluency, in comparison to the effects of home Spanish usage, may have been due to the more immediate causal role of an offspring's own language fluency in adulthood.

The total effect which *fluency* yielded on GPA is an indication that the sum of the component effects, direct and indirect, was strongly positive. The significant affirmative direct effect reveals that subjects who were more fluent in Spanish earned higher grades in school. Even though this relationship was in the predicted direction, its statistical significance was not actually expected. It was felt that a subject's Spanish fluency, or bilingualism, would yield only significant indirect effects because only direct psychological impacts were predicted. Then, it was thought that the enhanced confidence of respondents would promote their achievement.

It is possible that increased Spanish fluency may have some unanticipated direct educational advantages. Some bilingual education advocates have argued, for example, that Spanish language ability promotes the learning of English. Further, it is possible that having communicative skills and experiences in two ethnic communities increases the amount of knowledge which is learned and which can be applied in school.

An indirect effect of the type expected was found. *Fluency* yielded a significant item-set indirect effect upon GPA via the psychological characteristics. Thus, subjects who were more fluent in Spanish developed more confident general psychological characteristics and, because of this, they earned higher grades. Yet, this was not the only indirect effect which *fluency* was predicted to yield. Significant individual-variable indirect effects were also expected. Figure 10.1 shows that *fluency* did not yield any effects of this type because none of the direct effects involved, between *fluency* and any of the intervening individual psychological variables, and between the latter and GPA, were of sufficient magnitude.

These findings reveal that a subject's Spanish fluency led to higher grades only if the overall level of confidence rather than just a specific psychological characteristic was enhanced. It may be that each individual psychological trait is a too limited and insignificant part of the general self-confidence of subjects for each trait to be involved in mediating significant effects of this particular nature. However, the greater importance of the aggregate over component psychological traits in mediating effects is probably more a function of the role of the Spanish fluency independent variable. Beyond this, it is difficult to understand why these findings were derived.

Results not central to this study were generally consistent with those of other investigations. For example, it was found that lower income homes tended to be associated with the greater use of Spanish and with the derivation of children who are more fluent in Spanish. However, lower income homes produced offspring with less ambitious plans (this was the second strongest effect in the model) and lower confidence that they could achieve such plans. Lower income homes did not directly affect the academic success of offspring, which is inconsistent with current research. However, a significant indirect effect suggests that such homes negatively affected the grade point averages of students only after lowering the general confidence of offspring.

## SURVEY RESULTS

Results from a 1977 mail survey of Chicano college students from Texas demonstrate that high family Spanish usage yields both negative direct effects and positive indirect effects on the psychological and academic success of college students who have achieved a high level of English fluency. Negative effects are partially offset, or sometimes reversed, when families (or other agents of socialization) promote the Spanish fluency of students. Thus, Spanish dominant homes with children learning English through elementary and secondary schools will help children more if they also promote their bilingualism. In our model, high fluency in Spanish, an indicator of bilingualism in this sample, promotes the self-confidence and academic success of Chicano college students.

In general, the findings suggest that the role of a family's linguistic socialization in the psychological and academic development of children is a very complex one. The varied effects may be an indication of just how *marginal* the Chicano family really is in American society. That is, perhaps it is because there are push-pull forces toward Spanish language maintenance and linguistic acculturation originating both from outside and within the Chicano community that families yield such discrepant effects. This does not mean that there is something inherently wrong with the Chicano family. Rather, the effects may be an indication of how such families are attempting to adjust to clashing social forces within a pluralistic and often hostile society.

To an extent, it is surprising that such family and offspring language characteristics continue to be as important as they are among college-age students. Previous research has tended to focus on the roles of such variables among younger cohorts, especially within the context of elementary and secondary school settings (D. Lopez 1976). Too many investigations have erroneously presumed that *problems* in language and cultural identity are largely resolved before adulthood, especially among the upwardly mobile who are perceived survivors of an earlier language and cultural selection process (D. Lopez 1976).

Investigations have probably underestimated the continuing importance of language variables among Chicano adults. Some authorities have argued that as socioeconomically mobile minority individuals venture beyond the security of the ethnic/racial community and family, there is often an increased rather than decreased need to maintain such ties (Pfeifer and Sedlacek 1974). Further, it is also possible that such individuals may face more potent forms of discrimination than less mobile ethnic group members because the successful minority group subject represents a greater economic and political threat to the status quo. Such forces may also encourage the maintenance of community and primary group support systems.

An important qualification must be made: it is not correct, given the findings of this study, to view any and all manifestations of non-bilingualism, whether in the home and/or offspring, as inevitable determiners of degenerated psychological and academic outcomes. Certainly, the sample of less bilingual college students surveyed in this investigation demonstrated that they had sufficient levels of confidence and educational skills to have survived public school and the push-pull forces which were probably stronger prior to the time that the students entered college. This is an achievement in and of itself which very few Chicanos have been able to accomplish. All that has been argued in this study is that, comparatively speaking, bilingualism will have more beneficial effects.

In general, this study has shown that home *and* offspring language maintenance have important effects on Chicano college achievement and on those psychological characteristics which are essential for educational and overall socioeconomic success. However, it is likely that, when compared to investigations done on samples of younger and/or less educated cohorts, those conducted on more highly educated Chicanos, as in this study, will probably lower the amount of variation and the effects of home socioeconomic status, offspring bilingualism, and confidence because of the higher typical level of these characteristics among such older individuals. Investigations should be conducted on public school students and noncollege educated adults to determine how, in fact, the importance of family and offspring language maintenance varies among different samples of Chicanos. Of course, subsequent studies on Chicano college students are also necessary to determine the resiliency of the findings of this study.

## REFERENCES

Alexander, K. L., Eckland, B. K., and Griffin, L. J. "The Wisconsin Model of Socioeconomic Achievement: A Replication." *American Journal of Sociology* 81 (1976): 324–42.

Alwin, D. F., and Hauser, R. M. "The Decomposition of Effects in Path Analysis." *American Sociological Review* 40(1975):37–47.

Barth, F. "Introduction." In F. Barth, ed. *The Social Organization of Cultural Differences*. Boston: Little, Brown, and Company, 1969.

Barth, E. A., and Noel, D. L. "Conceptual Frameworks for the Analysis of Race Relations: An Evaluation. In T. Pettigrew, ed., *The Sociology of Race Relations: Reflections and Reform*. New York: The Free Press, 1980.

Carter, Thomas P., and Segura, R. *Mexican Americans in School: A Decade of Change*. New York: College Entrance Examination Board, 1979.

Coleman, J. S., et al. *Equality of Educational Opportunity*. Washington, D.C.: U.S. Department of Health, Education, and Welfare, Office of Education, 1966.

Del Buono, X. A. "The Relationship of Bilingual/Bicultural Instruction to the Achievement and Self-concept of Seventh Grade Mexican-American Students." Unpublished doctoral dissertation, Michigan State University, 1971.

Derbyshire, R. L. "Adolescent Identity Crises in Urban Mexican-Americans in East Los Angeles." In E. Brody, ed. *Minority Group Adolescents in the United States*. Baltimore: Williams and Wilkins, 1968.

Duncan, O. D. *Introduction to Structural Equation Models*. New York: Academic Press, 1975.

Firme, T. P. "Effects of Social Reinforcement on Self-esteem in Mexican-American Children." Unpublished doctoral dissertation, Stanford University, 1969.

Garcia, H. D. C. "Chicano Social Class, Assimilation, and Nationalism." Unpublished doctoral dissertation, Yale University, 1980.

Garcia, R. L. "Mexican-American Bilingualism and English Language Development." *Journal of Reading* 17(1974):467–73.

Gordon, M. M. *Assimilation in American Life: The Role of Race, Religion and National Origins*. New York: Oxford University Press, 1964.

Grebler, L., Moore, J. W., and Guzman, R. C. *The Mexican-American People: The Nation's Second Largest Minority*. New York: Free Press, 1970.

Hirsch, H., and Gutierrez, A. *Learning To Be Militant: Ethnic Identity and the Development of Political Militance in a Chicano Community*. San Francisco: R and E Research Associates, 1977.

Kenniston, K. *Radicals and Militants: An Annotated Bibliography of Empirical Research on Campus Unrest*. Lexington, Massachusetts: Lexington Books, 1973.

Long, K. K., and Padilla, A. M. "Evidence of Bilingual Antecedents of Academic Success in Groups of Spanish-American College Students." *Journal of Cross-Cultural Psychology* 11(1970):400–406.

Lopez, D. E. "The Social Consequences of Chicano Home/School Bilingualism." *Social Problems* 24(1976):234–46.

Novack, M. *The Rise of the Unmeltable Ethnics: Politics and Culture in the Seventies*. New York: Macmillan, 1973.

Pfeifer, C. M., Jr., and Sedlacek, W. E. "Predicting Black Student Grades with Non-Intellectual Measures." *Journal of Negro Education* 43(1974):67–76.

Poussaint, A., and Atkinson, C. "Black Youth and Motivation." In J. Banks and J. D. Grambs, eds. *Black Self-Concept*. New York: McGraw-Hill, 1972.

Ramirez III, M. "The Relationship of Acculturation to Educational Achievement and Psychological Adjustment in Chicano Children and Adolescents: A Review of the Literature." In O. I. Romano V, ed., *Voices: Readings from El Grito, 1967–1973*. Berkeley: Quinto Sol Publications, 1973.

Rand Corporation. *A Million Random Digits*. Glencoe, Illinois: The Free Press, 1955.

Rogers, Dorothy D. B. "Personality Traits and Academic Achievement Among Mexican-American Students." Unpublished doctoral dissertation, The University of Texas at Austin, 1971.

Selltiz, C., Wrightsman, L. S., and Cook, S. W. *Research Methods in Social Relations*. New York: Holt, Rinehart, and Winston, 1976.

Shaw, M. E., and Costanzo, P. R. *Theories of Social Psychology*. New York: McGraw-Hill, 1970.

Troike, R. C. *Research Findings Demonstrate the Effectiveness of Bilingual Education*. National Clearinghouse for Bilingual Education, 1979.

Weisberg, H. F., and Bowen, B. D. *An Introduction to Survey Research and Data Analysis*. San Francisco: W. H. Freeman and Company, 1977.

Zeller, R. A., and Carmines, E. G. *Measurement in the Social Sciences: The Link Between Theory and Data*. Cambridge: Cambridge University Press, 1980.

# PART THREE
# Policy Issues

# 11.
# Limited English-Proficiency: Analytical Techniques and Projections

*Louis G. Pol, Rebecca Oxford-Carpenter, and Samuel Peng*

IN THE FOLLOWING PAPER, we present both a set of techniques designed to create a surrogate measure of English-language proficiency, and a set of projections of limited English proficient persons to the year 2000 utilizing one of these techniques. Information about the number of children with Limited English Proficiency (LEP) is needed by federal and local policymakers to assess the extent to which the educational needs of these children have been met. To enhance the availability of such information, the 1974 Education Amendments authorized the National Center for Education Statistics (NCES) to determine the number of LEPs. Congress further amended the Bilingual Education Act in 1976 to authorize the NCES, the National Institute of Education (NIE), and the Commissioner of Education to work together to determine the size of the LEP population of various minority language groups in each state, as well as in the nation. Consequently, several studies were conducted, including the Survey of Income and Education (SIE),[1] the Children's English and Services Study (CESS),[2] Projections of Number of Limited English Proficient Persons to the Year 2000,[3] and some independent analyses of CESS data.

These studies have provided not only information needed by policy makers, but also a basis for obtaining a better understanding of the issues for identifying and projecting the number of LEP persons. The first crucial issue is the

---

1. *Survey of Income and Education (SIE)*. A survey completed by the Bureau of the Census in 1976.
2. *Children's English and Services Study (CESS)*. L. Miranda & Associates, Inc., Westat, Inc., and Resource Development Institute under a contract with the National Institute of Education, the National Center for Education Statistics, and the Office of Education completed in 1978. See O'Malley (1981, 1982) for further details.
3. *Projections of Number of Limited English Proficient (LEP) Persons to the Year 2000*. A study conducted by InterAmerica Research Associates, Inc., under a contract with the National Center for Education Statistics in 1980.

specification and definition of the concepts of non-English language background (NELB) and limited English proficiency. Without this conceptual development, any projections produced are of little use. As documented by Waggoner (1978), various definitions of LEP persons have been used by state education agencies. Definitions have ranged from the extremely simple, *non-English dominant children* to the very elaborate (1) *children who were not born in the United States, whose native tongue is a language other than English, and who are incapable of performing ordinary classwork in English*; and (2) *children who were born in the United States of parents possessing no or limited English-speaking ability and who are incapable of performing ordinary classwork in English*. Because of the wide variation in ways of defining LEP children, no meaningful comparisons or aggregations of state information can be made. Thus, a common definition of the concept of LEP is needed.

From previous studies, it is found that LEP is a subset of NELB, because not everyone with non-English language background is limited in English proficiency. Thus, the task of identifying LEP persons is twofold: first, the specification of NELB, and then the identification of LEP. In defining NELB, previous studies generally used the following criteria: persons in households in which languages other than English are spoken; persons with non-English mother tongues; and/or foreign-born persons who speak languages other than English, regardless of their household language.

Identifying LEP persons is rather complex. As defined in the Bilingual Education Act, as amended, LEP persons are those who are denied the opportunity to attain achievement levels comparable to others at their appropriate age and grade levels because of limited English language skills. The 1978 Amendment of the Act expanded the language skills domain to include speaking, reading, writing, and understanding the English language. Operationally, the identification of LEP persons requires a test that measures these skills. The Language Measurement and Assessment Inventories (LM & AI) used in the CESS are an outcome of an extensive search by a group of specialists for empirical criteria for determining LEP persons. Although performance on the LM & AI may be related to factors other than language skills, the test is generally acceptable, given the current state-of-the-art in the assessment of language proficiency (DuBois 1980).

The second issue addressed in previous studies concerns the design and procedures for determining the numbers of LEP persons in various minority language groups in each state and in the nation. One means of ascertaining these numbers would be to administer an English proficiency test to all NELB children. Those children whose scores are below the criterion (cut-off) score then can be identified as LEP persons. This approach, however, would be extremely expensive and time consuming. It is also doubtful that the full cooperation of all children and local educational agencies could be obtained.

Another approach would be to estimate the LEP population on the basis of existing data or data from regularly conducted surveys of households, such as the Current Population Surveys and the 1980 Census. The problem with this approach is that there are no test scores on English language skills in these surveys, and it is unlikely that an appropriate test covering all age groups of interest will be included in future surveys.

The need for information about the number of LEP persons, and the improbability that a language skills test will be administered to all NELB persons in a large national survey, have prompted educational researchers to look for alternative means of estimation. As mentioned earlier, it is generally conceded that LEP should be defined on the basis of scores on a language skills test, but, given the constraint of limited funds, test scores can be obtained only from a sample of NELB persons. Thus, the central issue is how to link the test scores of a small sample of NELBs both to a data set that is large enough for state estimates, and to a data set compiled at the same or different points in time.

Currently, the CESS contains test data, but its sample size of 1,909 cases is too small to allow reliable estimations for detailed state and language groups. The use of CESS data can be expanded if a proper linkage can be established between those data and a larger data set, such as the 1980 Census or the SIE. Various analytic approaches have been suggested in previous studies.

The purposes of the present paper are to review these analytic approaches and then present projections of the LEP population to the year 2000, utilizing one of these techniques. Furthermore, modifications to the technique used that might improve future projections are introduced. Finally, the policy implications of these projections for bilingual planning are discussed.

## TECHNIQUES

### Discriminant Function Analysis

Basically, two analytic procedures have been employed to link current CESS test scores to a set of census-type questions such as, "How well does the person speak English?," and "How well does the person understand English?," and to other variables, such as age, sex, and grade level. The first procedure employed discriminant analysis to determine an optimal linear combination of selected survey-type items that differentiates an LEP from a non-LEP person. A linear combination of these discriminating items is known as a discriminant function. The function can be expressed as:

$$D_i = \Sigma d_{ij} x_j$$

where

$D_i$ is the score on the ith discriminant function;

$d_{ij}$ are weighting coefficients; and

$x_j$ are census-type variables, expressed in equal units (i.e., standardized).[4]

This approach attempted to classify an NELB as an LEP or a non-LEP based on the score of the selected discriminant function. From this approach one would hope that only a few items (i.e., the x's in the function) are needed to produce a discriminant function which can yield a high degree of correct classification, or that the misclassification of LEPs as non-LEPs can be balanced by the misclassification of non-LEPs as LEPs.

This approach can be illustrated by an analysis of CESS data performed by the Resource Development Institute (1979). In that analysis, the following steps were implemented:

1. selecting questionnaire items from the CESS survey;
2. computing the degree of relationship between the selected items and the criterion (i.e., LEP vs. non-LEP status);
3. identifying items most highly related with the criterion (i.e., LEP status);
4. utilizing varying sets of selected items as models in a series of discriminant function analyses, with LEP and non-LEP status defining group membership;
5. comparing the efficiency of the models with respect to percentages of correct classification, and;
6. selecting the best model and applying its discriminant function weights to other survey data that have the same kind of questionnaire items to obtain state and national estimates of the number of LEP children.

The questionnaire items selected for the analysis were mostly language-related. These items were labeled Candidate MELP Items (CMIs). Those CMIs found to be significantly related to the criterion were: language often spoken in household; usual language of household; child's usual language; language often spoken by child; language spoken by siblings; where child was born, if not the U.S.; how well child speaks English; language spoken with

4. Census-type variables include items such as income, age, educational level, usual household language, and usual individual spoken language.

friends; how well child understands spoken English; language subgroup; age of child; and highest grade attended.

From these items, five models, each including items of particular interest, were tested on the whole United States sample. The best three were tested on the ten subgroups defined separately by region (i.e., California, Texas, New York, and the balance of the U.S.), by language (i.e., Spanish and other language), and by region and Spanish language, taken together.

The discriminant function analysis did not produce highly satisfactory results. The proportion of correct classification was generally around 60 percent. This percentage was too low to be acceptable for national estimates.

Recognizing the problems of a non-normally distributed dichotomous criterion variable and categorical predictor variables in the discriminant function analysis, Rowlett, Calkins, Brockett, and Sheffield (1980) used an alternative logistic discriminant analysis. This analysis, however, did not produce any results that are significantly different from those of the discriminant function analysis described previously.

The relatively low percentage of correct classification that emerges from the discriminant analysis technique means that it is not usable. The inclusion of predominantly language related items in the model poses an additional problem in that most of these items are not found in Census data; thus, the model cannot be used without further modifications.

### Probabilistic Procedure

The second procedure, employed in the 1980 study by InterAmerica Research Associates, Inc. (Oxford et al. 1980), was a probabilistic approach. It consisted of identifying subgroups of NELB persons included in the CESS and computing the probability of a member in a group being LEP. This probability was determined by dividing the weighted total of individuals in that subgroup. Specifically, for each subgroup of a population, the probability of a member being LEP is computed as follows:

$$P_i = \Sigma W_{ij} X_{ij}$$

where

$P_i$ is the probability for the *ith* group;

$W_{ij}$ is the weight for the *jth* person in the *ith* group;

and

$X_{ij}$ is the LEP status of the *jth* person in the *ith* group,

determined by test scores, 1 being LEP, and 0 being non-LEP.

**TABLE 11.1**
**Specification of Categories**

| Category | Ability to speak and understand English | Family income |
|---|---|---|
| 1 | No response | — |
| 2 | Very well | No response |
| 3 | Very well | < 15,000 |
| 4 | Very well | ≥ 15,000 |
| 5 | Well | — |
| 6 | Not well (< few words) | — |
| 7 | Not well (a few words) | — |
| 8 | Not at all | — |

Note: "Speak" and "understand" were two separate questions. Whichever response indicated better proficiency, if they differed, was the one used. Family income was only used for responses of "very well."

The derived LEP-to-NELB ratios (also known as LEP rates) from the CESS then were applied to SIE data to estimate the number of LEPs in this country and in each state by age cohorts and major language groups. The SIE was selected for linkage because it is a larger data set, has the relevant variables, has a similar sampling frame, and allows for estimates at the state level.

The characteristics included for determining subgroups were region of the country, ability to speak and understand English, and family income. The five language/region categories used were: Spanish speaking in California, Texas, New York, and rest of nation, and non-Spanish speaking for the nation as a whole. These five categories were then cross-classified with the eight categories shown in Table 11.1 to produce a total of 40 population subgroups.

The results for the forty subgroups of the NELB population are presented in Table 11.2. These probabilities were applied to SIE data by first defining the NELB subgroups outlined previously, and then by multiplying the $p$ value by the weight of the sample member. The sum of the products of the probability and weights is the estimated number of LEP persons. For example, the total number of LEPs of Spanish language background in California was 505,100, which is the sum of the products of the LEP rates in column 3 of Table 11.2 and the estimated NELBs of corresponding groups from the SIE.

The probabilistic approach has several advantages over the discriminant analysis technique. First, it eliminates the problem of misclassification resulting from the inefficiency of discriminant functions. Second, it requires only a few key language items. As shown in Table 11.1, only the variables of speaking and understanding abilities were used. The fewer language items needed, the more likely that such data are available. In fact, as can be seen in Table 11.3, the language items can be limited to only the *speaking ability* item. The $p$ values derived for subgroups using this item are as good as, if not better

**TABLE 11.2**
**LEP-to-NELB Ratios for Forty Subgroups of NELB Population**

| Category | Spanish | | | | | | | | | | | | Non-Spanish | | |
|---|---|---|---|---|---|---|---|---|---|---|---|---|---|---|---|
| | California | | | Texas | | | New York | | | Rest of nation[2] | | | Nation as a whole[3] | | |
| | LEP/total[1] | Percent | Sample size | LEP/total | Percent | Sample size | LEP/total | Percent | Sample size | LEP/total | Percent | Sample size | LEP/total | Percent | Sample size |
| 1 | 15.2/15.2 | 100.0 | 8 | 31.8/31.8 | 100.0 | 16 | 7.7/7.7 | 100.0 | 6 | 16.2/30.2 | 53.6 | 21 | 32.0/51.9 | 61.6 | 8 |
| 2 | 114.6/128.4 | 89.2 | 36 | 31.5/45.1 | 69.9 | 34 | 39.6/50.5 | 78.3 | 43 | 95.2/126.7 | 75.1 | 87 | 116.4/245.2 | 47.4 | 87 |
| 3 | 143.6/191.5 | 75.0 | 79 | 108.5/147.4 | 73.6 | 130 | 174.2/193.7 | 89.9 | 98 | 110.3/155.0 | 71.1 | 124 | 145.8/259.1 | 56.2 | 87 |
| 4 | 40.6/76.6 | 53.0 | 20 | 41.2/60.1 | 68.5 | 38 | 15.8/17.2 | 92.2 | 8 | 38.5/114.3 | 33.7 | 46 | 88.2/374.6 | 23.5 | 84 |
| 5 | 110.9/130.5 | 84.9 | 75 | 213.9/250.0 | 85.5 | 170 | 46.0/48.9 | 93.9 | 39 | 151.1/250.1 | 60.4 | 177 | 277.2/364.2 | 76.1 | 124 |
| 6 | 37.2/44.8 | 82.9 | 26 | 15.0/16.0 | 93.8 | 20 | 19.2/22.6 | 85.2 | 16 | 37.3/37.3 | 100.0 | 30 | 71.3/73.2 | 97.4 | 22 |
| 7 | 65.3/65.7 | 99.4 | 31 | 49.4/49.8 | 99.0 | 47 | 22.3/22.3 | 100.0 | 15 | 54.7/56.1 | 97.4 | 39 | 46.6/51.2 | 91.0 | 13 |
| 8 | 1.1/1.1 | 100.0 | 1 | 1.1/1.1 | 100.0 | 1 | .6/.6 | 100.0 | 1 | 0.0/0.0 | 100.0 | 0 | 2.6/2.6 | 100.0 | 2 |

Notes: 1. LEP/Total gives the weighted numbers of LEP and (NELB) total in the category in 1,000's.
2. This set of LEP ratios was used to make estimates for states other than California, Texas, and New York.
3. This set of LEP ratios was used for all non-Spanish language groups in each state as well.

**TABLE 11.3**
**Comparison of LEP-to-NELB Ratios Derived From Groups Defined by One Language Item and by Two Language Items**

| Region | Category* | Analysis 1** | | Analysis 2** | |
|---|---|---|---|---|---|
| | | Spanish children | Non-Spanish children | Spanish children | Non-Spanish children |
| California | No response | 1.00 | 0.62 | 1.00 | 0.62 |
| | Very well (NA) | 0.89 | 0.47 | 0.89 | 0.50 |
| | Very well (< $15,000) | 0.75 | 0.56 | 0.76 | 0.62 |
| | Very well (≥ $15,000) | 0.53 | 0.24 | 0.54 | 0.27 |
| | Well | 0.85 | 0.76 | 0.84 | 0.72 |
| | Not well (< few words) | 0.83 | 0.97 | 0.82 | 0.97 |
| | Not well (a few words) | 0.99 | 0.91 | 1.00 | 0.90 |
| | Not at all | 1.00 | 1.00 | 1.00 | 1.00 |
| Texas | No response | 1.00 | 0.62 | 1.00 | 0.62 |
| | Very well (NA) | 0.70 | 0.47 | 0.72 | 0.50 |
| | Very well (< $15,000) | 0.74 | 0.56 | 0.75 | 0.62 |
| | Very well (≥ $15,000) | 0.69 | 0.24 | 0.69 | 0.27 |
| | Well | 0.86 | 0.76 | 0.86 | 0.72 |
| | Not well (< few words) | 0.94 | 0.97 | 0.95 | 0.97 |
| | Not well (a few words) | 0.99 | 0.91 | 0.99 | 0.90 |
| | Not at all | 1.00 | 1.00 | 1.00 | 1.00 |
| New York | No response | 1.00 | 0.62 | 1.00 | 0.62 |
| | Very well (NA) | 0.78 | 0.47 | 0.79 | 0.50 |
| | Very well (< $15,000) | 0.90 | 0.56 | 0.90 | 0.62 |
| | Very well (≥ $15,000) | 0.92 | 0.24 | 0.94 | 0.27 |
| | Well | 0.94 | 0.76 | 0.92 | 0.72 |
| | Not well (< few words) | 0.85 | 0.97 | 0.86 | 0.97 |
| | Not well (a few words) | 1.00 | 0.91 | 1.00 | 0.90 |
| | Not at all | 1.00 | 1.00 | 1.00 | 1.00 |
| Other | No response | 0.54 | 0.62 | 0.64 | 0.62 |
| | Very well (NA) | 0.75 | 0.47 | 0.75 | 0.50 |
| | Very well (< $15,000) | 0.71 | 0.56 | 0.71 | 0.62 |
| | Very well (≥ $15,000) | 0.34 | 0.24 | 0.34 | 0.27 |
| | Well | 0.60 | 0.76 | 0.62 | 0.72 |
| | Not well (< few words) | 1.00 | 0.97 | 1.00 | 0.97 |
| | Not well (a few words) | 0.97 | 0.91 | 0.95 | 0.90 |
| | Not at all | 1.00 | 1.00 | 1.00 | 1.00 |

*See Table 1.
**Analysis 1 used 'speak and understand' and 'income level' to define categories (see Table 1); Analysis 2 used only 'speak' and 'income level' to define categories.

than, those derived for subgroups using the *speaking* and *understanding* items combined. This finding is particularly helpful, since the 1980 census only includes *speaking ability*, and since the probabilities of LEP can be applied to 1980 census data.

## LEP PROJECTIONS

### Cohort Component Prevalence Rate Method

The LEP projection method used in the study is the Cohort Component Prevalence Rate Method. This method links the previously discussed probabilistically derived LEP rates to an independent set of population projections. The Cohort Component Prevalence Rate Method begins with the simple equation:

*Equation 1*
(a) Projected LEP for Year $Y$ = (b) NELB 1976 ÷ Total
Population 1976 × (c) Population Projection for Year $Y$ × (d)
LEP Rate

where (a), the LEP projection for Year Y, is the product of the following elements: (b) the NELB-to-total-population ratio, based on the 1976 SIE (NELB Rate); (c) Census Bureau's noninstitutionalized population projection for Year $Y$ (U.S. Bureau of the Census 1977a); and (d) the LEP rate.

This is called the Cohort Component Prevalence Rate Method because (b) and (d) involve calculation of prevalence rates, while (c) utilizes Census Bureau population projections, which are based on a method that uses age cohorts and accounts for population change resulting from the interaction of such components as fertility, mortality, and migration. Explicit in this formula are our own assumptions that not only does the LEP rate remain constant across time, but so does the NELB rate. We also assume that these NELB rates are age-band specific and not cohort specific; that is, as the five- and six-year-olds in 1980 become ten- and eleven-year-olds in 1985, they do not carry with them the 1980 five- and six-year-old NELB rate, but exhibit the 1985 projected ten- and eleven-year-old NELB rate.

The overall methodology involves two basic steps. First, the NELB population is projected. Then LEP rates are multiplied by the projected NELB population to produce the number of LEPs.

Equations 2 and 3 below are other ways of expressing the elements in Equation 1.

*Equation 2*
Projected NELB Population for Year $Y$ = NELB Rate (from SIE)
× Projected Population for Year Y (from Census Bureau
Population Projections)

*Equation 3*

Projected LEP Population for Year Y = LEP rate (derived from CESS and SIE using MELP) × Projected NELB Population for Year Y

The projections utilize the U.S. Census Bureau's illustrative projections of state populations by age, Series II-B. Series II-B assumes: (1) a cohort total fertility rate of 2.1, which is consistent with the birth expectations seen in survey data; (2) an increase in life expectancy from 69.1 to 71.8 years for males and 77.0 to 81.0 for females between the years 1976 and 2050; (3) net immigration of 400,000 persons per year; and (4) a continuation from 1975 to 2000 of the civilian, noncollege interstate migration patterns by age for 1970 to 1975 (U.S. Bureau of the Census 1977a, 1979a). While other Census Bureau projections can be used, it was decided that Series II-B has the most-likely-to-occur set of assumptions concerning future levels of fertility, mortality, and migration. It has been mentioned above that Equation 1 assumes constant LEP and NELB rates. However, it is likely that the two rates will not remain constant, and that the further from the 1976 to 1978 period, the larger the error will be, especially with respect to the NELB projection. In particular, the NELB population most likely is growing at a rate somewhat different from that of the total population.

A differential growth rate was applied for Spanish NELBs, because they are growing at a much faster rate than the rest of the NELB population, in general, as well as faster than the total United States population. This differential growth rate was calculated from figures in the Current Population Surveys, Series P-20. The growth rate of the total United States population is now about .7 or .8 percent per year, and by the year 2000 the Census Bureau projects that it may fall to about .4 percent per year, or it may stay constant, depending on future fertility. The .8 figure for the total United States population was chosen. The growth rate of the Spanish-origin population, in contrast, is approximately 2.2 percent per year. The differential growth rate is 1.4 percent per year (2.2 minus .8). This differential growth rate is projected for more than one year by using the basic compound interest or geometric progression formula. The annual growth rate for each projection year is calculated for each state/age group, and the differential of 1.4 percent per annum greater is applied to the Spanish NELB group.

It was necessary to manipulate published data by age to correspond to the age categories required in this study. While SIE data are available by single years and therefore can be aggregated in any way desired, Census Bureau population projections for states are produced in intervals varying from five to forty years. Therefore, it is necessary to utilize two standard demographic techniques to disaggregate these data. The first technique (Arriaga 1968) makes use of a quadratic equation and reduces ten-year intervals to five-year intervals. Following that was the use of Beer's oscillatory interpolation procedure (Shryock and Siegal 1971:600–702), which is a six-term minimized fifth-difference formula designed to produce single-year categories from five-year intervals.

## Categories for Projections

The categories for projections included:

*Language*. The nineteen non-English language groups included in the SIE, plus combination groups: Asian; non-Spanish; non-Asian; non-Spanish and non-Asian, and total non-English.
*Geographic Area*. Nation, all states, and District of Columbia.
*Age*. For policy purposes, three sets of age categories were selected: contiguous ages, birth to fifty-five and over, school ages, five through fourteen only, and miscellaneous ages. The contiguous age set included seven mutually exclusive categories, the school age set included six nonmutually exclusive categories, and the miscellaneous age set included eight nonmutually exclusive categories. It was possible to use all age groups for calculations of NELBs. However, for estimates and projections of LEPs, only the five-through-fourteen age group was usable because the CESS, one of the determinants of the LEP rate, included only that age band.

A rather stringent criterion was used to determine which language by geographic area by age categories would be projected. Only those cells which had population estimates (in the 1976 SIE, the necessary basis for all the projections) equal to or greater than three times the standard error of the cell sample size were included in the data base for projection. This criterion insures a nonnegative 99 percent confidence interval.

## LEP Overview

The discussion which follows is concerned exclusively with LEP children in the five-through-fourteen age band. The total number of LEP children ages five through fourteen in 1976 approximated 2.5 million, with a drop to 2.4 million in 1980 and a gradual increase to 2.8 million in 1990 and 3.4 million in 2000. The 1976 figure of 2.5 million can be compared with the finding of 2.4 million LEP children in the same age band in the 1978 CESS.[5] This com-

---

5. It should be noted that the figure of 3.6 million LEPs found in the CESS was for the entire four-through-eighteen band and was based on extrapolation.

parison is not surprising, because the LEP projections showed a decline from 2.5 million in 1976 to 2.4 million in 1980 and 1985, and the CESS result also captured this decline. These data also reflected the fact that the United States population projections showed temporary declines in younger age groups for about the same time.

### LEP Results by Language

Between years 1976 and 2000 there was an increase of 880,000 LEP persons. Of this increase, 840,000 persons (95.5 percent) were accounted for by the Spanish LEP population. This result is a product of the higher growth rate for Spanish speakers, the concentration of this group in the five-through-fourteen age band, and higher LEP rates for this group.

Results of LEP by language are displayed in Figure 11.1. Spanish LEPs numbered 1.8 million in 1976, dropped to 1.7 million in 1980, returned to 1.8 million in 1985, and rose to 2.1 million in 1990, 2.5 million in 1995, and 2.6 million in 2000, *an overall rise from 71 percent of all LEPs in 1976 to 77 percent of all LEPs in 2000.*

Asian LEPs in this age band also showed a temporary decline. In 1976 there were .13 million, dropping to .12 million in 1980 and .11 million in 1985, returning to .12 million in 1990, and rising to .13 million in 1995 and 2000.

Non-Spanish and non-Asian LEPs ages five through fourteen, when combined, totalled .6 million in 1976 and 1980, declining to .5 million in 1985, and returning to .6 million for the remainder of the century.

A portion of the differing language results can be explained by variations in LEP rates. Children five-through-fourteen-years-old, of Asian or other non-Spanish language backgrounds, with occasional exceptions, had LEP rates in the range of .41 to .53, with a composite ratio of .50, meaning that *50 percent of the NELBs in these groups were also LEP*. LEP rates for five-through-fourteen-year-olds which were lower than .50 were found for such NELB groups as Filipinos, French, German, Greek, Japanese, Korean, and Polish. LEP rates of .50 to .60 occurred for Chinese, Italian, and Portuguese NELBs. Yiddish and Navajo NELBs had LEP rates of .60 and .70. The highest LEP rates were found for Spanish and Vietnamese NELBs, .75. Newer arrivals and those culturally separated from the mainstream of society, the most noteworthy was Navajo, had higher ratios.

While LEP rates for individual languages were assumed constant across time for the projections, the predominance of growth by the Spanish group raised the national average LEP rate from .65 in 1976 to .68 in 2000. The .65 figure was the result of 2.5 million five-through-fourteen-year-old LEP children (1.8 million Spanish and .7 million non-Spanish) versus 3.8 mil-

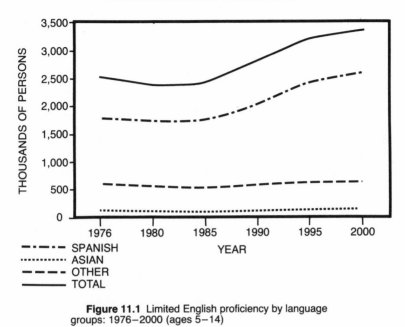

**Figure 11.1** Limited English proficiency by language groups: 1976–2000 (ages 5–14)

lion five-through-fourteen-year-old NELB children (2.4 million Spanish and 1.4 million non-Spanish) in 1976. The .68 figure was the result of 3.4 million five-through-fourteen-year-old LEP children (2.6 million Spanish and .8 million non-Spanish) versus 5 million five-through-fourteen-year-old NELB children (3.5 million Spanish and 1.5 million non-Spanish) in 2000.

### LEP Results by Age

The five-through-nine-year-old LEP group numbered 1.3 million in 1976, dropped to 1.2 million in 1980 and 1985, and rose to 1.5 million in 1990 and 1.8 million in 1995 and 2000. The ten-through-fourteen-year-old LEPs numbered 1.3 million in 1976, 1.2 million in 1980 and 1985, 1.3 million in 1990, 1.4 million in 1995, and 1.6 million in 2000. Thus, there was a slightly greater overall increase in five-through-nine-year-old LEPs than in the ten-through-fourteen-year-old LEPs. These results are shown in Figure 11.2

One might assume that the LEP rate will drop as children grow older because of their longer exposure to an English-speaking environment. This assumption, however, was not fully supported by the results. Except for Spanish language background children, the twelve-to-fourteen-year-olds had a higher LEP rate than the ten-to-eleven-year-olds. Reasons for such patterns are not quite clear. One possible explanation is that there are more immigrants of

*Pol*

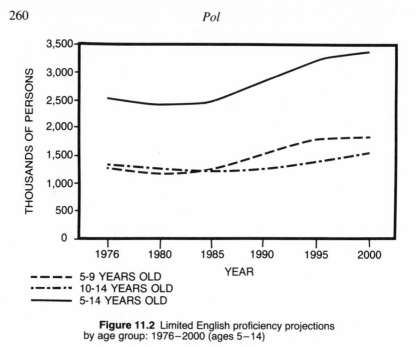

**Figure 11.2** Limited English proficiency projections by age group: 1976–2000 (ages 5–14)

ages twelve to fourteen or older entering the country. Legal immigration data seem to provide evidence supporting this suggestion. In 1978, the proportion of all immigrants ten-through-nineteen years of age was about one-third greater than that for immigrants less than ten years old (9.5 percent versus 7.3 percent) (U.S. Department of Justice 1968). This pattern was consistent for all language categories.

### LEP Results by State

State LEP projections are presented in Figure 11.3. Two of the three main states in which LEPs are concentrated showed overall increases to the year 2000, despite some temporary plateaus. California LEPs numbered .6 million in 1976, 1980, and 1985; and then rose steadily to .7 million in 1990; .8 million in 1995; and .9 million in 2000. In Texas, LEPs totaled .5 million in 1976 and 1980, .6 million in 1985, .7 million in 1990, .8 million in 1995, and .9 million in 2000. By way of contrast, New York showed .5 million LEPs in 1976; .4 million in 1980, 1985, and 1990; and .5 million in 1995 and 2000.

The percentage of the total LEP population which was concentrated in these three states rose from 63 percent in 1976 to 67 percent in 2000. These figures compare with 45 percent of all NELBs concentrated in these three

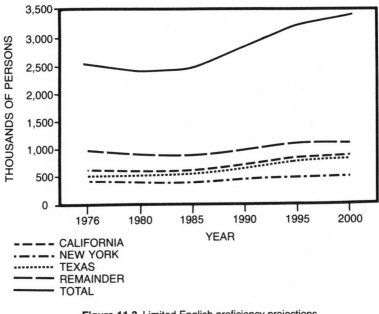

**Figure 11.3** Limited English proficiency projections
by major states: 1976–2000 (ages 5–14)

states in 1976 and 48 percent of all NELBs in 2000. The indication is clear: LEPs are more highly concentrated than NELBs in these three key states.

There was a large variation in LEP rates by state. While the Spanish LEP rate in New York was .92, it was only .58 in Florida. Comparable to the national Spanish LEP rate were the figures for Texas and California, .79 and .77. This seems to suggest that the Cubans, concentrated in Florida, are much more proficient in English than the Chicanos of Texas and California, who in turn are much more proficient than those of Puerto Rican background in New York. This is a speculative explanation, but it is intriguing and plausible.

Another possible explanation for the variation in LEP rates by state is that the LEP rate of a language group is positively related to the concentration of the language group members in a region; that is, the greater proportion of NELBs in a community, the higher the LEP rate. However, California, which in 1976 had a far larger share of all five-through-fourteen-year-olds of Spanish language background than did New York (27 percent versus 15 percent), had a LEP rate for this age group of .77, scarcely larger than the comparable national rate. Therefore, this explanation, while attractive, may not be valid.

## LEP Results by Language and Age

Spanish LEPs, ages five through nine, went from .9 million in 1976 to .8 million in 1980; .9 million in 1985; 1.1 million in 1990; and 1.4 million in 1995 and 2000. Ten-through-fourteen-year-old Spanish LEPs totaled .9 million in 1976, 1980, and 1985; 1.0 million in 1990 and 1995; and 1.2 million in 2000. These figures show that younger Spanish LEPs grew a little faster in number than did older Spanish LEPs between 1976 and 2000.

Asian LEP children, ages five through nine, totaled 70,000 in 1976; 63,000 in 1980 and 1985; 74,000 in 1990; 84,000 in 1995; and 81,000 in 2000. LEPs ages ten through fourteen of Asian language backgrounds numbered 56,000 in 1976; 52,000 in 1980; 49,000 in 1985, and 1990; 52,000 in 1995; and 54,000 in 2000. Thus, there was a pronounced increase in the number of younger Asian LEPs between 1976 and 2000 and a slight drop in older Asian LEPs during that period.

Non-Spanish/non-Asian LEPs, ages five through nine, totaled .3 million in 1976, 1980, 1985, and 1990; almost .4 million in 1995; and .3 million in 2000. Ten-through-fourteen-year-old non-Spanish/non-Asian LEPs approximated .3 million in 1976, 1980, 1985, 1990, 1995, and 2000. There was little change in numbers for both of these age groups in the non-Spanish/non-Asian category.

The LEP rate exhibited little variation within a language group, but considerable differences across language groups. The Spanish LEP rates were clustered around .75 for all age groups, while all non-Spanish LEP rates tended to cluster around .50. In general, though, the Spanish five-through-nine age group had a slightly higher LEP rate (.76) than the ten-through-eleven and twelve-through-fourteen-year age groups, which had rates of .74 and .73. In contrast, the non-Spanish groups had LEP rates for these age groups (five through nine, ten through eleven, and twelve through fourteen) of .50, .48, and .51, respectively.

## LEP Results by Language and State

The major concentration of 1976 LEP children was for Spanish speakers in three states—California with 500,000, Texas with 480,000, and New York with 330,000. Together they accounted for 52 percent of all LEP children. However, by the year 2000 they had grown to a 60 percent share of all LEP children, or 780,000 in California, 820,000 in Texas, and 410,000 in New York. Of the total growth of 880,000 LEP children projected between 1976 and 2000, a full 700,000 (79.5 percent) came from just the Spanish-speaking LEPs in these states. Of these three states, Texas showed the most dramatic growth with 70 percent, followed by California with 56 percent and New York with 25 percent growth. Also notable was the growth of Spanish LEPs in Florida; from 76,000 in 1976 to 150,000 in 2000 (97 percent growth) and in Arizona from 52,000 to 103,000 (96 percent growth). While Texas surpassed California in numbers of Spanish LEPs in 1980 (547,000 versus 513,000), California maintained its lead as the state with the largest number of LEPs (902,000) followed closely by Texas (853,000) in the year 2000.

The total gain in non-Spanish LEPs from 1976 to 2000 was only 40,000, which was widely dispersed, nationally. Non-Spanish LEPs actually declined in the states of New York, Pennsylvania, Illinois, and Ohio, where they were most concentrated. The non-Spanish LEP total for those four states declined from 225,000 in 1976 to 204,000 in 2000. However, this was almost compensated for by the gain from 104,000 to 117,000 in California alone.

There were also significant variations in LEP rates by language and state. The highest LEP rate was .92 for the Spanish in New York, and the lowest was .41 for the Filipinos in Hawaii. Within the Spanish group, the range was from .54 in Oregon to the previously mentioned .92 in New York. Texas and California, where the Spanish population is most concentrated, had LEP rates of .77 and .79, respectively. Despite the fact that most other states had lower Spanish LEP rates, the presence of high rates in California, New York, and Texas brought the national Spanish LEP rate up to .75. In contrast, the Asian group ranged from .46 in Alaska to .63 in Oregon, with a national Asian LEP rate of .50. The group that is neither Spanish nor Asian ranged from .43 in Iowa to .63 in Arizona, and had a national non-Spanish/non-Asian LEP rate of .50.

## CAVEATS TO THE PROJECTION

Three issues must be raised concerning the base population projections: (1) lack of usable information about illegal immigration; (2) lack of reliable information on refugees; and (3) inability to differentiate the growth rates and age structure of the base population by all specific language groups.

The most serious caveat regards immigration of illegal or undocumented aliens. The Census Bureau has summarized all the available studies, and it has found that the number of illegal immigrants present in the United States is estimated by various studies to be anywhere from 2.9 to 12.0 million (Siegel, Passel, and Robinson 1980). Many of these studies are strictly guesswork. Furthermore, the rate of flow into and out of the United States is indeterminate. With no definitive source to draw upon, and with an overwhelming probability of error, it was decided not to address the question of illegal immigration in making projections in this study.

The recentness and volatility of the Indochinese and Cuban refugee influx indicates the difficulty of considering world political events in making population projections. A 1980 NCES study by Goor indicated almost 100,000 Indochinese children ages five through eighteen resided in the United States as of October 31, 1979—almost double the reported number for the 1977–78 school year. The trends of such political refugee immigration are so unpredictable that it is impossible to involve them in a systematic projection methodology. Although the 1980 Census can provide some data on Indochinese refugees, reliable information concerning recent Cuban refugees will have to emerge from a later census.

Another important caveat concerns our inability to differentiate the growth rates and age structure of the base population by all relevant language groups. Because of this inability, projections for some of the specific non-Spanish European language groups may have been overestimated (e.g., Polish) and projections for some of the Asian language groups (e.g., Vietnamese) may have been underestimated. It is impossible to adjust the figures further in any realistic way without knowing more about the growth rates and age structure of the language groups.

Four problems were presented by Oxford et al. (1980, 1981) with regard to LEP prevalence rates: (1) language shift through intermarriage and acculturation; (2) immigration; (3) lack of information on the expected effect of school experiences on LEP rates; and (4) use of a single set of non-Spanish LEP rates to apply to the SIE.

While the strength of the probabilistic approach to projecting LEPs lies in its efficiency and simplicity, it is not necessarily free from weakness. As may be recalled from Table 11.2, some subgroups in the sample had such a small number of cases that they may not be sufficient to produce a reliable estimate of $p$ value. In fact, the first response category (i.e., no response to the "speak" and "understand" questions) and the eighth category (i.e., "not at all") had only a few cases included in the sample. The estimated $p$ values for those subgroups may be unreliable.

The use of language items in classifying subgroups may also pose the problem of varying criteria used in self-rating of language ability. The response categories to the language items range from "very well" to "not at all". It is assumed that older NELB children will be more likely than younger ones to give themselves "very well" or "well" ratings, reflecting in part the result of education and other intervention programs. It is also not clear whether respondents in one survey interpret categories in the same way as respondents in other surveys. Thus, the difference in response distribution for those self-rating items between, for example, the SIE and the CESS may be due to varying rating criteria used by respondents. This problem is complicated further if a certain response category appears in one survey but not in the other. For example, the "refusal" category in the SIE was not included in the CESS. Thus, no $p$ value derived from the CESS can be applied to this group.

## NEW PROJECTION TECHNIQUE TO BE TESTED:
## SYNTHETIC ESTIMATE PROCEDURE

In view of the measurement problems cited above, one may ask if it is necessary to use those language-related items to define subgroups for deriving LEP ratios. The answer to this question is: the items used to define subgroups for deriving LEP ratios should be determined by the way one wants to present the estimated number of LEP persons. In the projection just presented, the number of LEP persons in subgroups is defined by three variables: state, age cohort, and language group. Thus, the subgroups needed for computing LEP ratios can be defined sufficiently by those variables. Detailed or further breakdowns of a group do not add any precision if the weighted marginal total is the statistic of interest, since the total weight remains fixed.

What this analysis tells us is that CESS data can be linked to other survey data that do not include language items, except those needed to construct selected NELB subgroups. For example, if one is interested in the number of LEP persons by country of birth and by household language, a certain set of LEP probabilities is required. However, if one needs to further classify LEP persons by geographic region, a different set of probabilities will be needed.

Once the subgroups have been selected, the $p$ values of LEP for these groups can be derived from one study and then applied to another study, conducted at a different time and having estimates of the NELB population. This procedure is commonly labeled the synthetic estimate procedure. The probabilistic approach described above, in fact, uses the synthetic estimate procedure.

Specifically, the steps to estimate LEP persons are as follows:

a) For a study that has language test scores: define NELB test scores; determine the subgroups of NELB for which the number of LEP persons is to be estimated; and compute the LEP $p$ value for each subgroup.

b) For a study to which derived $p$ values are to be applied: define NELB as in (a) above; determine subgroups of NELB as in (a) above; calculate the total NELB in each subgroup (i.e., the sum of the weights of NELB persons in the subgroup); and multiply the proper $p$ value by the total NELB to obtain the estimated LEP persons in that group.

The above procedures assume that the LEP $p$ values remain stable over a short period of time. If this assumption is not supported, adjustment in the $p$ values will be needed. The application of the above procedure also can accommodate the sampling errors for both the $p$ value and the total NELB. Assuming that at a 95 percent confidence level, the $p$ value for a subgroup from survey A is: $p \pm 1.96\sigma_A$, and the total NELB (N) for the same subgroup from

Survey A is: $p \pm 1.96\sigma_A$, and the total NELB (N) for the same subgroup from Survey B is $N \pm 1.96\sigma_B$, where $\sigma_A$ and $\sigma_B$ are standard errors for $p$ and N, respectively, from Surveys A and B. The actual estimation of LEP persons can have the following four figures:

$$(p + 1.96\sigma_A)(N + 1.96\sigma_B) = \chi_1$$
$$(p - 1.96\sigma_A)(N + 1.96\sigma_B) = \chi_2$$
$$(p + 1.96\sigma_A)(N - 1.96\sigma_B) = \chi_3$$
$$(p - 1.96\sigma_A)(N - 1.96\sigma_B) = \chi_4$$

Obviously, $\chi_1$ will be the upper limit, and $\chi_4$ will be the lower limit of the estimate for a subgroup. It is important to provide ranges such as these for planning purposes. Decision-makers need to know both maximum estimates and the minimum estimate in order to allocate resources in the most reasonable way.

The above procedures can be used for projecting the number of years by varying the $N$s to reflect changes in the NELB population and refining the $p$ values, if data permit. A simplistic way is to use the same $p$ value but different $N$s over the year to reflect the increase or decrease of the NELB population, an approach that takes into consideration varying growth rates for different subgroups.

## POLICY IMPLICATIONS

The results and techniques presented above have implications for bilingual education, social services, and military manpower planning. First, it is clear that Spanish LEPs will become an increasingly important factor over the next two decades. Spanish language background persons are already the largest group of non-English language background persons, and their share of LEPs will increase. This is due in part to the fact that they have higher LEP rates than do most other NELBs, indicating that a greater percentage of the Spanish language background children ages five through fourteen are limited in English than children of the same ages from most other NELB groups. Together, these facts indicate that educational, social, and military planners in many agencies will need to find ways to meet the bilingual education needs of a growing Spanish clientele.

However, the sheer number of Spanish NELBs and LEPs should not mask the needs of other groups. The very high LEP rates among smaller groups, such as Vietnamese, Navajo, and Yiddish, are important for policy planning. Nevertheless, planning for these groups in areas where their concentration is not high most certainly will present difficulties.

The geographic concentration of NELBs and LEPs within three states—California, Texas, and New York—should significantly influence the allocable funds and programs for the next few decades. However, an important caveat is that the projections cannot foresee and take into account such phenomena as the increasing Cambodian refugee influx or the massive Cuban sea-lift operation, both of which have affected geographic concentrations of LEPs in untold ways. In addition, changes in United States immigration policy would certainly affect our projections.

One interesting result that affects policy planning is that LEP children and younger NELB groups temporarily appear to decrease in number during the decade of the 1980s, although they all increase again by the end of the century. This reflects the projected temporary decline of younger age groups in the total United States population and is a factor in educational planning.

Clearly, new projections should be made using 1980 Census data. It is important to use the latest and most accurate data possible in order to make projections. In the meantime, the projections reported here offer the best available information for policy planning for language minority groups until the year 2000.

## REFERENCES

Arriaga, E. E. New life tables for Latin American populations in the nineteenth and twentieth centuries. *Population Monograph Series No. 3.* Berkeley: University of California Press, 1968.

Dubois, David D. *The Children's English and Services Study: A Methodological Review.* Washington, D.C.: United States Department of Education, National Center for Education Statistics, Publication Number 80-503, August 1980.

Goor, J. *Indochinese children: A survey of selected states and districts.* Washington, D.C.: National Center for Education Statistics, 1980.

Oxford, Rebecca; Pol, Louis; Lopez, David; Stupp, Paul; Peng, Samuel; and Gendell, Murray. *Changes in number of non-English language and limited English proficient persons in the United States to the Year 2000: the projections and how they were made.* Rosslyn, Virginia: InterAmerica Research Associates, Inc., 1980.

Oxford, Rebecca; Pol, Louis; Lopez, David; Stupp, Paul; Gendell, Murray; and Peng, Samuel. "Projections of Non-English Language Background and Limited English Proficient Persons in the United States to the Year 2000: Educational Planning in the Demographic Context." *Journal for the National Association for Bilingual Education* 5(1981): 1–30.

Resource Development Institute. *Analysis of MELPs among respondents.* Austin, TX: Author, 1979.

Rowlett, K., Calkins, D., Brockett, P. L., and Sheffield, J. *A comparison of linear discriminant function and logistic regression using categorical predictors and a binary criterion variable.* Paper presented at the annual meeting of the American Educational Research Association, Boston, Massachusetts, April 1980.

Shyrock, H. S., and Siegel, J. *The Methods and Materials of Demography.* Washington, D.C.: United States Government Printing Office, 1971.

Siegel, J. S.; Passel, J. S.; and Robinson, J. G. *Preliminary review of existing studies of the number of illegal residents in the United States*. Washington, D.C.: United States Bureau of the Census, 1980.

United States Bureau of the Census. Illustrative projections of state populations by age, race, and sex: 1975 to 2000. *Current Population Reports, Series P-25, No. 796*. Washington, D.C.: United States Government Printing Office, 1979.

United States Bureau of the Census. Projections of the Population of the United States: 1977 to 2050. *Current Population Reports, Series P-25, No. 704*. Washington, D.C.: United States Government Printing Office, 1977a.

United States Bureau of the Census. Persons of Spanish Origin in the United States: March 1976. *Current Population Reports, Series P-29, No. 329*. Washington, D.C.: United States Government Printing Office, 1977b.

United States Department of Justice, Immigration and Naturalization Service. *Immigrants admitted by country or region of birth, sex and age*. Washington, D.C.: Author, 1968.

Waggoner, D. *State education agencies and Language-minority students*. Washington, D.C.: National Center for Education Statistics, 1978.

# 12.
# Bilingualism and Hispanic Employment: School Reform or Social Control

*Craig Richards*

WHILE THE GREAT SOCIETY PROGRAMS of the 1960s failed to break the vicious circle of urban poverty, they did succeed in increasing minority professional employment. The public sector, in particular, stimulated by an infusion of federal dollars, has been credited as the most receptive employer of minority professionals. In the case of Hispanic professionals, it is widely presumed that within the public sector, public schools—through expanding bilingual programs—have also been a major source of employment since the late 1960s.[1]

This paper describes and interprets changes in California's public school Hispanic employment practices and the contribution of bilingual categorical funding and regulations to such increases in the period from 1967 to 1981. At issue is understanding the role of public schools in providing employment for Hispanic professionals in terms of both its public policy and political-economic ramifications.

1. The term "Hispanic" is used throughout this study as an umbrella term for people of Ibero-American origin, which includes virtually every racial and ethnic grouping. Hispanics have been recognized as a cultural minority by the courts and the term Chicano is a narrower term which applies to Hispanics of Mexican national origin. In recent years, California's Hispanic population has come to include a significant number of Central Americans who, while subjected to similar cultural and color barriers to employment, have an historical experience different from Chicanos. Moreover, the consistent use of the term "race" as a substitute for the cumbersome phrase "race and ethnicity" is not meant to obfuscate the point that many Hispanics share a common Caucasian racial background with Anglos. The study uses the term "race" to differentiate Anglos from Blacks and Hispanics since discrimination on the basis of group characteristics is common for both Hispanics and Blacks in distinction from Anglos. The term "race" in this sense is used not as a precise anthropological term but rather as a cultural category in a society where ascription based on social features is the basis for access to employment. The terms 'minority segregation,' 'school segregation,' and 'Anglo, Black or Hispanic segregation' refer only to the level of student segregation, not to the level of teacher segregation in public schools. Finally, the term 'segregation' is applied equally to minority and nonminority schools that are racially isolated. In this study Black and Hispanic teachers are treated as "minorities" (although in many school districts they are in fact in the majority) since that is a conventional term in educational policy.

California is an important test case for this investigation because it has been an educational laboratory, and, whether intentionally or unintentionally, California has been involved on a number of fronts in relevant issues, including statewide financing, desegregation, bilingual education, and teacher layoffs. It is still unclear what impact this combination of federal, state and local initiative has had on Hispanic employment. This paper offers some preliminary insights.

### Social Reform or Social Control

There are at least two competing interpretations of state employment reform—the social *reform* and the social *control* perspective—and both must be sifted through a screen of demographic, economic and institutional changes which accompany, and undoubtedly affect, Hispanic employment outcomes.[2] Each of these related topics will be treated in greater detail in the following pages.

The American common school system has a long history of ideological association with democracy and social reform.[3] Indeed, it has been a major locus of reformist pressure for much of the past century. More recently, the nation's schools have been the target of the federal policy reforms of the Great Society in the 1960s. Similarly, the teaching profession *itself* has long been viewed as an occupation conducive to the social mobility aspirations of young adults from working class and minority backgrounds. Consistent with this perspective, proponents of increased employment of Hispanic teachers have argued that such hiring is desirable for equity, legitimacy, and role-modeling reasons.[4]

2. There are a number of recent and excellent reviews of the literature on recent theories of the capitalist state. See in particular: Martin Carnoy, *Theories of the State*, Unpublished, Stanford University 1981; Bob Jessop, "Recent Theories of the Capitalist State," *Cambridge Journal of Economics* 1, no. 4, December 1977, David A. Gold, Clarence Y. H. Lo, and Erik Olin Wright. "Recent Developments in Marxist Theories of the Capitalist State," in *Monthly Review* 27, Nos. 5 and 6, October 1975. Theda Skocpol, "Political Response to Capitalist Crisis: Neo-Marxist Theories of the State and the Case of the New Deal," *Politics and Society* 10, no. 2, 1980.

3. Lawrence A. Cremin (1964): *The Transformation of the School: Progressivism in American Education*, New York: Random House, Vintage Books; John Dewey (1966): *Democracy and Education*, New York Free Press; Wirth, Arthur (May 1981): "Exploring the Links Between Dewey's Educational Philosophy and Industrial Reorganization," *Economic and Industrial Democracy*, vol. 2, no. 2, p. 121–40.

For an excellent review of the debate surrounding the potential of education for reform in the present period see, Hurn, Christopher (1978): *The Limits and Possibilities of Schooling*, Boston: Allyn and Bacon. On internal colonialism, see: Mario Barrera, (1979): *Race and Class in the Southwest: A Theory of Racial Inequality*, University of Notre Dame Press, Indiana; Stokely Carmichael and Charles Hamilton (1965): *Black Power*, New York; Harper and Row; Martin Carnoy (1974): *Education as Cultural Imperialism*, New York: David McKay and Co.

4. Beatriz Arias (October 1979): "Desegregation and the Rights of Hispanic Students: The Los Angeles Case," *Evaluation Comment* 6(1): 14–18; Beatriz Arias (1981): "Towards an Understanding of Desegregation Remedies for Hispanics," (Unpublished). Presented at the Ameri-

In light of this history, interpreting the patterns of Hispanic employment in California's public schools has at least two important public policy implications. First, if Hispanic educators experienced significant and permanent employment gains, it suggests that existing political institutions are capable of responding to demands for social reform. Additionally, such gains support the reformist thesis that the public sector is a critical arena within which minorities, women and other under-represented groups can first establish employment gains which can then be used as models for the wider society. Therefore, verifying the success of employment gains by Hispanic teachers lends support to advocates of an expanded role for the state in ameliorating the inequities of our economic system.

Second, nested within this general question of the role of education as an employer of Hispanic professionals is the related issue of the contributions of bilingualism to the increased employment of Hispanic professionals. Evidence of dramatic increases in Hispanic employment attributable to bilingualism would be additional support for a reformist conception of public education. Indeed, Title VII legislation and proponents of bilingual education have been frequently attacked precisely because bilingual education is perceived to be no more than a *jobs program* for Hispanics.[5] Ironically, given the rapidly changing demographics of California and the shortage of bilingual certified teachers, non-Hispanic teachers may be benefitting as much as Hispanics from bilingual-related employment. As yet, however, there is little evidence to either support or reject the claim, a problem this study attempts to address.

In contrast to the reformist perspective, there is a less sanguine interpretation of Hispanic employment practices in the public schools. A *revisionist* school of critical scholarship has established a dissenting interpretation of public schooling and questions the viability and permanence of reforms with an egalitarian thrust. Some revisionist scholars have argued that schools are more accurately portrayed as institutions of social control and social reproduction.[6] Thus, to the extent that schools are situated in a wider society that is

---

can Educational Research Association, Los Angeles. Abdin Noboa (Fall 1980): "Hispanics and Desegregation: Summary of Aspira's Study on Hispanic Segregation Trends in U.S. School Districts." *METAS*, 1–24; Anthony G. Dworkin (April 1980): "The Changing Demography of Public School Teachers: Some Implications of Faculty Turnover in Urban Areas." *Sociology of Education* 53(2):66.

5. Betsy Levin (March, 1982), "The Making (and Unmaking) of a Civil Rights Regulation: Language Minority Children and Bilingual Education," Institute for Research on Educational Finance and Governance, Stanford University Project Report No. 82–A4.

6. Samuel Bowles and Herbert Gintis, (1976) *Schooling in Capitalist America*. New York: Basic Books. David Nosaw (1979) *Schooled to Order*, New York: Oxford University Press. Paul C. Violis (1978) *The Training of the Urban Working Class*, Chicago: Rand McNally. Jerome Karabel and A. H. Halsey, editors, (1977), *Power and Ideology in Education*, New York: Oxford University Press.

highly unequal, schools cannot be expected to become significantly more equal than the larger society, either in their treatment of pupils or in their employment practices. This view certainly negates a leadership role for the public schools as a model employer of minority professionals.

The social control perspective also has an explanation for apparent employment gains by Hispanics in the public schools: Hispanics have been hired only to teach Hispanic children. Thus, it could be argued that the *apparent employment gains* of Hispanic teachers occurred only because Anglo teachers fled to jobs in the suburbs. New vacancies were filled by Hispanics for pupil control purposes and to appease angry Hispanic leaders. Revisionists argue that few Hispanic educators are hired in predominantly Anglo school districts. In short, their argument is that public schools have created what Stokely Carmichael originally called "welfare colonialism," a form of internal colonialist theory developed within the American Black nationalist movement.

Similarly, Mario Barrera has developed an internal colonial model for the Chicano experience in the Southwest in terms of race and class. He argues that Chicanos, as an internally colonialized people, have interests that transcend their class positions and simultaneously class interests which potentially conflict with their racial and cultural interests, depending on their locations in the class structure. Quoting Barrera:

> Chicanos also constitute a colony with a certain coherence across class lines in the sense that they are liable to be in frequent contact with each other. Thus the bilingual Chicano teacher, a member of the professional-managerial class, comes into contact with Chicano parents from the working class. Chicano social workers are liable to have a largely Chicano clientele, as are other Chicano professionals.[7]

Thus, in the absence of highly politicized Hispanic interest groups, Hispanic educators can find themselves racially functional to the reproduction of a segregated and class based public school system—a system which at the same time is ideologically committed to ameliorate race and class bias.

If, indeed, there has been an increase in the number of Hispanic professionals employed in public schools in the post–Civil Rights period, how would this increase be interpreted in light of the foregoing discussion? Frances Piven and Richard Cloward have argued in their provocative book, *Poor People's Movements*, that independent action and disruptive tactics are the most effective strategy for the poor to improve their conditions, and this "politics of disorder" stimulated the dramatic increases in the employment of

---

7. *Op cit.*, Barrera, p. 216.

minority professionals within the public sector during the Civil Rights era. Sharp disagreements exist, however, over the extent, permanence, and political significance of these apparent changes in employment practices.[8]

The social reform and social control perspectives advance competing views of the institutional role Hispanic teachers play within a larger system of education. A third view, the most plausible, is that advanced by Ira Katznelson and by Levin and Carnoy who agree with Piven and Cloward on the importance of public schools as an institutional terrain within which to advance the equity demands of minorities, but also believe that these reforms are being eroded due to fiscal crises and a lack of institutional protections sufficient to sustain such reforms.[9] The following sections attempt to clarify these related issues of fact and interpretation by describing first the relative levels and direction of change in the employment of Hispanic teachers; and second, the specific contribution of bilingualism to increased employment of Hispanic teachers; and finally, by interpreting these changes in light of the social reform and social control theses.

## THE IMPETUS FOR BILINGUAL EDUCATION

As early as 1968, Congress established, under Title VII of the Elementary and Secondary Education Act, a demonstration program to address the educational needs of low-income children with limited proficiency in the English language. Prior to 1968, virtually every state required that English alone be used as the principal medium of instruction.[10] The impetus for bilingual education, however, followed the 1974 U.S. Supreme Court Decision *Lau v Nichols* (414 U.S. 593), which held that language minority children were entitled to public school instruction in their native language. Evidence of this impetus can be found in the changes in the level of federal funding for bilingual programs before and after 1974. From 1969 to 1974 annual federal appropriations grew from $7 million to $45 million; from 1974 to 1980 they grew from $45 million to $158 million.

In California that impetus was furthered by a profound demographic shift

8. For an interesting debate on the merits of the "politics of disorder" as a strategy to empower minorities see the exchange between Piven and Cloward and Roach and Roach in *Social Problems*, December 1978; and Robert B. Albritton (December 1979), "Social Amelioration through Mass Insurgency? A Reexamination of the Piven and Cloward Thesis," *The American Political Science Review*, pp. 1003–1011. Also see D. K. Newman, *et al.* (1976) Chapter 4, in *Protest, Politics and Prosperity*, New York: Pantheon Books.

9. Henry Levin and Martin Carnoy (1983): *The Dialectics of Education*, unpublished manuscript, Stanford University; Ira Katznelson (October 1978): "Considerations on Social Democracy in the United States," *Comparative Politics*.

10. See Richard Navarro and Beatriz Arias, (Autumn 1981), "Bilingual Education for Hispanics, Issues of Language Access and Equity," *IFG Policy Notes*, vol. 2, no. 4.

in the school-age population.[11] In 1981, California had 810,605 students whose primary language was not English; of these, 612,362 (76 percent) were Spanish speaking. Among students who spoke Spanish, 136,689 could not speak English and another 148,875 had limited proficiency in speaking English. In short, nearly half of all Spanish-speaking students either could not speak English or could speak English only with great difficulty. Together, judicial mandates, legislative reform, and profound demographic shifts generated a new demand for bilingual teachers.

A number of studies have been conducted on the supply and demand for bilingual teachers, both nationally and in California.[12] In the Burnett study, a national shortage of 75,000 bilingual teachers was estimated. Similarly, supply and demand studies in California, which have been mandated by the state legislature, consistently point to a shortfall of bilingual teachers. According to the California Commission for Teacher Preparation and Licensing (1981), the 1981 supply of elementary teachers with bilingual certificates was 5,026 while the demand was 9,627. Supply is meeting just over 50 percent of demand. Furthermore, the gap between supply and demand was not expected to close over the next two or three years. Anticipated increases in supply, based on current college enrollment, were expected only to match corresponding increases in demand. In absolute terms, the number of language minority children not provided access to qualified bilingual teachers will be increased.

## CATEGORICAL FUNDS FOR BILINGUAL TEACHER TRAINING

California, with the largest and fastest-growing Hispanic population of any state in the nation, also receives the largest percentage (26 percent) of federal aid directed at Hispanic students. Additionally, California supports bilingual categorical programs from state resources. For the 1980–81 school year, eighteen California State Universities and Colleges received a total of twenty-nine state and fourteen federal bilingual grants. The state grants totaled $2,046,407 while the federal grants amounted to $5,441,301, for a total of $7,487,708. As Table 12.1 demonstrates, 1,299 students were in bilingual programs related to the above funds at an average of $5,764 per student.

11. See Dorothy Waggoner, (October 1978), "Place of Birth and Language Characteristics of Persons of Hispanic Origin in the United States, Spring 1976." U.S. Department of Health, Education and Welfare, National Center for Education Statistics. And more recently, California State Department of Education, (Spring 1981) *Language Census Report*.

12. The most recent of these studies include: California Commission for Teacher Preparation and Licensing (February 1981) *Status Report on Bilingual-Crosscultural Teacher Preparation in Accordance with California Education Code Section 10101*, Sacramento; Joanne Binkley, (September 1980), "Bilingual Education Program Graduate" unpublished, SRI, Menlo Park, California; estimated that approximately 1500 bilingual certified teachers were generated by Title VII sponsored programs and 870 from non-Title VII sponsored programs in 1980.

**TABLE 12.1**
**California State University and College Bilingual Grants by**
**Source, Amount and Students Served, 1981**

| Grant Source | Amount | Students |
|---|---|---|
| Federal | | |
| Multi-Year | | |
| Title VII Project | $3,041,400 | — |
| ESEA Title VII | 2,399,901 | — |
| Federal Total | 5,441,301 | 382 |
| State | | |
| Bilingual Teacher | | |
| Corps (AB 2817) | 1,283,050 | 629 |
| Bilingual Teacher | | |
| Development (AB 1329) | 763,357 | 288 |
| State Totals | 2,046,407 | 917 |
| Overall Totals | 7,487,708 | 1,299 |

Source: California Commission for Teacher Preparation and Licensing, *Status Report on Bilingual-Crosscultural Teacher Preparation*, February 15, 1981, Table 6.

Title VII Bilingual Grants are awarded directly to prospective teachers to become certificated classroom teachers. This legislation is a part of the Elementary and Secondary Education Act (ESEA). Funds are also available under Title VII for currently certified teachers to pursue advanced degrees in bilingual education or to institutions of higher learning, local education agencies, or non-profit corporations to provide specific services related to bilingual staff development. As of 1981, California passed two major pieces of legislation intended to increase the supply of bilingual teachers. California Assembly Bill 2817 established a bilingual teacher corps program which is designed to prepare instructional aides to become certified bilingual classroom teachers. The grantee enrolls in a state-approved community college or four-year public institution of higher education. The Bilingual Education Improvement and Reform Act of 1980 (AB 507) is a grant program which provides a stipend to upper-division and graduate students enrolled in bilingual-bicultural programs. Grants may be awarded to currently practicing teachers as well.

## CHANGES IN HISPANIC PROFESSIONAL EMPLOYMENT

California's public schools were not always a significant employer of Hispanic professionals. In 1959, the California State Board of Education established the Commission on Discrimination in Teacher Employment to address the problems minority teachers confronted when seeking a public school position. The establishment of the commission followed the passage of State Education Codes which made it a violation of California state policy to refuse

**TABLE 12.2**
**Totals and Percentages for California Public School Teachers by Race**
**Comparing 1967, 1977, and 1980**

| Classroom Teachers | Anglo | Black | Hispanic | Other | Total |
|---|---|---|---|---|---|
| 1967 Totals | 163,523 | 8,137 | 4,189 | 4,003 | 179,852 |
| (Percent) | (90.9) | (4.5) | (2.3) | (2.3) | (100) |
| 1977 Totals | 146,195 | 9,645 | 8,227 | 6,642 | 170,709 |
| (Percent) | (85.6) | (5.6) | (4.8) | (4.0) | (100) |
| 1980 Totals | 121,323 | 9,400 | 8,826 | 7,568 | 147,117 |
| (Percent) | (82.5) | (6.4) | (6.0) | (5.1) | (100) |

Note: This table was adapted from Foote, et al., 1978, Table 15, page 35, and The California State Department of Education, 1980 (Figures in parentheses are percentages.) The category other includes: Asian, Pacific Islander, Filipino, American Indian, and Alaskan Native.

employment because of an applicant's race, color, religious creed, national origin, age, or marital status. A 1959 survey by the Commission concluded that the most significant type of discrimination problem confronting teachers was that "members of certain racial and ethnic groups, particularly Negroes, still face limitations in finding jobs." [13] The commission also found that the total number of Hispanic teachers in California public schools was even lower than that of Blacks.

California's public schools have altered their earlier employment practices. Table 12.2 shows that in absolute terms Hispanic teachers increased their presence in the classroom by over 100 percent from 1967 to 1980, while Anglo teachers lost about 25 percent in the same period. These changes took place at a time when the total school age population decreased by over 3 percent, and the number of students from racial and ethnic minorities, particularly Hispanic, rapidly grew. Nevertheless, while Hispanic pupils now represent well over one-third of all California pupils, only one out of every twenty teachers is Hispanic. By 1985, Hispanic students are projected to represent nearly one-half of the California student population, while the one to twenty ratio of Hispanic to non-Hispanic teachers is unlikely to improve given current hiring practices. For example, of the 9,678 new teachers hired in 1980 in California's public schools, about 84 percent were Anglo and 10 percent were Hispanic. [14]

The ratio of Anglo teachers to Anglo pupils in 1967 was 1:20; by 1979, that ratio was up, 1:17, a 15 percent increase in Anglo representation. The

13. Commission on Discrimination in Teacher Employment (1961): *Toward Equal Employment Opportunity for Teachers in California's Public Schools.* Second Annual Report, California State Department of Education, p. 1.

14. California State Department of Education, Office of Intergroup Relations (Fall 1979): *A Racial and Ethnic Distribution of Students and Staff in California Public Schools.*

ratio for Hispanic teachers to Hispanic pupils changed from 1 : 147 in 1967, to 1 : 104 in 1979. These figures confirm that the employment gains of Hispanic teachers have more than kept pace with the rapid increases in Hispanic pupils. Given continued fiscal retrenchment in California, however, the absolute number of newly hired Hispanics has been very low and will continue to be so. In short, the employment of Hispanic teachers has more than doubled since 1967, but that doubling occurred over an extremely small base.

## A COMPARATIVE PERSPECTIVE

Although Table 12.2 demonstrates that Hispanic employment in California did increase substantially in relative terms, Table 12.3 shows that education's contribution to the employment of Hispanic professionals was smaller than the state civil service and approximately equivalent to levels in the private sector. Contrary to conventional wisdom, these results suggest that California public schools are not model employers of Hispanic professionals. While Hispanic employment gains in the public schools have been significant, they are *not* so relative to the gains in comparable occupational categories in other sectors of the economy. Finally, if private sector professional Hispanic employment appears relatively impressive, one should note that while 55 percent of the *total labor force* was employed in higher status white-collar occupations in California, only 29.7 percent of the *total Hispanic employed labor force* was working in these types of jobs. In short, Hispanics would nearly have to double their 1978 levels of employment in upper level white-collar jobs to be employed at the same rate as non-Hispanics in California.

## THE CONTRIBUTION OF BILINGUALISM TO HISPANIC EMPLOYMENT

Teaching jobs requiring bilingual certification have been a major avenue of entry for Hispanics into the educational labor force: 39 percent of all Hispanic teachers in California are bilingually certified. At the same time, however, the overall contribution of bilingual certification to Hispanic employment in the total teacher force has been relatively modest. There are two reasons for this. First, employment generated by bilingual education has also provided a significant number of new jobs for Anglo teachers in absolute terms (about 2,400 in 1980), if not in relative terms. Moreover, even if all bilingual education teachers were Hispanic, the contribution of bilingual certification to the total labor force would be less than 5 percent. Given present hiring patterns, the net addition of Hispanic teachers to the *total labor force* as a direct result of bilingual programs was roughly 2 percent during 1980.

Keeping these qualifications in mind, an important corollary question is

**TABLE 12.3**
**Professional Employment in California, by Race and Sector**

| | Public School Teachers (1980) | State Civil Service Professionals (1980) | Private Sector Professionals (1978) |
|---|---|---|---|
| Hispanic | 11,804 | 5,180 | 37,011 |
| Percent of Total | (5.9) | (7.7) | (5.0) |
| Black | 9,400 | 5,246 | 24,681 |
| Percent of Total | (6.4) | (7.8) | (3.4) |
| Anglo | 121,323 | 51,143 | 627,290 |
| Percent of Total | (82.5) | (76.3) | (85.0) |
| Other | 7,568 | 5,429 | 45,647 |
| Percent of Total | (5.1) | (8.2) | (6.2) |
| Total | 147,117 | 66,998 | 734,629 |
| | (100) | (100) | (100) |

Sources: California Labor Market Issues: Hispanics, September, 1981; California Department of Education, Office of Inter-Group Relations, 1980; Annual Census of State Employees, Report to the Governor and Legislature, July 1981, California.
Note: The Category for State Civil Service Professionals includes technical workers but not administrators. The Category for Private Sector Professionals does not include officials and managers, occupations that have slightly higher participation rates for minorities.

whether state and federal bilingual education programs have themselves contributed to racially determined employment patterns. It seems reasonable to expect that the demand for bilingual certified teachers of all races would be greatest in schools, especially elementary schools, with the most Hispanic students. This should occur for three reasons. First, 60 percent of all Hispanic students are enrolled in grades K–6.[15] Second, the incidence of limited English-speaking students is greatest in these schools because Hispanics are the largest language minority in California. And third, demand for these specially trained teachers outstrips supply by more than 100 percent. Three-fourths of all bilingual teachers were in such schools in 1980.

## PUPIL SEGREGATION AND HISPANIC EMPLOYMENT

Cursory evidence suggests student segregation is an important determinant of minority employment. To assess more accurately its impact, estimates were generated that measure the probability of a Hispanic teacher being employed in a school with specified racial concentrations of students while controlling

15. California State Department of Education, *op. cit.*, Table 2.

statistically for the independent effects of selected variables commonly recognized to influence teacher demand and supply. This model takes the 1981 supply of employed California public school teachers and isolates the importance of teacher race in predicting the level of student segregation in the schools where teachers are assigned. Given the categorical nature of the dependent variable (levels of pupil segregation), these methodological objectives were best satisfied through a set of statistical procedures known as *multinomial logit analysis.*[16]

Multinomial logit modeling provides a methodology for estimating the relative weight given to a teacher's race in predicting that teacher's likelihood of being employed in a school with a certain proportion of minority pupils, as compared to teachers in other schools with different proportions of minority pupils. In the analysis that follows, schools with 70 to 100 percent Hispanic students will be used as the principal, common point of comparison against which all other teacher assignments will be compared. From this, the first stage of the analysis is to estimate the dependent variables: (a) the log-odds of a teacher being assigned to a school with less than 10 percent Hispanic students rather than being assigned to a school with more than 70 percent Hispanics; (b) the log-odds of being assigned to a school with 10 to 30 percent Hispanic pupils compared to greater than 70 percent; (c) the log-odds of being assigned to a school with 30 to 50 percent Hispanic pupils compared to greater than 70 percent; and finally, (d) the log-odds of being assigned to a school with 50 to 70 percent Hispanic pupils as compared to a school that is higher than 70 percent Hispanic. The choice of these five levels and the four sets of comparisons specified in the model satisfy the objective of examining a broad range of racially segregated schools, constrained only by the statistical requirement that sufficient numbers of teachers for a given race are assigned to schools with these levels of minority pupil concentration.

To compute these log-odds, variables reflecting other supply and demand conditions are introduced simultaneously and their separate effects are controlled statistically. These variables include a variety of personal characteristics which, in addition to race, include the teacher's sex, education, teaching experience, and teaching credentials (bilingual or not). Job-related, that is, school-related characteristics must also be introduced; in addition to measures of the racial segregation of students, these include the grade level of the

16. Takeshi Amemiya (December 1981): "Qualitative Response Models: A Survey." *Journal of Economic Literature*; Aaron S. Gurwitz (1980): "School Finance Reform and Residential Choice: A Multinomial Logit Approach," Rand Corporation Draft; Morley Gunderson (Spring 1980): "Probit and Logit Estimates of Labor Force Participation," *Industrial Relations*, vol. 19, no. 2, pp. 216–20; Peter Schmidt and Robert P. Strauss (June 1975): "The Prediction of Occupation Using Multiple Logit Models," *International Economic Review*, 251–259.

school, whether elementary or secondary, and the recent (1979–80) change in Anglo, Black, and Hispanic student populations in the school to which the teacher is assigned. Given the simultaneous introduction of these supply and demand conditions, the multinomial logit model is said to be of *reduced form*; that is, it is not possible to separate formally the determinants of labor force supply and demand. For example, it is impossible from this model to determine whether Hispanic teachers occupationally prefer teaching in racially segregated schools or whether they are only accepted for employment in segregated schools.

Once the log-odds of teacher assignment by level of pupil segregation are computed, the beta coefficients can next be converted into probability estimates. These conditional probabilities specify the likelihood that an Anglo or Hispanic teacher will be assigned to a school with one of five levels of racial segregation, while controlling for other personal and job-related characteristics. It is these probability estimates which are reported in the text. Tables 12.8 and 12.9 report the beta coefficients and t-tests from which these probabilities are derived and a formal presentation of the general form of the multiple logit model.

The statistics reported below were estimated on data derived from the 1981 teacher surveys conducted as part of the California Basic Education Data System (CBEDS). These surveys canvass the entire population of elementary and secondary teachers employed by local educational agencies in California. The estimates derived from these data reflect the relative importance of personal and job-related characteristics on the actual assignment to racially segregated schools of Anglo, Black, and Hispanic teachers.

The probability estimates of employment for Hispanics and Anglos with nonbilingual credentials are presented in Tables 12.4 and 12.5, showing variation by teacher race, teacher sex, school grade-level, and level of Hispanic pupil segregation. Different racially determined patterns of employment in Hispanic segregated schools are observed for Anglo and Hispanic teachers— patterns that hold even after controlling for the independent effects of other personal and job-related characteristics. First, at the secondary level, Anglo teachers are up to twice as likely to teach in schools with less than 10 percent Hispanics, while on the opposite extreme, Hispanic teachers are four times as likely to teach in the most Hispanic segregated schools, those with an Hispanic enrollment greater than 70 percent. Second, at the elementary level, Hispanic teachers are even more likely to teach in segregated schools: 40 percent of all Hispanic elementary teachers teach in schools with over 50 percent Hispanic students, compared to under 15 percent for similarly trained Anglo teachers. Again, at the other extreme, Anglo elementary teachers are three

**TABLE 12.4**
**Probability of Hispanic Teacher Employment for**
**Each Level of Hispanic Segregation[a]**
**1981**

| | Hispanic Pupil Concentrations in Public Schools[b] | | | | |
|---|---|---|---|---|---|
| | 0–10% (N = 265) | 10–30% (N = 508) | 30–50% (N = 490) | 50–70% (N = 386) | 70+ % (N = 636) |
| Hispanic Elementary School Teachers with Regular Credentials | | | | | |
| Male | .10 | .30 | .21 | .13 | .27 |
| Female | .11 | .26 | .20 | .15 | .28 |
| Hispanic Secondary School Teachers with Regular Credentials | | | | | |
| Male | .21 | .35 | .25 | .08 | .12 |
| Female | .23 | .30 | .25 | .10 | .12 |

[a]Controlling for the effects of average education, experience, changes in Hispanic pupil growth, and changes in Anglo pupil growth.
[b]N is the number of Hispanic teachers in a random sample of 2,285 Hispanics who teach in schools with these levels of Hispanic pupil concentration.

**TABLE 12.5**
**Probability of Anglo Teacher Employment for**
**Each Level of Hispanic Segregation[a]**
**1981**

| | Hispanic Pupil Concentrations in Public Schools[b] | | | | |
|---|---|---|---|---|---|
| | 0–10% (N = 782) | 10–30% (N = 821) | 30–50% (N = 317) | 50–70% (N = 155) | 70+ % (N = 157) |
| Anglo Elementary School Teachers with Regular Credentials | | | | | |
| Male | .37 | .38 | .13 | .06 | .06 |
| Female | .31 | .38 | .15 | .07 | .07 |
| Anglo Secondary School Teachers with Regular Credentials | | | | | |
| Male | .41 | .39 | .12 | .04 | .03 |
| Female | .36 | .40 | .14 | .05 | .03 |

[a]Controlling for the effects of average education, experience, changes in Hispanic pupil growth, and changes in Anglo pupil growth.
[b]N is the number of Anglo teachers in a random sample of 2,232 Anglos who teach in schools with these levels of Hispanic pupil concentration.

times more likely than their Hispanic counterparts to teach in schools with fewer than 10 percent Hispanics. Third, these trends apply irrespective of the teacher's sex. At no level of Hispanic pupil segregation does a teacher's sex appreciably alter the employment patterns of Anglo and Hispanic teachers within segregated elementary and secondary schools. In short, gender is not an important predictor of internal assignment in a labor market where three out of every four employees are women.

Multinominal logit analysis also allows generation of conditional probability estimates of employment for Hispanics and Anglos with bilingual cer-

**TABLE 12.6**
**Probability of Employment for Hispanic Teachers with Bilingual**
**Certificates for Each Level of Hispanic Segregation[a]**
**1981**

| | Hispanic Pupil Concentrations in Public Schools[b] | | | | |
|---|---|---|---|---|---|
| | 0–10%<br>(N = 265) | 10–30%<br>(N = 508) | 30–50%<br>(N = 490) | 50–70%<br>(N = 386) | 70+ %<br>(N = 636) |
| Hispanic Elementary School Teachers with Bilingual Credentials | | | | | |
| Male | .02 | .14 | .24 | .22 | .38 |
| Female | .02 | .12 | .24 | .25 | .38 |
| Hispanic Secondary School Teachers with Bilingual Credentials | | | | | |
| Male | .05 | .20 | .36 | .18 | .21 |
| Female | .05 | .17 | .36 | .20 | .22 |

[a]Controlling for the effects of average education, experience, changes in Hispanic pupil growth, and changes in Anglo pupil growth.
[b]N is the number of Hispanic teachers in a random sample of 2,285 Hispanics who teach in schools with these levels of Hispanic pupil concentration.

**TABLE 12.7**
**Probability of Employment for Anglo Teachers with Bilingual Certificates for Each**
**Level of Hispanic Segregation[a]**
**1981**

| | Hispanic Pupil Concentrations in Public Schools[b] | | | | |
|---|---|---|---|---|---|
| | 0–10%<br>(N = 265) | 10–30%<br>(N = 508) | 30–50%<br>(N = 490) | 50–70%<br>(N = 386) | 70+ %<br>(N = 636) |
| Anglo Elementary School Teachers with Bilingual Credentials | | | | | |
| Male | .09 | .44 | .21 | .06 | .20 |
| Female | .07 | .42 | .22 | .07 | .21 |
| Anglo Secondary School Teachers with Bilingual Credentials | | | | | |
| Male | .11 | .52 | .21 | .05 | .10 |
| Female | .09 | .51 | .24 | .06 | .11 |

[a]Controlling for the effects of average education, experience, changes in Hispanic pupil growth, and changes in Anglo pupil growth.
[b]N is the number of Anglo teachers in a random sample of 2,232 Anglos who teach in schools with these levels of Hispanic pupil concentration.

tificates. These estimates are presented in Tables 12.6 and 12.7. Several findings are especially noteworthy. First, the demand for bilingual education teachers regardless of race or grade level is extremely low in schools with less than 10 percent Hispanic pupils. This empirically verifies the previous hypothesis that the demand for teachers with bilingual certificates should be greater in schools with ever larger concentrations of Hispanic students. Second, at the secondary level, where only one out of four bilingual teachers

## TABLE 12.8
### Multiple Logit Modeling of Hispanic Teacher
### Employment in California by Level of Hispanic Pupil Segregation, 1981
### Coefficients and t–ratios
### (N = 2285)

| Dependent Variable | C | Sex | Level of Ed | Years of Experience | Bilingual Credential | Elem | Hispanic Growth | Anglo Growth |
|---|---|---|---|---|---|---|---|---|
| LOGe | .72 | .07 | −.16 | .07 | −2.07 | 1.51 | −.16 | −.01 |
| | (−1.75) | (−.42) | (−1.78) | (6.51) | (−8.69) | (7.47) | (−7.10) | (−.63) |
| LOGe | −.01 | .17 | −.14 | .04 | −1.18 | .96 | −.13 | −.12 |
| | (−.04) | (1.25) | (−2.05) | (3.76) | (−7.91) | (5.46) | (−7.59) | (−7.40) |
| LOGe | −.68 | .03 | .03 | .02 | −.19 | .99 | −.09 | −.08 |
| | (−1.99) | (.23) | (−.40) | (2.05) | (−1.49) | (5.54) | (−5.38) | (−5.11) |
| LOGe | −.73 | −.14 | .02 | −.01 | .19 | .36 | −.03 | −.06 |
| | (−1.99) | (−.91) | (.22) | (−.70) | (1.42) | (1.69) | (−1.83) | (−3.65) |

The dependent (polychotomous) variable is constructed on the following five levels of Hispanic pupil segregation: $P_1$ = 0–10 percent Hispanic pupils (n = 265), $P_2$ = 10–30 percent Hispanic pupils (n = 508), $P_3$ = 30–50 percent Hispanic pupils (n = 490), $P_4$ = 50–70 percent Hispanic pupils (n = 386), and $P_5$ = 70+ percent Hispanic pupils (n = 636). It should be noted that the n for each level is the number of Hispanic teachers assigned to schools with the corresponding percentage of Hispanic pupils.

## TABLE 12.9
### Multiple Logit Modeling of Anglo Teacher
### Employment in California by Level of Hispanic Pupil Segregation, 1981
### Coefficients and t–ratios
### (N = 2232)

| Dependent Variable | C | Sex | Level of Ed | Years of Experience | Bilingual Credential | Elem | Hispanic Growth | Anglo Growth |
|---|---|---|---|---|---|---|---|---|
| LOGe | 1.63 | .24 | −.03 | .02 | −2.54 | 0.97 | −.24 | .001 |
| | (3.59) | (1.11) | (−.34) | (1.84) | (−3.99) | (3.46) | (−9.10) | (−.04) |
| LOGe | 1.49 | .07 | −.04 | .02 | −.95 | .91 | −.20 | .10 |
| | (3.33) | (6.33) | (−.42) | (1.97) | (−2.28) | (3.26) | (−7.80) | (−4.15) |
| LOGe | .52 | −.03 | −.01 | .02 | −.67 | .80 | −.07 | −.03 |
| | (−5.00) | (−1.27) | (.18) | (1.05) | (2.67) | (−1.47) | (1.34) | (−7.48) |
| LOGe | .15 | −.16 | −.08 | −.01 | −1.05 | .50 | −.02 | −.04 |
| | (.27) | (−.59) | (−.61) | (.34) | (−1.76) | (1.50) | (−.84) | (1.34) |

The dependent (polychotomous) variable is constructed on the following five levels of Hispanic pupil segregation: $P_1$ = 0–10 percent Hispanic pupils (n = 782), $P_2$ = 10–30 percent Hispanic pupils (n = 821), $P_3$ = 30–50 percent Hispanic pupils (n = 317), $P_4$ = 50–70 percent Hispanic pupils (n = 155), and $P_5$ = 70+ percent Hispanic pupils (n = 157). It should be noted that the n for each level is the number of Anglo teachers assigned to schools with the corresponding percentage of Hispanic pupils.

worked in 1980, Hispanic bilingual certified teachers are over twice as likely as their Anglo counterparts to work in Hispanic segregated schools, that is, with greater than 50 percent Hispanic student enrollment. At the other extreme, Anglo teachers with bilingual certificates are over twice as likely as Hispanic teachers with bilingual certificates to work in schools with the fewest Hispanic students. Third, this pattern of racial assignment is even more exaggerated at the elementary level: Hispanic teachers with bilingual certificates are almost three times *more* likely to work in the most segregated schools and are three times *less* likely to work in schools with less than 30 percent Hispanics than are Anglo teachers with bilingual certificates. Finally, we again find little variation in employment patterns between the sexes.

To determine whether bilingual certification contributes to the assignment of teachers in segregated schools independent of the race of teachers, Tables 12.4 and 12.5 must be compared with Tables 12.6 and 12.7. Looking first at Hispanic teachers only from Tables 12.4 and 12.6, Hispanic teachers who are bilingually certified are 20 percent more likely to teach in schools with a majority of Hispanic students than are Hispanic teachers without that certificate. This trend holds in both elementary and secondary schools. In schools with enrollment of less than 30 percent Hispanic students, the opposite holds: Hispanic teachers without a bilingual credential are at least twice as likely to teach there; in elementary schools that ratio more than doubles, becoming five to one.

Looking next at Anglo teachers only, Tables 12.4 and 12.7, we see that bilingual education programs have partially ameliorated the impact of employment segregation for Anglo teachers. Anglo teachers with bilingual certificates are three times as likely to teach in the most Hispanic segregated schools than Anglo teachers without this certification. Again, these trends apply equally to elementary and secondary schools. Despite these apparent differences, the impact of a bilingual credential on Anglo employment must be kept in perspective: over 50 percent of all Anglo teachers—those with bilingual credentials as well as those without—teach in an elementary or secondary school which is less than 30 percent Hispanic in its student enrollment.

And finally, the most telling comparisons can be drawn between Hispanic teachers *without* bilingual certification and Anglo teachers *with* a bilingual certificate, comparing Tables 12.4 and 12.7. Despite the integration effects of bilingual-related employment on Anglo teachers, they are still less likely to teach in schools where more than 50 percent are Hispanic students and are more likely to teach in schools which are less than 30 percent Hispanic. In other words, a Hispanic teacher with a general credential is more typically found in schools with greater levels of Hispanic segregation than an Anglo teacher with a bilingual certificate. Thus, race—and not credential—remains the most important predictor of teacher assignment. Taken together, these findings are consistent with earlier research: bilingual education programs contribute to the contradictory effects of increased Hispanic employment and increased Hispanic staff segregation.

Demographics play a complicated role in relation to Hispanic teacher employment. Declining enrollments have a strong negative impact on Hispanic employment because minorities lacking special credentials, for example, bilingual certification, are more likely to be at the end of the seniority queue. At the same time, minorities may face better than average employment opportunities in predominantly Hispanic pupil districts, which also have higher growth rates, because Anglos avoid employment in segregated districts and because minorities may be selected for social control and legitimacy purposes. For example, the Los Angeles Unified School District lost nearly 5,000 Anglo students in 1981. School Board member Roberta Weintraub observed, "Current enrollment trends suggest the city's school system will become nearly all Hispanic in the next decade." [17]

The result of these simultaneous demographic pressures seems to have a chilling effect on staff integration efforts. On the one hand, a major objective of social policy is to secure increased employment of teachers who can guarantee Hispanic children equal educational opportunity; on the other hand, a racially balanced school staff is also a critical social policy goal. Existing incremental Hispanic employment reform strategies seem unable to resolve this conflict, particularly because the absolute number of Hispanic teachers employed in recent years is so low.

Despite the fact that the current demand estimates for bilingually certified teachers exceed supply by 100 percent, it seems that Hispanic teachers with a bilingual credential are contributing to the policy objectives of improving the educational opportunities of Hispanic children to the extent that Hispanic teachers provide role models, cultural compatibility, and a linguistically supportive environment for Hispanic children. Nonetheless, a contradictory outcome of teacher assignment based on bilingual certificates has been to increase the segregation of the public school labor force. The present research is consistent with previous investigations on Hispanic segregation by Aspira (see footnote 4) which also concluded that bilingual education contributes to the contradictory effects of increased Hispanic employment and greater educational opportunity for Hispanic children, and simultaneously increased Hispanic staff segregation.

17. *San Francisco Examiner*, November 24, 1981.

## HISPANIC SOCIAL REFORMS

The purpose of this study was to analyze the role of California public schools as employers of Hispanic teachers and to determine how and why that role changed in the post–Civil Rights period. Three perspectives on Hispanic employment reforms were described. Consistent with the social control thesis an argument was presented that genuine or *structural* reforms did not, in fact, occur. To the extent that Hispanics were hired, it was primarily to teach Hispanic children and administer Hispanic schools. Nevertheless, while Barrera's and Carmichael's models are at least partially accurate descriptions, they failed to explain changes in employment policy in terms of ongoing legislative, judicial, and social struggles—struggles which did result in increased employment of Hispanic educators.

The social reform perspective, on the other hand, is consistent with the argument advanced by Piven and Cloward that the "politics of disruption" during the Civil Rights Era forced a government response.[18] This response was then translated into employment reforms in the public schools because schools were a ready pipeline into Hispanic communities by their very nature as segregated institutions. Yet, the reformist perspective also fails to address the persistence of racial segregation of pupils and staff and the limited nature of employment reforms which have occurred. Recent theoretical work by Hans Weiler on education and the crisis of legitimacy among modern democratic capitalist societies complements the arguments of Levin and Carnoy and of Katznelson that the state can be an important political terrain for expanding the political power of minorities and other under-represented groups. Weiler argues that the state pursues a strategy of "compensatory legitimacy."[19] It attempts to increase its legitimacy among disaffected segments of the population without undermining its legitimacy with established interests. This would be consistent with observed increases in educational legislation, funding, and employment directed at Hispanic segregated schools, and the absence of successful pupil and staff integration efforts in predominantly Anglo school districts. The crucial distinction between a compensatory legitimacy

18. Social unrest clearly played a role in increased Hispanic employment in the public schools in California. For example, in negotiations with the school board following the East Los Angeles student walkouts in 1968, students demanded schools be taken over by Chicano personnel where enrollments indicated the majority of students were Chicanos. Carlos Munoz, Jr. (1974): "The Politics of Protest and Chicano Liberation: A Case Study of Repression and Co-optation," *Aztlan* 5 (1 & 2): 119.

19. Hans Weiler (June 1982) "Education, Public Confidence, and the Legitimacy of the Modern State: Is There a 'Crisis' Somewhere?" Institute for Research on Educational Finance and Governance, Stanford University. Program Report No. 82-B4.

perspective and the social control perspective is that the former implies that disaffected members of society play a part in creating a crisis and are not merely acted on by existing institutional structures.

In summary, Hispanic teachers benefitted from the post-1967 employment reforms, but the relative level of increased Hispanic public school employment is modest compared to both state civil service and higher level white-collar increases in Hispanic employment. Further, these public school employment reforms took place in a manner calculated to increase the presence of Hispanic educators in Hispanic segregated schools and communities but not in Anglo segregated schools. This employment pattern persists because the combination of fiscal, demographic, and political pressures which keep schools racially and ethnically segregated are stronger than existing institutional remedies to segregation. Bilingual employment has marginally increased Hispanic participation in the California public school labor force, and it has also, ironically, contributed to the segregation of Hispanic staff. As Arias and others have suggested, it is crucial for social policymakers, including the courts, local school districts, labor unions, and legislators to develop a more comprehensive model which incorporates both desegregation goals and bilingual remedies. The current trend away from categorical programs and affirmative action, combined with declining Anglo enrollments and the decreased desirability of teaching as a career for minorities, will further erode even those gains which have been made.[20]

## Policy Implications and Recommendations

The policy implications are straightforward, if somewhat pessimistic. Only a concerted planning effort directed at the state level and supported with significant increases in state and federal funding will reverse the direction of this trend. Given current state and federal disinterest in pursuing equitable employment policies in education, the fiscal crisis facing the state of California in the post-Proposition 13 period, and the absence of a politically volatile Hispanic constituency, employment reforms are unlikely in the short run.

These conclusions in no way detract from the fact that Hispanics have made important employment gains in the public schools. This study suggests, however, that these gains were limited in order to minimize the structural

20. According to recent figures by the National Center for Education Statistics (Report on Education Statistics, 1983, 14:26) 86 percent of all prospective education majors are white, 5 percent are Black females, 3 percent are Hispanic females, and the remaining 6 percent are minority males. In light of the demands on minority schools for minority faculty, staff integration of suburban schools remains highly unlikely. The above figures which were taken from surveys of graduating seniors show nearly 100 percent decreases from a similar study conducted in 1972.

changes necessary to accomplish increased employment. Finally, these research findings are consistent with advocates of a stronger role for public-school labor-force planning at the state level. To the extent, however, that the state is a potential arena for structural employment reforms, it will become necessary to abrogate the *racial logic* of decentralized public school employment practices and explicitly consider affirmative action, equity, and legitimacy goals.

# 13.
# The Problems of Language, Education, and Society: Who Decides

*Richard A. Navarro*

SINCE THE FIRST ENACTMENTS of bilingual education as national and state policies, lawmakers have striven to clarify the purposes of the program. The use of the native language of children with limited or no proficiency in English has been a political football, tossed among various interpretations of the goals for bilingual education. This is illustrated in the use of the term *bilingual* education to describe a program whose purpose is *not* to develop the ability to speak two languages, but the use of the primary language as a pedagogical tool for transferring the child to English "as efficiently and effectively" as possible.[1]

That no legislative body has formally recognized that bilingual education is not an "encompassing unitary phenomenon" as critics describe it, but is a diverse set of activities as Otheguy (1982) argues, lends credence to the suspicion that lawmakers do not want to make the politically difficult decision of clarifying the purposes of the law to the extent that some groups may feel that their interests have been excluded. As a result, several interpretations have emerged. While these are generally stated in terms of optional programs, their implications are often more far-reaching. The three most dominant options for educating the language minority child are: maintenance bilingual education, transitional bilingual education and immersion. While the most divergent objectives exist between maintenance and immersion approaches, the focus of debate most recently rests on the differences between transitional bilingual education and immersion (de Kanter and Baker, 1983; Hernandez-Chavez, et al. 1981).

Beginning with Fishman's pioneering work, *Language Loyalty in the United*

---

1. Assembly Bill 507, Chacon, Chapter 1339, Statutes of 1980.

*States*, there have been a growing number of scholarly appraisals of the functions of language on social behavior in multilingual societies. Advocating a
closer connection to the "historical dimensions in the sociology of language,"
Fishman (1973:145–55) advises that if societal dimensions are needed—as I
believe they are—to productively understand the socio*linguistic* facts-of-life,
then surely historical dimensions are needed to productively understand the
*socio*linguistic facts-of-life. By discerning the *linguistic* issues from the *social* issues during the historical period in which bilingual education policy
was formulated, the objectives of bilingual education may be more clearly
understood.

C. B. Paulston (1974, 1978, 1983) is perhaps one of the most critical theo-
rists to take up Fishman's call to distinguish between "matters of society and
nation" and "matters of language." Writing from a conflict paradigm, Paulston describes her own position: "Unequal opportunity, the existence of which
is most certainly not denied, tends to be seen as a result of a condition of
inequality rather than as a cause of school failure" (1978:416). Paulston goes
on to argue that research on bilingual education must also pay attention to
those *language policy* issues which are based on the political logic within the
decision-making process, as well as the *language problem* issues which are
based on linguistic criteria and are benefited by scholarly input.

Complementing Paulston's earlier work, Heath suggests that language *interests* are determined before groups enter the political arena. That is, different interest groups have a different "language ideology—the self evident ideas
and objectives a group holds concerning roles of language in the social experiences of members as they contribute to the expression of the group"
(1977:53). The process of formulating a policy from among these interests is
the essential dynamic of politics—the use of power for the satisfaction of
one's interests or those of a constituency. Heath notes:

> Within the U.S., we know more about language planning than we do
> about language policy, i.e., the ideology from which policy must de-
> rive. Until our level of knowledge of the two are equalized, bilingual
> education will continue to be caught in its entanglement of conflicting
> ideology bases (1977:55).

Heath calls for research which will lay bare the range of interests which are
characteristic of groups involved in bilingual education as a "*sociopolitical
program.*" Students of bilingual education policy cannot be content with defining the problem and then studying the conflict over the solution to resolve
the problem, but must step back and first examine how the problem gets defined and then look at the solutions which flow out of this formulation pro-

cess. Selecting the political arena—the legislative process—as the *field* of study portends additional benefits as patterns of behavior are observed as they relate to uses of power. Bilingual education policy analysis might be guided by the following questions:

What is the problem and how is it defined?
Who has the power to define the problem and what system-specific mechanisms are used to legitimate this definition?
How are political relations structured in the policy formulation process?
How does the outcome of this policy formulation process articulate with social as well as language issues? What are the symbolic and the substantive aspects of each?

Bilingual education is a relatively new approach to English language instruction, appearing during an era when compensatory efforts were considered to be a sound educational response to the call for equality of educational opportunity. A common assumption of the enacting legislation is that children with limited proficiency in English from low-income backgrounds can be helped out of poverty by overcoming their language barrier through compensatory programs. Hispanics are the principal beneficiaries of Title VII, representing over 80 percent of the nation's language minority population. Bilingual education also shares the stage with other social action programs of the 1960s and has benefited from the gains achieved by the civil rights movement (Matute-Bianchi 1979). However, since 1978 the definition of the problem has changed from *equity* concerns in society to *effectiveness* concerns in the schools. This shift in definition of the problem has fundamental ramifications for the outcomes that flow from the policy-making process.[2]

## SOCIALIZATION VS. DISTRIBUTIVE OBJECTIVES

Transitional bilingual education has most recently been defined in a publication by the Office of Planning, Budget, and Evaluation of the U.S. Department of Education as, "Using the student's native language to teach subject matter until he or she achieves English proficiency" (Birman and Ginsberg, 1983:ix). Transitional bilingual programs generally include English-as-a-

2. The research for this paper was supported by funds from the National Institute of Education (Grant No. OB-NIE-G-80-111) to the Institute for Research on Educational Finance and Governance at Stanford University. The analyses or conclusions do not necessarily reflect the views or policies of NIE. For a description of the research and extended discussion of the findings, see Navarro (1983).

second-language instruction as well as a multicultural component. Immersion, or structured immersion as it is referred to in some cases, implies the use of the "target language as the principal medium of instruction" (Tucker and D'anglejan 1975:67). The child is treated as a native speaker of the target language with three important conditions: first, immersion teachers are fully bilingual; second, students may ask questions in their primary language but the response by the teacher is usually in the target language; and third, the content of the language is limited to the ability of the students to understand it. "Structured immersion *may* include home language-arts classes" (Birman and Ginsberg 1983:xii, emphasis added). And, at least in the Canadian case, the primary language is also used to teach selected content subjects. Although, at a theoretical level, the two approaches reaffirm the purpose of bilingual education to teach the target language as quickly and efficiently as possible, the historical circumstances which gave rise to the two approaches differentiate them according to socialization goals vs. redistributive purposes.

Merrill Swain, a Canadian scholar, points out that "the origins of bilingual education are as varied as the community, societal, and political settings in which they are located." She goes on to distinguish between the United States experience, which has largely been experimenting with the transitional approach, and the Canadian experience, which has contributed to our knowledge of immersion programs. She writes:

> In the United States, for example, the recent resurgence of interest in bilingual education has largely been a consequence of a society which claims to provide equal opportunity to all. It has come to be recognized that equal educational opportunity to minority-language children whose facility in the school language (English) is limited can best be achieved through the provision of instruction in the children's dominant language while proficiency in English is being developed. In Canada, however, the recent growth of bilingual education has largely been a consequence of political entities which are committed to providing services in the country's two official languages (1978:420).

Swain goes on to describe the immersion program in Canada as attempting to maintain a balance in social relations between French-Canadians and English-Canadians. Most importantly, the French form the base of the Canadian bilingual population and French continues to be the language of instruction. For English-Canadians, the dominant majority in Canada (dominant minority in Quebec), bilingual skills are seen as providing economic opportunities in both employment and as special bonuses. In other words, since the country is officially bilingual, the ability to communicate in French has become a condition for maintaining the dominance of English-Canadians in traditionally English-controlled sectors of society (Hache, 1983:5).

In the United States, the introduction of bilingual education was seen as a means of addressing discrimination against language-minority students, especially Hispanics and Asians. While conducting reviews of school districts suspected of violating the Civil Rights Act of 1964, the Office for Civil Rights of the Department of Health, Education, and Welfare discovered practices which discriminated against language minorities because of their lack of proficiency in English. On the basis of this evidence, school superintendents received a memorandum from the Office for Civil Rights on May 25, 1970, stating that each school district was required to rectify the "language deficiency in order to open its instructional program to these students." In 1974, the purpose of the memorandum for extending equal educational opportunities to language minority children was affirmed by the Supreme Court in its *Lau vs. Nichols* (1974) decision.[3] Essentially, the Court found that "there is no equality of treatment merely by providing students with the same facilities, textbooks, teachers, and curriculum; for students who do not understand English are effectively foreclosed from any meaningful education."

In addition to mandates for bilingual education based on civil rights policies, the U.S. Congress also funded the development of bilingual programs beginning in 1968.[4] Recognizing the high dropout rates among Hispanics and the increasing pressure to raise the economic standing of this growing minority, lawmakers in Washington passed the Bilingual Education Act as their response toward improving the educational opportunities for language minorities. The point of the Congressional action as well as that of the Courts and the Department of Health, Education, and Welfare was to address equity concerns first by recognizing the structural *imbalance* of social relations, and second, by introducing bilingual education as a social lever for causing a redistribution of opportunities to offset past discriminatory practices.

While limitations in space do not permit a thorough analysis of the formation of bilingual education policy (see Hache 1976, 1983), for the purposes of this paper it suffices to say that the policies in Canada have continued to support the status quo, that is, English-Canadian domination. While it is true that English-speaking children are learning French in the Francophone provinces, it is still the case that for French-Canadians to be socially mobile they must have a knowledge of English. Although Canada is an officially bilingual country, English-Canadians are not required to know French in order to progress economically, politically, or socially. The power to define the problem in Canada is controlled by the English majority and the policies have been legiti-

---

3. *Lau vs. Nichols*, 414 U.S. 593 (1974).
4. Title VII of the Elementary and Secondary Education Act (E.S.E.A.), The Bilingual Education Act of 1968.

mized by such conciliatory commissions as the Royal Commission on Bilingualism and Biculturalism (1967) and the Task Force on Canadian Unity (1979).

In the case of Canadian immersion programs, bilingual education is intended to fulfill the social obligation of the state by providing bilingual skills. Schooling is a means of socializing its citizenry in the instrumental and normative values necessary for the continuation of the social system which are consistent with bilingualism, especially for English-Canadians. This view is in agreement with the findings of Lambert and Tucker (1972) that the success of the Canadian immersion programs is attributable to the assumption that bilingualism is a *desirable* end, the middle class social standing of the students, and the fact that the primary language is the socially, culturally, politically, and economically dominant language. Furthermore, since both English and French are recognized as the official languages of the country and English is the dominant language of the majority of the population, there is little chance that English-Canadians will lose their proficiency in their mother tongue while learning French. More recently, Lambert has reiterated that the context in which bilingual education is implemented differs substantially between the two countries:

> It is totally wrong to ignore the contextual factors of the St. Lambert [Canada] experiment in evaluating the efficacy of an immersion approach in the United States public education context. These factors include the higher prestige of the L1 [primary language] of the immersion students, a factor which is reversed in the non-English speaking children in the U.S.; the middle-class status and average educational attainment of the parents of those children, which do not match the characteristics of the parents of the LEP/NEP [limited and non-English proficient] students in the U.S. schools.[5]

Clearly, the socialization mode is not appropriate to the stated purposes of bilingual education in the United States. Whereas bilingual education in Canada is based on maintaining social equilibrium through the socialization of its English-speaking youth for a bilingual environment, the purpose of bilingual education in the United States is to alter the existing social order which has discriminated against language minorities, and increase the conditions of equity in society. The dilemma is that this purpose cannot be confined to a purely language issue, but must be approached from both a linguistic perspective *and* a redistribution orientation, which requires a more comprehensive social ini-

5. Lambert, W., Personal Communications, December 1981. Quoted in Hernandez-Chavez et al., 1981.

tiative than bilingual education can possibly provide. C. B. Paulston notes, however, that policy makers are quite content to avoid this apparent conflict and continue to lump both language and redistributive aspects together in the formulation of bilingual policy. She outlines the conflicts in the assumptions embodied in the Congressional act:

> (1) The lack of social and economic success on the part of these minority groups is due (a) to "unequal opportunity" as manifest through different language, different culture, and different learning styles, and (b) to a lack of scholastic success as a group because of poor English-speaking ability; (2) with the provision of English skills, merit and IQ will lead through scholastic skills gained in a "meaningful education" to social and economic success (1978:407).

In this passage Paulston points out that the purpose of bilingual education is to provide *compensatory training* in English, assuming that solving the *language problem* will erase decades of discrimination and socio-economic status differences in society. In other words, although the Congress recognizes that inequalities exist, rather than seeing these inequalities as a result of stratification in the social structure, the low status of language minorities is attributed to language differences which can be resolved by increasing their proficiency in English. The contradictions in the Congressional intent can be linked to the unwillingness to distinguish between social and linguistic issues.

Bilingual education policy in the United States has managed to skirt the basic issues it was established to address. This has been accomplished by defining the problem in such a way that school failure and the social disadvantage of language minorities is attributable to their limited proficiency in English rather than as symptomatic of a society which stratifies its members and the opportunities they enjoy on the basis of their language and their culture.

By comparing the purposes of transitional bilingual education programs with immersion programs in Canada, we see that the two are oriented toward the fulfillment of fundamentally different social objectives. This contrast raises doubts regarding the efficacy of pursuing consensus goals in the policy formulation process. A consensus assumes that there can be agreement from among competing interests on one approach. However, ethnic interests—the improvement of life chances for language minority students—are subordinated by the dominant interests which are disproportionately represented in the political system. In other words, the *language ideology* of the dominant groups will persist and find legitimation in the policy-making process (Lukes 1974; Therborn 1980). The hierarchical structuring of political power is evident in the history of bilingual education policy formulation, particularly if we examine the shift from *equity* concerns in society to *effectiveness* concerns in the schools.

## BILINGUAL EDUCATION POLICY MAKING IN CALIFORNIA

The formulation of bilingual education policy in California is significant not only because the state enrolls one of the highest percentages of language minority students (27.5 percent of the total in the United States), but also because the major bilingual education legislation in the state has been sponsored by a Chicano legislator. Furthermore, in 1979, when the State Board of Education attempted to pass a bill in the legislature to repeal the bilingual education mandate, a coalition of bilingual education interest groups was formed to do battle with the proposed law. Not only were the coalition members successful in blocking the bill, but they were also successful in achieving a consensus in the legislature to enact their own reform bill to address the concerns of the critics of the program by making the program more flexible. It would appear, therefore, based upon these events, that there is no conflict between equity goals—as expressed by the participation of minority interest groups to establish, expand, and/or defend programs to enhance their life chances in society—with the effective and efficiency goals of mainstream interest groups— to reduce dissension and assimilate marginal groups within the existing pattern of social relations. Thus, an important question arises which will be briefly addressed: what is the impact of the incorporation of minority elites into the political system on the articulation of minority interests in policy making?

### Background

As of 1959, California law provided that "all schools shall be taught in the English language."[6] It was not until 1967 that the law was changed to make statutes conform to new federal legislation and permit the state to receive federal monies for bilingual education.[7] By 1972, forty-eight federally funded bilingual education projects were established in the state under Title VII. Although about 19,000 students with limited or no English-speaking ability were involved in the program, the California Legislative Analyst concluded that a substantial number of language minority students were not being served by bilingual education.

During the same year, the California Legislature enacted Assembly Bill (AB) 2284, the Bilingual Education Act of 1972, sponsored by Assemblyman

---

6. California Education Code, Section 71, (West 1975).
7. Senate Bill 53, Short, Chapter 200, Statutes of 1967.

Peter Chacon. The purpose of bilingual instruction, the new legislation stated, was "to develop competence in two languages." The law, enacted during Ronald Reagan's term as governor, was intended to develop a "positive self-image" among language minority students "and to develop intergroup and intercultural awareness among pupils, parents, and staff in participating school districts." [8]

The Bilingual Education Act of 1972 was the first major voluntary state-wide bilingual education program in California. Since the State Department of Education did not have a reliable means of counting the number of language minority students in the state, an important provision of the bill included a requirement for school districts to undertake an annual census of limited English-speaking students. A bilingual teacher described the effect of AB 2284 in her school district, a rural region of Northern California:

> [In one school district where I taught] it was a real struggle. It was a racist area. Growers owned the school board and there were no Chicanos on the school board and no Chicano teachers could get hired there. [The teachers] were all white. I was the only one who was able to get hired because I "WASN'T THAT MEXICAN" to them.
>
> We were able to start a bilingual classroom the second year I was there. [Then] we got the state funds and all of a sudden we were legitimate. All of a sudden we were a legitimate bilingual classroom and bilingual needs were being legitimated by the state.
>
> The school is still racist and the area is still racist, but Chicano parents and students are more legitimate now. The district realizes that they have to meet their needs. [9]

One important effect of Title VII was to increase public awareness of the learning needs of language minority students and to orient the states to recognize the interests of language minorities in education. AB 2284 further legitimized the interests of language minorities in educational policy-making and the expectation that the state should attempt to achieve equity in educational programs by providing instruction which met the needs of language minority students. However, AB 2284 was a voluntary program and the ultimate responsibility to provide such programs remained with the local authorities. Once state monies were received for bilingual education, implementation at the local level varied and the State Department of Education did not effectively monitor compliance with the law. The statement from the bilingual

---

8. Assembly Bill 2284, Chacon, Chapter 1258, Statutes of 1972.
9. To maintain the anonymity of informants, names are not used. Interviews were ethnographic (Spradley 1979) and none were conducted with more than one informant on the same date. For this reason the following notation has been used to distinguish informant interviews: Informant Interview, June 21, 1980.

teacher indicates that the parents of language minority students were not in a position to influence decision-makers and there was no bilingual education constituency to act on behalf of the students. While AB 2284 began to change these conditions by legitimizing the needs of language minority students, the program was not implemented to the full extent of the law or to meet the objectives of the program.

One of the most credible sources of information regarding injustices suffered by disenfranchised groups in society was the U.S. Commission on Civil Rights. The Commission's nationwide studies in the 1960s and early 1970s were highly influential in legislative decision-making and in exposing critical areas of neglect (Schneider 1976). In addition, the California Advisory Committee to the Commission conducted its own studies within the state. The first report issued by the Advisory Committee in April of 1968 focused on Los Angeles County.[10] The report recommended that the Office for Civil Rights of the U.S. Department of Health, Education, and Welfare (HEW), monitor educational programs in Los Angeles, and it cited several violations of HEW regulations. In 1972, the Advisory Committee conducted field investigations and held open meetings on educational practices in Santa Maria, Guadalupe, and Pismo Beach. All of these studies described the problems of language minority students in the schools and focused on the U.S. Commission on Civil Rights' recommendations for increased federal and state involvement with local school districts.[11]

Some of the complaints received by the Commission and the Advisory Committee alleged inadequate monitoring by the State Department of Education. In 1975 the Advisory Committee, in conjunction with Commission staff members, decided to study the effectiveness of the Department in ensuring statewide compliance with state and federal laws and regulations affecting language minority children. Several individuals and organizations participated in the Advisory Committee's hearings and expressed concern that bilingual programs were misapplied, that the law was not fully implemented, that compliance reviews were inadequate, and that support from the state did not meet the needs of local districts. One witness criticized the implementation of the law by state and local authorities by asking, "If the money isn't being used for what it's supposed to be used for, then how is it benefiting minority children?"[12] An attorney for California Rural Legal Assistance told

10. *Education and the Mexican-American Community in Los Angeles County.* California Advisory Committee to the U.S. Commission on Civil Rights. Sacramento, April 1968.
11. *The Schools of Guadalupe . . . A Legacy of Educational Oppression, and Educational Neglect of Mexican American Students in Lucia Mar Unified School District.* California Advisory Committee to the U.S. Commission on Civil Rights. Sacramento, 1972.
12. Teresa Perez, Chicano Advisory Board of Fresno. Quoted in *State Administration of Bi-*

Commission staff members that the State Department of Education had not made even a minimal effort to define a *bilingual teacher* for the purposes of carrying out the AB 2284 mandate. He added, "It is not enough to appropriate money for programs and label them 'bilingual' when nothing, in fact, has changed in the classroom. Such a policy is destined to result in the failure of bilingual bicultural education because it is not bilingual or bicultural or education." [13]

At the conclusion of its study, the California Advisory Committee determined:

> The [State] Department of Education did little to oversee the data collection and evaluation of non and limited-English-speaking students or of bilingual programs established to assist these students. The department provided districts with inadequate testing instruments for census collection and inadequate evaluation instruments for bilingual programs. Uniform definitions for bilingual education were unavailable. The department had no formal procedures for verifying the accuracy of district data. As a result, what little information exists on the numbers of language-minority students and the quality of bilingual programs is unreliable. Most significantly, when the department became aware of local district noncompliance with State or Federal laws or regulations, it made little effort to enforce compliance. [14]

In light of the delinquency of the State Department of Education in the implementation of the Bilingual Education Act of 1972 and continued violations of limited minority students' civil rights by local education authorities, new legislation was proposed. Most of these bills were sponsored by Assemblyman Chacon and sought to increase the state's capacity for the provision of bilingual education. One bill which was adopted authorized establishment of the Bilingual Teacher Corps Program in recognition of the fact that there was an insufficient number of bilingual teachers in the state.

In addition to strengthening the delivery of services, such legislation also contributed to the development of a constituency within the education community for bilingual education. One organization, the California Association for Bilingual Education, formed in 1975, has become a major interest group for bilingual education in the state. Other related organizations which became active in bilingual education included the Association of Mexican American Educators, founded in 1965. In 1969, the English-as-a-second-language

---

*lingual Education—Si o No?* A Report of the California Advisory Committee to the U.S. Commission on Civil Rights. Sacramento, June 1976:31.
13. *Ibid.*, pg. 33.
14. *Ibid.*, pp. 86–87.

teachers organized under the California Association of Teachers of English to Speakers of Other Languages. Finally, both of the major teachers unions (California Teachers Association and the California Federation of Teachers) began to experience the formation of subgroups made up of bilingual teachers who advocated support of the new program within the two powerful education lobbies. Although these ad hoc bilingual interest groups were only marginally influential in the passage of the mandatory bilingual education legislation in 1976, they played a major role as advocates for bilingual education after 1978.

### Formation of AB 1329

Armed with the *Lau* decision of the U.S. Supreme Court and the scathing criticisms of the Advisory Committee on the implementation of the 1972 Bilingual Education Act, Assemblyman Chacon requested the formation of a legislative subcommittee to determine the effectiveness of the bilingual programs and their compliance with the *Lau* decision, and to make recommendations to the legislature. After six public meetings across the state, the legislators proposed several policy, program, and administrative changes. Most importantly, their recommendations supported strengthening the Bilingual Education Act of 1972 to specify the "Lau Remedies" as a minimum program requirement as well as making the provisions mandatory rather than voluntary.

At the next legislative session, Assemblyman Chacon introduced a modified bilingual education bill, AB 1329, which incorporated the major recommendations and concerns raised by the *Lau* decision and the public hearings on the state's administration of bilingual programs. AB 1329 was the most ambitious educational policy in the nation to address the learning needs of language minority students. The bill mandated that each limited and non-English-speaking student enrolled in California public schools from grades kindergarten through twelve receive instruction in a language understandable to the pupil. Cosponsored by Senate President *Pro Tempore* George Moscone and several other legislators, the bill passed on the last day of the 1976 legislative session and was signed into law by Governor Jerry Brown on September 4, 1976.[15]

Favorable public opinion, support from mainstream educational organizations for a *mandatory* bilingual education bill, as well as the election of a Democratic governor who was closely allied with Hispanics through the farmworkers' movement were credited for the passage of the legislation. Assemblyman Chacon noted that the assembly subcommittee hearings were particularly beneficial in cultivating grassroots support. Chacon commented:

15. Assembly Bill 1329, Chacon-Moscone, Chapter 978, Statutes of 1976.

The role [of grassroots organizations] was rather unique with respect to the things that community groups do. [At the subcommittee hearings] we discussed the make up of 1329 and we reached a tentative consensus of what the bill ought to provide . . . So really, 1329 was a result of input from the field—as it should be.[16]

Grassroots organizations, however, did not play a role in the passage of the legislation. It was an elite process of policy formation. Although AB 1329 was sponsored by a Chicano legislator, more importantly, it was sanctioned by key majority politicians and legitimized by environmental factors such as the *Lau* decision, HEW regulations and "Lau Remedies," 1974 amendments to Title VII, and continuous agency reports which documented unequal opportunities for language minorities in the schools and society.

In addition to patronage relations and environmental factors, other characteristics of the early period of policy formation and implementation included: the use of public hearings to define the problems of inequality of language minorities as a *language issue* and legitimize the solution, that is, stronger mandates for bilingual education, the use of legislation to develop a program constituency, and a strong orientation toward local autonomy, even at the expense of program objectives. Dobb (1983) has arrived at similar findings in a separate study of the implementation of language census requirements in the state. In short, while a unique period of social unrest in American history during the 1960s and 1970s affected the awareness of inequalities in society, the solutions which were legislated to deal with these problems were incorporated into the existing pattern of relations based on the dominant interests. The outcome, as we have come to realize, reflects the structural inequalities of society. While a few Hispanics have benefited from these programs, the Great Society dreams have failed to translate into real hope for disenfranchised peoples as a whole. The real problem, as defined in this paper, is the hierarchy of influence in decision-making and the powerlessness of minority interests in the process of policy formation. The process of incorporation as powerless participants in the political system is reflected in the redirection of equity concerns following Proposition 13 in the state.

## Imperiled Progress: The Undoing of AB 1329

Even before the implementation of AB 1329, a vocal opposition to bilingual education had begun to emerge in California. Problems associated with the implementation of the 1972 bilingual bill coupled with continuous disagreements regarding methods of instruction set the stage for controversy

16. Informant Interview, November 12, 1981.

over the new state policy. In addition, several social, economic, and political factors at the national and state levels undercut the ideological support for bilingual education as a remedy for inequalities in educational opportunity.

At the national level, public debate over bilingual education—its philosophy, effectiveness, and future—became increasingly intense and hostile (e.g., Bethell 1979; Epstein 1977). At the state level, several major newspapers carried critical editorials asserting that bilingual education was not serving its original purpose of helping students achieve English fluency. For instance, the *Sacramento Bee*, in its editorial on July 18, 1978, charged, "Bilingual education is, in fact, a maintenance program fostering indefinite dependence on Spanish or one of the several other languages in which bilingual programs are offered. . . ." Other factors were also contributing to what Assemblyman Chacon called "an anti-bilingual mood." The passage of AB 65 (school finance reform bill) in 1977, the overwhelming voter support and enactment of Proposition 13 (property tax initiative) in 1978, and the anxieties of retrenchment due to declining student enrollment created a greater awareness of the need to cut services, consolidate educational programs, and establish priorities over funding of programs in the public schools.[17]

The most important among the changes affecting the political mood of the state regarding categorical programs generally and bilingual education in particular was the passage of Proposition 13. On June 6, 1978, California voters decided two to one to cut property taxes by roughly 50 percent. Proposition 13 took away local revenue-raising capacity at a time when schools were already having difficulty balancing their budgets due to inflation and dwindling revenues. In a study of five San Francisco Bay Area school districts, it was found that four of the districts faced a deficit in their 1978–79 budgets before the passage of Proposition 13. The success of the state's tax revolt served to increase the schools' dependence on state funding. California leaped from 30 percent to 80 percent state assumption of school costs in 1978 (Kirst and Somers 1980). Comparable figures nationally for the same year, estimated by the National Center for Education Statistics, show that state governments provided 44.1 percent of school funds, local 47.8 percent and federal 8.1 percent.

Many local school districts were unable to cushion themselves from the combined effects of declining enrollment and reduced revenue from Proposition 13. Where districts had to make reductions, these tended to be concentrated in the areas of classified personnel, support services, and supplies, in order to avoid cutting programs. Teaching personnel were not cut except for instructional aides and substitutes. Still, teachers' salaries and benefits made

17. Peter R. Chacon, "The California Legislature Looks at Bilingual Education," California State Assembly, Sacramento, January, 1979.

up approximately three-fourths of the budgets of most districts, and local administrators attempted to reduce certified personnel by not replacing teachers who left the system and by reallocating teaching assignments among the existing staff (Katz 1979). However, AB 1329 virtually flew in the face of budget-cutting measures, which frustrated local administrators. The law required that bilingual classes be taught by an accredited bilingual education teacher or a teacher with a State Board of Education waiver who was earning a bilingual education certificate. Reallocation of teacher responsibilities and seniority rules to govern staff reduction were sharply inhibited by the mandate in districts with large language minority populations. This conflict led many critics of bilingual education to charge that the program was no more than a jobs program for Hispanics (see Richards' chapter in this volume).

Another condition which adversely affected the political climate toward bilingual education was the growth of the number of Hispanic students in relation to other subgroups in the school-age population. Although overall student enrollment was declining by approximately 9 percent, the proportion of ethnic minority students was increasing. According to the State Department of Education Racial and Ethnic Student Survey of 1977, the percentage of white students dropped from 75 percent to 63.5 percent, a loss of 586,000 students, while minority students in grades K through 12 increased to 36.5 percent of the total between 1967 and 1977. Hispanics significantly increased their numbers in the statewide student body during the decade to nearly 21 percent of the total, compared to 10 percent black student enrollment.

The effect of these demographic changes, particularly the dramatic increase in Hispanic students, was noted by a Los Angeles radio station in an editorial: "KNX suspects that some critics of bilingual education . . . resent the growth of the Hispanic population here. So they feel threatened by things like bilingual ballots, signs and classrooms" (December 3, 1978). In a more scholarly analysis, State Board of Education President R. Kirst and academic colleague G. Garms wrote, "Those segments of the population that are increasing their proportion in education today may prove to be a mixed blessing." Lumping together children who are nonwhite, poor, and born to teenage mothers, Kirst and Garms wrote, "Thus while those with no direct interest in public education are increasing in numbers, an increasing proportion of those who have a direct interest will also be among those who tend to be politically powerless—voter turnout is lower as well as opportunity to provide resources for campaigns . . . [and] many of them will also require expensive, special programs for the disadvantaged" (1980:21).

The perception that the increases in Hispanic enrollments would adversely affect the education establishment's ability to compete with other social programs in fending off imminent cutbacks was also reflected in the political language at the time. Assemblyman Chacon worried that "the public has established priorities in terms of programs it is willing to support and bilingual education is not one them." Chacon assessed the arguments against the program and concluded, "Survival of bilingual education as a state-funded program will ultimately be decided politically." [18]

Although political support for bilingual education was critical for its continuation, there was no recognizable interest group to which public officials would be held accountable as they sought new ways to reduce spending for education. In this sense, Proposition 13 marked a turning point in government outlays for addressing equity issues in education. Language minorities, who were just beginning to enjoy the legitimization of their interests in education, were on the verge of losing bilingual education to adversity and their own political powerlessness.

Following the implementation of AB 1329, particularly in the aftermath of Proposition 13, several public hearings and legislative committee meetings took place in order to collect information on concerns with implementing the law and determining what changes were needed to more effectively address the needs of language minority students. Assemblyman Chacon convened two meetings of the Special Subcommittee on Bilingual/Bicultural Education in 1977 and 1978. The State Department of Education convened a special convocation in 1978 to identify salient issues related to bilingual education, to examine current and alternative educational practices, and to make recommendations for the improvement of the program. At the request of the State Board of Education, an Ad Hoc Bilingual Education Community Interaction Committee was formed to advise the Board on possible improvements in the program. Finally, the State Board of Education and the Assembly Education Committee each held separate meetings to critically examine the state's bilingual education programs.

All of these actions, in a period from October 1977 to March 1979, were instrumental in focusing attention on the problem of implementing bilingual programs and legitimizing the need to change the law. One striking difference from the pre-AB 1329 hearings was the concern for determining the effectiveness both of the program in teaching English to language minorities and of bilingual instruction as the most efficient means for integrating students into mainstream classes. Equity was a concern, inasmuch as it was required under *Lau*. Three recently decided New York court cases served as a reminder to the state that it was required by federal mandate to meet the needs of all its students. [19] However, with the pressure of limited resources, policy makers were strongly inclined to do the minimum necessary for minority interests.

18. *Ibid.*, pg. 9.
19. *Aspira of New York, Inc. v. Board of Education* [394 F. Supp. 1161 (S.D.N.Y. 1975)];

That changes were inevitable was assumed by all: problems with implementation and administration of bilingual programs as well as an unfavorable political climate gave the impression that it was necessary to alter the program to provide more local flexibility in the implementation of the mandate. Several program supporters advocated making these changes through administrative fiat in the program regulations. In setting up the Ad Hoc Bilingual Education Community Interaction Committee, the State Board of Education suggested to program supporters that they be open to recommendations for making such changes. Top officials in the State Department of Education further reassured program supporters that the department would not propose any new legislation to change the bilingual mandate. Meanwhile, the department hired two consultants, Heide Dulay and Marina Burt of Bloomsbury West, Inc., a San Francisco consulting firm, to develop program options for bilingual education; the options developed eventually found their way into legislation. The ad hoc committee, like the earlier public hearings, served as a pretense for seeking public input on the changes to be made in the program while the real power to decide the changes to be recommended was controlled by a few members of the State Board of Education and officials of the State Department of Education, with the assistance of the Bloomsbury West consultants.

The recommendations by Dulay and Burt were seized upon by the state board and the Department of Education because they provided a means of legitimizing the interests of the latter in bilingual policy. Based on their own research findings, Dulay and Burt suggested that bilingual education programs were being misapplied and most language minority students would be better served by intensive English programs such as ESL. The research claimed that the majority of students (65 to 85 percent) in bilingual programs were English dominant, that is, language minority students "whose English language skills are not on par with those of native English speakers their age, but whose level of Spanish skills is equally low or substantially lower." This led the consultants to argue that "most of these children can communicate in English; they simply have not scored at norm levels in English language skills—a problem many native English speakers also have." Since the intent of bilingual education was to teach language minority students academic courses in their strongest language while providing intensive English instruction until a transfer could be made into an all-English classroom, Dulay and Burt concluded that the program was being misapplied. They claimed that "in the United States, the rationale for teaching subject matter in the limited English proficient child's native language has been the assumption that the native language was the child's stronger language. For English superior limited English

---

*Rios v. Read* [73 F.R.D. 589 (E.D.N.Y. 1977)]; and *Cintron v. Brentwood Union Free School District Board of Education* [455 F. Supp. 57, 62-64 (E.D.N.Y. 1978)].

proficient children the native language is the weaker language."[20] The program options proposed to do away with bilingual instruction for the English-dominant language minority student to be replaced by intensive English instruction. In one of the more controversial sections of the recommendation, bilingual certification was not required; instead a special ESL and other "extended English" skills were recommended for teachers.[21]

When the State Board of Education approved the Dulay and Burt proposal and directed its staff to seek a legislative sponsor, the action set off a furor among some legislators and bilingual educators and split the Department of Education into several factions. Although the three top Anglo members of the Board said they knew all along the department was developing a bilingual education bill, supporters of bilingual education, including Lorenza Schmidt, a Chicana member of the Board, said they were unaware of it. Schmidt challenged the decision of the board, saying that the department had been insensitive to objections raised by educators, parents, teachers, administrators, and local school board members in drawing up its plan. Charging the board with condoning "an act of racism," Schmidt accused the Department of "working in conjunction with members of the State Board who intended to write new bilingual legislation which reduced the legal mandate on local districts to provide bilingual education."[22]

Although there had been several public hearings to determine the changes which were *necessary* in the law, the actual formulation of the policy proposal was determined by a few members of the State Board and the Department of Education. The most striking outcome of this unmistakable orchestration by nonminority interests was its effect on bilingual advocates, particularly Hispanics. The ad hoc committee, which was set up to advise the board, was never used for this purpose. However, when the members, who included major activists in teaching, law, policy and research in bilingual education convened from across the state to discuss their differences, they found that they had much more in common than they had previously believed. When the State Board approved the Dulay-Burt proposal, many members of the ad hoc committee banded together to oppose it and to advocate more moderate changes in the law. The threat to bilingual education as represented by the State Board action was a motivating force for coalescing. Although Hispanics and bilingual advocates would not be unified in a concerted effort to support the same proposal for another year, bilingual education became a significant sym-

20. Marina Burt and Heide Dulay, "Hispanic Students May be Misdiagnosed." *California Federation of Teachers Innovator*, April, 1980.

21. Richard Alatorre and Dennis Mangers, "Untangling the State's Educational Controversy: Major Change is Needed to Eliminate Waste and to Create New Flexibility." *Los Angeles Times*, August 12, 1979.

22. Lorenza P. Schmidt, "Statement Presented to the State Board of Education," April 11, 1979; "Letter of Information," April 23, 1979.

bol of Hispanic political identity and meaning for enhancing their role in the political process.

The controversy over reforms in the bilingual education law took two years to be resolved in the California State Legislature. In the first year, the competition focused on two bills, both carried by Chicano assemblymen. Richard Alatorre, sponsor of AB 690, carried the bill backed by the State Board of Education and the Department of Education to repeal the law and replace it with a program that emphasized intensive English instruction without bilingual teachers (Dulay-Burt proposal). This plan was also supported by a majority of the mainstream educational organizations such as the California Federation of Teachers, the California School Boards Association, and school administrators. Peter Chacon, sponsor of AB 507, introduced his bill late in 1979 as a rival solution to the problems accompanying implementation of the existing law which he coauthored in 1976. Chacon's bill was supported by a coalition of the bilingual interest groups as well as several Hispanic political organizations in the state.

The threat to bilingual education by the bill sponsored by the State Board served to underline the importance of bilingual advocates taking an active role in the political process. Twenty organizations, including the California Association of Bilingual Educators and the Association of Mexican American Educators, the two largest groups, formed the Bilingual Community Coalition to seek changes in the Alatorre measure that would build the existing law rather than repeal it. As opposition to the program increased, the identity of the coalition was strengthened among their own constituency. One member of the coalition characterized their role as a "true case of David and Goliath . . . twenty or thirty people did the work and did not give up, [and] we never really felt we were going to win, we were just going to make sure they knew they had been in a fight." [23] Melinda Melendez, another member of the coalition, wrote in a Chicano student newspaper at Stanford University that "as in other situations where Chicanos have been coerced into accepting remedies that are 'good for us,' Chicano educators and parents united to protest this threat to a bilingual education for Chicano students and to support AB 507. . . . In a historic effort to coalesce with other bilingual communities, the Bilingual Community Coalition was formed . . . to educate the community about the bills and to clarify misleading information being circulated by the opposition. Now the Bilingual Community Coalition and Chicano community must work together in a concerted drive to support the strong Bilingual Education Act which presently exists." [24]

Several attempts were made to compromise, first in Alatorre's bill and then in resolving the differences between AB 690 and AB 507. But rather than

23. Informant Interview, January 28, 1982.
24. Melendez, Melinda, "Bilingual Education Legislation," La Onda, Stanford University, December, 1979.

building grounds for consensus and resolving their differences in the first year, adversaries on both sides of the issue were more polarized. The conflict escalated to a dramatic Senate Finance Committee meeting in which several compromise solutions were proposed, including one by the Chicano Legislative Caucus. The committee members rejected the Chicano Caucus' proposal which prompted both authors to withdraw their bills. The Chicano Caucus and the coalition succeeded in averting last minute attempts to pass a bill to repeal the existing law, thereby stalling a resolution until the following year. Again, Melendez wrote, "By the end of the 1979 Legislative Session, the Coalition was able to secure a narrow victory . . . a temporary respite in the continuing flurry of neoconservative *movidas* [a pre-planned political move] against Chicanos in California."[25] When the legislature recessed in September 1979, Hispanic politicians, educators, and other special interest organizations across the state had finally succeeded in forming a symbolic bond to support bilingual education. It was symbolic because, although many differences continued to divide them, the threat was so great that Hispanic interest groups united to counter "any efforts by other legislators to undermine or eliminate this program."[26]

In 1980, the second year of the bilingual education controversy, the coalition gained the support of several key politicians who signaled to the rest of the legislature that the interests of the Hispanic community were to be represented in deliberations on bilingual education. The governor provided increased credibility to the politically inexperienced coalition and strengthened its position by appointing a technical aide to develop a compromise among embattled forces in the legislature. In a speech before an international convention of bilingual educators in Anaheim, Governor Jerry Brown announced his support of the coalition-backed bill and pointed to the growing Hispanic population saying, "There's power out there and as that power becomes conscious of itself and links up with other groups, then I think we're going to see a shift in the political structure of this country."[27] The governor's assistant for Hispanic affairs also provided political counsel to the coalition members on how to gain the necessary votes and favor of legislators through effective political activity in the legislature and in legislators' home districts. Through their combined efforts, the governor and others who contributed political support despite their distance from the conflict, helped to incorporate the participation of the coalition into the routines of decision-making.

As the competition wore on in the second year and the coalition continued to make in-roads into the policy-making process, many key legislators and in-

25. *Ibid.*
26. Richard Alatorre and Peter R. Chacon, Press Release, August 30, 1979.
27. Kim Murphy, "Brown Backs Bilingual Education," Santa Ana Register, April 23, 1980.

fluential interest groups began to realize that the coalition would have to be a part of a solution if it was to pass the legislature and be signed into law by the governor. From the beginning of 1980, Chacon and the coalition had advocated a course of compromise and consensus. Recognizing that they did not control enough influence in the legislature to succeed alone, the coalition was forced to accede to many of the concerns and interests of mainstream educational organizations and legislators whose support was critical for the passage of AB 507.

Eventually AB 507, the coalition-backed bill, was enacted by the legislature. However, the final bill had been transformed to the degree that any *real* strengthening of the law or increase in the commitment of the state to guarantee the constitutional rights of language minority children had been removed. While the coalition was successful in averting more negative proposals that would have repealed the law, their *victory* in passing AB 507 should be perceived, to be more accurate, as a symbol of influence without the substantive criteria to determine the outcome. The real power for determining the outcome continued to be controlled by nonminority interests who dominated each stage of decision-making. Besides the initial State Board action, there were other examples of dominant interests in the policy formation. For instance, the teachers unions wanted and won weaker protection from layoffs for bilingual teachers. A key legislator for gaining Senate approval demanded and received several revisions in the bill, including language that clearly specified the purpose of the program to teach children English as effectively and efficiently as possible. Finally, critics of the bilingual concept fought for and won program options which included intensive English instruction and experimentation with immersion and High Intensity Language Training (HILT) approaches. Rather than altering the relationships of powers within the political system, the coalition's own position changed significantly, conceding their limited ability to prevail and participating within the constraints of the situation. The system demands that competing groups negotiate a compromise with *relative* political resources despite the obvious imbalances in power.

Although the outcome of participation in the decision-making process was more symbolic than substantial for the interests of the bilingual community, the coalition members, and in particular Hispanic political elites who participated as members of the coalition representing organizations from across the state, enhanced their own roles as leaders. The results of the incorporation of Hispanic political elites into the political system were two-fold: first, they used their limited influence not as a base for separatism and increased fragmentation, as some critics feared, but as a means to further integrate Hispanics into mainstream political action; second, Hispanic political elites, like mainstream politicians, recognized the boundaries of their own political behavior imposed by the system. Since their own interests as leaders of the bilingual community became closely identified with the success of their bill in the legislature, it was to their benefit, as well, to justify the outcome in ways which heightened their own importance and appeared to address the interests of their constituencies. In this manner, the integration of Hispanic political elites helped to rationalize and legitimize, to the Hispanic community, the resolution of the competition which bound them to a common interest with other elites in the political process. Modifying the conclusions reached by J. Q. Wilson more than twenty years ago, we can confirm that the limitations on minority political influence are due to constraints imposed by the political system in the form of rules of effective political behavior and the exigencies of maintaining a political organization (1960:22).

    The stratification of power and the inability of Hispanic political elites to provide tangible benefits to their group collectively have a direct bearing on the efficacy of political action and reinforce the stigma of powerlessness among Hispanics. While we have acknowledged that bilingual education originated in a unique period of history when the social environment provided the impetus for majority/minority relations to be renegotiated generally, this brief California history demonstrates how the goals which were established *then* have shifted to fundamentally new goals, *now*. The concern for equity and the redistribution of opportunity have given way to *efficiency, basics*, and *meritocracy*—all symptoms of lower priorities for investments in human capital, while our national destructive capabilities continue to increase.

    This paper has been concerned with the objectives of bilingual education and who decides its purposes. Rather than differentiating between social and language issues involved in bilingual education, the confusion of the two has led many well-meaning political activists astray. Scholarship on bilingual education has yet to distinguish the language ideologies that converge in the policy-making process or the implementation of bilingual programs as Heath has called for. And, culture, which was a cornerstone of bilingual education programs in the beginning, today is a relic of the past. No doubt, since the mid 1960s bilingual education has matured and needed to change in order to better fit the social realities, but what has been lost? For instance, research has shown that there is a substantial difference between the interaction of a non-Hispanic teacher with a predominantly Hispanic class and a Hispanic teacher.[28]

28. R. Carrasco, A. Vera, and C. B. Cazden. "Aspects of Bilingual Students' Communicative Competence in the Classroom: A Case Study." *Latino Language and Communicative Behavior*, edited by Richard P. Duran. Norwood, N.J.: Ablex Press, 1981. Also C. Cazden, R. Carrasco, A. Maldonado-Guzman, and F. Erickson, "The Contribution of Ethnographic Research to Bi-

These differences go beyond the language issue and they are not resolved by the inclusion of a Spanish-speaking aide, celebrating Cinco de Mayo once a year, or breaking the private/public language barrier as Rodriguez has suggested (1982). This is not to imply that Hispanic children should be taught exclusively by Hispanic teachers; rather, our preparation of teachers and structuring of the school environment (i.e., allocation of resources, assignment of teachers, segregation of students, etc.) in schools where Hispanic students matriculate are extremely poor and in need of immediate attention! Language is only one aspect of these grim conditions (cf., Olivas 1981).

Education is once more in a period of reevaluation. It has caught the public's eye through the National Commission on Excellence in Education and attention has been focused on the mediocrity which has beset the schools. But I wonder, will the *solutions* that will undoubtedly emerge from this reflective state look like what we have already seen? Will complex social problems be reduced to simplistic notions of deficiencies in the learner, as in the case of language minorities? Will insufficient resources and the absence of institutional support for a program like bilingual education be ignored in evaluations sponsored by the government and instead find that the concept is to blame for not producing reliable evidence that the program is working? Ultimately the questions boil down to: Who decides the standards to judge? Who has the authority? As we have seen in California, it is unlikely that the judges will also be those whose interests are the improvement of life chances for minority students. Minority interests are not linked to the institutionalized arrangements which maintain the "constellation of differentiated resources" and the power to access these resources (Hill-Burnett 1976:37).

Finally, the California experience has given us another valuable lesson— that educators *are* capable of political mobilization and playing a role in the formulation of policy. Changing the stratification of power to decide the outcome of policy making is a long process and the politicization of education is a *pro*active response toward realizing this objective. For Hispanics, effectiveness in schooling should be measured by the degree to which current trends are reversed and by a reduction in the number of Hispanic school dropouts. Because the population is young, the power to change the social conditions for Hispanics is in the schools.

## REFERENCES

Bethell, T. 1979. "Why Johnny Can't Speak English: Against Bilingual Education." *Harpers* 258 (February):30–33.

cultural Bilingual Education." *Current Issues in Bilingual Education*, edited by J. Alatis. Washington, D.C.: Georgetown Roundtable on Languages and Linguistics, Georgetown University Press, 1980.

Birman, B. F. and A. L. Ginsberg. 1983. "Introduction: Addressing the Needs of Language-Minority Children." In de Kanter and Baker, *Bilingual Education*: A Reappraisal of Federal Policy. Lexington, Mass.: Lexington Books.

de Kanter, A. A. and K. A. Baker. 1983. *Bilingual Education: A Reappraisal of Federal Policy*. Lexington, Mass.: Lexington Books.

Dobb, F. 1983. *Compliance Management and Manipulation: The Case of the California State Language Census*. Unpublished Ph.D. Thesis, Stanford University.

Epstein, N. 1977. *Language, Ethnicity, and the Schools: Policy Alternatives for Bilingual-Bicultural Education*. Washington, D.C.: Institute for Educational Leadership, The George Washington University.

Fishman, J. A. 1966. *Language Loyalty in the United States*. The Hague: Mouton.

———. 1973. "Historical Dimensions in the Sociology of Language." In *Report of the Twenty-third Annual Round Table Meeting on Linguistics and Language Studies*. R. W. Shuy (ed.), Washington, D.C.: Georgetown University Press, pp. 145–55.

Hache, J. B. 1983. "The Politics of Bilingual Education Policy Development and Implementation in Canada." A paper presented to the Annual Meeting of the American Educational Research Association, Montreal, Canada (April).

Heath, S. B. 1977. "Viewpoint: Social History." In *Bilingual Education: Current Perspectives*, vol. 1. Social Science. Arlington, VA.: Center for Applied Linguistics, 53–71.

Hernandez-Chavez, E., et al. 1981. *The Federal Policy Toward Language and Education: Pendulum or Progress?* Sacramento, CA.: Cross Cultural Resource Center, Monograph No. 12.

Hill-Burnett, J. 1976. "Commentary: Paradoxes and Dilemmas." *Anthropology and Education Quarterly* 7:4.

Kirst, M. W. and S. A. Somers. 1980. *Collective Action Among California Educational Interest Groups: A Logical Response to Proposition 13*. Stanford, CA.: Institute for Research in Educational Finance and Governance.

Lambert, W. E. and G. R. Tucker. 1972. *Bilingual Education of Children: The St. Lambert Experiment*. Rowley, Mass.: Newbury House Publishers, Inc.

Lukes, S. 1974. *Power, A Radical View*. London: Macmillan.

Matute-Bianchi, M. E. 1979. "The Federal Mandate for Bilingual Education," *Bilingual Education and Public Policy in the United States*. Ethnoperspectives in Bilingual Education Research, vol. 1. R. V. Padilla, ed. Ypsilanti, Michigan: Department of Foreign Languages and Bilingual Studies, Eastern Michigan University.

Navarro, R. A. 1983. "Identity and Consensus in the Politics of Bilingual Education: The Case of California 1967–1980." Unpublished Ph.D. Thesis, Stanford University.

Olivas, M. A. 1981. *Research on Hispanic Education: Students, Finance and Governance*. Stanford, CA.: Institute for Research in Educational Finance and Governance.

Otheguy, R. 1982. "Thinking About Bilingual Education: A Critical Appraisal." In *Harvard Educational Review* 52(3):301–314.

Paulston, C. B. 1974. *Implications of Language Learning Theory for Language Planning: Concerns in Bilingual Education*. Arlington, VA.: Center for Applied Linguistics.

———. 1978. "Rationales for Bilingual Education Reforms: A Comparative Assessment." In *Comparative Education Review* 22(3):402–419.

———. 1983. *Swedish Research and Debate About Bilingualism: A Critical Review of the Swedish Research and Debate About Bilingualism and Bilingual Education in Sweden From an International Perspective*. Stockholm: National Swedish Board of Education.

Rodriguez, R. 1982. *Hunger of Memory: The Education of Richard Rodriguez*. Boston: Goldine.

Spradley, J. P. 1979. *The Ethnographic Interview*. New York: Holt, Rinehart and Winston.

Schneider, S. G. 1976. *Revolution, Reaction or Reform: The 1974 Bilingual Education Act*. New York: L.A. Publishing Co.

Swain, M. 1977. "School Reforms Through Bilingual Education: Problems and Some Solutions in Evaluating Programs." In *Comparative Education Review* 22(3): 420–33.

Therborn, G. 1980. *The Ideology of Power and the Power of Ideology*. London: Verso.

Tucker, G. R. and A. d'Anglejan. 1975. "New Directions in Second Language Teaching." In *Proceedings of the First Inter-American Conference on Bilingual Education*. R. Troike and N. Modiano, eds. Arlington, Virginia: Center for Applied Linguistics, pp. 63–72.

Wilson, J. Q. 1960. *Negro Politics: The Search for Leadership*. Chicago, IL.: The Free Press.

**PART FOUR**

**Reference Material**

# About the Contributors

ADALBERTO AGUIRRE, JR., has been on the faculty of the Department of Sociology at the University of California, Riverside, since 1980, and Chair of the Linguistics Program since 1983. He is author of *An Experimental Study of Chicano Bilingualism* (1978), *Chicanos and Intelligence Testing* (1980), and *Language in the Chicano Speech Community* (1985).

ROBERT BERDAN, director of the Bilingual Special Education development program at California State University, Long Beach, has done extensive work in the area of language variability and the syntax and phonology of Black English. For several years he was senior researcher at the National Center for Bilingual Research.

STEPHEN DIAZ became co-director of the Community Educational Resource and Research Center, University of California, San Diego, in 1984, a center which he founded. Since 1984 he has been working to develop and analyze the effectiveness of computer-mediated activities in enhancing the basic skills development of low-achieving bilingual students. He has been widely published in linguistics journals.

HOMER D. C. GARCIA, an assistant professor at Pitzer College, has also been a member of the staff at the Chicano Studies Center of the Claremont Colleges since 1982. He conducted post-doctoral research at the Center for the Social Organization of Schools at the Johns Hopkins University from 1980 to 1982. He has taught at Yale University, the University of New Haven, and the University of Arizona.

MARYELLEN GARCIA, a member of the Department of Spanish and Portuguese at California State University, Long Beach, has focused much of her research on the Spanish and English of Mexican-Americans, especially their norms for Spanish language use, the linguistic features of their English and Spanish, and English-language use in social contexts.

MARIA GONZALEZ-BAKER, computer-education coordinator for the Kingsville Independent School District in Texas, previously served as the director of curriculum (K–12) of Robstown Independent School District in that state.

She has worked for more than fifteen years in bilingual and migrant education as a public school teacher, administrator, and teacher trainer.

FERNANDO J. GUTIÉRREZ, a counseling psychologist at the University of Santa Clara (California) Counseling Center, received his doctorate in counseling psychology from Boston University. In 1978–79 he was a Title VII H.E.W. Fellow, and he served on the Children's Committee of the Advisory Council to the Commissioner of Mental Health of the Commonwealth of Massachusetts during 1979–80.

RODOLFO JACOBSON, a professor of linguistics and bilingual education at the University of Texas at San Antonio, has investigated Spanish-English code-switching from a sociolinguistic viewpoint for many years and has developed the *New Concurrent Approach* in bilingual methodology which is used widely by teachers of bilinguals.

DENNIS LEASHER MADRID, associate professor of psychology and mental health at the University of Southern Colorado, has worked for a number of years in the field of language acquisition. His particular focus has been in second-language acquisition of bilingual children and adolescents.

LENTO F. MAEZ, who holds a Ph.D. in language acquisition and reading development from Arizona State University, Tempe, has done extensive research in the effects of microcomputer-assisted instruction with fourth, fifth, and sixth-grade bilingual students in an attempt to understand how bilingual children acquire knowledge.

LUIS C. MOLL has been assistant research psychologist at the Laboratory of Comparative Human Cognition at the University of California, San Diego, since 1978. He has done extensive research on the use of the computer in the bilingual classroom, and he is co-editor of the *Quarterly Newsletter of the Laboratory of Comparative Human Cognition*, which is distributed in more than thirty countries around the world.

RICHARD A. NAVARRO, senior researcher at the Institute for Research on Teaching and assistant professor in the Department of Teacher Education at Michigan State University, earned a Ph.D. in international development education from Stanford University. Since that time he has co-directed a Title VI-sponsored project to add an international dimension to teacher education and conducted research on schools and communities in multi-cultural environments and on the politics of bilingual education.

REBECCA OXFORD-CARPENTER has devoted several years to work concerning language minority issues. She was director for an inter-America project that resulted in demographic projections of non-English language background and limited English-proficient persons in the United States, and she also created the Army's first demographic projections of Hispanic soldiers.

SAMUEL PENG is a statistician in the Longitudinal Studies Branch of the National Center for Educational Statistics, Washington, D.C.

LOUIS G. POL has been an associate professor of marketing at the University of Nebraska at Omaha since 1984. Much of his research has focused on the national policy implications of the projected increase of persons with limited English-language proficiency in the United States. His most recent work has been in the areas of the impact of demographic change on marketing strategies.

CRAIG E. RICHARDS, an assistant professor of educational administration at Rutgers University, has longstanding interest in Latin American affairs. He is co-editor of *Revolution in Central America*, published in 1983.

JOSEFINA VILLAMIL TINAJERO, an assistant professor in the College of Education at the University of Texas at El Paso, has coordinated a public school-university collaborative demonstration project designed to implement a model of supervision. She has worked extensively as a teacher trainer and evaluator of bilingual programs.

BENJI WALD has focused research on the study of acquisition and use of English and Spanish in the urban Mexican-American communities of Los Angeles while working at the National Center for Bilingual Research. As a sociolinguist, he has also worked extensively on speech behavior, multilingualism, and vernacular languages.

# Index